AMERICAN LIBERALISM

John McGowan

AMERICAN LIBERALISM

An Interpretation for Our Time

The University of North Carolina Press

CHAPEL HILL

© 2007 The University of North Carolina Press
All rights reserved
Manufactured in the United States of America

Designed by Heidi Perov
Set in Cycles with Meta display

This book was published with the assistance of the H. Eugene and
Lillian Youngs Lehman Fund of the University of North Carolina Press.
A complete list of books published in the Lehman Series appears at
the end of the book.

The paper in this book meets the guidelines for permanence and
durability of the Committee on Production Guidelines for Book
Longevity of the Council on Library Resources.

Library of Congress Cataloging-in-Publication Data
McGowan, John, 1953–
    American liberalism : an interpretation for our time /
    John McGowan.
        p. cm.
    Includes bibliographical references and index.
    ISBN-13: 978-0-8078-3171-7 (cloth: alk. paper)
    1. Liberalism—United States. 2. United States—Politics and
        government—2001–   I. Title.
    JC574.2.U6M355 2007
    320.510973—dc22   2007015456

A Caravan book. For more information, visit www.caravanbooks.org.

11 10 09 08 07   5 4 3 2 1

To Allen Dunn, James Thompson, and Tyler Curtain,
synecdochically,
but mostly for their incomparable selves

CONTENTS

AMERICAN LIBERALISM

America at the Crossroads

Democracy ain't worth a damn if it's not liberal. And liberalism isn't worth much if it isn't democratic. Americans are in danger of losing both because they have forgotten what liberalism is—what it aims to achieve and how, against all odds, it has succeeded throughout our history.

Contempt for liberalism characterizes the populist right and the academic left both. Not surprisingly, their relentless assault has undermined the nation's allegiance to its liberal heritage and its liberal institutions. The intertwining of liberalism and democracy in America has been misunderstood and attacked. An illiberal version of democracy has been brought forward as a replacement for the liberal democracy that evolved from the founding of the republic through the civil rights era of the mid-twentieth century. The attempt to disconnect liberalism from democracy is one manifestation of America's still unresolved relationship to the changes wrought during the second half of the twentieth century: the altered status of blacks, women, and gays; shifting public standards of decorum; transformations in understanding what it means to be American in the face of our actions and defeat in Vietnam and in response to a new wave of immigration to this country, this time including many nonwhites; changes in America's economy, especially in employment patterns/conditions and in the distribution of wealth and income, changes that began with the first oil crisis (1973) and that are usually viewed as the effects of "globalization"; the end of the post–World War II welfare state consensus, which accepted the New Deal and underwrote the attempt to form the Great Society; and last, but not least, America's transformed role in a post–Cold War world in which civil wars and terrorists, along with states' responses to them, are the primary source of conflict.

We stand at a crossroads in American history. From 1890 to 1970, American society moved slowly, but steadily, toward a wider distribution of wealth, bringing unprecedented prosperity to an ever larger portion of the population. At the same time, social insurance programs protected most people from the ill effects of cataclysmic events like unemployment, severe illness, natural disasters, and workplace accidents. Social Security provided baseline economic support for the elderly, while various welfare programs aided the nonelderly poor. Since 1970, these programs have been under attack, and many of them have been eroded. Even more significantly, the distribution of wealth and income has moved dramatically in the other direction, with the most well-off significantly richer and the vast majority treading water at best and losing ground at worst. (See Appendix, items 2–3, 6–8, for documentation of these changes.) This transformation in most people's economic well-being is accompanied by a greater volatility in incomes, a loss of job security, and an erosion of benefits, especially of pensions and of health insurance. In short, while most Americans' economic position has, at best, remained the same over forty years even as the nation's aggregate wealth has greatly increased, their economic vulnerability has increased. In what Jacob S. Hacker has called "the great risk shift," ordinary Americans are now much more likely to suffer sudden economic downfall as a result of catastrophic illness, or losing a job, or having their retirement funds undermined by corporate failures or market downturns.[1]

This concentration of economic power at the top is matched by the increasing power of money in our politics and an increasing power in the executive branch of government. Although the decline of liberalism is now forty years old, the particularly blatant pandering to the super-rich and to American businesses during the past six years, combined with the enlargement of executive power in the name of national security, has dramatized, in our current moment, the choice between a liberal and a nonliberal future. That we stand at a crossroads, faced with a dramatic choice between two very different visions of what America can and should be, is the impetus for this book. My goal is to articulate, as fully and persuasively as I possibly can, a vision of American liberalism as the path our country should take.

For many on both the left and the right, liberalism is their favorite whipping boy, the all-purpose cause for everything they do not like about contemporary American reality. And most of these critics also trumpet democracy as their political ideal. I highly doubt they could deliver a democracy we would wish to endorse if they purged it of its liberal elements. But I do not doubt that some of our actual or would-be political leaders are hostile to a liberalism that I will do my best to convince you is well worth supporting. My fear, quite simply, is that Americans do not understand what liberalism is or how it relates to democracy. Armed with a better understanding, they might choose to reject liberal democracy. I hope and believe otherwise. I offer here a vision of liberal democracy that explains its benefits and its frustrations, so that at least our polity can make the momentous decisions it currently faces with a clear sense of what it is choosing between and in the name of what goods it makes those choices.

Understanding liberalism is complicated by the fact that, as a set of political principles and strategies, liberalism is not exactly the same now as it was in 1776. The story I tell emphasizes a strong continuity between the liberalism of Thomas Jefferson and James Madison and the liberalism of the early twenty-first century, but it requires a fairly detailed account to illustrate that continuity. Although this story of liberalism's evolution is complex, my political position is simple. I think liberal democracy gives us our best chance of living at peace with other Americans—and with the people in the rest of the world.

The founding fathers were liberals. The Declaration of Independence and the Constitution provide us with a mixture of noble ideals (especially of freedom and equality) and of clear-eyed legal and institutional tools for approaching those ideals. That mixture of idealism and realism is characteristically American, but also characteristically liberal. On the idealistic side, liberalism is America's best self, articulating the goal of enabling the freedom and prosperity of all citizens. That idealism gives us both the belief that these ideals are achievable and the will to work toward their achievement. On the realistic side, liberalism recognizes that we are often not our best selves, and thus creates a system of checks and balances that prevents the accumulation of power in the hands of the few. No elite—be it political, economic, religious, or ethnic—is entitled to dominate in a polity founded on the premise that all are created equal. As I was always taught that Jefferson said, the price of liberty is eternal vigilance.[2] America can be its best self when citizens know its founding ideals—and when the checks and balances that protect those ideals are maintained and utilized. This book aims to remind Americans of those ideals—ones I believe most Americans still cherish—and to provoke them to consider what it would mean to honor them in today's world, one that is very different from the world of 1787.

I present an American version of liberal democracy. As will become clear soon enough, I have been influenced by political philosophers from John Locke and John Stuart Mill to the present, but I constantly try to process the general reflections and observations found in the philosophers' work through the history of the United States. My American focus means that I begin with the American founders, depending rather heavily on the Federalist Papers written by James Madison and Alexander Hamilton, to highlight the salient features of liberalism. And when I move into the twentieth century, my understanding of "modern liberalism" follows from the work of a quartet of American political philosophers who have tried to articulate a liberalism that speaks to contemporary conditions: John Dewey, Franklin Delano Roosevelt, John Rawls, and Martha Nussbaum.[3]

I want to establish a "usable past" for those currently engaged in American political debates on the liberal side—thus my focus on American ideals and American history. Politics can be defined as the actions through which humans in a particular society establish, maintain, reproduce, and reform/ transform the conditions of their living together. Better yet, substitute "interactions" for "actions" in that last sentence. Politics attends to our being-with-others, to the interactions and negotiations through which we build a social space we occupy together and through which we achieve individual identities, purposes, commitments, and loyalties. Politics entails (at least partially) negotiations about dividing up resources, arguments about what it is possible to do, and contention over what it is desirable to do. Disagreements on all three of these matters are the basic stuff of politics—and at the heart of a liberal democracy with its processes of deliberation, publicly staged advocacy, regular elections, and adversarial legal and legislative procedures. Liberalism, like any political philosophy, aims to articulate a vision of the best way to understand the fact that humans everywhere live in societies and to articulate a set of principles recommended as guiding us toward the best possible way for humans to organize their social relations. That more general philosophy is then taken to have consequences in terms of the positions adopted on more local, substantial political debates. Political philosophy (or political theory), then, both undertakes to describe/explain the basic conditions of human political communities *and* to advocate a particular way of living together. Political scientists, at times, attempt to separate these two by offering a "value-neutral" description or explanation of some political institution or interaction. That might well be possible, but its reverse is not. Any political vision that advocates one set of choices over alternatives will be built upon claims about the facts (the nature) of the human condition or, more modestly, the facts of the ways a specific historical polity has been and currently is organized. I strive to offer a compelling as well as reasonably comprehensive vision of American political reality and of how we could/should best live that reality.

If readers do not recognize my portrait of liberal democracy as representing a set of American ideals and experiences, I have failed. Precisely because this account of liberal democracy is so American specific and so driven by my understanding of America's contemporary situation, I have chosen to emphasize in the subtitle that what I offer here is "an interpretation for our time." There will, of course, be family resemblances to the liberalism found in the English tradition and to democracy as understood and practiced elsewhere, but my account is almost entirely refracted through American history and American thought, while also strongly shaped by my understanding of the crossroads at which America currently stands. My emphasis is primarily on liberalism rather than on democracy because it is the liberal part of our heritage that is so badly misunderstood at present. Of course, liberalism and democracy are deeply intertwined in American history and politics, so democracy is a constant presence in these pages. I address issues of democracy directly at the end, but that fairly brief discussion makes no pretense to being comprehensive. The topics considered there are dictated by the larger goal of providing a fairly complete overview of liberalism. The "interpretation" of liberalism offered here presents a particular (obviously contestable) interpretation of what America has aspired to be, has understood itself to be, and has, in some historical moments and at some specific locales, actually managed to be.

I have described this book to friends as an attempt to lay out the basic principles, values, and commitments of American liberalism. One crucial dimension of publicly articulated principles is that they are "essentially contestable."[4] To make one's views public is to solicit others' agreement, but also to acknowledge that the arguments and reasons that convince me will not necessarily convince others. The "interpretation" of American liberalism offered here is my best attempt at a full-scale liberal vision. Undoubtedly, it will prove more useful to many readers because it clarifies their own different beliefs than because it expresses what they have often felt but never put so fully into words. Either response would thrill me. I do think of this book as a basic civics lesson. I am trying to present an American liberalism that I think is an indispensable part of our political history and political ideals, a part we are in danger of losing through ignorance, misunderstanding, misrepresentations (willful in some cases), and inattention. But that hardly means I only succeed if I convert all my readers to my vision of liberalism. To the contrary, more important is to spur readers to reflect upon their own understanding of the politically feasible and desirable.

The civics lesson aspect of this book leads me, since I want to be comprehensive yet relatively and readably brief, to portray liberalism in fairly broad strokes. Here it is probably an advantage that I am not a professional political theorist, but rather a citizen addressing other citizens. I have been deeply influenced by the political philosophy and theory that I read avidly (and sometimes teach), but I am trying to do something no academic political theorist would want to do. Namely, I pay scant attention to the fact that liberalism comes in many variants—and is characterized by a whole series of internal debates. I offer an "interpretation" of liberalism that I find compelling without getting much sidetracked into specific objections from liberals themselves to the ways I present and argue for various components of my view. My rhetorical aims for this book are the only justification for not embroiling myself in debates internal to the field. In doing so, I have run roughshod (sometimes knowingly, undoubtedly often unknowingly) over distinctions, disagreements, and issues that adherents to various varieties of liberalism deem crucially important. In so doing, I never intend to suggest that liberalism is monolithic and has a once-and-for-all definitional identity, or that there is a consensus about what liberalism is or what it has to say about specific topics. My understanding of political concepts is always "situational"; such concepts are deployed in specific contexts to advance and advocate certain beliefs and commitments. The relevant context for me is the current political climate in American society, not academic debates—hence my subtitle, "An Interpretation for Our Time."

That said, where I am aware of the academic debates that surround this account of liberalism, I have used notes to refer my readers to those debates. But my nonacademic goal leads me to keep my eye on the ball in the body of the text, and this book is designed to be completely comprehensible to the reader who never once looks at the notes. For readers who want a better sense of the public and academic debates surrounding the main text's claims, the notes will point them toward learning more—and toward finding proponents of opposing views as well as the works of the authors who have influenced me. I have also provided an appendix that gathers together statistical and other data that underwrite some of my claims about current conditions in our American polity. But the main attraction is the text of the book, which presents what I hope is a coherent and comprehensive interpretation of what the terms "liberalism" and "democracy" mean in an American context and what is entailed in allegiance to them. These terms are used every day in political and journalistic discourse, but they are never defined—as if everyone already and always knew what we were talking about.

If concepts are deployed situationally, then they cannot, in the final analysis, function noncontrastively. The implied contrast throughout Book One (on liberalism) is to conservatism and illiberalism, even though the contrast mostly remains implied. In Book Two, I present an account of contemporary

American conservatism that makes the contrast explicit. More problematic for some readers will be the fact that, by and large, I do not engage with leftist critiques of liberalism. Partly that is the result of the attempt to keep this book of reasonable length. A fully adequate engagement with nonliberal leftist thought would have taken me far afield. But, at the end of Book Two, I do offer more substantive reasons for neglecting leftism in a consideration of contemporary American politics, as well as paying some attention to the left's objections to liberalism.

So much for preliminaries. Now readers are entitled to a foretaste of the book's substantive argument to orient them as they move into the main body of the text. Liberalism, I contend, provides our best guarantee of liberty and the peace in which to exercise it, while its commitment to equality provides the ever-elusive ideal that makes it a dynamic, restless, and radical political position. That commitment to equality explains the historical transformation from the founders' vision to the liberalism of today, as well as illuminating the main fault lines in our contemporary political debates. Whether we insist that the founders were liberal, conservative, or republican (everyone agrees that they were not democrats) makes little difference beyond propagandistic appropriations that merely muddy the waters. The key is that a distinctive understanding of freedom and of its interrelation with the ever-elusive goal of equality characterizes American political culture. I think there is a demonstrable continuity—both in political sensibility and through a series of concrete historical steps—between the views of Jefferson and Madison and contemporary, twenty-first-century liberalism. Succinctly put, "classical" liberalism develops a distinctive understanding of liberty, one that links freedom to individual agents, that relies on the rule of law and of legally established civil liberties to counter arbitrary and/or absolute power, and that responds to the pluralism (religious and otherwise) of modern societies by enshrining liberty of conscience, freedom of association and expression, and autonomy in choosing how to live one's life. The liberalism of the founders, as the Declaration of Independence makes dramatically evident, already possesses a strong attachment to the notion that "all men are created equal," but the full ramifications of that ringing assertion take a long time to become clear. (We have no reason to believe that they are completely understood, not to mention realized, even today.) The unfolding of what equality means and how a liberal democratic polity might better put it into practice encompasses the transition from the founders to "modern" liberalism. That historical story is complicated because, in the second half of the nineteenth century, the referents of the labels "liberal" and "conservative" reverse themselves almost completely. If we keep our eyes firmly on the concept of equality, however, that reversal is not so baffling.

To lay my cards fully on the table: the liberalism I espouse is "egalitarian liberalism," a phrase I take from Thomas Nagel, who characterizes this position as favoring "not just individual rights but a form of distributive justice that combats poverty and large inequalities." Nagel adds that "the term 'liberalism' applies to a wide range of political positions, from the libertarianism of economic laissez-faire to the democratic egalitarianism of the welfare state. In its European usage the term suggests the former rather than the latter; in American usage it is the reverse."⁵ John Dewey noted this divergence between American and "other countries'" usage in 1927: "In the United States the name 'liberal,' as a party designation, is still employed to designate a progressive in political matters. In most other countries, the 'liberal' party is that which represents established and vested commercial and financial interests in protest against governmental regulation."⁶ I employ the term "liberalism" in its American usage throughout this book. Linking the term "liberalism" with this focus on equality dates from the Progressive Era in American history and becomes firmly entrenched during the New Deal, which is emphatically not to say that agitation for equality was absent in nineteenth-century America, but only that a politics inspired by that ideal had not yet been given the name "liberal." The more usual name for nineteenth-century advocates of equality was "democrat," as is most obvious in Alexis de Tocqueville's *Democracy in America*, which almost never uses the word "liberal," but associates democracy with the drive toward equality.

Equality is the most complicated and contested of the primary liberal values—and I locate liberalism's other components in relation to its commitment to equality. Democracy is then, in turn, interpreted through its relation to equality. Conservatism is best characterized by its indifference or outright hostility to equality. Norberto Bobbio, in his elegant little book entitled *Left and Right*, concludes that the "distinction between left and right corresponds to the difference between egalitarianism and inegalitarianism."⁷ That is certainly the place to start, although there are other significant differences as well.

My extended description of liberal democracy will not win universal acceptance, but it is presented in a positive, assertive form as representing what I consider the best thinking and experience on these matters. I offer some assertions more confidently than others. Generally speaking, throughout the book I avoid the first person when I present traits or principles of liberalism or of democracy that I am fairly confident would find wide agreement among self-described liberals. However, I do, in certain instances, discuss ideas or arguments that are attributable to specific liberal or democratic writers. In those cases, I identify the writer in question and reconstruct his or her position. Finally, when I offer interpretations of liberalism or of its consequences that I think (or know) are subject to more disagreement, I usually switch to the first person in order to signal that, here, my way of understanding liberalism is influencing the exposition.

The book's organization is simple. In imitation of David Hume's *A Treatise of Human Nature*, I have organized the text into books with numbered sections, instead of the more usual chapters. (Hume, whose thought defies easy characterization as liberal or conservative, greatly influenced Madison and Dewey. My account of liberalism is also indebted to him.) Book One provides a long description of American liberalism's primary principles and values, paying particular attention to how those principles and values were present at the founding moment and how they are understood today. The presentation of liberalism is followed, in Book Two, by an engagement with conservative positions and a brief discussion of nonliberal leftists. Book Three offers a historical sketch of how the liberalism of the founders became the "modern" (or egalitarian) liberalism of today. I hardly do justice to America's complex history, but I do name some of the key historical transformations germane to liberalism's evolution. The appeal to certain well-known moments in the republic's political history indicates why a claim of continuity between the founders and today's liberals is plausible. Book Four moves on to a discussion of democracy and toward an understanding of "liberal democracy." The term "liberal democracy" is just about universally used by political scientists to characterize the form of government that currently prevails in the Western democracies. But egalitarian liberalism has come under extended attack in the past forty years at the same time that democracy has been elevated as a universal ideal beyond criticism. This development suggests that we live during a transitional moment in which our current political arrangements (and their historical and ethical justifications) are poorly understood—and that there is considerable impetus from various quarters to place a nonliberal or illiberal democracy in liberal democracy's stead. This book aims to clarify what is at stake during this transitional period, and thus it concludes with a short account of the contrast between liberal and illiberal democracy.

BOOK ONE

Liberalism: Principles and Values

1

LIBERALISM AND DEMOCRACY

Liberalism and democracy are not identical and, to some extent, not even very compatible. My contention is that they end up working well together, especially if we take into account the imperfections of this world. Do they complement one another? To some extent. But at times they also pull in different directions, sometimes to good effect, sometimes not.

Historically, democracy dates back to the ancient world whereas liberalism is a modern invention. (By modern, I mean the world after 1500, a world characterized by greatly increased European contact with non-Europeans following Columbus's voyages; by the splintering of Christianity into various sects following Martin Luther's break from the Catholic Church; by the increased dissemination of knowledge and the growth of science that accompanied the Renaissance and the invention of the printing press; by the movement from a feudal to a capitalist economic order; and by the growth of the nation-state and its slow movement away from absolutism toward some version of popular sovereignty.) Liberalism originates as a loose set of responses offered to the problems attending social organization and authority after the demise of a single, unifying religion and as an alternative to arbitrary and absolute power lodged in a monarch. Thomas Hobbes, at the beginning of the modern era, recognizes that, in the absence of a religious authority accepted by all citizens, the basis of order will have to be secular and human. Unlike most liberals, however, Hobbes is willing to sacrifice almost all liberty to secure order. More characteristic are John Locke, Montesquieu, Adam Smith, Immanuel Kant, Thomas Jefferson, and James Madison, all of whom want to maintain, even increase, individual liberty (especially freedom of opinion and belief, but also rights of free enterprise and property) while at the same time ensuring some modicum of public order. In the simplest terms (terms I will revisit later and complicate somewhat), liberalism responds to modern conditions of plurality, conditions most dramatically portrayed in the multiple religious disputes—some more violent than others—spawned by the Protestant Reformation. Modern plurality also manifests itself in the economic competition generated by capitalism. If members of a society do not share the same religious beliefs and are competing against one another economically, what could possibly hold society together? Spurning Hobbes's drastic solution—a monarch whose power derives from the people, not from God, but who, once appointed, has absolute authority—the other liberal writers work to achieve a balance between the individual freedoms they recognize in modern plurality and the need to secure those freedoms by providing a peaceful and ordered setting for their enactment.

I will return to this central dilemma posed by modern plurality, but the key point right now is that liberalism precedes democracy in modern political thought—and in modern political reality.[1] From 1650 on, liberalism—the attempt to end the disastrous religious wars by figuring out some way to institutionalize religious tolerance—dominates not only political philosophy, but also actual political reforms in England and Holland (at least). Democracy is not really on the table until, arguably, 1750, with the work of Jean-Jacques Rousseau, who is very influential but also a marginalized outsider. The French Revolution brings democracy onto the political stage—and demonstrates that it is a short step from liberalism to democracy; the two go hand in hand. The collapse of the revolution into Napoleonic despotism and the restoration of the Bourbon dynasty in 1815 delays the full emergence of democracy in Europe to the latter half of the nineteenth century. In America, democracy is not firmly established until the Jacksonian era. According to Stanley Elkins and Eric McKitrick, "'Democracy' was not to emerge as a fully legitimate cultural value in America, commanding more or less universal approval, until the 1830s, with the appearance of a national system of mass political parties."[2] In other words, democracy is mostly a mid-nineteenth-century phenomenon, whereas liberalism is a seventeenth- and eighteenth-century one. The crucial point for Americans is that the founding fathers were liberals intent on creating a republic; they were not democrats. That is why we are saddled with the Electoral College. The founders aimed to secure liberty and prevent tyranny. They were not committed to democratic procedures that rested political decisions on the will of the people, even though they accepted that the authority of political institutions did, ultimately, derive from the people. Hamilton and Madison understood a "republic" as distinct from a "democracy," with the main difference being that a republic refracted and refined the people's will through a series of filters that insulated the government from direct pressure from the demos.[3] For Madison especially, a commitment to religious freedom and civil liberties was distinct from commitment to a government directly responsive to the people's will. In general, liberalism is the attempt to maximize individual freedom within a legal order that distributes power. Democracy, on the other hand, refers to the location of sovereignty in the people and to mechanisms of decision-making at various sites, most notably within the government, but also potentially in the workplace and other locales.

2
PREVENTING TYRANNY, PROMOTING FREEDOM

By calling the founders "liberal," I mean to direct attention to their suspicion of concentrated governmental power, their fierce attachment to liberty, and their emergent commitment to equality. Their "republicanism" was both antidemocratic and not yet full liberalism to the extent that they resisted full social, political, and economic equality and that they focused on the "general welfare" and not the prosperity of isolated individuals as government's responsibility. American liberalism has never looked liked its European counterparts because, prior to the Gilded Age, there was never a strong voice in American politics favoring the kind of laissez-faire liberalism found in Britain in the 1820s, a liberalism that is built on the model of self-interested economic man as the best possible citizen. That British "liberal" position is the hallmark of American conservatism. I cannot emphasize this point enough. I agree with Louis Hartz and Sean Wilentz (and, hence, disagree with Joyce Appleby) that the laissez-faire position did not make a (significant) appearance in American politics before 1880—and that the laissez-faire position in American politics is always "conservative" because it is oriented toward preserving an unequal status quo.[4] It is only when the captains of industry feared that the state would take the workers' part in the labor struggles of the Gilded Age that laissez-faire arguments arrived on the American scene.[5] For Hartz, American liberals (in stark contrast to their British counterparts, notably Jeremy Bentham and John Stuart Mill) of the pre–Civil War years did not distrust the state because it was *their* state, a servant of the people. The British Benthamites, on the other hand, were trying to undercut the legitimacy and power of a state that was still in aristocratic hands. Alexander Hamilton's use of the state to aid commerce (through the establishment of a national bank, and through tariffs and infrastructural investment in roads and canals) set the pattern for American intertwining of state and economy.

Jefferson and Madison's protests against Hamilton's actions are sometimes cited as proof of their nascent embrace of a laissez-faire philosophy. But Jefferson and Madison did not object to state action per se. What they objected to was the way that Hamilton's economic policies favored those who were already economically most well-off. They mistrusted this combination of economic and political power because it would concentrate power in the hands of the few. Jefferson and Madison's liberalism combined a liberal commitment to equality with "republican" ideas about a common good that transcended, and justified limitations on, individual interests. Neither man ever espoused a "rugged individualism," and American liberalism has retained their moderation of the individualistic pursuit of self-interest. The historical transformation of liberalism in the United States (the story told in Book Three) has more to do with changing notions of the proper role of the state than with movement away from or back toward an individualistic politics and psychology based on a certain reading of Adam Smith. Thus, the interpretation of liberalism I offer is distinctly American—and it reflects the emergence of modern American liberalism out of both the liberalism and the republicanism of the founders. The founders' liberalism finds expression in Jefferson's ringing statement about the "the pursuit of happiness" and in the Bill of Rights, both of which have no precedent in a republicanism that takes Rome as its model.[6]

The American Constitution is, to repeat, not a democratic document.[7] Many of our democratic practices are either explicit later amendments to the original document (like the direct election of senators) or evolved, extra-constitutional procedures (like our whole process of nominating presidential candidates or, for that matter, electoral campaigns themselves, which would have appalled the founders). For this reason alone (although there are many others), it is simply impossible to take the Constitution at its word (granting for the moment the dubious proposition that we could know, unproblematically, what its word is). America has evolved away from its founding to a commitment to democracy not held by the founders. But the seeds of democracy are already contained in the framers' acceptance of the ultimate authority of the people. Similarly, the seeds of egalitarian liberalism are present in the Declaration of Independence's insistence on the equality of all.

The crux is the issue of liberty and the potential threats to it. To call the Constitution "conservative," as Russell Kirk does, is way too hasty because the Constitution eschews the authoritarianism of much conservative thought, and it places so much weight (especially in the Bill of Rights) on enabling individuals.[8] In the widest view, because of his emphasis on civil liberties and his suspicion of any and all accumulations of power, Madison was a liberal. He contrasted with the more conservative Hamilton on precisely these grounds. Hamilton wanted a stronger national government than Madison.[9] Madison's declaration (in Federalist No. 47) that "the accumulation of all powers legislative, executive, and judiciary in the same hands, whether of one, a few or many, and whether hereditary, self appointed, or elective, may justly be pronounced the very definition of tyranny" underwrites his differences with Hamilton.[10] As James Read puts it, "What especially distinguished Madison, besides the seriousness of his commitment to civil liberties, is his appreciation of the extremely broad range from which threats to liberty can proceed."[11]

In a narrower view that focuses on Madison's fear of democracy, he does appear conservative. One threat to liberty is what Alexis de Tocqueville would later name "the tyranny of the majority." Madison wanted the Constitution to safeguard against that form of tyranny as well as others. There is little doubt that Madison recognized the rich as a minority and the poor as the majority. For that reason, his antidemocratic republicanism was a defense of privilege—and hence recognizably conservative. But he, unlike many conservatives, never thought the privileged deserved or should be allowed overriding political power. His idea instead, famously expressed in Federalist No. 10, was to effect a distribution of powers among the states and the national government, a distribution mirrored by the partial power held by various "factions" in the polity, none of which would be dominant, so that the common good, rather than the interests of any particular group, would emerge as the focus of the (various) governments' activities. Madison's views became central to liberal political theory and practice: no power without a counterbalancing power somewhere in the system, no social group accorded outsized privilege or influence, a distribution of powers so that individuals and institutions are able to act on the freedoms the polity establishes and protects.

Madison's liberalism had two aims: to safeguard against the tyranny of consolidated power and to provide a modus vivendi in a world characterized by intractable conflicts among people with different beliefs, goals, interests, and values. Here we can locate the "realism" for which he is (and the founders more generally are) rightly celebrated. The Madison of Federalist No. 10 does not expect any political order to erase conflict, so he focuses on creating political institutions and arrangements that mitigate conflict, "refine" self-interest, and, crucially, prevent any particular faction from gaining the upper hand, especially from gaining the upper hand permanently. "To break and control the violence of faction" ranks very high among the "advantages" (51) that the proposed Constitution will bring, Madison assures his readers.

Liberalism, in short, is a set of political expedients meant to prevent tyranny and to promote peaceful coexistence in a pluralistic society, while fostering individual freedom. These expedients are various, do not form a coherent or even completely consistent whole, are justified entirely on the basis of promoting the desired goals, and are related to one another as a series of trade-offs among desired goods and in reference to the overarching aims of limiting tyranny, maintaining civil peace, and maximizing freedom. In the absence of agreement on such fundamental matters as religion, expanding the individual's freedom of decision on these questions appears preferable to forceful conversion, especially in view of the spectacular failure of war in the sixteenth and seventeenth centuries (as well as during other historical periods) to accomplish such conversions.

Liberalism's temperament is pragmatic. Achieving its goals of preventing tyranny and promoting peace is the measure of a constitution's or government's success. Jefferson thought it would be a good idea to revisit and revise the whole apparatus of government once in every generation.[12] Think of his notion as a version of a yearly checkup with one's doctor. What's working, what isn't, where do things seem headed for a breakdown, what new circumstances require our attention, what can we do to improve short-term health and long-term prognosis?

The founders were especially concerned with two forms of tyranny: that of governments and that of a particular faction or portion of the population. This faction might be the majority. But it need not be the majority. The more general way to state the danger is that some group might seize control of the government or exercise extragovernmental social power in such a way that it is able to abrogate privileges to itself and to deny freedoms/privileges to others over a substantial, even if not permanent, period of time. Steven Lukes offers a "three-dimensional" model of power on which I will rely throughout this book. Power, first and foremost, is the ability "to prevail over the contrary preferences of others." Power is the capacity to obtain what I want (the positive side of power); it can also mean that I have the ability to enlist your unwilling aid in furthering my projects or to prevent your achievement of your own projects (the negative side of power, or what is meant by having power *over* another human being). Second, power is manifested when someone or a group "controls the agenda," is able to place certain projects or issues on the table (for governmental or societal action/consideration) while keeping other issues from ever being raised or addressed. Finally, a "three-dimensional view incorporates power of the first two kinds, but also allows that power may operate to shape and modify desires and beliefs in a manner contrary to people's interests."[13]

Liberalism is committed to any and all strategies that will prevent such accumulations of power in any particular hands. The premise is that power will be abused, so we need to devise ways to maintain its circulation, its movement from one set of hands to another. The founders strove to protect against governmental tyranny though the rule of law, the separation of powers, and various forms of "checks and balances."[14] They strove to protect against "factions" by limiting democracy (understood here as the ability of the people to set governmental policy—or even to elect governmental officials—*directly*) and, albeit only geographically, by distributing representation across the polity.

Madison derived from "the celebrated [French political philosopher] Montesquieu, the oracle who is always consulted and cited on this subject" (Federalist No. 47: 268) the conviction that one important and effective way to combat tyranny—either of government or faction—is the multiplication and fragmentation of power. It does not matter where power is located or who holds that power. Any and all consolidations of power in a single institution or in one group's hands are to be feared. But the solution is not an attempted erasure of power. Instead, power should be multiplied. Social and political arrangements should aim to empower, to give citizens as much autonomy, as much independence, as feasible. The Bill of Rights, then, can be understood positively as well as negatively. It is not just a check on governmental power, a list of things government shall not do. It also empowers citizens by proclaiming that their religious beliefs and their political opinions should be self-chosen and that they should express those opinions in public and, crucially, form "associations" to promote those opinions.[15] Liberalism does not battle tyranny merely by limiting the scope of politics, although it does rely on that tactic in some cases. It also battles tyranny by expanding the range of politics and the extent of citizens' involvement in it. Liberalism aims to create, foster, encourage, and maintain a public sphere apart from the government, a realm sometimes referred to as "civil society."[16]

In the first instance, civil society is a response to the possible abuse of power. I have already suggested one possible consequence of power: the ability to abrogate a disproportionate share of social privileges or goods to oneself and to deny them to others. But power, viewed more positively, is the capacity to make decisions, to act on those decisions, and to have a reasonable chance that those actions will yield their aimed-for results. (Note that

I have not identified "who" has this power; it could be an institution, a nation, a particular group, or an individual. Also note that power can be limited at any point in this chain: in decision-making, in the capacity to act, and in the ability to secure desired outcomes. Finally, keep in mind that various factors—from physical and psychological disabilities to opposing humans to natural conditions—might serve to frustrate the capacity to decide and act independently and to get what is wanted through action.) Liberalism seeks to distribute power throughout society; it wants to do everything it can to enhance the capacities of its citizens.

Freedom without power is useless. This fact leads to the difficult balancing act any liberal polity must perform: it can empower its citizens by, in certain instances, ensuring that some citizens do not gain power *over* other citizens. Hence, distributing power necessarily entails taking power away from some. In the absence of this redistribution, the promise of liberty is empty. We find here the first connection between liberty and equality. Where there is an unequal distribution of power, the freedom of those with less power is threatened.

For this reason, the famous "negative" definition of freedom offered by Isaiah Berlin is unsatisfactory, even though its simplicity and its appeal to common sense are attractive in the face of the elaborate, counterintuitive philosophical accounts found in (for example) Spinoza and Hegel. Berlin writes: "The extent of my social or political freedom consists in the absence of obstacles not merely to my actual, but to my potential choices—to my acting in this or that way if I choose to do so."[17] By focusing on the negative side of power (obstacles that stand over and apart from the agent), Berlin neglects the positive side of power as capacity. (This connection of freedom to capacity is more fully developed in my discussion of equality.) When we consider capacity, it becomes obvious that power (as soon as it does not simply consist in brute physical force) is a function of the agent's position in a set of social relations and within a context shaped by political institutions.

A polity, in other words, structures and distributes power; individuals do not possess power apart from the political and social order in which they are embedded. So it is wrong to think the individual possesses some kind of primordial freedom to act that is subsequently hampered by external obstacles. Action is only possible and meaningful within a social context. Consequently, one of the most pressing questions for any politics is how to empower citizens and which citizens to thus empower. Liberalism, from its inception, works to distribute power more widely than in a monarchy or oligarchy. Egalitarian liberalism pushes that distribution further than Madison's liberal republicanism would. Against Berlin, the egalitarian liberal insists that effective freedom requires the ability to form and to act on one's choices—and that the conditions for such freedom are not simply the absence of constraints, but substantive social and political arrangements that distribute power among the polity's members.[18]

This positive fostering of the power to act underwrites the civil liberties (freedom of speech, of religious belief, of association) that are absolutely essential to any liberal vision of the polity. Civil liberties are necessary, but not sufficient, to an achieved liberalism. Viewed one way, as I have tried to suggest, these liberties are a positive good that a liberal polity tries to provide, with the hope that establishing these possibilities will encourage their enactment and thus spur the proliferation of power and of enjoyed, lived freedom. Freedom is fostered by habit and practice; the Bill of Rights provides the conditions of empowerment, but making freedom a reality rests in the hands of those who exercise that freedom daily.

From another point of view, civil liberties are a check against governmental action and are tied to the more general liberal expedient commonly called "the rule of law." We see here liberalism's propensity to work both sides of the fence, positive and negative. All instruments for achieving the goal of preventing tyranny are worthy as long as they actually do promote that goal. Hence liberalism will work both to multiply sites of power in order to *balance* forces in society and to establish outright limits in order to *check* power as well.

There is much more to say about the intertwining of the liberal commitment to freedom and the notion of equality. But first I want to develop the liberal conception of the rule of law (central to the establishment and maintenance of a liberal government) and liberalism's relation to pluralism (central to an understanding of liberal society). With that more full-bodied account of liberalism in hand, we will be ready to address the complexities introduced by a commitment to equality.

3
THE RULE OF LAW

That liberalism predates—and exists in some tension with—modern democracy is most evident in liberalism's commitment to the rule of law. Democracy locates sovereignty in the demos, in the people. A pure, direct democracy would render all decisions by plebiscite, in a vote by all citizens on the issue at hand. The populace's decisions would be final. A pure, indirect democracy would make the assembly of elected representatives supreme. The legislation that the assembly passed would immediately become governmental policy—and it could change today what it decreed yesterday. The only check on its powers would be the periodic elections by which the populace expressed its approval of or disagreement with the assembly's decisions and the executive's enactment of those decisions.

Liberalism, however, erects another, independent source of authority to exist alongside the popular will to which democracy appeals. As a matter of historical fact, the expedient of a constitution as a constraint on arbitrary power was first developed as a check on monarchial and/or aristocratic rule. In intellectual as contrasted to political history, we can trace the notion of limits on what power can do to debates in medieval theology about whether God is constrained by reason or natural law or some other independent set of principles that even He cannot violate. A totally "arbitrary" power—unfettered by natural laws, by canons of logic and consistency, by moral principles, by cultural and historical traditions, or by institutional procedures—would make all human action untenable. Human agency relies on a felt capacity to make decisions on the basis of imaginatively projecting certain results from undertaking certain actions. Only if humans successfully move much of the time from decision through action to something fairly close to the desired result can they develop a sense of human power, of the capacity to influence the course of events and the course of their own lives. Human power is, of course, hardly unlimited. An individual constantly experiences the various contingencies that frustrate his best-laid plans and encounters other powers (especially those of our fellow human beings) that work against what he strives to accomplish. But the existence of an arbitrary, unchecked power that transcended the individual—whether divine or an absolute monarch or the collective power of society—would make individual agency impossible, simply pointless. The individual would not have the capacity to determine and enact anything. We should recognize that many (perhaps most) human beings throughout history have lived in that powerless condition, or at least in a condition in which what capacity they possessed to determine for themselves was extremely limited.

Liberalism desires to expand, as far as practicable, the individual's powers of self-determination. (I will return to the complications entailed by this baseline individualism in the section on liberalism's values.) That commitment requires the limitation of transindividual powers. It is not enough to multiply sites of power and to distribute power among all citizens. There also has to be checks on the exercise of power at those various sites, just as there will be legal constraints on what individuals can do. Institutions, in many ways, are to be feared more than individuals since they can command greater resources and act more effectively than a single person. In any case, institutions—whether political or civil—must be situated within a framework that prevents them from acting arbitrarily and that checks any tendency toward the accumulation of power at the expense of either other individuals or other institutions.

A constitution—and the legal apparatus established to maintain it—functions as a site and a source of power that is separate from, and in a necessary tension with, the demos. From whence does the constitution derive its authority? From the demos.[19] Liberalism, in its founding moment, cannot appeal to either God or tradition to legitimate its establishment of the rule of law. The recourse to divine sanction is barred because modern peoples do not follow the same God. A state grounded in religion will be subject to the endless religious squabbles that liberalism strives to sidestep. Liberalism places human authority where divine authority was. In the founding moment, the demos binds itself by a law, a constitution, that its representatives write and the people ratify. David J. Siemers explains why Madison placed such emphasis on ratification of the U.S. Constitution by the people:

> To ensure its sacred character, Madison's constitutional scripture
> would receive its form above and outside normal acts of legislation.
> Its power would be officially sanctioned by clearly recognized acts
> of popular consent occurring in historical time. . . . Madison strongly
> advocated that the Constitution be ratified by ad hoc conventions.
> This extraordinary arrangement would mark the Constitution as an
> exceptional legal entity, a true act of popular sovereignty outside,
> above, and unalterable by mere statutory law.[20]

Humans give their laws to themselves, a position most fully worked out in Kant's practical (moral and political) philosophy—and Madison wanted to invest that act with as much majesty as possible. The people, in freedom, constrain themselves, creating legal institutions and authorities that will now have power over them.

Being modern, however, entails the recognition of historical change. The very term "modern" marks a temporal break; used as an adjective, "modern" indicates that this practice, artifact, belief, or institution did not exist at some point in the past. "Modern" says that the life I lead is substantially different from the life my ancestors led and implies that my descendants will, in turn, lead a life different from mine. The Constitution, no matter how solemnly instituted, should be open to change. As Madison argues in Federalist No. 37, "a faultless plan was not to be expected" since the founders were subject to the "fallibility" to which all humans are "liable" (195). Under the circumstances, "the most that the [Constitutional] Convention could do . . . was to avoid the errors suggested by the past experience of other countries, as well as of our own; and to provide a convenient mode of rectifying their own errors, as future experience may unfold them" (175). The demos that established the rule of law can also revise it. There needs to be an active and continual interchange between the sovereign people and the law if that law is not, in its own turn, to be experienced as arbitrary and despotic.

We experience yet another of liberalism's precarious balancing acts here. It is precisely this sense of liberalism's delicacy, its fragility, that motivates this book. In search of the greatest possible freedom and peace, liberalism continually establishes—and strives to maintain—sophisticated expedients that balance opposing needs and tendencies. There is—and can be—nothing simple about liberalism. It has neither a simple view of our needs nor a simple view of how they can be best met. And it can never rely on simple—and direct—modes of enforcement because the dilution of power and its abuses is always one of its central aims. That's why liberalism is and should be frustrating. It checks our desires to act forcefully; it frustrates any individual or institution that strives to take matters into its own hands. What to critics looks like liberalism's paralysis, its wishy-washiness, is actually liberalism's abiding dedication to the principle that one person, one agency, one institution should never be allowed to do the job. It should always be limited, be held in place, by its relations to other people, other agencies, and other institutions with which it must negotiate. The self-determining individuals that liberalism aims to empower are still always embedded in legal and social relations to others that check exercises of untrammeled will.

The balancing act here is between the law as servant of the people and the law as tyrant over the people. The law must be both subject to the people (thus revisable by them) and a check on the actions of the people. So the power invested in the demos and the power invested in the law should be separate, but they should also be related to and capable of influencing one another. The law, of course, will inevitably influence people insofar as its enforcement will constrain people's actions. For that reason, liberalism believes the influence should also work in the other direction. There must be means established for the people to influence the law.

American liberalism provides three crucial mechanisms for revising the law—and, ultimately, the Constitution. The first are the explicit rules for formal amendment. The second is normal legislation. The Constitution hardly claims to be a complete body of law. Rather, it establishes the framework within which the people and their representatives engage in the ongoing task of devising and elaborating society's laws. Thus, the Constitution's gaps, its silences, are as important as its specific strictures.[21] While it rules some decisions and actions out of bounds, its silences indicate that other decisions and actions are possible and permitted, but hardly mandated. Thus, the writing, passing, and enacting of laws (by its representatives in the legislature) becomes the central (although not the sole) way the demos governs itself and manifests its power. The rule of law becomes the very form through which the "superior" power of the people expresses itself. That form, like all forms, both constrains and enables. Or, to be more precise, it enables by constraining. It provides the means for organization and articulation, giving the inchoate desires of the demos a way to come into public existence. Described this way, the tension between legal forms and the people's power might seem simply productive, utterly benign. But their intersections are more fraught than that, as indicated by the last scene for their meeting: the courtroom.

The legislature is hardly conflict-free. There are, and should be, substantial disagreements over what the government can and should do. But the legislative process produces new laws that are positive articulations of collectively made decisions to act. These decisions are constrained by the Constitution's established guidelines of the permissible—and, thus, all laws in the American system are subject to judicial review. The means for review, however, seem peculiar at first glance. The judges do not simply read each act passed by Congress and rule on its constitutionality. Rather, all judgments—no matter how wide-ranging their application will prove—are made in the context of, in relation to, individual cases. No law is reviewed unless its enactment in some particular instance causes some citizen to challenge it. And the challenge to the law is staged in a courtroom setting that is deliberately—and elaborately—adversarial. Why?

The answer is partly historical. The American founders retained the English case law system even though the Americans also wrote a formal Constitution. The founders provided for the evolution of the Constitution through its continual testing by difficult, unexpected, and debatable cases. In other words, they understood that they could hardly expect, as they tried to project the new nation's future needs, to anticipate every contingency that might arise. They also understood that no set of laws would eliminate conflict. So the legal system had to provide a place where conflicts could be aired and adjudicated. Crucially, it had to provide a place where the law itself could be contested. The people must be able to question the law, to challenge it. A court case stages the fact that the people are not above the law—but neither is the law above the people. Finally, trial by case law enables the law to be responsive to new circumstances and unexpected social interactions. Only a flexible, evolving law could hope to prove resilient enough to provide a framework for a modern, ever-changing society. The law must generalize, but its generalizations need to be continually tested against conditions on the ground—as represented by specific cases and by the variety of positions that can (and will) be taken in relation to those cases. Madison makes this point well: "All new laws, though penned with the greatest technical skill, and passed on the fullest and most mature deliberation, are considered more or less obscure and equivocal, until their meaning be liquidated and ascertained by particular discussions and adjudications" (Federalist No. 37: 198).

We reach here the much contested—but also, I think, badly misconstrued —question of how much leeway judges should have in their interpretation of the Constitution. Conservatives claim that the only safeguard against arbitrary "judicial activism" (the buzzword of our day) is adherence to "original intent."[22] Liberals argue that the Constitution is, necessarily, an evolving document—with the means for its evolution built in by the original framers themselves. The liberal position only makes sense if we see the Constitution as existing between two sources of extralegal authority: the demos and morality. I have already discussed how the law is established as a constraint on pure democracy. The people—or the legislature as their instrument—cannot simply suspend civil liberties or declare Buddhism the state religion. On the other hand, the law also constrains morality. Most fundamentally, it takes the power to judge crimes and to punish criminals out of all private hands and locates it in the legal system. But the law also refuses to involve the state in the judgment or punishment of various behaviors that morality condemns— from various forms of sexual behavior to vices like gambling, drinking, or laziness. Most dramatically, the law imposes its version of "justice" over and against the passionate sense of what is just that morality affords many individuals in many instances. Few participants in a court case are fully satisfied by the outcome. The gap between what the law decides and what morality, in the eyes of some individuals, demands often yawns wide. Courtroom experience is frustrating, even infuriating.

As already noted, the law must constrain, but also allow productive (revisionary) interaction with, the demos. The same dynamic informs the law's relation to morality. Liberalism strives to resist a tyranny exercised by some citizens over others in the name of morality. Precisely because moral values differ, liberalism refuses to give any particular moral viewpoint (treated here like any other faction that has pretensions to being given full sway in the polity) absolute authority.[23] The law is not—and should not be—the articulated morality of the society. That is because any such articulation of a morality would never capture the moral convictions of every member of that society. Liberal law, in other words, exists as much to protect a citizen from the imposition of another's morality as it does to instantiate the community's morality. Morality is a source and a form of power that liberal law serves to constrain—just as it works to constrain various other forms of power in society.

Here is the main point—a crucial one because misunderstanding this point is the source of endless and harmful confusions. Law in a liberal society is political, not moral. The law is political because its aim is to establish and maintain the conditions in which the people can live in peace and security while each person possesses as much power of self-determination as possible. The law establishes a polity and a modus vivendi for social interactions within that polity. It is political because it addresses the difficulties that arise from human beings living, consorting, and acting together—and provides the frameworks, procedures, and sites for the ongoing negotiation of those difficulties (among which are conflicts in moral views).

But the law is hardly disconnected from morality. The political cannot be divorced from the moral, but liberalism insists that to collapse the two into one another is disastrous. Again, liberalism's preferred model is the proliferation of sites of power, of sources of authority. The dividing lines here are fuzzy, so this paragraph offers tentative distinctions. But the important thing is not whether the details convince you, but whether the notion of a distinction between the political and the moral makes sense—and whether the rationale for maintaining that distinction is compelling. That said, I think "peace" and "security" are political goods. The law is political insofar as it works to secure those goods by ordering our relations to those with whom we share the polity and, ultimately, the world. Freedom (or self-determination) seems to be more ambiguous. I am inclined to call freedom a political good but can see why tyranny might be thought a moral issue as much as, even more than, a political one. Justice, however, seems to me a moral category—and the moral category that most inevitably and consistently interacts with the political. Laws that violate many citizens' sense of justice will generate resistance, either in the form of nonobservance or in reform efforts. Similarly, laws that violate other deeply held moral tenets will meet resistance, if only from the individuals who have those moral beliefs. The means of resistance are multiple, ranging from political organizing to civil disobedience to various forms of violence. Any law (from the Constitution on down) is only effective if the vast majority of citizens voluntarily comply with it. The classic American case is Prohibition, which tried to make illegal an activity many citizens thought morally and socially permissible. When a large number of citizens (just how large is an interesting question—where is the tipping point?) feel morally justified in breaking a law, that law becomes unenforceable. Law, then, cannot ignore morality, just as it cannot ignore the demos. It must remain in a productive, yet tension-laden, dialogue with morality, just as it keeps open its avenues of communication with the demos.

The founders' retention of the adversarial case law system suggests that they understood that morality evolves. In modern conditions, moral beliefs clash. Moral positions are always being contested by those with different views—and sometimes a society's prevailing views change. At other times, there isn't anything that can be easily identified as the prevailing view since there is widespread diversity of opinion. It certainly seems the historical case that Americans changed their position on the morality, not just the legality, of slavery between 1787 and 1887. And it also is arguably the case that some of the founders hoped for and expected that change. Thus they wanted to establish a legal framework that could evolve in relation to such wide-scale changes in moral outlook. At any given moment in a society's history, some moral issues will be fairly uncontroversial, with most citizens holding roughly similar views, while other issues will be hotly contested. Those contests will be waged in the public square, in elections, in legislative debates, and in courtrooms. Much of the contest will be rhetorical—with citizens trying to persuade others to change their views. But the contests can also become more physical. What did more to change American views of slavery—the rhetorical work of the abolitionists or the Civil War? The process of change was neither neat nor simple—nor, unfortunately, without a high cost in human lives. The law has the delicate task of being aligned with uncontroversial views, of curbing the strictures of zealots in the controversial cases, and of keeping its ear to the ground so as to register movements from controversial to uncontroversial (and vice versa). The continual arguments staged and waged in the courtroom are the law's most reliable means of contact with the moral convictions of the citizenry.

Not all law cases, of course, hinge on moral disputes. Much more common are conflicting interests. Liberal law strives not merely to protect life and liberty from despotic power, but also to secure property. It is precisely here that leftist critics insist that "the rule of law" simply provides for the state's aiding and abetting the appropriation of the lion's share of society's goods by the wealthy few.[24] Liberal law, so they argue, defines as "private"—and hence outside the public jurisdiction, control, or use—resources that can be gained and held only because of that enabling definition. The very structure of liberal law creates the possibility of large-scale inequalities in command of and access to material goods and resources. Thus, the political (or legal) "freedom" afforded by a liberal polity is a sham because it fosters economic inequalities that make that freedom ineffective. If I cannot afford to act on various options, then what good is my putative freedom?

I think such leftist arguments misdiagnose the causes of the problem. (This is not to say that the problem of inequality does not exist or is insignificant. To the contrary.) Liberalism's commitment to establishing a distinction between "private" and "public" domains does not necessarily generate the kinds of inequality in wealth that currently prevail in America. The fault lies in the content, not the structure. The private/public distinction is justified—and crucial—precisely as a limitation on state power. But much depends on how that distinction is drawn. And we should fully expect that the lines between public and private will be continually contested and will shift over time. America's current economic inequalities are certainly a symptom of consolidated power—and, as such, call for strengthening countervailing powers. To be absolutely concrete for a moment, the freedom of workers to associate and to gain some leverage against their employers through association has been undermined by an ensemble of forces—some legal, some economic, some cultural—over the past forty years, with most lamentable results.[25] It is utterly consistent with liberal efforts to combat consolidations of power to institute legal mechanisms that protect workers' interests. A minimum wage law is just one tiny example, while the actual level at which the minimum wage is set illustrates the prevailing balance of power between employees and employers. (See Appendix, item 3.) Freedom depends—only in part, but still in part—on citizens retaining some independence from the state, which means, among other things, not being totally dependent on the state for their livelihoods. Only citizens with a separate source of economic well-being can then stand up to the state, contesting its various dictates in courts of law or in various forms of political agitation. By the same token, citizens need the means to avoid total dependence on their employers.

In a liberal polity, certain "private" realms exist outside the government's purview. Vibrant, ongoing, and deeply engaging activity in those realms multiplies the sites at which freedom is enjoyed and action undertaken. The ongoing issue is where to draw the public/private line. What should law dictate—that is, forbid or make obligatory? What should law regulate—that is, permit but establish parameters within which the permissible unfolds? What should law leave entirely alone—that is, set no limits and remain utterly silent? These questions are continually negotiated and renegotiated in a liberal polity. The public/private line does not remain in a single place. A good example in our time involves questions of child and spousal abuse. Before 1970, the state generally turned a blind eye toward domestic relations. But society has gradually moved to a sense that the law should actively interfere in physical violence that occurs within the family.

Liberalism is messy because it eschews simple or final solutions. It strives to balance different claims and powers, to find trade-offs among conflicting views, imperatives, and goods that will get the contending parties as much of what they want as possible. No one is likely to get everything that he or she wants. All settlements are thus inherently unstable because all the involved parties will keep contending for a new arrangement that suits them better—and new parties to the dispute will arise. The temporary settlements liberalism achieves place competing interests in wary, but still peaceful, relations to one another. The contending parties are held in place by a sense that everyone loses big time if no settlement can be reached, if civil peace yields to civil war. But we can fully expect each party to push things to the brink, to strive to get as much as possible without driving the other side into violent resistance. And thus we can also expect the parties to feel some considerable hostility to liberalism's moderating mechanisms, to the legal contrivances by which it tries to regulate, contain, and adjudicate conflicts.

Liberalism acknowledges an imperfect world and provides constraints that we put upon ourselves to curb our tendencies for unrestrained conflict. In the heat of the conflict, it is all too easy to forget that these laws exist to protect us from ourselves and to experience them instead as impediments to our desires. The liberal legal framework almost never grants anyone an absolute victory because today's absolute triumphs breed tomorrow's wars. If you leave someone powerless, without the political and legal means to advance their interests, then you have invited them to step outside the legal and political framework to wage war. Hence, liberalism shuns drastic, final solutions. It only offers makeshifts and frameworks, fully expecting them to change as needs and circumstances change. Liberalism values flexibility and reversibility over dogmatic certainty. It is more interested in establishing ways of living in peace with others than in being right. (I hear in imagination's ear the howls that this statement will elicit. A more extended defense of this statement is offered in the section on "Values.") Liberal law—poised between morality and the demos, between public need and private property, between enunciated general principles and thorny individual cases—embodies, to the frustration of nearly all, these unsatisfying, impure, never-final decisions on how to proceed here and now to the best of our abilities in ways that keep social relations intact.

To some extent, the rule of law is smoke and mirrors. To self-proclaimed radicals on both the right and the left, liberal legalism is dangerously naive. If the law is self-created, grounded in human authority alone, then it stands on nothing but whim. What humans did yesterday they can undo with impunity today. The cynical response to this abyss is to declare that might rules all. Liberal law is a delusion, a mask. It is a laughably feeble effort to restrain power—and it cannot possibly do the job. Those who trust in the law to protect them will be crushed. Those strong and ruthless enough (think Machiavelli and Nietzsche) to recognize that power is all and to pursue it full bore will be the world's masters. Whatever power the law possesses comes from the force with which it is made to prevail. Only violent enforcement makes the law effective—and it is made effective solely to serve the accumulation of power by some in face of the desire of others to grab that power for themselves. It is all struggle all the time, and no liberal expedient can hope to mitigate the conflicts. Power cannot be distributed and multiplied, nor can competition be moderated by compromises and trade-offs. Humans strive for absolute power, and contrivances short of violent conflict cannot stop that headlong rush.

The response to this drastic view can only be that the proof is in the pudding. Neither abstract thinking, nor general claims about "human nature" and "social laws," nor projective thought experiments can tell us in advance whether liberal expedients can produce societies in which citizens manage to live together in peace for a relatively long time because enough of them possess a large enough portion of freedom, security, and prosperity to make risking it all seem a bad bet. Their motives need not be so calculating; they may also avoid risking the liberal peace—despite its inevitable frustrations—out of the desire to pursue other interests (religious, aesthetic, intellectual, etc.) or out of a sense of commitment to their neighbors' well-being or out of a more abstract sense of justice. But let's stick for the moment to prudential considerations. Liberalism justifies itself pragmatically when it says that it can, precisely by forefronting peaceful coexistence along with individual autonomy, deliver peace and security. The price for these not inconsiderable achievements is that you won't get everything; you will inevitably have to accept some frustration of your desires. And the stratagem for achieving this result includes submission to a law that is admittedly human in origin and in execution. Humans living in society with one another will bind themselves to constraints underwritten by a humanly contrived law and a set of institutions/arrangements that instantiate and perpetuate the rule of that law.

David Hume is the thinker who has most fully thought through this pragmatic understanding of the rule of law. He takes the example of promises to illustrate the social dynamics involved here.[26] Making promises is a completely human contrivance. It is a language game that humans have invented—and it establishes a distinctive relation between one person and another. (Hannah Arendt goes so far as identifying promises as the foundation of all polities, as the fundamental way that people bind themselves to one another.)[27] Promising is a social institution because its conventions—the procedures for making a promise and for determining what counts as a promise—are neither individualistic nor subjective. But promising is not natural either. It is something that exists only between humans who share a language. A human child must learn from other humans what a promise is and how to make and understand one. No other animals, from all that we can observe, make promises. So the establishment of the social institution of promising is a matter of human ingenuity responding to human needs.

How, Hume asks, is this social institution preserved? It is transmitted through education; it is legitimated by an appeal to its benefits for social intercourse; it is enforced by social sanctions (disapproval, shunning, and perhaps even legal proceedings in breach-of-contract cases); but, primarily, it is maintained by repeated acts of promising by various people who have mastered the ability to make and receive promises and who have internalized its rules to such an extent that they experience a "wrong" when they themselves or someone else abuses the convention by uttering a false promise. Hume highlights that human beings, in society, have this capacity to bind themselves to norms of their own devising—and that habit, social approbation, and an interest in peaceful, stable, and secure relations with one's fellows can give the norms sufficient authority to make them effective and relatively long-lasting. They are "relatively" long-lasting because all things—even the earth itself—exist within a temporality of impermanence.

Liberals believe that the law is no different in kind than promising. Yes, we have established much more elaborate mechanisms, the whole apparatus of the state, to preserve and enact the law, but its origins and its rationale are continuous with those of promising. We reach here a crucial difference from some conservatives. Many conservatives insist that grounding the law on human authority means we are a short step away from declaring that everything is permitted. (Not all conservatives take this position. Edmund Burke and Michael Oakeshott base their conservatism precisely on the need to preserve humanly created institutions. Hume himself, for that matter, was a conservative political thinker for the most part despite the fact that his atheism led his contemporaries to see him as a "radical.")[28]

Why, some conservatives ask, should any individual bind herself to dictates that emanate from another human being? Only a suprahuman source of authority can command respect and obedience. Conservatives of this stamp tend to locate that suprahuman source in the divine, or in Nature.[29] By way of contrast, Burke and Oakeshott try to instill a reverence for tradition in their readers, but they never claim that the origin of those traditional ways and established institutions is anything but human. Their thought is motivated by their sense of the fragility of the humanly created, but they do not deny its legitimacy or question its ability to be effective.

Liberals agree that the law is fragile—and responsibility for its preservation lies solely in our human hands. So we should—as part of our civic education—be impressed with a sense of the law's benefits and of our having to do our part in both its preservation and its evolution. No one else can do this work for us. But liberals generally want to temper a reverence for tradition, for what is currently in place, with continued examination of its rationale and of its appropriateness in changed circumstances. An over-rigid refusal to revise the law out of a sense of its fragility is as likely to undermine that same law as to protect it. The law, as I have argued, must remain responsive to, even while somewhat independent of, the claims of politics, morals, reason, and social changes. A law that is out of touch with current realities and current moral and political sensibilities invites widespread disrespect and disobedience.

Beyond this pragmatic appeal to people's practices and their results, the secularist and humanist asks those who insist that we need a suprahuman origin for the law: What historical evidence do we possess that appeals to nonhuman grounds for authority are effective? When it comes to injustice, killing, and general mayhem, the historical record offers little proof that more mystical forms of authority command greater allegiance than secular ones. Sectarian violence alone should give pause to anyone who thinks that divine authority would produce better human behavior toward other humans. More generally, however, any argument about the law's source of authority should take care not to confuse the law's articulation of certain norms and the law's ability to shape behavior. The law articulates a desideratum. The very need to state these principles, rules, and guidelines reflects the knowledge that humans will often act to violate them. In establishing its laws, a society states what it hopes to encourage human beings to become. The law is akin to morality in at least this respect: it sets up ideals that people are urged to live up to. That urging is partly positive, partly negative. On the positive side of the ledger are the benefits accruing from law-abiding behavior, benefits that range from peace and security to the perfectionist achievement of self-referential virtues such as integrity, honor, and altruism (to name just a few). On the negative side of the ledger, most obviously, stands punishment. No legal code—or even a more loosely organized social institution like promising—can allow all deviant behavior to pass unsanctioned.

The real question, it seems to me, is not whether divine authority is more effective than an openly acknowledged human source for the law. The questions of moment are, instead, (1) the extent to which the inducements to obedience are effective, and (2) the authority that legitimates punishment. Every legal code provides for punishment in this world, no matter what it might say about the real penalty being enacted in another world. Thus, in practice, appeals to suprahuman authority show little confidence in that authority's effectiveness. They invariably supplement the punishment to come in the hereafter with a more immediate punishment here and now. Furthermore, punishment within a system that appeals to a suprahuman grounding passes the buck. The human agents of punishment insist that this punishment is performed in the name of, is authorized by, something beyond the human. The punisher is only an instrument of a higher power. Liberalism sees this sleight of hand as just another example of certain humans abrogating power to themselves. It seems pretty generally the case that punishments are more severe when the punishers are convinced that they are serving the purposes of a larger, more-than-human power. It is certainly the case that such an understanding legitimates the concentration of power in the hands of the righteous, who then wield it against the reprobate. Liberalism is always suspicious of any arrangements that lead to power inequities.

To take it upon oneself to punish another human being is an awful thing. Liberals believe that nothing should obscure that awfulness. We should ensure that we feel the full weight of the responsibility we humans take upon ourselves when we decide to punish other humans. The law—and its agents—should recognize that its authority is merely human. We humans are responsible for everything the law accomplishes and does, both for good and for evil. The law is not exempt from human imperfection and from the human tendency to abrogate power and misuse it. That's why it is crucial that the law contain within itself mechanisms for its revision and its contestation. The law is an expedient to protect us from some of our worst human tendencies, but it cannot save us from ourselves each and every time. It can itself become an instrument for the enactment of those tendencies. The law is not a deus ex machina. It does not come from elsewhere to ensure justice. Whether or not it serves more to secure justice than to prevent it is entirely in the hands of its human practitioners. And that, for the most part, is a hopeful fact since a nonhuman understanding of the law and its foundation all too often licenses the most inhuman treatment of human beings by other human beings, while also placing the law beyond question and reform.

The law, then, articulates norms (or ideals) that can only be instantiated by human action. The norms are alive, have a real presence in the world, only insofar as some people believe and abide by them. Social institutions (like the legal system) provide trans-individual and cross-generational (i.e., persistent over time) sites that help, but cannot guarantee, the collectivity's attempt to make its norms thrive. The example of language itself is instructive here. It is possible to codify the rules of language, to produce a "grammar" and a dictionary, but it is not possible to keep a language alive unless there is a community actively using that language day in and day out to conduct its relationships among its members. There are social mechanisms—from schooling to the chiding of nonconformists—for maintaining relatively "standard" usage, but the language will change over time. However, language's fluidity, its shifts in both syntax and semantics over time, does not undermine its ability to function adequately at any given historical moment. Even though it is built on shifting sands, the interest each speaker has in maintaining the ability to communicate with his neighbors motivates adherence to prevailing practices. Finally, language is not subjective. Even the person who introduces a new word to the language cannot do so single-handedly. His word will not become part of the language unless other speakers adopt and use it. In short, language is thoroughly human—and socially but not subjectively relative (different societies have different languages, just as different societies have different legal systems and different currencies). The human and relative characteristics of language do not render it so unstable that it fails to satisfy the human needs it exists to serve. Yes, language is imperfect, but it would probably be a lot worse if placed on more stable foundations, ones that prevented it from changing along with the times. Flexibility is to be highly prized—in law as well as in language. Case law gives us the ability to respond to individual cases, just as our linguistic ingenuity is tested by our unfolding experiences and aided by the open-ended structure of our language.

Legal norms, like the grammar of a language, are given a real presence in the world by their ongoing practice, their instantiation in human actions. Even at the best of times, norms are a tenuous bulwark against abuses. Nothing underwrites the law—or the convention of promising—except the continued and continual practices of lawful behavior and of promising. The law is reaffirmed anew and reinforced each time it is enunciated, followed, and enforced. And the temptation to circumvent the law, to rewrite it to accommodate one's current beliefs and interests, is ever present. Hume identifies this ever-present temptation by distinguishing between the arrant and the sensible knave.[30] The arrant knave is the simple thief, the person who acts in direct defiance of legal prohibition in trying to grab goods and power to which he is not entitled (where, of course, the terms of entitlement are established through the legal system). The sensible knave, however, is more insidious. He is someone who aims to secure the goods provided by social institutions like the law without engaging in the practices that alone can underwrite those institutions' continuance. More recent liberal theorists call the sensible knave "the free rider." This knave makes a false promise that gives him an advantage in his dealings with another—fully cognizant of the fact that his false promise only works because of the general practice of making and keeping promises. Enough sensible knaves and the institution of promising will collapse altogether. Enough use of the law to enable or to cover up consolidations of power and/or of wealth and the law itself, with its dependence on voluntary compliance and its continuance through observant practices, will collapse. To think that divine authority or reason could shore up a law undermined by sensible knaves who maneuver within the social framework it establishes to thwart its informing norms is to misread history and to misunderstand how the law is judged by its subjects on the ground. Widespread abuse—what we nowadays tend to call "corruption"—renders the law nugatory.

The law, as we say, is no respecter of persons. With that generalized suspicion that characterized the founders, especially Madison, the law looks askance at each individual's propensity to make an exception of herself.[31] Whether blind self-love is derived from an assurance in one's virtue or from one's pursuit of material well-being (worse still are those who combine the two), the law points to each individual's partiality (in every sense of that word) and urges or persuades or forces the individual to understand and undertake her actions within a social matrix. Each individual has a stake in maintaining these social institutions since each benefits from them. And those institutions establish procedures—most crucially, adversarial contests between equal parties before a judge who is not a party to either side of the dispute—that serve to contain individual partiality. Hence the emphasis on an independent judiciary.

Impatience with the law is endemic since it so often frustrates immediate individual desires or conflicts with strongly held moral intuitions. The point is hardly to render the law immune to contestation. Rather, the rule of law is one component among several in a liberal polity. It is a crucial site of social power and has the specific functions outlined here. But it does not reign supreme—or on its lonesome. It exists in tension and in relation to the demos, to morality, to the getting and spending of economic life, and to the various individual exercises of freedom through which a life is forged. Liberalism, however, has a huge stake in maintaining the rule of law because it locates sovereignty in the people who create the law to which they subject themselves and who maintain that law through their continual acts of rearticulating, enacting, and obeying it. A law that is both responsive to and semiremoved from the endless debates that characterize a pluralistic society serves as a fundamental safeguard against tyranny.

I want to turn now to liberalism's understanding of and relation to that pluralistic society, but must first address one last issue raised by the rule of law. The American Constitution begins "We, the people of the United States. . . ." But, of course, the United States did not exist prior to the Constitution. That nation is what the Constitution constitutes. The law—its articulation, its ratification, its enactment, its ongoing practice and enforcement, and the interactions and contestations among citizens that take place within its framework—creates the nation and sustains it. The origin is the establishment of the rule of law. Without the law (as embodied in the Constitution), the nation does not exist. That is why new citizens, new soldiers, and those newly elected to office swear to uphold the Constitution, which is the palpable and indispensable source of nationhood.

But what about the people? Liberalism, in almost all concrete cases (England provides the most important historical exception), has been fundamentally democratic insofar as it locates sovereignty in the people. (Yet, as I have argued, liberalism is not purely democratic since it provides checks and balances to the people's sovereignty.) The Constitution has to be ratified by the people in order to be legitimate and to take effect. This law is to be respected, is to be established, only if it is a law the people impose on themselves. Who is "the people"? The odd use of the singular verb "is" here, just like the use of the definite article "the," indicates that "the people" is understood as a single unit even though it is comprised of multiple persons. If the Constitution—and thus, ultimately, the nation—derives its authority from the people, then what constitutes the people? It would seem that the people must preexist the nation. But how can there be an American people prior to there being an American nation?

The straightforward liberal response is that the people constitute themselves as a people in their ratification and ongoing enactment of the Constitution. Existence as a nation and as a citizen is performative.[32] A nation becomes a nation through a verbal ceremony, just as a wedding establishes a new relationship between two people through a few words being spoken. Those words change everything. But they are only empty words if not followed up by countless corresponding actions over a long span of time. The new relations established by the wedding ceremony or by the ratification of the Constitution must be given flesh (as it were) through the way they are lived day in and day out. The people self-consciously designate (declare) themselves a people at the founding moment. They give themselves the task of unfolding the meanings and ramifications of that declaration through their history.

Liberalism, in this respect, is forward-looking. It recognizes the crucial importance of the origin in establishing the framework, the ensemble of relationships, for action. But it insists that the origin, while constraining, is not determinative. The rules of a game like baseball allow the activity to occur, but they only provide a general structure. Everything from batting stances to the development of different pitches to tactical decisions about positioning the fielders and attempting to steal bases is completely unscripted. The actual game—as played on the field—is created by its practitioners over time. Similarly, the nation and the people are brought into existence by the ratification of the Constitution, but the concrete character of that nation and that people unfolds through their actions as time moves forward from the starting point. Patterns and habits are, of course, created, so the nation's history displays various continuities and even settled arrangements that can prove difficult to change. But revisions and novelties are also introduced as time rolls on. The nation and the people are always a work in progress, attentive to, but not slavishly bound by, the origin.

That, at least, is the ideal. As a matter of historical fact, since its origins in the seventeenth and eighteenth centuries, liberalism has been shadowed by conceptions of "the people" that posit determinative and definitive origins.[33] Having lost any shared religious belief that united people, the modern era has evidenced a continual anxiety about what "social glue" will bind together people who live within a single polity.[34] If everyone followed his own conscience, believed in his own god, and pursued his own interest (as the new economics of capitalism encouraged him to do), what would prevent the chaos of endless doctrinal and political disputes set against the backdrop of unmitigated economic competition? Various candidates for a centripetal force to poise against all the centrifugal forces of modernity are advanced. Most notably: ethnicity, culture, and/or nationalism. (Usually, in practice, some combination of all three, with a shared language thrown into the mix, is proffered.) A quasi-mystical entity, understood as preexisting the establishment of a legal framework in the Constitution, is designated as the source of the people's "identity" as a people. These entities are quasi-mystical because, while not strictly speaking nonworldly, they can never be called into presence. Rather, they are invoked as the substance or category that underlies and unites a multiple set of people and/or practices even though this underlying principle of unity is notoriously difficult to specify. There is no blood test to prove ethnicity, no way to settle the issue of whether the Bible or Shakespeare is part of American culture, and no uncontestable litmus test of one's nationalistic fervor. The law—for those who elevate ethnicity, culture, or nationalism in this way—merely expresses and subsequently preserves the essence of this primal source of our existence together as one people. And that essence, crucially, must be protected against everything that would dilute it, that would change it. Those who locate a source of nationhood or identity prior to the establishment of the rule of law are almost always oriented toward origins and faithfulness to them. The anxiety about social unity that is indicated in their positing of these quasi-mystical entities also expresses itself in their conviction that it will be "chaos come again" if those entities are revised or dethroned. Here, then, we find another set of pressures (apart from those that stem from the demos or from morality) to which the rule of law is commonly subjected.

My presentation of this issue has made it clear where my sympathies lie. Even while I, in this book, invoke the American founding, I do not believe that origins are determinative. That America was founded, to a large extent, on the "original sins" of slavery and the displacement/extermination of indigenous peoples does not doom us to perpetual racism or enduring injustice. Those origins are hardly irrelevant—and should be both acknowledged and rectified. I have been willing—even eager—to place the law in productive tension with the demos and morality. Can I find my way to a similar understanding of the law's relation to the origins located in ethnicity, culture, nationalism, and a violent history often driven by those abstractions? Certainly, as a matter of sheer necessity, a realistic liberal must acknowledge passionate attachments to these representations of the sources of personal and group identity—just as the realistic liberal must recognize passionate attachments to religious beliefs. These attachments are facts about human motivations that a liberal Constitution must take into account if it is to have any hope of creating a peaceful, well-ordered society. But, as with morality and the demos, liberal law stands apart from, refuses to grant immediate or unqualified authority to, the particular social identifications to which people are passionately attached. A society that only looked forward, that possessed no reverence for tradition, for established ways of doing things, would be as monstrous as one that insisted on ritualistic repetition of its origins. The rule of law, as we have seen, is balanced between constraint and the enabling of freedom, between establishing firm rules and allowing for those rules' revision. Liberalism does not entail complete impiety (Santayana defined piety as "loyalty to the sources of one's being"), although liberalism does tend to locate an individual's being out in front of her, as something she will create through her actions, not something which she was given at birth. (The whole historical shift from an aristocratic to a liberal society is summed up in that last sentence. That one's eventual identity was not determined by one's social place at birth seemed to John Stuart Mill *the* defining characteristic of the transition to modern societies.)[35]

The quandary here can be best illuminated by returning to the puzzle of "who is this people" who get to ratify the Constitution. Who is eligible to participate in this first vote? Since it is not the whole of humanity, there must be some setting of limits. The first—and most obvious—limit is territorial. The Constitution only has pretensions to establish itself as the law over a limited physical domain. Thus, it is the people living in that domain who get to vote. A people, then, has at least (it would seem) a geographic unity. Of course, there are various cases where even that unity is tenuous. More importantly, geographic proximity can foster as much conflict as cooperation. No one has ever thought living in the same territory is sufficient to render various persons "a people." And that is the rub. Because, invariably it would seem, the next step is to limit, by some other criteria, who gets to vote on the Constitution. Liberal principle aims for the inclusion of all. But the historical fact is partiality; some people in the relevant territory are allowed to vote and some are not. The tension in this case is between liberalism's commitment to inclusion and the fact that actual liberal law, bowing to the pressure of those who invoke preexisting entities to define who belongs to the people, excludes some. The history of liberal nations such as the United States follows a fairly predictable path toward greater inclusiveness, as excluded groups use appeals to liberal principles (especially equality) to shame or coerce the law to recognize their right to participate in political and social processes. But it would be foolish to think this history of conflicts over inclusion will ever end. So long as the world is divided into separate nations, there will be disputes about who belongs to this nation and who does not. Those disputes, in our time, have come to be centered around citizenship. It was hard finally (not that the effort was not made) to deny African Americans their civil rights in the middle of the twentieth century because no parties to the dispute denied that blacks were citizens. Blacks had already been accepted (in the one hundred years since the Civil War) as part of "the people," even if they were a part that was discriminated against. But, today, a large number of individuals who live in our midst are not deemed part of the people because they are not citizens. That the "illegal immigrants" live amid us is relevant to the conflicts about how to categorize these people legally, how to treat them morally and politically, and how to live with them sociably, but they have no established claim (as blacks did) on the polity. So the battleground is precisely whether or not to give them that established claim, whether or not to open the way to citizenship.[36]

My point is that all-inclusion is not an option. We cannot simply declare everyone in the world an American citizen. So our legal system will have to designate the conditions under which an individual is eligible for citizenship or not. Precisely because liberal law is no respecter of persons, liberalism rejects ethnic, cultural, or nationalistic criteria for citizenship. Such criteria are too "personal." They insist that someone possess a preexisting identity, whereas liberalism is more interested in what you will make of yourself. But the current dilemmas posed by illegal immigrants are a salutary reminder that the law must have some criteria on this issue. Those criteria will be subject to revision as they are contested in our courts and legislative assemblies, but it is ingenuous at best and covertly discriminatory at worst to claim that we have no criteria, that we stand for total inclusiveness.

The best current candidate for that criterion is contribution to the nation's well-being. I think (I don't claim that this argument necessarily follows from the principles of liberalism) that some kind of work visa (so that we honestly and legally recognize those whose labor our society makes use of) should be offered to all noncitizen workers and that there should be established ways of moving from those visas to citizenship. We should offer citizenship precisely to those who have a track record of using the opportunity our economy and its labor market have given them. Such a program would have the additional benefit of curbing the abuse of illegal workers, who accept poor working conditions and low wages out of fear of being turned over to the U.S. Immigration and Naturalization Service.

These speculations about current immigration policies do bear on liberal principles insofar as they suggest that patriotism can be grounded in an appreciation of the opportunities afforded by a peaceful, well-ordered society that extends the protection of law to all who are legally recognized—and that strives to legally recognize all who work in the society. The larger point is that the rule of law, the nation it establishes, and the benefits that follow from that establishment and that rule can be a completely sufficient source of patriotism. At times, writers have spoken of feelings inspired in this way as America's "civic religion." The name is neither here nor there. At stake is whether the nation—understood as a political entity created by the people to promote the general welfare of all—can inspire a devotion that binds the people to its laws and to one another. Liberals insist that this nation can produce all the patriotism we need.[37] The rule of law does not need to be grounded in ethnicity or culture or some mythos of the nation. David Hollinger highlights the contrast between what he calls (borrowing from Michael Ignatieff) "civic nationalism" and an "ethnic nationalism [that] claims . . . 'an individual's deepest attachments are inherited, not chosen.'" Civic nationalism asserts, instead, "'that the nation should be composed of all those—regardless of race, color, creed, gender, language, or ethnicity—who subscribe to the nation's political creed. This nationalism is called civic because it envisages the nation as a community of equal, rights-bearing citizens, united in patriotic attachment to a shared set of political practices and values.' . . . A civic nation is built and sustained by people who honor a common future more than a common past."[38] The fact of our living together in peace, sharing a history of struggles to maintain that peace and better our lot, is enough. The more we can convince ourselves that that is enough, and the more we can abandon appeals to and nostalgia for more mystical sources of union, the better off we will be because we will be abandoning desires for shared essences that prove, in practice, to be sources of division.

4

PLURALISM

Liberalism, both as a contingent historical fact and as a matter of its most fervently held principles, is a response to pluralism. We reach here the closest liberalism ever gets to a metaphysics. By metaphysics, I mean a claim to have identified an unalterable and universally present fact about the universe. Mostly, liberalism is empirical and antimetaphysical. It values openness to the world in which we find ourselves and to the others with whom we share that world—and it accepts that the passage of time brings with it dramatic changes in the conditions under which humans act and in human motivations themselves. Metaphysical (or ontological) assertions about the nature of things or about human nature, especially when those assertions identify those "natural" entities as permanent and unchangeable, are implausible in the face of historical and individual differences. "Unnatural" is a term almost always applied to something that some human somewhere has actually done, so clearly humans have the ability to do that thing; it is not rendered impossible by the facts of "human nature." Such appeals to "human nature" are ways of trying to establish limits that have already been violated. More direct arguments about the desirability—or lack thereof—of the behavior in question are preferable because they allow for an examination of reasons for and against.

Trying to keep preconceived notions from clouding its ability to apprehend and appreciate the ever-surprising unfolding of events, liberalism is slow to form overarching explanatory schemas and quick to revise them. Its temperament is watchful, undogmatic, curious, intellectually humble, and wary of condemning the strange, the new, or the different. In matters scientific (claims to describe the nature of nature, the architecture of the universe), liberalism adopts the fallibilism recommended by the American pragmatists and the open-ended process of continual inquiry, testing, and questioning advocated by Karl Popper.[39] Everything in human history to date suggests that our current scientific theories are "good enough" for various purposes but will be revised someday in ways unforeseeable to us now. For that reason, an instrumental as opposed to a metaphysical or dogmatic attitude toward prevailing theories makes the most sense.

When liberalism turns to social issues—to the relations between people—the same temperament and attitudes come to the fore. The social arrangements that best promote peace and the general welfare are preferred. Those arrangements are cheerfully revised without regret when better ways to promote the basic ends are devised. This process of revision will be, so far as we know, endless because the perfect society eludes us. But liberalism is idealistic in the sense that it is committed to the constant pursuit of improvement, of moving closer to the ideals of "perpetual peace" (to use Immanuel Kant's phrase) and a "just, well-ordered society" (to use John Rawls's phrase).[40]

Liberalism can be agnostic about scientific progress (Does each new theory brings us closer to the truth, to the way that things "really are"?) and about progress in cultural achievements (Does it even make any sense to wonder if music today is better or worse than it was in Mozart's time?). However, liberalism cannot be agnostic about progress in social matters. Of course, a liberal does not have to insist that actual progress has been accomplished. Things might very well be getting worse. But liberalism stands on the assertion that progress is possible, that human action can make things better. We measure progress in relation to the goals that we identify as what our actions aim to accomplish.

We reach here the first plank of the liberal metaphysic. Humans are not so corrupt or sinful or inept that improvement of their lot is rendered impossible. Humans can form worthy ideals, and they can improve their individual selves and their societies by acting in ways that move them toward those ideals. Human history and the present (with its diverse cultures) argue against overly restrictive accounts of "human nature." All the evidence, for example, suggests that humans sometimes act selfishly and sometimes act altruistically. Both are possible for humans, and there is no reason to claim that one is more "natural" or fundamental than the other. The founders' "realism" was based on a clear-eyed view of the evils (including domination) of which humans are capable, but it also relied on the "virtues" of which humans are equally capable. Their aim was to create social arrangements and institutions that provided checks against those tendencies to misuse power, but that also encouraged and gave scope to the exercise of civic virtues. In Federalist No. 55, Madison writes:

> As there is a degree of depravity in mankind which requires a certain degree of circumspection and distrust: So there are other qualities in human nature, which justify a certain portion of esteem and confidence. Republican government presupposes the existence of these qualities in a higher degree than any other form. Were the pictures which have been drawn by the political jealousy of some among us, faithful likenesses of the human character, the inference would be that there is not sufficient virtue among men for self-government; and that nothing less than the chains of despotism can restrain them from destroying and devouring one another. (312)[41]

Such deliberate framing of institutional arrangements to activate certain potentials in humans and discourage others ("political and social engineering," to use the pejorative term sometimes applied to it) is not necessarily futile, although unexpected consequences, unforeseen circumstances, and human evil all make the translation from intention to result contingent and uncertain. Armed with a strong sense of human fallibility and attentive to the feedback offered by unexpected results, purposive human action can, in the realm of politics as elsewhere, have beneficial consequences.[42] Such action should be based on a shrewd sense of the human desires and tendencies that history and the present reveal, but also open to the wide variety of human motivations and capabilities.

Pluralism also means that there will be disagreement over the meaning of action's results. There is no way to "prove" to everyone's satisfaction that some result is an improvement or that human evil, perversity, self-seeking, and corruption won't, in the long run, win out over action inspired by lofty ideals. Liberalism's faith at this juncture is metaphysical, even dogmatic if you like. William James most dramatically articulates liberalism's core assertion that the world is an open-ended, "unfinished" one that is susceptible to change by human action.[43] Our motivation—the engagement of our energies—stems from this sense of work that can be done. We inevitably imagine future results for which we, in the present, devise the means of achieving and then set out to accomplish. The alternative is lassitude, cynicism, and outright nihilism: the enervating conclusion that there is nothing to be done. Of course, that conclusion can also be self-serving for those who are doing just fine—thank you—within the ways things are now.

James posits a "pluralistic universe," one in which there are many possible futures. There are plural paths into the future. The universe as it currently exists, the facts on the ground today, do not dictate or determine what the facts will be tomorrow. The current facts, of course, limit what is possible. There are not endless possibilities, but there is more than one possibility. There is always a space—the present—for human intervention. Those interventions can make a difference. Humans contribute to the ongoing constitution of the world, whether they act deliberately or not. Our actions alter nature (think of nuclear fission or genetic engineering) as well as culture, so James and his fellow pragmatists (especially John Dewey) urge us to act with the fullest consciousness of what we are aiming to achieve and of what consequences we actually produce.[44] We can then learn from experience which actions are most effective and what consequences (both good and bad) are most likely to follow from which actions. We probably won't ever attain either full consciousness or a perfect fit between actions and what they aim to achieve, but we can do better or worse in this regard.

This grand metaphysical claim about the world's plasticity and the efficacy of human action is merely the backdrop to the more specific, but still rather metaphysical, description of pluralism on which I will focus here. Our scene now is almost entirely social, and this social metaphysic has two primary tenets. The first, most fully associated with the work of Isaiah Berlin, is that there are many goods for which humans agents strive and that there is no reason to believe or evidence to suggest that these plural goods are entirely compatible.[45] In short, the achievement of one good can often only be achieved by relinquishing or delaying the achievement of another good. We might say that this is a metaphysic of imperfection. Perfect contentment, the attainment of all goods, with them all possessed in the same moment, is unlikely. Trade-offs, compromises, even the outright destruction or sacrifice of one good to advance another will be the order of the day. This assertion may be a statement about the nature of the universe and hence not seem specifically social as contrasted to natural. But I think it makes more sense to see the claim as one about "the human condition." It is humans who identify—and then value and attempt to acquire—various goods. So it is humans who have the problem of ordering those goods and deciding what trade-offs, compromises, and renunciations to make. Prior to, or apart from, human existence, it may (in a Darwinian sense) be true that there is competition for resources, but it requires a human presence to name the goods that motivate competition and to consciously shape courses of action in relation to those goods. Within human communities, the number of goods proliferates. In contrast to Darwin's paucity of goods—all related to the sustaining or reproduction of "life"—we find humans, in some cases, foregoing the production of offspring, and even sacrificing their own lives, in the pursuit of other goods.

This brings us to the next—and even more important—plank in liberalism's social pluralism. Simply stated: Given the diversity of goods, different human beings will be motivated by and will strive to achieve different ends. More complexly—and grandly—stated: Guided by different beliefs, values, desires, temperaments, talents, interests, and opportunities, individual human beings will develop and attempt to realize very different "life projects." Liberalism need not (although some liberal thinkers do try to) provide a theory or an explanation of such diversity. Whether individuals are born different or develop their differences as a result of social training is, I think, neither here nor there. Instead, the case for diversity rests on empirical observation, rather than on some explanation for that observed fact. In modern societies, at least, diversity of outlooks and pursuits is the rule. It is arguable whether even "traditional," premodern societies achieved a conformity that now eludes us. But whether they did or not is immaterial. Liberalism asserts that social unanimity cannot be produced in our world today, and—this is crucial—that attempts to create such unanimity are far, far worse than the disease they claim to be curing. The bedrock of liberal pluralism is the insistence that diversity is an unrevisable feature of modern social life. Therefore, we need to learn how to live with it. Madison is adamant in Federalist No. 10 that political and social diversity—manifested by the presence of "factions" in the polity—is ineliminable. Only the greatest tyranny—what we know today, after the horrible experiences of the twentieth century, as totalitarianism—could overcome pluralism.[46] Here is Madison's statement of this foundational liberal assertion:

> There are two methods for curing the mischiefs of faction: the one, by removing its causes; the other, by controlling its effects.
> There are again two methods of removing the causes of faction: the one by destroying the liberty which is essential to its existence; the other, by giving to every citizen the same opinions, the same passions, and the same interests.
> It could never be more truly said than of the first remedy, that it is worse than the disease. Liberty is to faction, what air is to fire, an ailment without which it instantly expires. But it could not be a less folly to abolish liberty, which is essential to political life, because it nourishes faction, than it would be to wish the annihilation of air. . . .
> The second expedient is as impracticable, as the first would be unwise. As long as the reason of man continues fallible, and he is at liberty to exercise it, different opinions will be formed. (52–53)

Madison concludes: "The inference to which we are brought is, that the *causes* of faction cannot be removed; and that relief is only to be sought in the means of controlling its *effects*" (55). You cannot get rid of pluralism, so you must learn how to live with it. Madison's great insight is that the "evils" of faction, the conflicts it engenders, are not mitigated by the fruitless (and usually violent) efforts to eliminate diversity, but by the opposite expedient of multiplying differences. Where there are many groups, no single group expects or can gain dominance. Just as the proliferation of Protestant sects quells the dream of converting all to one religion, so a large republic will thwart the efforts of any single faction to "concert and execute their plans of oppression. Extend the sphere and you take in a greater variety of parties and interests; you make it less probable that a majority of the whole will have a common motive to invade the rights of other citizens" (57–58).

Madison's formulation leads to two crucial observations. First, I have called liberal pluralism metaphysical because it rests on a claim about the nature of things, one that insists it has uncovered an inevitable, always-present fact about human togetherness in the modern era. We should always pay close attention to the place where a political or philosophical worldview locates necessity. That place is exactly where it digs in its heels, where it says that human action will be futile, where it indicates that we have moved from the realm of the possible to the impossible. The necessary is what we must accept, what we cannot change or revise through our actions. Liberal pluralism as I have described it is, in one way, geared precisely to opening up as far as possible the realm of the possible, is bent on being much less convinced than most philosophical positions that humans are hedged in by ineluctable realities that they must grin and bear. But even liberalism ends up identifying a necessity, marking a limit to what humans can achieve.

Second, limits play a strange role in human desire and human actions. Tigers, so far as we know, don't dream about flying. But humans are continually captivated by the impossible. The boundaries of the possible do get revised by human action. By refusing to take quietly various necessities, we as a species have changed the very terms of what is possible and what is not. The dream of a perfect community—where perfection is measured by complete agreement—surfaces again and again in human history. Pluralism may be a fact like cancer, a fact we reluctantly acknowledge, but one we hardly embrace and one we think it noble to continue fighting against. I have a friend who says we could replace all bumper stickers with the all-purpose slogan "Be more like me." How can the polity acknowledge and accommodate this persistent desire to win others over to my way of viewing the world, my sense of the proper and the good?

Madison offers a partial answer to this question. Federalist No. 10 describes the process through which members of the legislature will be chosen and the deliberations that will take place in the legislature. Because congressional districts will be large, Madison believes that a single- or special-interest candidate will not have much chance of winning. Only a candidate of larger views, someone who grants credence and support to opinions not necessarily his own, will be able to secure enough votes. Representatives will have to attend to various factional opinions but will not be captive to any particular one. Elections and legislative deliberations offer a full public airing of plural views while preventing any one view from dominating. Competition for office provides the impetus for articulating different views in a context where the conversion of other citizens to my view is the goal. The *form* of elections pushes advocates to understand the views of others, to express their own views in a language likely to appeal to those others, and thus to create positions that accommodate various needs and opinions. Madison hopes that political interactions between contending factions can be transforming, can lead to the enlargement of one's views. Aggressively defending my own faction and its views against all others will not be a winning strategy either in elections or in legislative deliberations in Madison's view. The Republican Party in the early twenty-first century, guided by political operative Karl Rove, abandoned this Madisonian position. Rove argued that winning elections depended on mobilizing your most ardent supporters by drawing sharp distinctions between your own views and strongly attacking the views of your opponents.[47] The jury is still out (since the Rove-led Republicans won in 2002 and 2004, but lost in 2006) about whether a polarizing strategy wins elections. But there is no doubt that such a strategy is hostile to pluralism in its continual insistence that political opponents are a threat to the nation's security and well-being. Madison sounds like our contemporary when, in 1792, he asked, "The Union: Who Are Its Real Friends?," and answered, "Not those who charge others with not being its friends, whilst their own conduct is wantonly multiplying its enemies."[48]

E pluribus, unum. The unity Madison suggests is formal and institutional. He does not believe we can ever attain substantive unity, an agreement in fundamental beliefs. All citizens, no matter what their views, will subscribe to the Constitution and the institutions it establishes because it provides the framework for allowing them the freedom to live out their substantive differences. Critics of liberalism, from both the left and the right, have always insisted that this is not enough. Only a substantive unity can give a community or a nation enough coherence to keep from falling apart. A common dream or purpose or identity is needed. The gap between the liberal limitation of unity to formal procedures/institutions and nonliberal appeals to substantive bases for unity yawns wide—and I consider it again in my discussion of conservatism.

For now, two further points must be made. The first is that form versus content is a significant difference here. Critics of liberalism love to point out that liberalism, too, must rely on unity at a certain point—and enforce that unity where it is lacking. Citizens are not free to flout the Constitution by abridging others' freedom to express their differing views. So formal unity can be oppressive—and undermine the claim of a pluralistic society. Even worse, the formal unity hides a substantive value that is imposed on all: individualism. A liberal polity denies religious and other communities any authority over their members. Individuals must be free to come and go as they please in relation to such communities, and to express their dissent when and where they wish. Pluralism is a sham in this view.[49] Such arguments are disingenuous, it seems to me, because they aim to obscure the real difference between living in a society where dissent and alternative values are tolerated and one where they are not. To equate the fact that certain forms (including the rule of law) are enforced with the enforcement of specific beliefs and/or ways of life is to think very abstractly indeed. There is an on-the-ground, lived difference between living in a society that aims, through its legal procedures and institutions, to grant individuals the freedom to live their lives in multiple ways and living in a society that tries to fit individuals into tightly defined patterns of acceptable behavior. True: all polities, including liberal pluralistic ones, will have points of unity. False: all polities are thus similarly intolerant of dissent, or their differences in toleration are only skin-deep and hence insignificant.

The second point is that we seem to reach a basic difference in political sensibility here. Every society is going to have centrifugal and centripetal forces. A liberal polity, like any polity, will have means for the achievement of conformity to basic laws, means that range from persuasion and political education to enforcement. What impresses liberals, however, is just how powerful the social and political forces pushing individuals toward conformity are. The biggest threat to the best possible lives comes from the concentrated power of states and other collectivities, not the efforts of individuals to break clear of those powers (which they will rarely do completely). Wherever and whenever we can push toward difference and plurality we should do so since power mostly works exactly in the opposite direction. Nonliberals, on the other hand, fear anarchy. They think that social power is on the verge of collapse, that permissiveness shows us that concentrated power has lost its "will" to govern, that there is a "crisis of authority," and that individual caprice is running wild. Pluralism, to them, is not a sign of a vibrant, free society, but of the scary flourishing of people whose outrageous behavior should not be tolerated.

A thoroughgoing pluralism (which I advocate, but which is not embraced by all liberal thinkers) tries, in every instance, to pluralize our thinking about problems and their solutions.[50] That effort underwrites my attempt to understand liberalism as a variety of political, social, and attitudinal expedients addressed to a variety of problems that arise from the fact of humans living in a world together. Liberalism in this view is not systematic; it does not all hang together, nor do all of its expedients neatly fit together. Liberalism is much more ad hoc than that, devising solutions as it goes along to problems—some old, some new—that crop up. Its decisions and actions are driven by those immediate problems, and its attitude is experimental. Let's see if this works to improve things; if not, we'll try something else. If so, we will still have to do other things in the future to deal with new problems—often problems created as a by-product of a fairly successful action taken in the past. Liberal action is guided by principles, by values, by ends-in-view, and by past experience of what works and what doesn't, but it is not much concerned with faithfulness to some overarching liberal worldview and is impatient with resistance to the novel and/or different just because it is new.

Liberalism's response to the challenge posed by pluralism of values and life projects follows this pluralistic path of multiple expedients. The first line of defense is to advocate and to cultivate tolerance.[51] One's difference from one's compatriots may well be a distasteful fact, but it would be well for all involved if everyone could manage to keep his distaste to himself. Tolerance doesn't require approval. It only insists on noninterference. The fundamental appeal here is to reciprocity. I should be able to recognize that my ways might be just as disagreeable to my neighbor as hers are to me. And I should also be able to recognize that I would resent any compulsion to give up my ways and adopt hers. So I should be able to see that it works the other way around. Why should my position be privileged over hers since we are both equally set in our ways, both equally convinced that we are right? A liberal polity strives, therefore, to create zones of mutual indifference—first, by clearly marking out in the law where neither government nor individuals can interfere with various beliefs and practices and, second, by working culturally to convert distaste to indifference. This emotional work of lessening the presence of disapproval and outrage is partly the effect of a "liberal education" (about which I'll have more to say shortly), but it also results from the polity's accumulated experience of living with difference. Over time, peaceful coexistence and occasional interaction with such others renders their differences less momentous. Nothing fundamental in my life is threatened by the fact that I live in a society in which others lead a life based on fundamentally different choices.

Of course, it isn't always going to work out so smoothly. As critics of liberalism never tire of pointing out, tolerance has its limits. Liberalism has never denied that fact. Tolerance is the first expedient because it is the most neutral one, the one that is least interfering. Where tolerance will do the job, we should let it. We should move on to other expedients only where tolerance does not work. And we should never allow a lack of faith in tolerance or some theoretical demonstration of its weakness or "contradictions" to keep us from attempting to practice it. One of the greatest historical achievements of the human race was liberalism's success in getting Catholics and Protestants in Europe (with the horrible and notable exception of Ireland) to stop killing each other after 1750. Yes, tolerance is a pale, negative, emaciated, egghead virtue, but we all have good reason to be thankful for its installation and cultivation in the modern West. Its benefits and its logic of reciprocity should be a central part of civic education in all of our schools. To disdain tolerance is to court enormous risks.

Yet, once again, I will concede that tolerance has its limits. The liberal principle that interference with another's life projects or property will not be tolerated successfully identifies many of the relevant cases where tolerance must be set aside and some person's activities forcibly curbed. In other words, criminal law is precisely aimed at identifying activities that will not be tolerated. Here, as elsewhere throughout the liberal polity, we will expect to encounter easy cases where there is fairly general agreement about what is intolerable and more contentious cases where the boundary lines of toleration are debated and, through legislation and court cases, over time revised.

Generally speaking, liberals will be extremely wary of adding any behavior to the list of criminal activities, to the category of the intolerable. This wariness stems from the core plank of liberal pluralism. Liberalism acknowledges that there is a persistent tendency in humans (negatively) to be outraged by behavior unlike one's own and (positively) to seek to convert others to one's own beliefs and practices in order to live in a community of the like-minded. The conviction that efforts to create that community must be unavailing (the bottom line of necessity in the liberal position) raises the worry that such efforts are, instead, a source of social conflict and/or domination. The founders clearly thought it a source of tyranny to place the power of the state and its laws on the side of a particular set of beliefs and practices—whether that set be defined as "religious" or "cultural" or "ethnic." Furthermore, the history of religious and ethnic conflicts offers substantial evidence that efforts to create social conformity lead again and again to violence against those who refuse (for whatever reason) to toe the line. The dream of unanimity exacts a terrible price, so liberalism not only repeats endlessly that pluralism is a fact that will not go away, but it also strives to cultivate a taste for, an appreciation of, that fact.

Thus far, I have presented only a negative case for the promotion of pluralism. We can't have nonpluralism, and the cost of trying to achieve social unanimity is truly horrific. Tolerance—although shaky because it goes against the grain of deeply felt emotions—has produced miracles of peace. Recently, we have become familiar with more positive efforts to cultivate a genuine taste for and pleasure in what nowadays gets called "diversity." Here, we might say, is liberalism trying to convert a necessity into a fact to be celebrated and embraced. Can this effort succeed? I don't know. But since I do believe that we will have diversity whether we like it or not, it certainly seems harmless to try to learn how to like it. And it certainly seems to me deeply pessimistic about human nature—and way too narrow-minded about what humans are capable of—to insist that we cannot learn to admire, take pleasure in, and learn from the different ways that others lead their lives. Yes, humans have deep-seated tendencies toward intolerance; that's why a liberal polity must remain vigilant against all the ways that intolerance underwrites tyranny, violence, and domination. But we need not deny—in some warping attempt to be "realistic"—the capacity of humans to be not only tolerant of, but also appreciative of, diversity in human practices and beliefs. Imperfectly to be sure, but far from disastrously, America has been a multiethnic and multireligious society from the start. Repeated predictions by "nativist" writers (whether in 1840, 1890, 1950, or 2005) that our coherence as a culture and a nation is about to dissolve in the face of this or that new wave of immigration have always proved wrong.

We reach here, in fact, one of the root meanings of the word "liberal." A liberal education, for instance, is one that aims to introduce the student to the whole range of human thought and action over history. Its all-inclusiveness—nothing human is alien to it—stems from the conviction that we can learn from everything that humans have thought and done. Its characteristic mode is openness and appreciation, not denigration and close-mindedness.[52] Certainly, a liberal education is not about condescending to the past or using it to assure ourselves of our own superiority. The much-derided liberal indecisiveness—the desire and ability to see all sides of the question—reflects an education that strives to give each moment in human history its due. The mistake is to believe that appreciation for the other's point of view is necessarily incompatible with passionate commitment. The antiliberal is terrified that society will fall apart if there is not some shared identity to hold the people together. And he thinks that the liberal is bloodless (the very term is suggestive)—eschewing allegiance to any particular group or any particular nation. The liberal is a cosmopolitan, a citizen of the world, a connoisseur of the human. And for that reason the liberal is seen as inhuman, as lacking the commitments that bind the individual to others in a localized time and place.

The liberal does not lack passion or commitment; those passions and commitments are just located elsewhere. The commitments are to peace, well-being, and freedom—and the liberal insists that we can only attain these goods by weaning ourselves of localized passions if those passions are understood as underwriting exclusive commitments or communities. ("Exclusive" is used here in the active sense of excluding certain persons from the polity's or the self's care and consideration because those people are not our kind or not those of whom we approve.) Diversity is a fact of the human condition demonstrated by the species' varied history and multiple cultures. But it is especially a fact of our contemporary situation because the movement of peoples has meant that every democratic society has become what the United States has always been: multiethnic and multicultural and multireligious. What holds this liberal polity together is patriotism—a patriotism underwritten by a love of our society's inclusiveness, by its noble struggle to maintain a rule of law that gives its varied citizenry the most ample opportunity possible to live the lives they freely choose and passionately desire to live. We would do well to cultivate a taste for diversity and a patriotic pride in our liberal institutions; both are bulwarks against the conflicts generated by those who believe that diversity threatens the polity instead of understanding that the polity exists to protect diversity.

Even to foster it. Maybe liberalism overreaches when it tries to enshrine diversity as a positive good, not just a necessity we must learn how to live with. But who would deny that, in American society, we encourage the development of a distinctive individuality? This is very tricky, since obviously the education we give to our children also promotes various kinds of conformity. Still, I think few Americans—no matter if they described themselves as liberal or conservative—would endorse educational methods that set out to squelch rather than to encourage individuality. (Think of how we contrast our schools with those in Japan. Their students get better math scores, but ours are more able to think for themselves—or so the stereotype goes.) So, on some level, diversity is recognized as a good—one that we should strive as a society to produce. Our (admittedly tenuous) commitment to liberal education stems from the half-conscious recognition that a purely technical education will not foster the kind of ingenuity and creative/critical thinking that a more open-ended education encourages. The education of the young is surrounded by such anxiety because the more conservative people in our society are afraid that education will introduce too much difference. They are afraid that the center will not hold if there is too much diversity in society. You are free to grow up and become a poet instead of an engineer, but not a homosexual instead of a heterosexual or an atheist instead of some variety of a Christian. The liberal response is that no education that you devise will prevent some people from becoming homosexuals or atheists. They will spring up again in each succeeding generation. And there is no compelling evidence that their existence threatens the ability of the society to exist or to thrive. Here, of course, the rubber hits the road. The "values conservative" insists that our society has already been severely harmed by the "tolerance" of sexual deviance or atheism. The liberal believes that the ills of our society are not the product of too much tolerance or of wayward individual behavior. These different interpretations of our current situation must slug it out in the public square, as described below.

Liberalism adds another expedient to the adoption of tolerance and the attempt to cultivate a taste for diversity: the endorsement, protection, and encouragement of a robust public sphere (or, to use another term for it, civil society). Between private (domestic and familial) space and the state, a liberal society has a "public square" or, more accurately, "public squares," places where fellow citizens meet, converse, argue, and contend. An emphasis on public spheres is an obvious extension of Madison's vision of political interaction in Federalist No. 10. These sites can be virtual or actual. Crucially, they should be as unregulated as possible, although the law must sometimes intervene to guarantee equal access to all. Civil society is "public" because it is a place where relative strangers meet, and because it is not owned by private interests that can dictate what gets said or done there. This space is held in common. But it is not public in the sense of governmental. The actual physical (a public park or a city square) or virtual (radio and TV frequencies) spaces may be maintained by the government, but the activities that take place there and the words spoken are not scripted by the state and cannot claim either the state's endorsement or its condemnation.[53] Those activities and words are permitted under the law, but are not obligatory for anyone. Some of the civil liberties to which liberalism is bound—freedom of speech, freedom of the press, freedom of assembly—are motivated by its commitment to allowing and promoting a vibrant commons. So it comes as no surprise that the historians tell us that civil society in the United States came into existence in the context of ratifying the Constitution and then putting its blueprint for a new government into practice.[54]

The reasons for sustaining civil society are multiple. As a response to pluralism, civil society offers a sublimation of conflict. Attempts to simply outlaw the effort to convert my neighbor to my way of life may prove too frustrating. Society will be better off if it does not require such saintly forbearance from its members, but offers every citizen the opportunity to proselytize. For physical compulsion, liberalism substitutes rhetorical persuasion. Some citizens will feel no need or desire to sway the opinions or lifestyle of other citizens. But for those who feel that need, they are welcome to articulate their own views, argue against the views of others, and display themselves as exemplars of one way of being in this world—with all of these (and doubtless many more) rhetorical moves enacted in full public view and protected from any censorship, abridgement, or revision by the state. Since such preachers can neither compel others to listen nor compel them to agree, the frustrations of pluralism for those who seek social unanimity remain. But such persons cannot complain that their worldview has been denied the same opportunity as all other worldviews to make its case.

Liberalism hopes, in fact, that the give-and-take of civil society will have other benefits besides undermining the legitimacy of any imposition of fundamental beliefs and values by nonverbal means. In liberal polities, there are plural sites of social interaction: the family, the workplace, the marketplace, churches, voluntary associations of every kind, formal and informal political organizations, schools, neighborhoods—and this list is suggestive, not exhaustive. The relation of citizen to state is not primary. Rather, liberalism places society above the state; it sees the relationships formed in various social activities as providing (along with familial relations) the key sources of motivation and meaning in citizens' lives. The state and the Constitution provide the framework for and the safeguard of the social—and for the individual lives that people carve out for themselves within the social. A liberal polity is judged by the quality of the social relations and individual lives that it enables. Proliferating the sites and opportunities for interaction with others pluralizes the ways that people can create rich, meaningful lives.

The public sphere is also where citizens concretely experience pluralism. What liberalism's critics can never believe is that a society in which people do not share fundamental values can hold itself together. Liberalism does walk a fine line here. It does rely on a common desire to live in peace with others. Those who would resort to violence of any sort and for any reason must be constrained. Beyond that, however, liberalism strives to allow maximum individual freedom in how one chooses to live his or her life. The liberal gambit is that each individual will recognize that he gains that freedom only through support of a social and legal framework that offers every other citizen a similar freedom. My individuality is possible through the acceptance, even promotion, of the other's individuality. The result, inevitably, is pluralism, not commonality, on the substantive level of beliefs and actions.

That's the abstract rationale for accepting pluralism. But the lived experience of pluralism comes in the public sphere in my interactions with other members of my society. Those interactions can be contentious and heated, but liberalism stakes its all on society remaining viable, even healthy, so long as citizens are engaged with one another. Society is a going concern so long as its members are still talking to one another. You exist in a living and ongoing social relationship not simply with those you agree with, but also with those you talk with. We can draw a parallel with marriage here. The two spouses are two different people, and they can have heated, passionate arguments. But the marriage depends on their continuing to talk to one another—or, to put it more abstractly, so long as they retain their commitment to being related to one another. Hence, in any argument within a marriage there is a kind of double perspective. There is the first perspective of what I believe and want to convince my spouse of in this particular argument. But there is the second perspective of whether this argument, this disagreement, is so fundamental that I will end the relationship altogether if I do not get my way. Liberalism does not take pluralism to mean that citizens disagree about everything all of the time. Instead, it understands pluralism to mean that agreement is never guaranteed and that forced agreement can, in many cases, be worse than agreeing to disagree. A society that is tolerant of disagreement offers greater latitude to individual autonomy—and thus will be a society that citizens will have reason to want to maintain. In their day-to-day interactions with others, therefore, there will be many incentives to reach modes of relating that do not push disagreements to the point of dissolving all social ties. Thus, we should expect—and, in fact, do observe—that people develop through those daily interactions various strategies to accommodate differences. The experience of pluralism on the ground—and of successfully negotiating the abstract threat it presents—takes much of the sting out of the many disagreements that exist between people. Encounters in the public sphere with those who are different from us can work practically to teach us how to live with differences and to demonstrate that society hardly depends on overwhelming agreement for its continued existence.

Of course, civil war, the breakdown of society into warring factions, is always possible—and it is, of all political evils, the worst. So we have every right to worry about what a society minimally needs to keep the peace. Liberalism's formula is, admittedly, counterintuitive. It seems, at first blush, that a society in which there was total agreement would be conflict-free, whereas a society with multiple disagreements would never be peaceful. But the empirical, historical record suggests otherwise. Maintaining agreement always requires authoritarian structures—and strictures. A constant policing effort is needed, with endless attempts to sniff out deviants and heretics, to keep the prevailing orthodoxy pure. Repression is bound to stimulate resistance. The seeming paradox that authoritarian regimes never seem to grasp is that social stability is much better guaranteed by an open civil society, by allowing the free expression of all views. To a large extent, simply allowing those views their opportunity to sway others' views is enough to keep people from resorting to arms. Given a fair chance to persuade others through words, the members of any particular group will find it hard to legitimate turning to force. (They will probably have to rely on theoretical sleights of hand like "false consciousness" to explain why their words were inadequate and force is justified.) Thus the historical record suggests that the counterintuitive liberal expedient of letting disagreements flourish and of letting them express themselves openly better succeeds in holding society together. (This expedient will be taken one step further in the discussion of democracy in Book Four, since the nonauthoritarian regime's tolerance of disagreement usually entails—and in a democratic society must entail—its acceptance that it will hand over power to its rivals if they sway a majority to their views.)

Experience in a vibrant public sphere thus teaches the lesson—hard to believe without firsthand experience—that disagreement is not fatal to social peace or stability, but can actually serve to produce and sustain those social goods. Civil society also plays a vital role in the formation of public opinion, which is centrally important in all democracies. And we can identify further social by-products of engagement in the public square. Interactions in the public square shape our concrete—as opposed to abstract or imagined (in Benedict Anderson's use of that term)—relations with other citizens. Anderson's argument is that modern societies are so large that they are, inevitably, "imagined" communities.[55] Citizens rely on various representations of the nation and of other members of the nation to ground their sense of connection to those others. In diverse societies, however, such representations are often fairly nonrepresentative, offering an "ideal type" that obscures the actual diversity of the citizenry. There also exists a tendency of groups (Madison's "factions" rear their head once more) to segregate themselves along lines of asserted sameness, whether they be shared interests, shared ethnicity, shared religion, shared values, or shared economic status. Just as liberalism multiplies power as an expedient against the human tendency to accumulate power, so its promotion of a public sphere works against tendencies toward segregation. We are better off, liberalism insists, if we have concrete experiences of interacting with a wide range of citizens. Our views of others are often changed when we have real relations with them. We accept, may even come to celebrate, the diversity of the citizenry as more and more interactions with people "unlike" us allay our fear of them.[56]

Liberalism's aims here are frankly pedagogical, to move people away from their tendency toward segregation, toward avoiding encounters with the different. For starters, certain public spaces must be accessible to all. This principle means that there are no "identity criteria" for entry into the public sphere. One need not be anything (ethnically, economically, culturally, etc.) to gain access. In most instances, one need not even be a citizen (to, for example, write a letter to the newspaper, take part in a public demonstration, or organize an ethnic or religious or social festival). Equally important, however, is the fact that one need not check one's identity at the door. Participation in the public sphere *as* a woman, or a Christian, or a doctor is not only possible, but also should be encouraged. Pluralism encourages interaction between fully differentiated individuals, not between some pale abstractions who place their differences on hold when encountering each other in public.

Crucially, the insistence on access for all has been extended over the past fifty years not just to governmental sites and to the public square that is my current focus, but also to economic sites. The law now states that you cannot offer employment or goods differentially. Economic enterprises must open employment to all and open the spaces in which goods are sold and consumed to all. This integration of public (here meaning nondomestic) spaces since the early 1960s in America has been somewhat successful. After the troubled period of the initial phase-in, there has been a general acceptance of racially integrated restaurants, places of employment, and public gathering places. None of the more drastic consequences of integration that were predicted by its most ardent foes has come to pass. Nevertheless, there remain significant social sites where integration has met far more resistance. Both schools and residential neighborhoods are almost as segregated now as they were in 1960. (See Appendix, item 4.)

Racial relations in the United States have bedeviled the liberal effort to promote and sustain a vibrant civil society throughout our history—an issue taken up in the more historical discussion of American liberalism offered in Book Three. For now, however, I will remain on the level of enunciating principles and expedients for their achievement apart from the concrete barriers that stand in the way of success. Liberalism's desire to maximize individual freedom logically extends to its interest in everything that might enhance that freedom. The public sphere is a site of articulation, a place where citizens announce, elaborate, stage, and exemplify their opinions, choices, and ways of life. In trying to convince others, citizens discover themselves, developing a firmer sense of what they truly believe, of what they are willing to take responsibility for in full view of their compatriots. The pressures of public performance serve to anneal self-understanding. And those pressures can have surprising consequences. Some people come to the public sphere without well-formed views and hope to learn something. But, most likely, the majority of people come to interactions with other citizens with fairly entrenched opinions. They are interested in convincing the other guy, not in being convinced by him. But persuasion is a two-way street. Entering into a dialogue, even into an argument, means that I might end up transformed. And if transformations are drastic and therefore rare, smaller changes are not. The dynamism of modern, liberal societies relies in large part on the continual conversations and debates those societies encourage and enable. Liberalism recognizes that opinions—both personal opinions and public opinion—are fluid. Each of us constantly revises our beliefs; at any given time, there are some things we believe wholeheartedly, other things we believe provisionally, and other things we believe out of unexamined habit—not to mention various things we have never considered at all. We might strongly resist being told what to believe; individuals within liberal societies take seriously their responsibility to, in all important matters and in many trivial ones, decide for themselves. But that hardly means such individuals are not influenced by what others say or do.

Under modern conditions of pluralism, no beliefs or ways of living are self-evident. Selves are always exposed to alternatives. Modern self-consciousness stems from this constant contact with difference. The inclination to give my own values and practices a name (to make them cohere into an entity that can be designated a "religion" or a "culture") reflects the need to identify where I stand amid a number of options that are being lived simultaneously by others in the world. Most people will feel the need to understand their own choices in reference to the other available possibilities—and even to justify their own choices in the light of perceived challenges from those other possibilities, even if the challenges are only implied.

Pluralistic civil society, in other words, fosters "public reason."[57] Conservatives and postmodern leftists alike assail liberalism's rationalism, claiming that liberals tyrannically impose the standard of rationality when judging the acceptability of all values, beliefs, and commitments. Such critiques miss the actual way that liberal rationalism works. Yes, liberalism insists that no individual should be compelled to believe or do something for which she sees no reasons. Everything in a liberal society is up for examination, is subject to criticism. There are no sacred cows. But reason itself is understood expansively—and in a public sense. It consists of the reasons, the articulated justifications, that one person can give to another in the public square. Kenneth Burke has it right: "The 'social' aspect of language is 'reason.' Reason is a complex technique for 'checking' one's assertions by public reference."[58] Reason, in other words, is the form our convictions take under the pressure of enunciating them in as convincing a fashion as possible to others who are not our intimates. Practically speaking, that means "the rational" is anything that might convince someone at some time. The full panoply of persuasive speech is allowed; there's no possibility of ruling some arguments out of court as "unreasonable" in advance or apart from the give-and-take of public argument. What counts as reasonable is forged in the very processes of public debate; that's why the result is appropriately called "public reason." And there's no reason to expect that "public reason" will ever achieve some finally settled form, or that, at any given moment, there will be a strong consensus about what is reasonable.

Thus, liberal rationalism is not about some substantive standard of what counts as reasonable or about the effort to enforce that standard. Rather, liberal rationalism boils down to two principles and one hope. The principles are (1) the wide variety of opinions in a pluralistic society are all on an equal footing; none is exempt from examination and/or criticism; none can compel adherence, and if it chooses (as it may) not to offer reasons (in public) for its adoption, it must accept that the number of its followers will likely remain small; and (2) only persuasion (through the articulation of reasons) is permissible in the advocacy of any opinion. Liberal rationalism, then, is primarily about the prohibition of compulsion and coercion. Rationality is anything that actually convinces people through speech alone. Any movement beyond speech directed at others to action directed at them is barred. If I think someone's speech is fatuous and wrong-headed, my recourse is to counter his arguments (and the facts he deploys to make them) with my own. Any claim that I make that his views are "unreasonable" must be a verbal claim and only based on my arguments about the absurdity of his. The distinction between rational and irrational, in other words, will always be established pragmatically through and in the very process of public debate. The distinction does not exist in some hard-and-fast way prior to its invocation and activation in the debate. Among the things contested in the public sphere will be the rhetorical modes deemed appropriate and found persuasive. Liberal pluralism—and the liberal rationalism I am advocating here through my understanding of "public reason"—should not and cannot delimit from the outset certain modes of argument, nor can it assume that any given mode is legitimate or effective by fiat or definition. The focus is on "reasons," not "Reason," and reasons are understood as what convinces people, nothing more, but also nothing less.

The hope is that the actual contestations in the public sphere and legislative deliberations in a liberal democracy will produce better beliefs and decisions. (I take up this hope again in the discussion of "deliberative democracy" in Part Four.) This is partly the hope that better arguments will prevail. For example, I find the argument that pluralistic tolerance more successfully promotes peace and stability than an effort to achieve social unanimity convincing—and thus offer it in this book as a contribution toward helping pluralism continue to thrive in American society. So, yes, liberal rationalism entails the hope that the success of good arguments will lead to a better society—and that individuals will be led by good arguments to work for and support social policies that improve all of our lives. But, even in cases where such success is not won, where neither side convinces the other, the process of verbally offering reasons in itself promotes civility and even empathy. Trying to persuade others to adopt one's views often leads to efforts to understand others' objections and different ways of viewing things. And the effort to persuade them already acknowledges their importance, that they are worth winning to one's side. In short, the hope is that conversations (even debates) across divides and factions will bind the participants in the public square together even when they do not reach agreement. They are conversing—and they are attending to the reasons, loyalties, values, and arguments that are most convincing to the others with whom they debate.

This last point indicates one further social effect associated with civil society: recognition.[59] The different cultures, religions, and lifestyles in a pluralistic society exhibit a desire to be recognized as valid, perhaps even cited as praiseworthy. This desire for recognition of our individual qualities from people beyond our family is widespread, albeit not universal. There are degrees of hunger for this recognition, ranging from those ambitious for fame or acclaim to those who only want the teacher or the boss to remember their name. In modern liberal societies, many want to be recognized as individuals. They want to be distinguished as just this person, not some other. This minimal insistence on one's own individuality can then extend to a desire for the acknowledgment that my individual difference makes a difference. I have made my mark. Others have recognized that their reality, their world, would have been different if I did not occupy it. Recognition from others registers the effects of my being here. We may witness various more-or-less desperate efforts to gain recognition. But certainly we can all understand how desolate it would be to feel that our presence went entirely unnoticed. Ralph Ellison caught the poignant terror of that possibility perfectly in the title of his great novel, *Invisible Man*.

Mentioning Ellison reminds us that issues of recognition in recent years have often centered around questions of nonwhite, "non-normal," or nonmajority populations. Groups, as well as individuals, desire recognition. Members of nonmainstream groups are hurt, resentful, and worse when society tries to render them invisible, either through various processes of segregation or by hiding their actual lives and realities under the mask of stereotypes. Pluralism begins from an acknowledgment of diversity and moves on from there to develop ways that our public life can maximize the staging of diversity, the interactions between diverse individuals, and the acknowledgment of the contributions to the society as a whole made by its diverse members and their subcultures (this last term serving as an awkward way of noting that there are factions bound together by similar traditions and practices as well as factions united by region or by economic interests). Of course, not all recognition is positive. Disapprobation as well as acclaim is expressed in the public sphere. Precisely because we do live in a pluralistic society, what is acclaimed by some will be ignored by others and derided by yet others. The public square is a noisy, messy, fairly incoherent, cacophonous place. Hannah Arendt stressed that it took "courage" to stand up and act in what she called the political "space of appearances."[60] Liberal law, especially in ensuring access to all and in insisting that all persuasion be verbal not physical, tries to create a safe public sphere, but it cannot—and should not—curb the jostling that follows from the encounter between different people with different passionately held views. Endless debates and disagreements are exactly what pluralism leads us to expect.

But isn't that a dystopian vision of our human lot? Wrangling among ourselves from now to the end of time? Think again. Would you really want to live in a world where everyone agreed with you, a world in which your views were never stretched by their encounter with well-articulated and well-argued contrary views? Such a brave new world of universal conformity would be static and boring. We continually experience pluralism as threatening and frustrating, but, like Midas, we should be careful what we wish for. Nonpluralism would be far worse. This leads to an odd paradox: I go out into the public square hoping to convince everyone of my point of view. Not only do I risk having my views changed in the process, but I actually would come to regret it if I achieved my original aim. A world in which everyone agreed with me would be as bad as a world in which everyone disagreed with me. Liberalism accepts and expects that most of us will always find a middle ground; we will mostly associate with those who mostly agree with us. Thus factions are formed. But the results will be catastrophic if there is no communication between factions or if the factions become so hardened that there is neither movement of individuals from one faction to another nor membership by individuals in multiple factions. A varied and vibrant public sphere with multiple sites of interaction provides the most important liberal expedient against a pluralism that degenerates into completely separated groups.

That's why communication, not agreement or consensus, is the hallmark of a healthy liberal polity. Conservatives keep insisting that national unity is threatened by dissent; they always feel that anarchy is just around the corner and offer various substantive beliefs that, if only they can get all to subscribe to those beliefs, will guarantee order. Liberalism insists that such fears are overblown; we do need a fundamental recognition (based on the principle of reciprocity) that the other guy has an equal right to be here and to live his life according to his own lights as I do. And we need a commitment to the procedural agreement (established by the Constitution and protected by the rule of law) that persuasion through words and exemplars is always permissible and that coercion by force will never be tolerated. But from that starting point, it is up to citizens themselves to form as tight or as loose bonds as they see fit. Everything in human history suggests that people will form various groups that are held together by various shared concerns and commitments. Our society relies on the formation of such groups—but liberalism remains vigilant against the acquisition by any such group of the power to prevent an individual from moving from one group to another or to keep another group from enjoying the full benefits of living in a liberal polity. I have elsewhere used the term "liberal diffidence" to characterize how liberalism as a way of organizing a polity refrains from, as far as possible, dictating anything in the way of substantive beliefs.[61] Politics offers the framework within which our lives are lived, not the content of those lives. One of the greatest freedoms liberalism has to offer is freedom from politics. So long as we can keep all things equal in a liberal polity (no easy task, obviously), individuals and groups can make their own lives and meanings in civil society. That is precisely why the literate and cultural expressions enabled by civil society acquire such significance, and are a site of such energetic commitment, in a liberal polity.

Liberal pluralism does not offer a perfect world—no matter if perfection is imagined as a society in which consensus on all basic questions is the rule or a society in which differences are perfectly recognized. Instead, liberalism tries to establish a society in which we can manage to rub along in peace, making progress toward agreement and understanding at times, but working even harder to ensure that the opportunities to disagree and the opportunities to insist that "you just don't get it" remain open, various, and plentiful. Many cannot simply renounce utopian dreams of unanimity, just as many cannot avoid desires for various impossibilities—hence the very real pain that the frustration of those desires produces. Such dreams and desires importantly impel our constant efforts to make our world a better place. Liberalism's persistent suspicion of utopian thinking can make it seem a killjoy. The rule of law sets limits to the accumulation of power and thus hampers any individual's or group's ability to remake the world. Similarly, liberal pluralism sets limits to any individual's or any group's ability to make its beliefs and practices hold sway in the entire polity. That's why liberal pluralism is a metaphysic; it does claim to designate limits to the possible, limits that humans constantly desire to cross. A liberal polity encourages the full and free expression of human imaginings and desires, but places some daunting, although not completely impassable, roadblocks to their enactment. Any such enactments should be small-scale and voluntary, established as experiments that are meant not just to improve the lives of their participants, but also to serve as a rhetorical display to others of the advantages of this way of living. Liberal pluralism thus encourages us to keep our options open, to expect the unexpected from human beings, and to learn how to delight in that diversity. But it also reminds us that diversity precludes worldwide harmony, while modernity renders segregated isolation impossible. It means misunderstandings, conflicts, disagreements, and having to develop a tolerance toward others whose lives we find distasteful or even abhorrent. Liberalism offers you the chance to convert others verbally from their way of life. But the power vested in the liberal state will not be used to assist you in your conversion efforts, only to thwart you if you cross the line from verbal persuasion over to some more forceful means of changing or preventing others' behavior.

5
LIBERTY AND EQUALITY

My description of liberalism thus far has focused on the two great political evils that humans living together in society can inflict on one another: tyranny and civil war. Liberalism distributes power while "checking" each instance of it to prevent tyranny and reciprocally maximizes freedom to individuals and groups with different beliefs to prevent civil war. There are social ills like racism and humiliation, economic ills like poverty and starvation, and existential evils such as illness and physical suffering. Modern polities also attend to these evils, as I will suggest shortly. But, before we reach those issues, liberalism can be described as aiming to create a polity—political institutions and laws, along with a distribution of power—to safeguard to the best of our human abilities against tyranny and civil strife.[62] Liberalism is not only focused on preventing evil, however. It also seeks to provide the positive goods of liberty and equality. The evolution of liberalism from 1776 to 2007 is primarily a consequence of changes in our understanding of what liberty and equality entail.

The Constitution begins by listing six goals in founding this new state: "to form a more perfect Union, establish Justice, insure domestic Tranquility, provide for the common defence, promote the general Welfare, and secure the Blessings of Liberty to ourselves and our Posterity." How did the founders understand the "Blessings of Liberty"? Much suggests that they generally thought of liberty negatively, as freedom *from*. An individual or a group or a nation possesses liberty when, unhampered by external influence or coercion, it can determine for itself how and when to act. Little is gained, however, if I have freedom *from* external coercion, but no freedom *to* accomplish this or that self-chosen goal. To enjoy the blessings of liberty, citizens need the power and wherewithal to act effectively. Citizens must be able to exercise their freedom. Franklin Delano Roosevelt captures this point when he declares: "'Necessitous men are not free men.' Liberty requires opportunity to make a living—a living decent according to the standard of the time, a living which gives man not only enough to live by, but something to live for."[63]

A focus on what people need to actualize their freedom in their daily lives leads to the "egalitarian liberalism" presented in this book. I trace the notion of "effective liberty" (or its cognate "effective freedom") to John Dewey, but the term and the notion are everywhere in modern liberalism. In 1935, a year before the FDR speech just quoted, Dewey writes:

> Liberalism is committed to an end that is at once enduring and
> flexible: the liberation of individuals so that the realization of their
> capacities may be the law of their life. . . . The liberal spirit is marked
> by its own picture of the pattern that is required: a social organiza-
> tion that will make possible effective liberty and opportunity for
> personal growth in mind and spirit in all individuals. Its present need
> is recognition that established material security is a prerequisite of
> the ends which it cherishes, so that, the basis of life being secure, in-

dividuals may actively share in the wealth of cultural resources that now exist and may contribute, each in his own way, to their further enrichment.[64]

Judith Shklar offers her own use of the key term "effective" when she writes: "Liberalism has only one overriding aim: to secure the political conditions that are necessary for the exercise of personal freedom. Every adult should be able to make as many effective decisions without fear or favor about as many aspects of her or his life as is compatible with the like freedom of every other adult. That belief is the original and only defensible meaning of liberalism."[65]

Amartya Sen's "capabilities approach" offers the most sophisticated version of "effective liberty" among contemporary liberal philosophers, while also having the additional benefit of explicitly tying questions of freedom to issues of equality.[66] Sen's basic idea is that the liberal commitment to liberty is empty unless the individual has the actual capability, the wherewithal as well as the freedom, to live the life he chooses. "Capability," he writes, "is primarily a reflection of the freedom to achieve valuable functionings. . . . In this sense it can be read as a reflection of substantive freedom. In so far as functionings are constitutive of well-being, capability represents a person's freedom to achieve well-being."[67] Describing freedom in this way, Sen insists, gives us a concrete way to assess the degree to which *every* citizen actually possesses freedom—and thus a concrete goal to aim for when attempting to achieve equality. A polity will have honored its commitment to equality when all of its citizens have the capability of effectively realizing their freely chosen versions of well-being.

Martha Nussbaum has adopted and elaborated the "capabilities approach," which she describes as "the ability of individuals to convert resources into meaningful human activity. The central question . . . is . . . 'What is [a person] actually able to do and to be?' . . . what she is in a position to do (what her opportunities and liberties are). . . . We then argue that in certain core areas of human functioning a necessary condition of justice for a public political arrangement is that it deliver to its citizens a certain basic level of capability."[68] Effective freedom requires having the means and the power to accomplish one's ends. Not just direct domination, but also the lack of adequate material and spiritual resources, can render individuals incapacitated. No liberal polity committed to truly providing individual liberty can tolerate an economic order that uses people and then throws them away, or social discrimination that humiliates certain categories of people and/or limits their access to some goods or public spaces. Egalitarian liberalism describes a fairly wide set of conditions and resources needed to make freedom actually available to citizens. Nussbaum's list of basic needs has ten items, ranging from life, bodily health, and bodily integrity to freedom of association and of imagination/play. In practice, modern liberalism begins with the attempt to achieve a "decent social minimum" for all people, a tough enough task in a world with deep poverty and dramatically unequal distribution of resources.[69] As prosperity is gained, however, the push is from securing the "minimum" for all to providing the conditions for the "flourishing" of all. This push comes under the banner of "equality" because it is grounded on the twin notions that each citizen is equally entitled to possessing the means for making freedom effective and that unequal distributions of power, resources, and/or liberty that diminish the capabilities of some are inimical to the basic liberal commitment to the equal provision of freedom to all.

It is in developing our sense of what freedom requires in order to be realized that modern liberalism revises the founders' liberalism. Roosevelt explains his sense of this revision in his Philadelphia speech of 1936:

> That very word freedom, in itself and of necessity, suggests freedom from some restraining power. In 1776 we sought freedom from the tyranny of political autocracy—from the eighteenth century royalists who held special privileges from the crown. . . . And so it was to win freedom from the tyranny of political autocracy that the American Revolution was fought. . . . But, since that struggle, man's inventive genius released new forces in our land which re-ordered the lives of our people. The age of machinery, of railroads, of steam and electricity . . . —all of these combined to bring forward a new civilization and with it a problem for those who sought to be free. For out of this modern civilization economic royalists carved new dynasties. . . . They created a new despotism and wrapped it in the robes of legal sanction. In its service new mercenaries sought to regiment the people, their labor, their property. And as a result the average man once more confronts the problem that faced the Minute-Man of seventy-six. . . . For too many of us the political equality we once won was meaningless in the face of economic inequality. A small group had concentrated into their own hands an almost complete control over other people's property, other people's money, other people's labor—other people's lives.
>
> For too many of us life was no longer free; liberty no longer real; men could no longer follow the pursuit of happiness.[70]

Acutely aware of where he stands—"Philadelphia is a good city in which to write American history," Roosevelt tells his auditors—FDR is at pains both to establish the continuity of his liberalism, his struggle to extend the freedom enjoyed by Americans, with the founding struggles of the nation *and* to explain the changing circumstances that make the struggle rather different now. The founders focused on the ways governments and/or a state-sponsored church made freedom impossible but paid less attention to social but nongovernmental impediments to the exercise of liberty. Not all accumulations of power into the hands of the few, or of a faction, take place within governmental or religious institutions. The fundamental liberal commitment to a truly achieved freedom leads, quite logically, to an expanded understanding of both the threats to freedom and the positive conditions and resources needed for the effective possession of it.

Note that Roosevelt's speech intertwines an emphasis on freedom with the language of "equality." The founders, of course, also used the language of equality, most famously in Jefferson's ringing statement in the Declaration of Independence that "all men are created equal." Yet Madison and Jefferson were both slaveholders, and Madison was party to the infamous decision to count slaves as three-fifths of a person in the U.S. Constitution. At the same time, as Ron Chernow documents, every one of the major founders expressed, some more strongly and persistently than others, their awareness that slavery was incompatible with their professed commitment to equality. Benjamin Franklin became president of Pennsylvania's abolition society; George Washington freed all of his slaves in his will; Alexander Hamilton was one of the founders of the New York Manumission Society; Jefferson and Madison both advanced schemes for emancipation, even though both did little practically to see such schemes become law and neither freed their own slaves. The crucial point is that the radical dynamic of equality was already readily apparent in the 1780s. "By 1784, Vermont, New Hampshire, Massachusetts, Pennsylvania, Rhode Island, and Connecticut had outlawed slavery or passed laws for its gradual extinction." As we will also see on the question of economic equality, we should be careful not to overstate the discontinuity between the founders and modern liberals. The implications of equality in relation to slavery and to the distribution of material resources were always on the table even if the programs we associate with the New Deal were a long time in coming and legal segregation persisted until the 1960s. On the founders' failure to end slavery, Chernow's conclusion seems exactly right: "The founding of the [New York] Manumission society and antislavery societies in other states in the 1780s represented a hopeful moment in American race relations, right before the Constitutional Convention and the new federal government created such an overriding need for concord that even debating the divisive slavery issue could no longer be tolerated."[71]

More globally, none of the founders—not even Jefferson—favored anything like full political equality, not to mention social equality. The best guess is that, for the founders, equality meant that each citizen is equal before the law and is equal in terms of the "rights" to which the Bill of Rights refers. It is worth realizing that, after the specific naming of various rights in the earlier articles, the Bill of Rights' Article IX reads: "The enumeration in the Constitution of certain rights, shall not be construed to deny or disparage others retained by the people." Apparently, the founders were relying on the English common law tradition of the "ancient rights and privileges" of the people. For our purposes here, the most plausible hypothesis is that the founders thought of equality in that same common law's terms: each person, regardless of rank or wealth, possessed those rights equally and stood as an equal before the law. The Constitution, at a minimum, asserts the legal equality of all citizens, but not of all people since the black slaves were not granted legal recognition as persons or citizens.

Legal equality is not yet—in fact, can be far from—political, social, or economic equality. But the notion of equality, once strongly asserted, would go on to become the joker in the pack. Did the founders realize that they had opened a door that could never be fully closed again when they signed a Declaration of Independence that expressed a commitment to the principle that "all men are created equal"? At times, it does seem that Jefferson understood the full implications of that statement. But even if he did not, Gordon S. Wood tells us that other Americans in the Revolutionary period were already pushing the idea of equality beyond mere legal equality. An early draft of the state constitution for Pennsylvania in 1776 declares that "an enormous Proportion of Property vested in a few Individuals is dangerous to the Rights and destructive of the Common Happiness, of Mankind," although more conservative views prevailed and the assertion does not appear in the final document.[72] The promise implicit in Jefferson's statement of equality might be (and certainly has been and still is) resisted by various factions in the United States, but it has persistently motivated other factions to demand that equality be made a reality. Because equality is an explicitly stated founding principle of the nation, it is extremely difficult, even for those who adamantly oppose the actual enhancement of equality, to base their opposition on the grounds of being against equality. As Jerry Z. Muller puts it: "An ongoing dilemma for American conservative thinkers . . . has been the perceived need to maintain popular reverence for the Declaration of Independence despite the fact that much of its content—from self-evident truths to the dogmatic assertion that 'all men are created equal'—is likely to be viewed with skepticism by many conservatives."[73]

A broad understanding of what equality requires characterizes modern liberalism. The issues here are enormously complicated—and central to the political battles of our history and of our own time. The key difference between liberals and conservatives in present-day America, I believe, is their respective understandings of and attitudes toward equality. So clarity on this point is crucial. Distinguishing between legal, political, social, and economic equality will help us understand what is at stake—and what an avowed commitment to equality can mean in different instances.

The founders, as I have described them, unquestionably believed in legal equality. The law is no respecter of persons; it treats everyone exactly the same. But the founders were not full-scale advocates of political equality, which can be defined as each citizen's having equal access to participation in political affairs and having an equal voice (minimally, a vote that is weighted the same as every other vote) in political decision-making. The Constitution violates the equal voice principle when it accords each state, irrespective of population, two U.S. senators. More directly, the founders also believed that women should not vote, and most of them also opposed universal male suffrage, favoring instead various qualifications that would exclude some citizens from voting.

Political equality, however, has proved to be a powerful principle over our nation's history. Once the principle is enunciated, various excluded groups will declare that their exclusion is illegitimate. Their claim is hard to resist. Conservatives will insist that the relevant group—women or blacks, for instance—are "not ready" for equality and will predict dire consequences if "they" are given such equality "prematurely," but it is the rare American who will contend that, forever and for all time, some group of people should be politically unequal, should be denied the vote. Racism and sexism in their most extreme forms do claim that a whole category of persons is inherently different from and inferior to other types of people—and thus should not be treated equally or granted the full rights of political participation. Such arguments have now lost their hold on most Americans and are not recognized, in either our courts or our legislatures, as legitimate reasons for denying legal and/or political equality.

The founders' ideal of equality, then, has stimulated multiple and mostly successful efforts to secure legal and political equality throughout American history. Liberalism is the reigning political position of all Americans in this respect. Of course, that does not mean that legal and political inequalities have been totally eradicated. There is ample evidence that the law treats blacks differently in criminal cases. (See Appendix, item 1.) But those who contribute to or even actively work to ensure the maintenance of such inequalities never openly espouse inequality and are, at least in principle, committed to change if prevailing practices are shown to promote inequality. Hence they will argue to their last breath that no such inequalities exist. These complications should not blind us to the fact that even the most conservative politician today is more liberal than the founders in regard to political equality. Not a single politician today (and few American citizens) would question that a woman or a black can sit on the U.S. Supreme Court or be president of the United States, whereas not a single one of the founders would have admitted that possibility. When it comes to political equality, we are all modern liberals. It has proved just about impossible to keep a lid on political equality. The notion of a "limited" equality available to only some people is so obviously a contradiction in terms that the very notion of equality appears to compel the movement from a limited to a full equality.

All of this is to say that the idea of equality has proved to be the recurrently radical thread in liberalism. It, even more than the commitment to freedom, drives the ongoing evolution of liberalism and has ensured that the classical liberalism of the founders—as well as the modern liberalism of our own day—is neither a static philosophy nor an unchanging set of political arrangements, but a dynamic response to changing circumstances and a never-ending attempt to better approximate the fundamental commitments. Equality and freedom are ideals that are always out in front of us, urging us on to more fully achieve them in an imperfect world. These principles call out to us, allowing us to gauge how far we have come and to see how far we still fall short. A liberal polity is judged not only on its ability to prevent tyranny and preserve the peace (after all, some authoritarian regimes manage that much), but also on its ability to enable actual, effective freedom and to afford that freedom equally to all.

What equality means becomes even more complicated, and much more fully contested (no American consensus here), when we turn to social and economic equality. Again, the founding fathers started this ball rolling because they did move partly toward social equality. The founders clearly—and explicitly—rejected any re-creation in America of the ranks and titles associated with the aristocratic societies of the Old World. There would be no official state-sponsored or state-recognized class differences in the United States.

To that extent, the founders were "levelers" socially as well as legally and politically. For Tocqueville, when he visited America before its fiftieth anniversary as a nation, the fact of social equality was what both fascinated and worried him. Tocqueville had no doubt that, in America at least, liberalism's commitments to liberty and political equality, along with its union with democracy, entailed a well-nigh irresistible push toward social equality as well. He was not completely convinced that order could be maintained in such a setting, and he suspected that vulgarity and mediocrity would triumph in the resultant society, but he did not believe that the grand American experiment would necessarily fail, and he thought it was likely to be tried elsewhere in the world before too long.[74]

Even in the absence of an aristocracy, there remain various sources of social inequality in the United States, most notably (but hardly exclusively) race, wealth, and gender. Modern liberalism pays a lot of attention to causes of and remedies for social inequality. The devil is in the details because there exists little certainty when we try to change through various kinds of interventions the outcomes of these processes. These uncertainties partially (but only partially) explain why social equality and economic equality as ideals are much more contested than legal equality or political equality in contemporary America. One crucial divide is how one understands the relation of social inequality to economic inequality. Liberals argue that it is just about impossible to disentangle the two. Those who have been historically socially unequal often remain economically worse off than those who have been socially privileged. (See Appendix, item 2.) Taking it the other way around, those who have more wealth are also socially and politically advantaged. In other words, if liberalism attends to accumulations of power in the hands of the few, it cannot ignore accumulations of social and economic power. The potential sources of tyranny are multiple—and liberalism is committed to preventing tyranny of all kinds.

Concerns about equality shade into issues of power when racism or vast wealth curtail the effective freedom of some citizens. Such concerns have been expressed popularly throughout the history of the United States but have had an uneven history in our courts and political institutions.[75] The Constitution does not attend to threats to economic independence that stem not from the government but from powerful players in the economic field itself. That silence, through much of American history, led the Supreme Court to invalidate many attempts to regulate economic activity—and still serves today to buttress the legal and rhetorical case of those who advocate various versions of laissez-faire.

Despite the Constitution's silence, economic matters quickly came to the fore once the new government was formed—and served to engender the split between Jefferson and Madison on one side and Hamilton on the other in the 1790s. Jefferson and Madison resisted Hamilton's economic policies (as secretary of the treasury in Washington's first administration) precisely because they thought those policies utilized the government to aid one particular class in the whole population: the "speculators" and "merchants," those whom we would today call "capitalists." Madison was moved toward the notion of what we now know as an "opposition party" by the consideration that economic power, working hand in hand with governmental power, must be checked. Madison originally thought that the formation of parties would be an unmitigated disaster, but he came to believe that an organized opposition to the government was a good antidote—even if hardly a sure-fire solution—to potential governmental overreach.[76] In his 1792 argument against Hamilton's plan, Madison had moved, by the very logic of his commitment to equality, from principles of legal and political equality to questions of economic equality. Here's Madison:

> In every political society, parties are unavoidable. A difference of
> interests, real or supposed, is the most natural and fruitful source
> of them. The great object should be to combat the evil: 1. By estab-
> lishing a political equality among all. 2. By withholding *unnecessary*
> opportunities for a few, to increase the inequality of property, by
> an immoderate, and especially an unmerited, accumulation of riches.
> 3. By the silent operation of laws, which, without violating the rights
> of property, reduce extreme wealth toward a state of mediocrity, and
> raise extreme indigence towards a state of comfort. 4. By abstaining
> from measures which operate differently on different interests, and
> particularly such as favor one interest at the expense of another.
> 5. By making one party a check on the other, so far as the existence
> of parties cannot be prevented, nor their views accommodated. If
> this is not the language of reason, it is that of republicanism.[77]

Madison recognized that political equality is threatened where economic inequalities are too great; he also feared that extreme economic differences would foster intractable social conflicts. He favored government policies that would redistribute wealth (point #3), and he worried especially about the way in which capitalism allows the accumulation of wealth by those who do not "merit" it (point #2).[78] As Sean Wilentz puts it, "After 1788, Madison, who understood the new regime perfectly, could see that the few instead of the many had become the chief threat to the American republican experiment."[79]

Conservatives since the 1780s have argued against political, social, and economic equality in various ways. Today, as we have seen, it would be hard to find someone who argues against political equality. And, for the most part, few remain who argue against social equality. Instead, present-day conservatives insist that social inequality and economic inequality are unconnected. They argue vehemently for the necessity and benefits of economic inequality. The most global liberal response is that conservatives in the past argued just as vehemently for the necessity and benefits of political and social equality. They were wrong on those counts, and they are wrong once again about economic inequality. The cat is out of the bag. Equality is too powerful an ideal to smother—and progress toward political and social equality has never brought the disasters that conservative opponents of such progress confidently predicted.

Conservative arguments against equality are considered more fully in Book Two. Right now, let's explore what equality has come to mean in everyday American political parlance. To some extent, the word "equality" is an unhappy label for the liberal ideas designated by the term. The term's popularity is understandable because it links to that sacred founding phrase in the Declaration of Independence and because it is economic inequalities that generate unequal possession of effective freedom. Appeals to "equality" are meant to alleviate the dispossession suffered by some. But "equality" in and of itself is never the goal. No liberal argues that one person's lack of a decent education or an adequate meal provides a reason for depriving others of these goods in order to achieve equality of condition. Rather, as already mentioned, the ideal labeled "equality," when translated into policy recommendations, means (at the least) providing a basic minimum necessary to the maintenance of life and (at the most) providing what is needed to render "flourishing" possible. That some will have "more" than the basic minimum or will flourish "more" than others is not disallowed if (and only if) everyone has the basics. This assertion is, undoubtedly, radical in its consequences. A full abiding by its implications would render a society that would deserve the name of "just."

Similarly, no liberal argues that "equality" entails sameness. In fact, Sen and Nussbaum's capabilities approach attempts to alert us to the obvious (but still too-often-neglected) fact that different people will need different things to be able to flourish. What a mother of three children needs is different from what a ten-year-old child or a seventy-five-year-old man requires. Giving everyone the same exact package of material resources would not achieve the effective freedom that is the actual goal. Moreover, the individuals who have been provided the means for flourishing will use those means in a wide variety of ways. Equality, despite conservative insistence to the contrary, is no enemy to pluralism. Quite the opposite. Pluralism can exist only where citizens are equal enough in power, resources, and effective freedom to actually be capable of choosing and sustaining a different way of life without fear of economic or political consequences. Dependents are hardly the people most capable of being different.

For contemporary liberals, it is an obvious—and disturbing—fact that some people have far more than they need for the exercise of effective freedom in this world, while others have far less than they need. The case against this state of affairs is not a rationale for equality of economic resources per se. And certainly it is not a rationale for everyone living the same way. Rather, it is a case for the good of effective freedom or (variably) of human flourishing, a good that should be equally available to all. If we affirm that good, then we should will the means toward it. That requires identifying what each person needs to be capable of flourishing and creating the political expedients that best provide those needs to each person. There is nothing easy about this task. What expedients can actually succeed in providing those needs is a very—but not hopelessly—difficult question. No society in human history has fully succeeded. But some societies have done much better than others, so the fatalistic conclusion (adopted by many conservatives) that nothing can be done on this score is refuted by concrete historical and contemporary examples.

This commitment to providing the means to effective freedom to everyone is what "equality" has come to mean in today's "egalitarian liberalism." I have explained how "equality" is probably not the best term for this ideal since it can mislead us in various ways. However, I think it undeniable that the current understanding of "equality" is an outgrowth of the ideal of equality enunciated by the founders and instantiated in the lived equality that Tocqueville found so amazing and disturbing. The better, because more encompassing and less ambiguous, term for the liberal position is "social justice." Its core principle can be stated as: *The society that more equitably distributes the means to individual human flourishing is more just.* Modern liberalism, at its core, is committed to this understanding of social justice, this extension of the notion of equality to include a distribution of fundamental resources to enable free individuals the capacity to act on their most basic aspirations and values. This understanding of what justice means has become commonplace enough to figure in George W. Bush's comment (quoted in the *New York Times*) that "a world in which some live in comfort and plenty, while half of the human race lives on less than $2 a day, is neither just, nor stable."[80]

John Rawls has been the great philosopher of this understanding of liberalism in our time. Sen and Nussbaum are concerned that Rawls's approach leads to a "one size fits all" account of the needed basic resources, but they are still building on the foundation that Rawls laid out. For Rawls, "justice" is the ultimate standard by which we judge a society, by which we decide its legitimacy, its being worthy of our allegiance, respect, and love. And the litmus test for Rawls is how a society treats the least well-off. That way of thinking led Rawls to his famous "difference principle," which states that differences in status, power, wealth, and other "primary goods" (a set of things people need in order to lead full and free lives) among the citizens of a liberal polity should be kept to a minimum. Rawls understands that inequities will remain, but in a just society, he insists, inequities are only tolerated to the extent that they are necessary to productive economic and/or sustainable social relations. The determination of how much inequality is permissible within polities that aspire to honor the difference principle is provided by a "maximin rule." The best (for Rawls, the most just) social relations would maximize the position of those who have the least (hence "maximin"). In other words, the society that managed to provide the most complete package of basic resources as a "minimum" available to all would be more just than a society in which many achieved much more than that minimum, but some achieved less than it.[81]

Rawls's moral prescription here follows William James's thought experiment in "The Moral Philosopher and the Moral Life." If, James asks, "millions [could be] kept permanently happy on the one simple condition that a certain lost soul on the far-off edge of things should lead a life of lonely torture, what except a specifical [*sic*] and independent sort of emotion can it be which would make us immediately feel, even though an impulse arose within us to clutch at the happiness so offered, how hideous a thing would be its enjoyment when deliberately accepted as the fruit of such a bargain?"[82] Rawls, in effect, reminds us that we often, perhaps somewhat unknowingly, make exactly that bargain. We accept, with varying degrees of complacency, the hideous poverty of other human beings, a poverty from which we benefit as we wear cheap clothes and eat cheap produce. A just polity would keep its eye firmly on the least advantaged as it made decisions that greatly influence (even if they cannot fully determine) the distribution of basic resources.

You can see why I think that we reach here a fundamental divide between liberals and conservatives. Modern liberalism has become committed to this model of justice that believes that actual equality across all dimensions is the most important indication that a society is just. Conservatives, as described in more detail shortly, deny the possibility and/or desirability of anything like economic equality, and insist that the unequal distribution of resources by the market is either a necessity to which we must submit or, in itself, just.[83] An approach toward equality that, at the very least, does not allow any citizen to fall below a certain standard of living underwrites the liberal understanding of justice. For modern liberals, conservatives have always resisted the movement toward equality (whether legal, political, social, or economic), so it is no surprise that today they resist economic equality. But the liberal believes that it is no more possible to quell the aspiration to economic equality than it was possible to halt earlier movements for legal and political equality. The unfulfilled promise of equality bequeathed to us by the founders motivates the evolution into modern liberalism.

We should, however, recognize that the modern liberal understanding of "social justice" is moral through and through. As such, it operates within the constraints of morality in a liberal polity. Different moral visions—and I am convinced that, at bottom, liberalism and conservatism are different moral visions—must compete in the public sphere and will find political and legal form only after the work of public persuasion is done. As already discussed, law and political institutions in a liberal polity lag behind the moral convictions of the citizenry, in some cases because those convictions are deeply plural, in others because a new consensus has emerged to which law and institutions have yet to catch up. It seems reasonably clear that the strong consensus of eighty years ago that homosexuality is immoral is currently eroding. Whether that erosion—which means we have dissensus on the topic today—portends the eventual formation of a new consensus that homosexuality is morally permissible, although hardly obligatory, cannot be currently known. The earlier consensus on this topic was so taken for granted that it did not even need to be argued for—and it was reflected in our laws and institutions. As the consensus began to dissolve, the law (fitfully, but correctly) began to decriminalize certain acts and to protect against some discriminations. But the law (in most cases) has stopped short of providing official legal sanction for homosexual acts and unions. Liberal polities fight shy of legal and institutional instantiation in the absence of a strong consensus on moral issues. In many instances, even a majority is not enough; a supermajority is needed to amend the Constitution. But this legal reticence in the face of moral disagreements is tempered by the bedrock liberal principles (in the common law tradition that the American founders adopted and adapted) of presumption of innocence and nondiscrimination. Where there is moral doubt and/or ongoing moral disagreement, the law is firmly set against any moralistic urge to rush to judgment, to ostracize, or to in any other fashion deny the rights of any individual or group. In that sense, it is indeed true that liberal law will, by certain lights, always be "permissive." It will permit, will refuse to exact penalties (legal or civic) for, certain behaviors that some members of the polis deem morally reprehensible. For conservatives, that often means the law tolerates vices such as gambling, drinking, and sexual deviance. For egalitarian liberals, that often means the law tolerates exploitive economic relations.

It is the very stuff of politics to do the rhetorical work required to win one's fellow citizens over to one's moral vision. We are never going to have complete moral agreement over the whole relevant field. Political disputes are often about the allocation of resources and/or of power, but they are also sometimes about competing moral visions of what the polity can and should be. The liberal moral vision has evolved into the concept of "social justice" outlined here. Liberals are committed to winning the public over to that vision and thus having it reflected in the laws and policies of American governments (federal, state, and local). But liberals, just like all the other players in the political field, cannot impose their moral vision. They can only expect it to become law and to hold the allegiance of the citizenry if they make that moral vision one that many hold dear and that others at least begrudgingly tolerate.

Who can doubt that great strides have been made in the liberal direction—or that huge strides are still to be made? We have come a long way toward the acceptance of African Americans as fully equal citizens, even as many African Americans still lack fully effective freedom. Programs like Social Security and Medicare have made inroads toward providing for the basic needs of the elderly—and, despite some conservative attempts to roll back these programs, they appear fairly firmly ensconced as features of our government desired by large majorities. But when it comes to social justice programs beyond Social Security and Medicare, the numbers are less conclusive. "A majority [of Americans]—50% to 35%—believes the government should do more to fight hunger and poverty, even if that would require increasing taxes on the middle class."[84] The liberal vision does not enjoy a vast majority and has been under increasingly aggressive attack during the past twenty years. My point is simply that "equality" and the understanding of "social justice" that goes along with it comprise the core of liberalism's moral vision of what a polity should be. But the distinctive liberal understanding of the relation of morality to law means that its moral vision cannot be directly translated into law and policy. Instead, that vision must go through the indirect route of articulation and contestation in the public sphere in the battle to win the consent and commitment of the demos. To attempt to bypass this difficult and often frustrating effort to forge a large majority is to succumb to what might be called the "autocratic temptation." Liberalism, especially when paired with democracy, can look like a formula for getting nothing done. It is famously (or infamously) inefficient and, repeatedly, generates the fantasy of or longing for a strong leader with a moral mandate. The "liberalism of fear" insists that such solutions are far worse than the disease they aim to cure.

The liberal expansion of what "equality" means and entails has, partially, won the battle in this effort to shape America's moral vision of what politics can and should aim to accomplish. That victory is evidenced by the progress toward social justice made in America since 1885. But that progress can be (and, to some extent, has been) undone, while making more progress depends on extending liberal principles of equality and justice even further. Progress is never guaranteed nor fully secure even once achieved. Fervent and persuasive advocacy is always needed. American liberalism has not distinguished itself on that front recently.

6
VALUES

Liberal diffidence—the abstention from using state power to tell citizens what to believe or how to live their lives—does not mean that liberalism is value-free. And it does not mean that liberals or pluralists are inherently or inevitably relativist about values. Liberals are perfectly able to say that murder is wrong and the law should forbid it. When it comes to values, liberalism does try to expand the range of the permissible. But it fully recognizes that some things will be obligatory and others forbidden.

The effort to expand the permissible is underwritten by a core value: liberty. It is also underwritten, as I have suggested, by the pluralistic conviction that there are many ways to live a good life. Liberty includes (although it is not simply comprised of) the freedom of each individual to make his or her own choices of what ends to pursue and how to pursue those ends within the broad field of the permissible. The broader we can make that field, the more freedom individuals will have. But some behavior must be forbidden. We should expect the need for constant trade-offs between goods that pull in opposite directions—here, freedom in tension with order. The liberal presumption is weighted toward freedom. The default position is permission. The burden of proof lies with order to justify any restrictions.

Focusing on the effort to extend the permissible leads pretty directly to just about all of liberalism's core values. It also reflects the English word's derivation from the Latin *liberalis*, which means "pertaining to a free man, noble, generous" and its core English meanings of "open- and broad-minded" and "not bound by authoritarianism, orthodoxy, or traditional forms in action, attitude, or opinion." Those values join the negative goal of limiting the power vested in institutional forms or particular social groups with the positive goal of enhancing each individual's control over her own choices and activities.

Liberalism has often been criticized, from both the right and the left, for its individualism. Yes, liberalism places a high—perhaps even the highest—value on individual life. The harm done by tyranny is registered in the suffering and deprivations endured by individuals, and the goods associated with freedom are enjoyed and utilized by individuals. Most simply put, life is located in the individual. Any polity, a liberal believes, should be measured by the quality of the individual lives it enables, with the important limiting proviso (underwritten by the asserted value of equality before the law) that no individual's good life can be achieved at the expense of other individuals. The liberal is suspicious of national glory, national wealth, or any other aggregate measure of the good that can be used to obscure attention to individual welfare. That individuals will, under various circumstances, sacrifice themselves to larger causes is, as history demonstrates, eminently possible. Other members of the society, who benefit from those sacrifices, will honor those individuals. But such sacrifices, as far as possible, should be chosen by the individuals, not exacted by the state or by others.

This liberal location of value in the individual life cannot be overemphasized. Liberalism always calls our attention to—and cries out in protest against—sufferings inflicted on individual human beings by the actions of other human beings. It is always suspicious of any state or any community that downplays such suffering in relation to some transindividual project. Always take seriously indeed the question of whether you would prefer to live in a society that routinely subordinates the good as understood and registered by the individual (starting from absence of suffering and moving from there to more positive pleasures and accomplishments) to other, overriding, goods and goals. Suffering follows inexorably where some humans have power over others. Even those who sincerely attempt to use power benignly (parents are a prime example) often hurt those in their care and, if they are honest and can transcend self-interest, know that their charges are, eventually, better off if given their freedom. Paternalism is of strictly limited benefit—and notoriously opens the door to various abuses and self-delusions.

Freedom to choose and enact one's own course in life is itself experienced as a great good, something cherished for its own sake. Increasing individual freedom also has beneficial consequences. A free people will move to minimize suffering, since few individuals, given the opportunity to forge their own course in life, will choose to suffer. The individual, as John Stuart Mill always insisted, is the best judge of his own interests and desires and should be left free to choose the means of advancing those interests and of satisfying those desires.[85] Humans have, unfortunately, shown themselves to be perfectly capable of indifference to, even enjoyment of, the suffering of others, but few are indifferent to or find pleasure in their own suffering. That's why it is best to place as much power as possible in the hands of individuals if the good one wishes to promote is, minimally, pain-free lives and, maximally, productive and happy lives. Here as elsewhere, liberalism acknowledges limits. No society can eliminate all pain. But a liberal society certainly should avoid enabling the pain humans can cause one another and will devote some of its resources to combating and alleviating the pains that Nature—in the form of sickness especially, but also in cases of natural disasters—deals out.

There are many competing theoretical accounts of the individual's relation to others and to social institutions. The liberal thinkers of the Enlightenment posit individuals as strongly independent of society, portraying selves who approach intellectual and emotional, and dream of material, self-sufficiency. Modern liberal writers, however, usually portray an individual firmly embedded in social relations that constitute and enable her very status as an individual. John Locke, Adam Smith, and John Stuart Mill are often cited as proponents of the first position, although none of them holds it in any simple way. In particular, Smith's *Theory of Moral Sentiments* makes it unlikely that anything remotely resembling pure individualism characterizes his understanding of the relations of individuals to others and to society;[86] similarly, Mill's *Subjection of Women* offers a strong version of the view that individuals are shaped and constrained by social circumstances, a perspective now called "liberal" in common parlance. It is conservatives today who espouse an atomistic individualism stronger than anything found in the works of the classical liberal writers. Rational choice theorists of our own day—most notably, Robert Nozick, Gary Becker, and Milton Friedman—offer a more sophisticated version of the position most notoriously enunciated in Margaret

Thatcher's pronouncement: "There is no such thing as society; there are only individuals."[87] This portrait of individuals is, as various liberals and nonliberals have taken pains to show, pretty implausible.[88] It violates just about everything we know about the long developmental periods humans undergo before reaching intellectual, emotional, and physical maturity, and it offers a skewed picture of how humans, who are found everywhere living together in social groups, relate to one another and of what humans characteristically need and want. In what follows, I present the more "intersubjective" position characteristic of much (although not all) modern liberalism. In this view, the individual is still the locus of action, life, bodily integrity and harm, and freedom. But that individual is constituted through her relations to others in a social matrix and experiences the need for a satisfactory arrangement of those relations as a primary motivation. The desires to be loved, respected, recognized, and cared for by others rank high among the primary goods that individuals seek.

Taking the individual as a primary political value (i.e., placing as much power as possible in individual hands and measuring the good of a polity in relation to the quality of individual lives it enables) need not be tied to an individualistic conception of human psychology or human nature. All that is needed is recognition of individually distinct bodies, so that the pain felt by one body is definitely located here, not there. But those individual bodies can be understood as standing in all kinds of complex relationships to one another and to having highly permeable boundaries. Not only do germs move from one body to another, so that your pain today might well become my pain tomorrow. But ideas, emotions, accents, bodily gestures, and habits also migrate from one body to the next. Various liberal thinkers—including George Herbert Mead, John Dewey, Charles Taylor, and Jürgen Habermas— have developed sophisticated accounts of how the individual's capacities, desires, and self-conception are developed socially in and through his or her intimate, sustaining, and inescapable relations with others.[89] Among these writers, Dewey in particular was deeply influenced by Aristotle's view of humans as political animals and Hume's critique of any social vision that did not recognize individuals as always and everywhere existing with others.[90] Alan Ryan's characterization of Dewey's position fairly summarizes a whole tradition that repudiates belief in an isolated, self-creating, and self-sustaining individual. "[Dewey] thought that our individuality resided in our biography, that individuals were more process than substance, that their substance was simply the process of their lives. Those lives were more social than individual, or perhaps we ought to say that human beings are *individual* only because they are *social*."[91] It is through her interactions with others within existing social structures that the person acquires individuality. Her inter-subjective relations are constitutive—and thus represent a crucial set of interests for the individual. The self-interested individual imagined by Gary Becker is seldom found in reality. Our interests and desires—in fact, our very selves—are complex and plural because they are forged within the social relations in which the individual is embedded from birth. Finally, even if some version of atomistic individualism can be found in Locke or Adam Smith, there is little evidence for such views among the American founders. It has become a truism that the founders were heavily influenced by Hume, who rejected "the selfish system of morals" found in Hobbes and Locke in favor of a view that saw "our selfish and vicious" propensities existing alongside "our social and virtuous" ones.[92] Individual liberty depends on government, not on some kind of liberation from government. As Madison saw it, the problem is to get enough government to secure liberty, but not so much as to occasion tyranny. "It is a melancholy reflection," he wrote to Jefferson in 1788, "that liberty should be equally exposed to danger whether the Government have too much or too little power, and that the line which divides these extremes should be so inaccurately defined by experience."[93]

The liberal focus on the individual, then, need not entail alienation from those original communities into which the individual was born or from whatever government the individual finds himself embedded within. Nothing in liberalism precludes an individual from declaring allegiance to this or that group, to subordinating her own inclinations or even her choices about how to live to a group's prevailing mores. Liberalism only insists that the subordination itself be freely chosen, that not all individuals in the society be compelled to find a place within such a group, and that such groups not be reinforced by state power. The liberal polity should (primarily through the education afforded each child) give each individual the capacity to judge for herself how she wants to understand and live her relationships to various social factions, some of which she is entangled in before she acquires that capacity for judgment. The individual, once she has the capacity to make that judgment, must also be given the freedom to make it and the power to act on it. Just as we can identify individuals by specifying which body is feeling a particular pain, we can identify an individual (especially what we might call the "political individual" who is particularly relevant to liberalism) as the site of a judgment made and of ensuing decisions and actions. Because judgments, decisions, and actions are not made in a vacuum, the language of "autonomy" can be misleading, indicating a self-sufficiency that is neither attainable nor desirable. Better to acknowledge that individual judgments are influenced by all kinds of things that surround the individual, but that there are still clear lines of demarcation between what I judge, decide, and do and what you judge, decide, and do. Liberalism is committed to enhancing the capacity of each individual to undertake these activities for him- or herself. Commitments, affiliations, vocations, beliefs, and courses of action freely chosen are stronger for having been achieved through that process of examination and endorsement. Such commitments are the basis of the voluntary compliance with supraindividual social forms and regulations. As far as possible, imposed compulsion (the original condition of being saddled with a life one did not ask for and in relation to others one did not choose) should be replaced with freely chosen cooperation. Many will choose to continue living among those they spent their childhood with. But not everyone will make that choice. And most everyone will, sometime in their twenties, be able to say that they have exercised some (if not total) freedom in the forms that those relations with others they have known since childhood now assume.

An emphasis on freely chosen association with others does not necessarily entail hostility to such associations. In fact, it is today's laissez-faire conservatives who sing the praises of agonistic, competitive relations between individuals as most productive of social goods and individual well-being. Liberals are much more likely to stress the benefits of cooperation over competition, and to see individual self-fulfillment as most apt to occur in the context of various ties to others. Dewey expresses this liberal position:

> The human problem is that of securing the development of each constituent so that it serves to release and mature the other. Cooperation . . . is as much a part of the democratic ideal as personal initiative. That cultural conditions were allowed to develop (markedly so in the economic phase) which subordinated cooperativeness to liberty and equality serves to explain the decline in the two latter. Indirectly, this decline is responsible for the present tendency to give a bad name to the very word *individualism* and to make *sociality* a term of moral honor beyond criticism. But that association of nullities on even the largest scale would constitute a realization of human nature is as absurd as to suppose that the latter can take place in beings whose only relations to one another are those entered into in behalf of exclusive private advantage.[94]

Writing in 1939, Dewey did not foresee the return of individualism, but he was clear that neither individuals mindlessly faithful to community nor the economic competition of all against all offer the conditions for the best possible society. Cooperation is between different citizens who work together across their differences not just to gain some common end, but, even more importantly, to enhance the development of each person's capabilities. Full realization of individual potential is only achieved in relation to others.

So far I have identified two fundamental liberal values: life and effective freedom. Crucially, life is lodged in individuals. It is individuals who have life—and who can lose it. Freedom consists in having control over that life— and, crucially, in having the capacity to protect, to develop, to utilize, and to live that life as one sees fit. The individual can dispose of his life, but the emphasis is more on his ability to compose it. We have seen already that these core commitments to life and freedom slide from simply possessing life to having a good life. Liberalism just about inevitably begins to attend to the quality of life, not just the having of it. On the legal, institutional, and political levels, that attention entails, minimally, protecting individuals from suffering—and death—inflicted by others. But less minimally, that attention leads to the notion of a just society as one that provides the means for a good life to all.

This focus on life and liberty as possessed by individuals is accompanied by two further core liberal assertions: each life is of equal value, and each individual has an equal claim (on the polity and in relation to others) to freedom. We generally take these assertions of equality for granted today, so it may be hard to remember just how revolutionary this liberal position was when first introduced by political philosophers in the seventeenth century and in actual polities in the latter half of the eighteenth century. Certainly, no plank in the liberal platform was as fiercely contested, both ideologically and politically. To a significant extent, the ideological battle over equality has been won by liberalism. Forthright denials of equality to certain citizens are fairly rare—although they do exist—these days.

Victory has its price: persistent obfuscation when it comes to questions of equality in contemporary liberal democracies. Nineteenth-century opponents of liberalism, and its coconspirator democracy, frankly argued that not all lives were of equal worth, that not every citizen was capable of full freedom (for example, non-Europeans and women), and that not every person was worthy of the privileges enjoyed by the superior few. Recall that Tocqueville's great *Democracy in America* devotes much of its attention to what it means personally and politically to live in a society of equals. Tocqueville tries to present dispassionately the pros and cons of equality—and he does so from the perspective of someone to whom it is an open question whether equality is to be endorsed or not. Today, however, everyone claims to be an egalitarian, even if the social practices and political policies they advocate directly favor some portions of the citizenry over others or indirectly afford some citizens privileges and/or opportunities denied to others. In America especially, but in contemporary liberal democracies more generally, it is very hard to acknowledge actual inequalities, or to discuss in the public square the ways in which those inequalities are produced and perpetuated. Are some inequalities inevitable and thus should be tolerated or even encouraged? Or, on the contrary, are those inequalities pernicious and inimical to our most fundamental values as a liberal society? The usual expedient is to use the notion of "equality of opportunity" to avoid any examination of real, existing inequalities. The general bowing and scraping before the god of equal opportunity has, it seems, rendered us incapable of apprehending, no less intelligently assessing or adequately working to remedy, various inequalities in our society. Unchallenged principles are always in danger of ossifying, and they often can serve (as in this case) to deploy piety toward the ideal in order to mask (and thus ignore) realities on the ground.

Similarly, liberalism's historical triumph is nowhere more evident than in the ubiquity today of the language of "rights." Readers will have noted that I have gotten this far into an account of American liberalism and have barely mentioned—or relied on—the notion of rights. In the actual political debates of our time, it would be highly unusual if the word was not uttered by the third sentence. We have come to understand each individual's equality in relation to the goods of life and freedom as a matter of that individual having a "right" to those goods. Thus, in their recent liberal manifesto, Bruce Ackerman and Todd Gitlin write: "We want to redirect debate to the central questions of concern to ordinary Americans—their rights to housing, affordable health care, equal opportunity for employment, and fair wages, as well as physical security and a sustainable environment for ourselves and future generations."[95] It is as if we understood the polity as a game of *Monopoly*. Each player in the game is given the same amount of money with which to start. Similarly, each player in a liberal polity starts with the same exact rights in her pocket. Rights are legal or political tender. The individual brings them forth to get her due.

I acknowledge that this vocabulary of rights has proved effective in any number of political battles over the past 250 years. As Cass R. Sunstein amply demonstrates, Franklin Roosevelt depended as heavily on the notion of "rights" when working to increase economic equality as he depended on the notion of effective freedom.[96] Even so, revising some received ideas about the individual and his rights (the two are entangled) need not hamper, but in fact may enhance, our understanding of and our liberal polity's ability to secure what I take to be liberalism's fundamental values, the goods that it aims to secure. I am certainly not hubristic enough to believe that my objecting to these received ideas and a now-habitual vocabulary of political demands will lead to their disappearance. The liberal principle of equality will continue to be cashed out by the tender of rights. But I worry that "rights talk" underwrites an adversarial relationship between the individual and the state. A more political—a more interactional and intersubjective—understanding of rights would go a long way toward changing the political climate in the United States for the better. Like individuals themselves, rights should be seen as the product of social interaction—more specifically, as politically created and sustained. Both Madison's original objection to a Bill of Rights and his subsequent embrace of the idea are instructive. Writing to Jefferson in 1788, Madison claims that "experience proves the inefficacy of a bill of rights on those occasions when its controul [sic] is most needed. Repeated violations of these parchment barriers have been committed by overbearing majorities in every State."[97] The danger to liberty is power—and no amount of talk about rights or claims about their inviolability will stand up to a power determined to ignore them. The protection of rights lies in the hands of the polis, of the others with whom one lives in society. But, for just that reason, Madison comes to change his mind. He recognizes that articulation of rights as fundamental commitments can be useful—and their establishment in law can serve as a safeguard, even if not as an ironclad guarantee, of their observance.[98] If I could be sure that rights were consistently understood as political creations that arise from and are underwritten by the ongoing constitutive relations between selves, I would use "rights talk" as glibly as the next guy. But I suspect that, when appealed to today, rights are tied to individualistic notions of a freedom disconnected from social relations and to a hostility to what gets called "governmental interference." So, for the most part, I refrain from relying on rights in my account of liberalism.

My argument, then, is that the liberal revolution in history was the conscious shaping of a legal and social world that took individual liberty as a basic value. Liberalism aimed to make possible a kind of freedom that had found only fitful expression in previous human societies. It is hardly clear that a great desire for liberal freedom preceded liberalism. Did the devout Catholic of the Middle Ages or the members of an Iroquois lodge long for individual liberty? Even many citizens in a liberal polity experience such freedom as more frightening and disorienting than exhilarating. Lots of people will choose to subsume themselves within larger groups. Individual liberty emerges as a good historically with the Protestant emphasis on freedom of conscience—and then blossoms within the wider political vision of a liberalism that aims to arrange social relations to cultivate, elaborate, and continually revise the practices of that liberty.

What difference does this argument that freedom is political, not natural, make? It is meant to combat the widespread feeling that the individual is pitted against the state or against society. Hobbes, Locke, and Rousseau all had it wrong. There is no "state of nature" for human beings. Individuals always exist within a society—and they are always deeply influenced by the relations in which they stand to family, neighbors, and more distant others. Individual liberty can only emerge within a society. And that liberty is best preserved when we consciously shape our laws and our social relations to promote and protect it. Simply to attack the state and its laws can never increase freedom; complete destruction of the legal order would destroy freedom's conditions. We can, of course, believe that only radical reform will yield true freedom. Radical reform can mean the complete abolishment of the current order in favor of a new one. But the anarchist or libertarian fantasy that true freedom means living outside all laws misunderstands how freedom is created and secured. We jeopardize the very freedom we claim to prize when we indulge— or encourage in others—a general hostility to the state.

If the idea of individual liberty was a historical novelty, the notion that all individuals should have the same access to that liberty was an outrage. Equality has to be established by law because it seems so obviously "unnatural." (This may just be a way of saying that it's easy to take my own "right" to individual liberty as natural. After all, who deserves liberty more than I do? But it's hard to swallow the other guy's right to the same liberty. Him? You've got to be kidding. You are going to give him liberty? Let me tell you all the dire consequences that will follow from that foolhardy course.) Different individual aptitudes are apparent, not to mention less relevant, but still glaring, differences of gender, size, inclinations, and skin/eye/hair color. In many ways, the history of Western liberal societies boils down to a stated commitment to equality and a fitful commitment to actually achieving anything even remotely like equality. The many rationalizations—from the crudities of racism and sexism to highly sophisticated justifications of the social need for elites or of the economic need for the extremely wealthy or the extremely poor— that have been used to justify inequalities in liberal societies testify both to liberalism's perpetual uneasy conscience on this score and to the ever-present resistance to accepting or allowing true equality. Liberal polities are so dynamic, in part, because they are committed to a value—equality—that has never been fully instantiated. Such polities contain an internal, legitimated standard by which they can always be found wanting.

This kind of argument—one that insists that rights and/or individual liberty can only exist within (or, more strongly, are products of) a particular political order shaped to foster and protect them—is of a piece with the modern liberal propensity to take a holistic view of human behavior. An individual's abilities, beliefs, and actions are deeply influenced by his social environment, which elicits various potentials in that person while obscuring others. That liberalism, including a liberal education, works to afford the individual some ability to disentangle himself, to distance himself, from those shaping influences is a tribute to their power. Contemporary critics of liberalism oddly fluctuate between bemoaning how liberalism undermines adherence to one's birth community (received patriotic or religious beliefs, for example) and claiming that individuals are solely responsible for their actions in ways that modern liberalism denies. Liberals are "soft" on crime and poverty because they are unwilling to squarely place the blame on the individual. The discussion just offered of the modern liberal understanding of the ways in which individuals are embedded in social and political relations underlines the fact that power of various forms mitigates any unhampered enactment of individual liberty. Thus liberty, like equality, serves as an ideal precisely because there are such persistent tendencies in human societies toward its limitation by various forms of accumulated power. To exact the price (full responsibility) of an achieved liberty while withholding its benefits (actual effective freedom) offends a liberal sensibility aware of how short our polity still falls of its stated ideals. The revision of Lockean liberalism's individualism by John Dewey and Charles Taylor accepts the insistence by David Hume and Edmund Burke (an insistence originally considered conservative) that individuals are social creatures through and through and, thus, best understood when we take into account the pressures, loves, desires, loyalties, values, and commitments that social relations entail. Where Dewey and Taylor depart from Hume and Burke is in valuing processes (of education and reflection) that enable the individual to examine those social relations. Hume and Burke think chaos lies that way. If everyone questions received tradition, then society will fall apart. That is too much freedom to give individuals, too much reliance to place on human reason. Dewey and Taylor insist, to the contrary, that modern individuals, in part because they encounter so many other ways to live a life and organize a society, will not grant legitimacy to a particular received form of life unless it stands up to examination, unless it can justify itself with a satisfactory account of its values and its means of achieving them. Of course, in a certain way, Hume and Burke already concede this liberal rationalism. What else are they doing in their writings but offering a statement of their values and arguments for the desirability of those values and the best means for making them prevail?

Liberalism also places a high value on peace, security, and stability. In one way, these values can be seen as ancillary to the emphasis on life. It is hard, if not completely impossible, to enjoy my freedom to live my own life if the peaceful, secure, and stable conditions that enable me to exercise that freedom do not exist. Taken that way, these values might seem self-evident—and less values than means toward the encompassing value of individual liberty. Nothing crucial hinges on whether peace, stability, and security are values or means to values. More germane is the constellation of character traits, worldview, and practices that are commonly called "bourgeois." That label is hardly ever a compliment. Historically, the antiliberal right contrasts an aristocracy that values honor, pride, and an insouciant carelessness about self-preservation with a cautious, calculating middle class that counts every penny, saves for a rainy day, and focuses its energies on commercial gain rather than military glory, social fame, or today's pleasures. The aristocrat is touchy, contentious, high-spirited, and gay (in the old sense of that word, the sense that Nietzsche uses in *The Gay Science* and that Yeats uses in his poem "Lapis Lazuli" when he tells us that "their ancient glittering eyes were gay"). The bourgeois are sourpusses, placating, even spineless, cravenly hoping for peace and quiet, to be allowed to go on about their business undisturbed. It is fair to say that an attraction to nonbourgeois style still clashes strongly with the mostly bourgeois values by which many contemporary Americans live their lives. Nowhere, perhaps, is that clash more vividly played out than in the utterly incoherent grab bag of emotional and cultural responses to the military in our country. We don't know whether to be enthralled by military derring-do and its glittering paraphernalia or ashamed of military brutality and the excessive masculinity it encourages. Thus, our culture at times attempts to domesticate the military by emphasizing that the soldiers are our "sons and fathers" (and, of course, today increasingly our "daughters and mothers"), or by treating military service as just another job. Other times, however, we go with the slightly embarrassed stance of "boys will be boys" and look indulgently at scared kids being urged to strike tough-guy and cowboy postures. Yet other times we encourage more traditional notions of manly valor and noble sacrifice. And always we veil in euphemism and protect ourselves by distance from the actual killing our military does. We are, officially, a peace-loving nation. We only go to war reluctantly—and compelled by the most terrible, but inexorable, necessities.[99]

Given the fatal attraction that militarism and war still hold, bourgeois values and the character traits that go with those values are less self-evident and less contemptible. Peace is a great blessing because humans are ever ready to come to blows. And figuring out how to behave in ways that promote peace proves no easy task. Overly aggressive behavior is read as a challenge or an insult—and inspires like behavior in response. But overly submissive behavior is read as weakness and can encourage further aggression as our antagonist pushes to see where we will draw the line. Our democracy used to love to tell itself that we were very slow to anger, but an implacable and dangerous foe once roused. That traditional view of ourselves is just one of the elements of our liberalism that appears on the wane these days. In its place, we seem to have developed an unstable mixture of sentimentality about our troops, aggrieved petulance about how the rest of the world misunderstands us, blustery bullying behavior toward one and all, and a willed ignorance about the realities of violence on the ground—violence that we have displaced elsewhere (geographically) and onto the shoulders of a small and marginalized portion of our population, our "volunteer army," so that we can carry on our "normal" (bourgeois) lives as if none of this is happening. Maybe the best way to state our dilemma is to say that we claim to desire peace, but then we do not will the means toward its achievement.

In any case, to pronounce peace as one of the greatest goods any society can secure for its members is to confront directly that the ways of peace are despised, ridiculed, and feared in many quarters. The grounds for this hostility appear to lie in a terror of weakness. Those who fear peace view life as an endless struggle in which I must strive very hard to wrestle the things I want away from a grudging world and from the others who also want them; then, once I have secured some portion of the means for life, I must protect those resources with all my might against others who want to steal them for their own or even just destroy them out of sheer malice and envy. To let down my guard a moment will be to make myself vulnerable. When we recall that "liberal" means, among other things, "open-handed and generous," we can recognize why the "life is a hard-fought struggle against circumstances and not-to-be-trusted others" outlook rejects liberalism as unrealistic. Peace, for this kind of nonliberal, is only a temporary cessation of hostilities.

Liberalism, in its infuriating, ever-reasonable way, can only answer this nonliberal by gently urging that he try out an alternative. Why does this response so often drive the militaristically minded to greater fury? Psychological speculations about uneasy consciences and threatened masculinity usually pop up at this point. Luckily, this is a political treatise, so I do not need to go there. The political question is, How can we arrange our civil life and political institutions so that citizens get to reap the benefits of peace most of the time, in all but the most extreme circumstances? Liberalism says: "Since we constantly claim that peace is a great good, let's work damn hard to make it a reality." Peace—like equality—is an announced ideal. That the ideal is always under threat—and probably never fully achieved—does not discredit the ideal. It stands, instead, as a continual prod to do better. And it also serves as a standard by which to judge actions actually undertaken. Do such actions promote peace? If not, why not? A heavy burden of proof should be placed on any political action that jeopardizes peace.

For liberalism, peace is a good because it provides the kind of stability and security that allows individuals to construct their lives. A life is a temporal project, with many actions undertaken today in light of the fruits they will yield in the future. If I cannot count on the basic structures of society or the most basic facts of my existence (economic well-being, freedom to move or to stay put as I wish) to remain stable, I cannot make long-range plans. Liberalism is committed to political arrangements that will make individuals' control over their own lives, over the paths they follow, a reality. War may be the most extreme instance of an event that completely cancels such individual control. Doubtless, there are always individuals who, in fact, greet the beginning of war with relief. They, for various reasons, have found freedom more burdensome than liberating, or they long (whether consciously or not makes no difference) to escape the life they have constructed for themselves. We might even condemn society for being too close-minded, too unimaginative, in the models of possible lives it transmits to its members. But liberalism remains committed to the political arrangements that maximize individual liberty and equality and to a peace that provides the stability that make freedom and justice, at least, a possibility.

At this point leftist critics of bourgeois values often enter the debate. Theoretically, they argue that individual liberty is a delusion, impossible to achieve and, hence, a false goal. Practically, they insist that liberty, pursued as a goal or even if achieved, has bad consequences. The bourgeois focus their attention on personal happiness and think that such happiness comes from "private" activities—notably economic well-being and domestic felicity. Success in achieving happiness is attributed entirely to individual effort (with, sometimes, an acknowledgment of the role luck may have played), and the fruits of success or failure are for the individual alone to enjoy or suffer. Individuals in liberal polities fail to recognize how dependent their well-being is on social and political structures. That's liberalism's theoretical flaw. And individual liberty in action is just a fancy name for massive—and appalling—selfishness. That's liberal individualism's moral flaw. Finally, some leftist writers join with some classic right-wing thinkers who are disturbed by the bourgeoisie's lack of public-mindedness, its indifference to the kinds of honor and acclaim that come with civic involvement.

I have indicated that I am sympathetic to the view that Americans often misunderstand that individual liberty is constituted and maintained by the polis. Liberty is not a natural possession. It is a product of a polity created to provide it to each citizen. That's why liberty is a value, a good that we consciously strive to attain. We are inevitably more or less successful in attaining it, but once we have designated it as valuable to us, as something we dearly wish for, then declaring it, by theoretical fiat, impossible is not the way to go. We should proceed empirically instead. Where has something approaching a satisfactory liberty been achieved? Given any set of human lives, which ones evidence more liberty as contrasted to which other ones? What social and political arrangements have, in actual historical societies, provided more liberty than have other societies? If we take off the theoretical blinders, we can examine our own desires for liberty and for equality honestly in order to consider in which contemporary societies we would find those desires intolerably thwarted. Individual liberty, like the other liberal values, is a standard and a goal. We cannot achieve it outside of society, and we may never be able to achieve it fully, but it stands as an ideal by which we measure our polity.

The selfishness worry seems, to me, of a different—and much more difficult—order.[100] Does liberalism, because it is individualistic, promote a disregard of the public good and a disinclination to contribute (time, talents, wealth, or whatever) to the public welfare? Liberalism believes, in this instance as in many others, that legal compulsion is both inimical to liberalism's core commitment to liberty and counterproductive because it generates resistance. The liberal legal structure exists primarily to constitute and protect liberty; hence, liberalism is always suspicious of laws that compel—either by forbidding some behavior or by making some other behavior obligatory. Such compulsion will, in some cases, be necessary. But, even then, liberalism will be more comfortable forbidding harmful behavior than in requiring beneficial behavior. What a free person will do voluntarily, he will often resist doing—or do badly and reluctantly—if compelled. (Any parent knows this fact about human psychology.) More crucial, however, in this instance is the question of the connection between the law and social relations. The various ties through and in which people in any society are bound to one another, with various obligations toward and commitments to the welfare of others in that society, are not created by the law and not, for the most part, sustained by the law. The law does work to protect the liberty of all parties in a relationship and will, in certain instances, set limits to what is permissible in order to counteract the potential of one party to wield undue power over the other. (The most obvious cases are labor and family law.) Criminal law will be used to curb abuses and civil law to handle disputes in these relations, but, beyond its ever-present attempt to create an equality among citizens, the law does not dictate the terms of the relationship. This balancing act between liberty and equality is, of course, not easy to maintain. Where and how to draw the line, what legal prescriptions are warranted and even necessary, will be constantly contested. But surely choosing the drastic way out—having the law establish and enforce the forms and lived realities of our social relations—would be far worse than liberal ambiguities.

My argument here is not a denial that social relations in the contemporary United States, especially as reflected in our growing economic inequalities, are seriously out of kilter. A liberal polity must address these issues because concentrated economic power limits the effective freedom of citizens. But what the law can achieve is limited, while liberalism remains wary of trying to compel individuals to be virtuous through legal means. Social, not legal, relations are the sources of commitments, obligations, and morality (as believed and practiced). The individual's most fundamental motivations and most profound senses of what is right and what is wrong stem from his entanglement with others. The law is abstract and alien compared with those on-the-ground lived relations. If the needs and wishes of those with whom he is connected do not mitigate an individual's selfishness, then why should we think the law will do the job?

In a society lacking any sense of commonality, the law will become a means for the individual to further pursue his selfish goals—and the site where those who resist his desire (and his power) to gather all to himself will have some chance of reining him in. But the ills of a society in which many pursue their individual interest with no regard—even contempt—for the general welfare or for the interests of others are not remediable by legal action alone, even if the law is a crucial site for combating such selfishness. In short, as the founders stressed, a polity relies heavily on "virtues" for its well-being.[101] These virtues, which include a commitment to the welfare of one's fellow citizens that can involve accepting the sacrifice of some personal benefits for the general good, cannot be created or guaranteed by law. They, in Brian Barry's words, depend on "a sense of common fate," on the belief that my destiny and well-being are inextricably intertwined with the destiny and well-being of my compatriots in this society. Any sense that I can exempt myself from that common fate, either because (in Barry's words) "I can buy my way out of trouble" or because suffering can be allotted to only some groups or individuals, undermines the polity.[102] In short, the modern liberal conviction that individual effective freedom is a good that cannot be achieved by individual effort alone, but must be understood as socially and politically enabled (or thwarted), leads fairly directly to an emphasis on cooperation. My liberty depends on others' supporting a social order that strives to maximize the freedom of all according to (even if rough) a maximin goal. To "free ride" on others' support is possible but violates the most basic terms of togetherness in a polity professing the ideals of liberty and equality.

The larger point is that there are social goods, things like promises and, I have been arguing, freedom itself that cannot be achieved without cooperation. In addition, a society needs a basic trust among its members that some are not gaming the system to their own advantage. A legal system for producing social goods and forbidding free riders is swimming upstream if the very notion of social goods is denied or the fundamentals of trust and cooperation have been lost. A liberal believes that we can best expect the cooperation and trust needed for a functioning society where we experience the polity as working toward an effective freedom offered to each and every individual.

Immanuel Kant and John Stuart Mill are the great liberal moral philosophers. All three of Kant's formulations of the categorical imperative in *Grounding for the Metaphysics of Morals* articulate crucial liberal principles.[103] First: "Act only according to that maxim whereby you can at the same time will that it should become a universal law" (30). Here Kant enunciates a key consequence of accepting the equality of all as well as the injunction against free riding: never make an exception of yourself. No status, privilege, attainment, or possession can justify allowing to oneself what would not be allowed to others. Second: "Act in such a way that you treat humanity, whether in your own person or in the person of another, always at the same time as an end and never simply as a means" (36). This assertion of the fundamental worth of each and every person underwrites the insistence that each should have the freedom to choose her own course in life and not be subject to serving as an instrument toward another's pursuits. The second version of the categorical imperative, then, is the injunction against tyranny, but it also supplies the crucial underpinning of modern liberalism's ethos of cooperation. Third is "the idea of the will of every rational being as a will that legislates universal law" (38). Here we get the principle of self-determination, that every people should only be subject to laws of their own devising, just as every individual should be able to recognize that those laws are ones to which she can rationally consent. The legitimacy of the law is based on its ultimately resting on the authority (the authorship) of those who are subject to it. Finally, Kant enunciates the key liberal principle that a legitimate government, one that operates within the rule of law, should always act in the full light of day:

> We may specify the following proposition as the *transcendental formula* of public right: "All actions affecting the rights of other human beings are wrong if their maxim is not compatible with their being made public."
>
> This principle should be regarded not only as *ethical* . . . but also as *juridical* (i.e. as affecting the rights of man). For a maxim which I may not *declare openly* without thereby frustrating my own intention, or which must at all costs be *kept secret* if it is to succeed, or which I cannot *publicly acknowledge* without thereby inevitably arousing the resistance of everyone to my plans, can only have stirred up this necessary and general (hence *a priori* foreseeable) opposition against me because it is in itself unjust and thus constitutes a threat to everyone. Besides, this is a purely *negative* test, i.e. it serves only as a means of detecting what is *not* right in relation to others.[104]

Since a right action is one that we could will that everyone perform and that does not use others as means, no such action need be afraid of becoming known. Some private acts of benevolence may do greater good if kept secret, thus lessening the burden on the person who receives the aid. But governmental actions are never improved by remaining secret since the state has the additional requirement of treating all equally. Governmental benefits given to some in secret are all too likely preferential treatment. Kant's publicity test shows how we implicitly acknowledge certain liberal norms by trying to keep secret actions that we know violate those norms.

Mill's contribution to liberal moral philosophy was his straightforward statement that the individual should be free to do what he chooses so long as his actions do not harm others. This idea seems so obvious to us now that it is hard to recognize what a service Mill performed in stating it so directly. Here is the relevant passage from *On Liberty*:

> The object of this Essay is to assert one very simple principle as entitled to govern absolutely the dealings of society with the individual

in the way of compulsion and control, whether the means used be physical force in the form of legal penalties, or the moral coercion of public opinion. That principle is, that the sole end for which mankind are warranted, individually and collectively, in interfering with the liberty of action of any of their number, is self-protection. That the only purpose for which power can be rightfully exercised over any member of a civilized community, against his will, is to prevent harm to others. His own good, either physical or moral, is not a sufficient warrant.[105]

Mill's utilitarianism, it is less often recognized, works from this same moral basis: actions that contribute to suffering more than to the alleviation of pain are unacceptable. Much is made of the difference between Kant's "deontological" morality based on a priori principles and Mill's "consequentialist" position with its stress on what an action produces.[106] More striking to me is that the two usually converge in their judgments of actual cases because they are committed to a basic equality of all persons—and that both articulate "principles" that float above any particular human context or society. Their formulations are legalistic in the sense of being general statements; what their thought usually neglects are the ways that individual cases—and lived human relations on the ground—inevitably complicate the ways in which the generalities come to be enacted.

As already indicated, Hume is the moral theorist who attends to the ways in which our actions, and our judgment of actions, are tied to a moral sensibility that is formed through our intimate and daily interactions with others. Hume himself was no liberal, but his approach to morality was adopted by William James and John Dewey in the early part of the twentieth century and by Charles Taylor and various feminist thinkers in the last twenty-five years of that century. Dewey insists that "morality is social," and James highlights the "claims" that others make upon us, particularly the call that comes from the suffering, which James characterizes as the "cries of the wounded."[107] When it comes to developing a sense of responsibility to the others with whom one lives in a political community, the law and general principles can only do so much.

The limits of what the law can achieve on this score remind us of the reason why liberal values are as crucial as liberalism's political expedients to maintaining a liberal society. The leftist who thinks that liberal individualism gives the green light to selfishness and, thus, is to blame for the inequalities of power and wealth in our society is as blind (or as hostile) to the liberal ethos of equality as the survivalist who is determined to defend to the death what he earned for himself. Equality is not simply a legal concept (either a legal fiction in the leftist's view or a pious fraud in the rightist's view). Equality marks my recognition that this person is here on earth with me, with a claim as legitimate as mine to have a good life, to enjoy what this life has to offer. Far from begrudging his presence and viewing it as a threat to my enjoyment of life, I strive to extend to him my best wishes and even, in some instances, my helping hand. If we insist, like the rational choice theorists, on reducing everything to selfish motives, we can say that the liberal, as distinct from "economic man," is someone who cannot enjoy life, cannot feel comfortable in this world and in his own prosperity, if he knows that somewhere someone is suffering.[108] The motives of or explanation for this feeling is neither here nor there. That it exists and that it is central to a liberal ethos is the crucial fact. The benefits of peace and stability are not individual; they redound to everyone who has the good fortune to live under such conditions. Liberals are committed to sustaining such conditions, are invested in the multiple social relations that can flourish under them, and work for making them the everyday reality for as many people in this world as possible.

Combining a commitment to peace and stability with the desire to extend their benefits to all generates a list of virtues that are distinctively liberal. Tolerance is the most famous of these—and the one that provides a minimal requirement for peace in a world where differences are encountered every day. From tolerance, we can move to open-mindedness; curiosity and generosity in the face of others' beliefs, needs, and desires; flexibility in terms of one's own needs and one's own responses to others and to situations; a willingness to compromise and a strong bias for verbal over physical conflict; an abhorrence, even horror, of violence. Rather than elaborating further, I will end this discussion of liberal values by pointing out that the listed virtues are widely praised and practiced in some quarters, but very much scorned in others. Liberalism asks, With which crowd would you choose, if you had the choice, to live out your days?

BOOK TWO

Liberalism's Critics

1
SITUATING AMERICAN LIBERALISM AND ITS CRITICS

American liberalism is different from its European and English counter-parts because established religion, an entrenched aristocracy, and an absolutist state never gained a serious foothold in the American colonies. In the absence of a landed aristocracy and a state that protected that aristocracy's wealth against the economic shift toward commerce and manufacturing, American liberals had no need to adopt the Benthamite laissez-faire economics. An easygoing acceptance of pluralism in matters of belief, accompanied by an acceptance that issues of conscience were outside the state's purview, was noncontroversial in the American context. Similarly, civil liberties, social equality (limited, it is true, to relations of one white man to another), and the notion that government's legitimacy rests on the consent of the governed were all generally accepted in the aftermath of the American Revolution and in the founding of the American republic.

Thus, if we flip the perspective, it is clear that many things that European and English conservatism attempted to defend and preserve against the onslaught of liberalism hardly existed in America at all and were never advocated by more than a small minority. There is no American Joseph de Maistre and barely even an American Edmund Burke. To put the case most bluntly and to stick solely to English conservatism: from Burke to W. H. Mallock at the end of the nineteenth century, English conservatives were frankly elitist, vehemently antidemocratic, strong defenders of an established church, in many cases anticapitalist, and consistently paternalistic, and they scorned the idea that the people's wishes or consent should be consulted by the state. John Henry Newman, writing in 1864, repudiates the liberal precept that "the people are the legitimate source of power" and its corollary: "Therefore, e.g., Universal Suffrage is among the natural rights of man."[1] Thomas Babington

Macaulay, in an 1853 letter to an American correspondent, predicts the coming ruin of the United States:

> You are surprised to learn that I have not a high opinion of Mr.
> Jefferson, and I am a little surprised at your surprise. I am certain . . .
> that I never . . . uttered a word indicating an opinion that the supreme
> authority in a state ought to be intrusted to the majority of citizens
> told by the head, in other words, to the poorest and most ignorant
> part of society. I have long been convinced that institutions purely
> democratic must, sooner or later, destroy liberty, or civilization, or
> both. . . . Either the poor would plunder the rich, and civilisation
> would perish, or order and property would be saved by a strong
> military government, and liberty would perish. You may think that
> your country [the United States] enjoys an exemption from these
> evils. I will frankly own to you that I am of a very different opinion.[2]

That American conservatism strikes a very different note is obvious the minute we turn to John Adams and James Fenimore Cooper, who wish to temper democracy and maintain some variant of social distinctions, of recognized and respected inequality. Adams argues that we are born unequal in capacities: "Inequalities are a part of the natural history of man." But he is careful to point out that these various individuals "were all born to equal rights." Most telling, however, is that Adams accepts that the people are to be the judges of superiority. Adams desires that "the natural aristocracy" rule, but that rule cannot be imposed. The people must choose. Crucially, then, the criterion of superiority becomes that one has been thus chosen. "By aristocracy, I understand all those men who can command influence, or procure more than an average of votes."[3]

Cooper (writing in 1838) nicely illustrates the bind American conservatives often find themselves in. He wants to insist that "equality is no where laid down as a governing principle of the institutions of the United States, neither the word, or any influence that can be fairly deduced from its meaning, occurring in the constitution." Furthermore, "desirable in practice, it [equality] cannot be, since the result would be to force all down to the level of the lowest." Despite that insistence, however, Cooper will not accept the inference English conservatives draw from such claims about inequality: namely, that the superior few should rule. Cooper states unequivocally that "no genuine liberty can exist without being based on popular authority." A privileged minority is just too apt to abuse its power, so popular sovereignty is required. Caught, Cooper can only urge other Americans to respect their betters and vote them into office. And he concludes with a phrase that will remind us of twentieth-century English conservative Winston Churchill's rueful acceptance of democracy as better than anything else that has been tried: "We do not adopt the popular polity because it is perfect, but because it is less imperfect than any other."[4]

American conservatives, in short, have never been in a position to deny popular sovereignty. They have rarely claimed that inequality of any sort should translate into greater political power. Attempts to limit the franchise were, of course, made by American conservatives, but we are now past the time when such attempts can be made openly. Only one set of American conservatives ever argued for feudal rights, an empowered aristocracy, a precapitalist economy, and natural castes: the apologists for Southern slave society. To their credit, many conservatives today have disengaged themselves from the historical entanglement of conservatism with racism, but battles over immigration remind us that the constant conservative effort to salvage some forms of inequality slides easily into nativist distinctions between "us" and "them." From the liberal perspective, there is little to choose between the genteel, astoundingly unconscious, Southern conservatism of Donald Davidson, who can write shortly after World War II that "the South at the outbreak of the Civil War was almost the only true religious society left in the Western World," and the more direct conservatism of Jerry Falwell, who "was in favor of Southern segregation [and] encouraged American Christians to invest in apartheid South Africa."[5]

While perfectly happy to have Southern conservatives' votes, neither the Democratic Party in the days of Woodrow Wilson and FDR nor Republicans today accept the extreme visions of absolute inequality that Southerners have been willing to espouse openly in American history. Certainly, hypocrisy and turning a blind eye have been prevalent on this score. But the larger point is that the conservative hankering for inequality has always, except for the Southern extremists, had to be trimmed in the American context in ways that were not true in England until well into the twentieth century. The result is that the weaves and bobs of American conservatism are especially difficult to track. We might even be tempted by the Louis Hartz contention that so many basic liberal principles are written into the very structure of the American republic that there is no true conservatism in American political thought at all, except among the Southerners who tried to secede from that republic.[6]

Hartz, writing in 1955, had no experience of the full-scale attack on American liberalism launched by self-described American conservatives in the aftermath of the 1960s. This conservatism is, undoubtedly, an odd mixture of liberal, conservative, and populist elements. But it knows that it hates liberalism (as it defines it), and it thinks that American history and society took a drastically wrong turn somewhere in the twentieth century. Was it during the New Deal or during the sixties? Were the 1920s or the 1950s America's golden age? Samuel Alito, applying for a job in the Reagan administration, hit many of this conservatism's key notes, including its understanding of itself as a fervently held faith. "I believe very strongly," he wrote, "in limited government, federalism, free enterprise, the supremacy of the elected branches of government, the need for a strong defense and effective law enforcement, and the legitimacy of a governmental role in protecting traditional values."[7]

That the first tenet and the last two are deeply incompatible points to one major fault line within contemporary conservative positions. There are other tensions as well within the contemporary conservative movement—and to make sense of that movement I find it necessary, in what follows, to identify and describe three variants of American conservatism. I do want to try to understand these variants in themselves, but the major focus is on their criticisms of liberalism as I have described it. To anticipate: traditional conservatism is primarily concerned with liberal permissiveness as a threat to social order, laissez-faire conservatism insists that every attempt to increase equality must come at the cost of liberty, and neoconservatism claims that liberals are "soft" and unrealistic about the threats other states and terrorist organizations pose to American security.[8] In each case, the attack on liberalism's perceived shortcomings entails fairly extreme revision or rejection of basic liberal principles and political arrangements.

American liberalism is also scorned by the nonliberal left in this country. The traditional leftist criticism is that equality and private property are incompatible, and that liberal claims to cherish equality are so much empty talk because liberals will never abolish private property. This essentially Marxist position is less in evidence these days, replaced by a more vague, if not less heated, critique of economic neoliberalism and the processes of globalization combined with a championing of various oppressed groups both domestically and abroad. It would take far more time than appropriate in this book to disentangle the contemporary left's relation to the socialist tradition and to the New Left "social movements" (such as feminism, black power, and gay rights) that are its most direct historical antecedents—antecedents that are now widely recognized by many of those leftists as inadequate guides to understanding the present and inadequate resources for effectively contesting contemporary injustices. But I will offer a short reflection on the relation of the liberalism I am espousing to leftist critiques.

2

TRADITIONAL CONSERVATISM

Traditional conservatism generally harkens back to Edmund Burke. Its great themes are the fragility of social order, the authority of inherited institutions and social relations, the emotional (as contrasted to rational) bases of allegiance and obedience, and the beneficial consequences of a paternalistic rule of the many by their betters. One great strength of traditional conservatism is its recognition that the extreme individualism of certain versions of liberalism offers an implausible vision of individual motivations and of the actual relations in any extant human society. Another great strength is its recognition that liberty is the result of a political order. Liberty and order are not opposites; the rule of law secures liberty rather than hampering it. Security and stability are crucial prerequisites for the enjoyment of liberty. The endless competition of all against all—either in warfare or in economic activity—does not offer a liberty to be enjoyed, but only a never-ending frantic effort to maintain life against constant threats.

Such insights led traditional English conservatives like Thomas Carlyle and John Ruskin (even Disraeli fits this mold) to view capitalism with deep suspicion because it dissolves traditional social bonds of deference, obligation, and cooperation in favor of (in Carlyle's famous phrase, which Marx adopted for his own ends) "the cash nexus." That some of the most devastating critiques of capitalism's impoverishment and maltreatment of factory workers came from conservatives earned these writers the label of "Tory Radicals." They set their faces against modernity and all of its manifestations. The economic individualism of capitalism was as repugnant to them as the political individualism of one man, one vote and the religious individualism of reaching a private judgment about belief in God. All such individualisms threaten social cohesion, the bonds that tie each to each in a common enterprise. Democracy is anathema because it opens politics to the same kind of competition that makes the marketplace a site of vulgar striving and the indulgence of even more vulgar tastes. Individual liberty really means license—and individuals freed from social restraints and the guiding hands of their betters will neither limit their desires nor make good choices.

Such a complete rejection of the modern and of individual self-determination is pretty much a nonstarter in the American context, although Allan Bloom's *The Closing of the American Mind* and Robert Bork's *Slouching toward Gomorrah* bewail Americans' persistent refusal to heed cultural and moral standards that are not self-generated, but come from "authorities" who should be respected.[9] Russell Kirk has been the American conservative intellectual who has most persistently attempted to develop a Burkean conservatism suited to American history and proclivities. To some extent, American Christian fundamentalists are closest to the wholesale hostility to modernity found in Burke and Carlyle—except that the Christian right consistently locates modernity's sins in its permissive culture and ignores (even embraces) the dissolving effects of free market capitalism. It is just about impossible to actually live a rejection of modernity, especially if one participates in the mainstream economy. Compromises with the devil abound. The contrast between the Amish and most evangelicals is instructive in this case. To truly reject the modern requires stringent separation from it. In the absence of such separation, conservatives almost invariably end up tolerating—or even becoming apologists for—certain aspects of modern life.[10]

Short of such separation, then, what does traditional conservatism look like in the present-day American context? For starters, its emphasizes traditional social bonds and the institutions in which those bonds are nurtured and maintained: the family, the church, and the nation. The subordination of the individual to authority (whether of the father, of God, or of the state) is stressed, as is an ethos of self-sacrifice for the good of the whole. Who would deny (or decry) the great sacrifices that parents make for their children or that soldiers make for their nation? Traditional conservativism insists, in contrast to much modern individualism, that self-fulfillment, that individual flourishing, occurs when the individual is subsumed in a cause or community larger than herself, one that pays limited or qualified attention to her individual needs and desires. Modern individualism, in this view, offers only anomie, a meaningless freedom that is burdensome and empty.

As already indicated, egalitarian liberalism also seeks to temper the extreme individualism of certain forms of classical liberalism and/or laissez-faire theories, thus suggesting an affinity between traditional conservatism and contemporary liberalism. Yet contemporary liberals are likely to find traditional conservatives the most frightening and incomprehensible cohort in the polity—and vice versa. Why? What's the difference that makes all the difference? Reverence for authority.

The great weakness of traditional conservatism is that it offers no criteria for acceptable change and no direct means for effecting change. It has no way of imagining a future better than the past. Addicted to narratives of decline, it can only criticize the present in terms of a lost past. The accumulated wisdom of tradition is the only standard. Authority derives from our way of life, and our institutions have stood "the test of time." Questioning these arrangements only breeds social turmoil and leads to chaos or civil war, both of which must (by definition) be worse than the status quo. In short, social order is so fragile in the conservative view, so liable to dissolve in the face of dissent, that authority must be maintained at just about any cost. The result is that traditional conservatives fear and detest pluralism of any sort, and they accept the swift and harsh punishment of all deviants.[11] Conservatives are "the party of order" and tend toward authoritarianism. In our day, of course, this consequence of conservatism manifests itself in the use of reasons of state ("national security") to curtail civil liberties, and in efforts to expand the state's enforcement of moral prohibitions, the presence and powers of police, the length of incarceration, and the use of capital punishment. Where conservatives see a besieged and threatened authority that must reassert its dominion, liberals see further concentration of power in persons and institutions that already had the upper hand. Whether, like Burke, one believes that anarchy is the great threat to liberty and social peace, or, like Madison, that tyranny poses the greatest threat to liberty, goes a long way toward determining if one is a conservative or a liberal. Where one places the emphasis makes a lot of difference. When Alito declares himself in favor of "limited government" and of governmental action to protect traditional values, he underscores contemporary conservatism's confusions on this score (or its attempt to have it both ways). American conservatives usually argue that liberty is maximized under current conditions and that uses of authority to curtail the activities of some are justified to secure an order without which liberty is impossible. The only alternative is the paleoconservatism theories of Bork and Bloom, who argue that we have been too tolerant of anarchistic license and must rein in individualistic excess to restore true liberty and beneficent order. Authority under threat equals freedom under threat. The conservative refuses to see any tension between the two and, in foreign and domestic affairs alike, will use the threat to freedom to justify all kinds of curtailment of liberties.

If not a reactionary calling for the restoration of a lost golden age, the traditional conservative apparently endorses the notion that we live in "the best of all possible worlds." We cannot make things better, so a ban on all political action makes sense. Such action can only make things worse, a position Burke at times advances. But Burke offers an ingenious solution to this dilemma of how to acknowledge that things do change and, in fact, sometimes even get better as history marches forward. His solution is taken up, albeit in very different ways, by all three variants of conservatism. Of course, Burke says, this sublunary world is not perfect. The empirical evidence of injustice and suffering is too obvious to ignore. We should and can hope for "improvement" (a key Burkean term). But such improvements come about through the slow evolutionary development of society over time. Our current arrangements and institutions grew anonymously and organically out of our community's pursuing its way of life together and making small, imperceptible, mostly unconscious, adjustments as it went along.

Think of how a language changes over time. There are few deliberate changes in syntax and vocabulary, and the language functions successfully as a tool of communication at any given moment of its history. But English in 1950 is very different from English in 1550. Human life is so complex—involves such an intricate weave of history, practices, beliefs, loyalties, and prejudices—that planned, rational, and deliberate reforms will almost invariably fail. Esperanto was inevitably a rationalist pipe dream. You cannot create a language out of whole cloth and actually get people to speak it, to incorporate it as an essential part of their daily practices. Other deliberate political schemes or reforms are no different than Esperanto. (Of course, the success of the U.S. Constitution indicates the limits of this analogy to language; there are deliberate, planned social innovations that work.) Burkean quietism, then, is not justified by a claim that the current world is perfect or even the best world possible given human fallibility and/or evil. Quietism is justified by the claim that deliberate action must be futile at best and positively harmful at worst. As Russell Kirk puts it: "'The wisdom of our ancestors' is one of the more important phrases in the writings of Burke. . . . 'The individual is foolish, but the species is wise,' Burke declared. In politics we do well to abide by precedent and precept and even prejudice, for 'the great mysterious incorporation of the human race' has acquired habits, customs, and conventions of remote origin which are woven into the fabric of our social being; the innovator, in Santayana's phrase, never knows how near to the taproot of the tree he is hacking."[12]

Mystery, our inability to know enough and thus to act wisely, and necessities (either of complexity, of order, or of human nature) that frustrate any human attempt to alter them—these are constant conservative watchwords against the dangerous human innovators who would dare to improve things. As Albert O. Hirschman has observed, conservatives persistently argue that proposed human action will be futile, that it will place what is already possessed into jeopardy, and that it will perversely produce effects the opposite of what was intended.[13] Traditional conservatives, especially, delight in the ironies of unintended consequences as proof that doing nothing is almost always better than doing something. It is not just that "if it ain't broke, don't fix it," but also "if it's broke, don't try to fix it because you will only make it worse." Trust to time, instead, which will make it better or, at least, make it so familiar that it won't bother you much any more. You'll probably even develop an affection for it as imperfect, but yours.

Yet improvements do occur—and conservatives are constantly in the embarrassing position of having to admit that innovations they fervently opposed in the past are actually changes for the better now that they have arrived. Jerry Falwell "has apologized for his segregationist views" and presumably Russell Kirk does think the abolition of American slavery a good thing even though he tells us that America's antebellum conservatives North and South "could not prevail against Abolitionists and Fire-eaters," which led to "the catastrophe of the Civil War."[14]

In short, the abiding conservative dilemma is that adoption of a wholesale theory that planned or deliberate change must be disastrous undermines the conservative's own passionate advocacy of certain changes and provides no criteria for which unplanned changes the conservative will endorse and which unplanned changes she will resist. For, truth be told, traditional conservatives do not peacefully accept each change that the nation's onward historical march introduces. They will act deliberately to roll back certain changes—as well as work actively to resist some changes. Quietism, it appears, has its limits. Are conservatism's deliberate actions to keep custom and nation from moving in certain directions always doomed to failure? There is, in fact, a deep strain of fatalism in much conservative thought, as well as a melancholy attachment to lost causes. Decline narratives and a consciousness of having fought the good fight against the degradations of the modern abound in traditional conservatism.[15] An appeal to necessity or providence or nature as overarching powers that render human action futile recurs in much conservative thought. But today's activist conservatives exhibit frequently enough a robust American can-do attitude to make one suspect that Kirk's portrait of the prudent, cautious, do-nothing conservative is rather obsolete.

One final cluster of themes and I can conclude this discussion of traditional conservatism. The emphasis on authority and order goes hand in hand with an easy acceptance of social hierarchy. Authority is held by some people over other people—and authority is located in social institutions like the family, the church, and the state.[16] At this point cautious conservatives usually stress the rule of law. They recognize that authority can be abused and that only an impersonal structure of law affords a place from which to identify and disallow such abuses. But these same conservatives will almost always resist "civic nationalism" or "constitutional patriotism," insisting that a more substantial "identification" with a larger social whole and subordination of individual autonomy to that whole is required to bind the citizen to the nation and its laws.[17] Rational allegiance to the law because it protects against abuses of authority and secures liberty is too bloodless to motivate obedience in the face of the temptation to do one's own thing. Obedience requires affectional bonds, which is why conservatives so routinely take the family as their model for social relations. Liberals (with a glance back to Aristotle) usually favor friendship as their model, since it is voluntary and between equals—unlike the unchosen inherited bonds between unequals found in the family.

The difference between an affectual and a legal bond *is* profound, as is the difference between a chosen and an unchosen one. Liberals deny that affectual bonds, untempered by legal checks or a moment of individual decision, are desirable in and of themselves. Affectual bonds can be an extremely effective cover for tyranny. Per usual, liberals want checks and balances, an external standpoint from which to judge affectual bonds and the demands they place on individuals. Conservatives, all too often, appear unable to distinguish between safeguards against abuses and an all-out attack against something. Liberals are not attacking the institution of the family per se; they are simply indicating the unfortunate, but also undeniable, fact that parental authority, like every other form of authority, is sometimes abused. Those subject to authority of any sort should always have another authority—often the law—within the liberal polity to which they can appeal for judgment and, where justified, redress. The liberal gambit is that subjecting hierarchical authority to its subjects' ability to question whether it is being exercised properly will strengthen the legitimacy and respect for that authority, not undermine it. The larger liberal point is that any authority that cannot survive such questioning does not deserve its authority. Conservatives find that approach "rationalistic" and a short step away from full-scale social anarchy. Apparently, their preferred strategy is that abused subjects stop whining and bear with it. We reach here once again the conservative propensity to feel authority is what is most threatened in such relations, whereas the liberal will argue that it is those subject to authority, the weaker party, who stand in most peril—and most require the assistance of the law and other political institutions.

In both the liberal and conservative views, authority is a check on unbridled passion, including passions for destruction and for the unlimited pursuit of one's own self-interest. In the conservative view, which is often (although hardly always) tied to a traditional Christian emphasis on man's sinful nature, an authority that rides herd on the self-indulgent individual is required. Father knows best, his word is law, and it is absurd to give the child the right or the wherewithal to question that word. The use of the family example here loads the case, since all must agree that the two-year-old is in no position to question his father's word or to choose whether to stand in this relation to the father. The true issue is when does childhood end, if ever? Do individuals ever acquire the right to question authority and to make voluntary choices about which social relations they will enter and which ones decline?

Liberals, ever attuned to abuses of power, think all individuals should be granted that ability to judge and choose. The larger point is that humans can and should be self-regulating. Yes, there are passions to be checked, temptations to be spurned. So humans establish institutions that aid in such curbing. Perhaps even more importantly, the social relations in which individuals stand to one another themselves offer various reasons to resist self-indulgence. Every human can see the reason for such institutions, for such establishments of authority—and, thus, understand and endorse their legitimacy while recognizing his own tendency to try to circumvent authority at times. Exempting authority from the ongoing task of explaining its rationality to those subject to its rule is merely a formula for tyranny. Authority, in other words, is not self-legitimating for liberals, and it is also not legitimated simply because it preserves social order. Some such orders exact too high a cost in terms of liberty. That's what tyranny is.

For all their talk of authority, traditional conservatives almost never talk about power. That's because "authority" always carries the connotation of a benign rule that is voluntarily followed by those under its sway, whereas power introduces the note of compulsion, of making someone do something against her will. But conservatives rarely consider how individuals might come to align their wills with authority. Kirk simply appeals to "something that we can call the conservative impulse or conservative yearning," that "transcending the differences of culture and history and race and national frontiers . . . exist[s] among all peoples," and Scruton tells us that "it is obvious that the bond which ties the citizen to society is likewise not a voluntary but a kind of natural relation."[18] These appeals to something that "naturally" exists in all humans are the prelude to the introduction of a "must," a necessity. After the velvet glove of authority's benign watch over us, its catering to our natural conservative craving for order and our desire for affectionate ties to our fatherly leaders, comes the iron fist of power.

Conservatism, at moments of stress, will insist that you must obey, no questions asked. Not surprisingly, traditional conservatives especially are fond of the velvet glove; thus, they will wax sentimental about the traditional family or small village, consistently revealing a sublime blindness to how tyrannical such settings can be to underlings and nonconformists. Kirk provides a wonderful instance of this willful unconsciousness to questions of power when he praises "the English people's aversion to change" (their persistent conservative impulse) and credits them with securing the Conservative Party's dominance of British politics from 1880 to 1960. "Had most of Britain's electors," he goes on to write, "belonged to the 'Celtic fringe' of Scotland, Wales, and Ireland, the Conservative party would not have found itself in a permanent majority."[19] That the madcap Celts' avidity for change might have had something to do with their relation to the power-holding British conservatives, who might have been resisting change to maintain their privileges in this unequal relationship, apparently never occurs to Kirk.

In sum, traditional conservatism's strongest critique of liberalism is its insistence that individuals must be understood in social context—and that individuals find much of their meaning in life through their relations with others. Furthermore, the political goods of liberty and peace are secured through political order, through the rule of law and other institutions of legitimate social authority. To that extent, as I have tried to show, contemporary American liberalism from at least John Dewey on has accepted the traditional conservative critique of liberal individualism, even though such liberals have most often found their inspiration in Hume, not in Burke. And since the founders, especially Madison, were deeply influenced by Hume, I think it true that an extreme liberal individualism has never been a key ingredient of American liberalism.

Be that as it may, traditional conservatism's untroubled acceptance of social and economic inequality marks its strong difference from liberal ideals. In addition, liberals will not agree that purposive human action is almost always futile. They can, for one thing, point to the American Constitution, which, unlike its British counterpart, is not the result of numerous anonymous actions over a long period. The conservative is right to insist that the time-honored practices and values that cohere into something we can identify as a "culture" must be taken into account when any change is considered. Rational planning from above has too often neglected such cultural factors and run into resistances it neither anticipated nor comprehends. But acknowledgment of a limit, of an obstacle, does not necessitate total surrender to it. Rational planning is improved, becomes more rational, the more fully we account for all the factors that will impinge on getting from the action taken to the desired result. The liberal will not accept that it is just all too complicated for us humans, and thus we should throw up our hands and sit patiently by to see how history or providence disposes. Conservative prudence is certainly not a bad thing; it only becomes so when it stymies all action.

Finally, and most crucially, liberals just flat-out disagree with traditional conservatives' strong tendency to claim that the fragility of authority means that it should be exempted from hard questioning or from having to legitimate itself constantly and explicitly to those who are subject to it. At bottom, conservatives do not believe, *pace* Hume and Kant, that people will obey a law that they give to themselves. Kirk, as so often, is explicit on this point, stating as his first principle of conservatism that "conservatives generally believe that there exists a transcendent moral order, to which we ought to try to conform the ways of society."[20] Our social relations are not something that we, in constant interaction and negotiation with others, attempt to shape in such a way as to increase our effective freedom, our peace, and our happiness, with structures of authority designed (and constantly revised) by us to achieve those ends. Rather, those human processes of building a decent society must be referred to ideals and standards beyond the human—and transcendence is thought to better secure those ideals and standards, to underwrite our allegiance to them, and to exempt them from the endless give-and-take of human disagreements. Where the conservative thinks order will be secured by removing authority from the realm of human questioning, the liberal sees a recipe for tyranny.

3
LAISSEZ-FAIRE CONSERVATISM

At first blush, laissez-faire conservatism looks like the exact opposite of traditional conservatism. Radically individualistic (in contrast to Burkean communitarianism) and focused squarely on this world, proponents of laissez-faire have almost as little use for tradition as ever-restless and innovative capitalism itself. Against traditional conservatism's prudence, it champions risk and honors the entrepreneur. It views all authority with suspicion, at its most extreme adopting the Nietzschean position that conventional morality, like state interference in economic activity, is just another way for the many to hamper the creativity of the individual. Liberty is its god term, although profit and wealth are not far behind. It sees these values as everywhere threatened by moralists, do-gooders, and the envious herd. The English Tory Radicals, especially John Ruskin in *Unto This Last* (1860), wrote compelling critiques of laissez-faire philosophy, and therefore it is not surprising that Friedrich von Hayek, the most important twentieth-century laissez-faire theorist, insisted that he was not a conservative.

Hayek recognizes that he is not quite a liberal either, especially given the movement of English liberalism, in the work of John Stuart Mill and Thomas Hill Green between 1855 and 1885, toward modern egalitarian liberalism.[21] The label Hayek proposes for his view is "Whig": "I am simply an unrepentant Old Whig—with the stress on the 'old.'" It comes as no surprise (everyone wants the founders on their side) that he hastens to insist that Whiggery "is the doctrine on which the American system of government is based. In its pure form it is represented in the United States, not by the radicalism of Jefferson, not by the conservatism of Hamilton or even John Adams, but by the ideas of James Madison, the 'father of the Constitution.'" But even Madison's Whig days were few, since Hayek tells us in a footnote that "we must remember . . . Madison's later 'surrender to the overweening influence of Jefferson.'" Every development of what Hayek calls Madison's "middle-of-the-road liberalism" after 1788 must be denied, hence the stress on "old" in Old Whig. "The crude and militant rationalism of the French Revolution" ruined liberalism of the Whig variety, and "our task must largely be to free that tradition from the overrationalistic, nationalistic, and socialistic influences which have intruded into it."[22]

I have two questions to answer in this section on laissez-faire conservatism: Why is Hayek, despite his self-labeling, best understood as a conservative? And how should we understand, in the contemporary American context, the rapprochement between a traditional, values-based conservatism and laissez-faire conservatism?[23] Democrats are baffled by today's Republican Party coalition, in which the upper middle classes vote their economic interest in the face of a moralistic conservatism they neither share nor admire, while the less well-off (the so-called Reagan Democrats) vote their social values in spite of their economic interests. I will suggest that this disconnect, while real, is not quite so wide as the Tom Frank analysis of it indicates.[24] There is as much continuity between laissez-faire and traditional conservatism as there is difference. But first I must offer a more detailed account of the laissez-faire position.

Laissez-faire thinking, as represented by Hayek in *The Constitution of Liberty*, begins with a simple dichotomy: liberty versus coercion. The two terms are linked together by definition: "Liberty or freedom . . . [is] the state in which a man is not subject to coercion by the arbitrary will of another or others" (11). Hayek then stoutly defends this definition against all attempts to understand liberty differently, including the "dangerous" notion of "effective power to do specific things," a position he associates with John Dewey and identifies as "widely accepted as the foundation of the political philosophy dominant in 'liberal' circles" (17). You may have the resources and, thus, power to do any number of things, but if you do them in the service of another (Hayek's examples include a contractor, a courtier, and a general), then you do not act freely. Freedom is simply and only that the individual is not being subject to another's will; it involves no provision of the means to enact his own will. Liberty, in other words, is entirely negative. The supreme good in Hayek's view is not measured by being able to do anything at all, but by the absence of any external interference. Quite literally, the free individual is one who is left alone. Laissez-faire, indeed.

Hayek just assumes that such freedom is desirable above all things. And he resolutely—and voluminously—argues against any and all proposals that would place freedom as one among a plurality of goods a polity or person might pursue. No trade-offs among plural goods is either desirable or possible. Reading Hayek can feel bracing (like reading Ayn Rand is for some people) because he is so resolutely uncompromising while drawing hard-and-fast distinctions that seem to cut through the crap and afford clarity where others prevaricate. Hayek's work is a formidable instance of "the rhetoric of reaction." Social justice is a mirage, as is equality of results or opportunity. "Attractive as the phrase of equality of opportunity at first sounds, once the idea is extended beyond the facilities which for other reasons have to be provided by government, it becomes a wholly illusory ideal, and any attempt concretely to realize it is apt to produce a nightmare."[25] Tenderhearted efforts to achieve social justice only lesson freedom while not moving society one inch closer to the stated goal. Face the facts, Hayek advises. Economic inequality is an inevitable necessity, and coercion, not increased equality or justice, is the only result of remedial action. We are presented with a stark choice: freedom or equality:

> From the fact that people are very different it follows that, if we treat them equally, the result must be inequality in their actual position, and that the only way to place them in an equal position would be to treat them differently. . . . The equality before the law which freedom requires leads to material inequality. . . . We do not object to equality as such. . . . Our objection is against all attempts to impress upon society a deliberately chosen pattern of distribution, whether it be an order of equality or of inequality. . . . If one objects to the use of

coercion in order to bring about more even or more just distribution, this does not mean that one does not regard these as desirable. But if we wish to preserve a free society, it is essential that we recognize that the desirability of a particular object is not sufficient justification for the use of coercion. . . . Economic inequality is not one of the evils which justify our resorting to discriminatory coercion or privilege as a remedy. (87–88)

Material inequality, Hayek insists, is inevitable if you have true equality before the law. Hayek poses the choice as either/or—and never addresses the possibility of degrees. Is there a point where material inequality—starving pensioners, sick people unable to afford health care—produces "evils" significant enough to "justify discriminatory coercion"? A similar refusal to think in degrees infects his use of the word "coercion." We are simply told: A policy to lessen inequality must be coercive and must fail. What is the historical evidence here? As a matter of fact, some societies are less unequal than others as the result of deliberate, chosen political decisions. If such decisions result from a democratic process and enjoy the wide-scale voluntary compliance of most citizens, then what justifies talk of "coercion?" If people don't value individualistic freedom as highly as Hayek does, if they are willing to make trade-offs between that kind of freedom and a more just, more cooperative, or less individualistic society, why should he object?

Furthermore, "coercion" is a sledgehammer of a word. Hayek presents our options as limited to full-scale permission or full-scale prohibition; there's freedom and there's coercion, and never the twain shall meet. But laws, especially regulatory laws, are much more supple than that. A society will permit all kinds of things conditionally. It will place limits, it will regulate, and it will set conditions. No one under sixteen can drive and only licensed drivers above that age; drive on the right side of the road; drunk drivers will lose their licenses. Are these coercions? In Hayek's world, they must be, but, if so, they seem perfectly reasonable ones and hardly great threats to the individual's freedom. There is no obvious, overall reason that similar conditions placed on economic activity must be freedom-destroying coercion. Of course, conservatives tend to endorse some of those economic coercions— like copyright law—even as they decry others—like minimum-wage laws. Complaining about "coercion" is rather a red herring since it turns out that even laissez-faire conservatives only object to some coercions, not all coercions on principle. The above-quoted passage from Hayek accepts that there will be some coercion in any society and only claims that such coercions must be "justified." Liberals will agree with that; they will only dispute Hayek's insistence that coercion in the economic realm cannot be justified because it is necessarily futile and counterproductive.

On this ground of necessary futility, the facts clearly indicate that there is much more room to maneuver than Hayek declaims. The United States is the most unequal economically of the thirty-two industrial nations, and "several new studies show parental income to be a better predictor of whether someone will be rich or poor in America than in Canada or much of Europe. In America about half of the income disparities in one generation are reflected in the next. In Canada and the Nordic countries that proportion is about a fifth."[26] (See Appendix, items 6–7.) Governmental actions do make a difference, and although conservatives mutter darkly about creeping socialism in Canada and the Scandinavian countries, has anyone ever made a credible argument that the citizens in those countries have seen their equality before the law or their civil liberties seriously curtailed because their governments promote economic equality more than America's does?[27] In fact, American conservatives are much more likely to decry the excessive permissiveness of those same societies. Is it just possible that more economic equality breeds less coercion? Certainly that's one logical conclusion to draw from the traditional liberal insight that a freehold, some secured property of his own, enhances a citizen's freedom. Here is where Jefferson—and Madison when he came under his influence—took his stand for the widespread distribution of economic well-being and against great concentrations of wealth.

Hayek can only respond to such awkward facts as Norway's prosperity by insisting that they don't matter. The only important thing is the titanic struggle between capitalism (the home of freedom) and socialism (the home of serfdom). A master of the slippery slope argument, Hayek will denounce every governmental attempt to mitigate the consequences of capitalism as tantamount to socialism. It is laissez-faire down to the last crossed *t* and dotted *i*. And the way to answer all that egalitarian liberal whining about social justice is simply to admit outright that capitalist outcomes are not just and have nothing to do with merit. The world's not fair—and all attempts to make it fair must fail and bring greater misery in the bargain. "Social justice" is "a will-of-the-wisp" and, "like most attempts to pursue an unattainable goal, the striving for it will also produce undesirable consequences, and in particular leads to the destruction of the indispensable environment in which the traditional moral values alone can flourish, namely personal freedom."[28]

The oddity, of course, is Hayek's fetishization of freedom when he paints humans so deeply hemmed in by necessity. We all must submit to the harsh realities of the market because that is the way to secure freedom—a freedom that will be lost if we make any deliberate attempt to better our lot in life. Under such terms, what is freedom good for? Work hard, compete against all others, eke out a living if you are lucky, and die. But at least you can know that you were free. Others didn't impose their will on you, only the existential conditions of human life and the market did. That's just the way things are; there's no one to blame. So buck up and face it like a man:

> We are of course not wrong in perceiving that the effects of the pro-
> cesses of a free society on the fates of the different individuals are
> not distributed according to some recognizable principle of justice.
> Where we go wrong is in concluding from this that they are unjust
> and that somebody is to be blamed for this. In a free society in which
> the position of the different individuals and groups is not the result of
> anybody's design—or could, within such a society, be altered in accor-
> dance with a generally applicable principle—the difference in reward
> simply cannot meaningfully be described as just or unjust.[29]

For all his talk of freedom, then, Hayek is a rather grim necessitarian. Not a determinist. The individual does have some choices to make about the paths he will follow. And presumably how individuals act does have some influence on the results of those actions. But necessity looms large because the scene of action and the rules of the game are set and cannot be significantly altered. Individual freedom on the micro level is matched by complete lack of freedom on the macro level. No individual or collective action can improve the basic operating conditions because the market—and, presumably, human society (the problem is whether Hayek thinks there is any distinction between the market and society)—is too complex for humans to understand. The parallel to Burke on society is almost exact, as Hayek notes.[30]

But all is not doom and gloom. The *deus ex machina* of the providential "hidden hand" lies in wait. Hayek is nowhere more conservative than in his enthusiastic endorsement of what social processes will produce of their own accord. Second only to his endless warnings about coercion's threat to freedom are his joyous encomiums to "those spontaneous forces . . . by which the efforts of society are co-ordinated [and] . . . a social order is maintained" (411). Hayek scolds worrywart conservatives who fear that chaos must result from the competition of all against all in the market. Such doubters lack "faith in the spontaneous forces of adjustment which makes the liberal [of the Hayek variety] accept changes without apprehension, even though he does not know how the necessary adaptations will be brought about" (400).

A free society is self-adjusting—but toward what? Not toward justice, as we have already been told. Toward more freedom? No, because individuals in that society are already free. There seem to be only three possible answers: greater productive efficiency, greater production of wealth (prosperity), or that old conservative standby: order. The first two are problematic; since it has been made clear that we cannot expect equal distribution of wealth, why should any individual contribute to its creation? Because of necessity, of course. But how is the more efficient contribution wrung from him an addition to, or even a preservation of, his freedom? It certainly looks like a mug's game: the individual pursues his self-interest by acting in ways he hopes will secure him wealth and freedom, but the actual rewards for his efforts are beyond his ability to secure. He just has to have "faith" that somehow, in some unspecified long run, he will partake of the "material progress" that "dynamic, highly competitive countries" achieve (49).

Given the theoretical and empirical embarrassments attendant on keeping the faith, Hayek (in fact) treads comparatively lightly in proclaiming the economic benefits of his ideal free society. What we might call "vulgar" laissez-faire theorists have, of course, shown no such reticence. Americans have been treated to an amazing variety of "voodoo economic" theories during the current conservative revival in the United States, ranging from various implausible "trickle down" theories and the insistence that cutting taxes will raise tax revenues to the claim that deficits don't matter.[31] Common to almost all of these scenarios is the claim that governmental actions that, on the face of it, serve to increase inequality will actually decrease it. Of course, the ever-growing gap between the rich and the poor in America since such policies first began to be implemented in the 1980s belies that claim. (See Appendix, items 6–7.) In short, American conservatives will not openly advocate increasing inequality, even as they pursue policies that promote such increases.[32] Even when contemporary conservatives argue for the necessity or inevitability of inequality, they never descend to details. Do we need the level of inequality we had in 1965 or the increased level we have today? Do we still need even more inequality than is currently the case? How much inequality are we talking about—and what specific governmental actions and laws influence how much inequality we actually get?

For Hayek, the benefits of the market are only secondarily economic. The main benefits are political: freedom and order. We can have the constant changes and innovations stimulated by capitalist competition, and order too, so long as we don't do anything to try to achieve such ends. We just have to do what comes naturally and not sweat the big stuff. How long periods of chaos might be before order spontaneously reasserts itself is not considered. Nor is the inconvenient historical evidence that players consistently try to game the system, to shift its rules and practices to favor themselves. Without checks and balances on both the macro and micro levels, the results are depressions, monopolies, environmental degradation, the use of child and/or slave labor, and a general breakdown of social comity reflected in violence between workers and employers. Pick your own favorite historical or contemporary example; I'll take the United States between 1875 and 1900.

But this is no time to let facts get in the way of theories or to undermine one's "faith." Hayek insists that he is no quietist, simply accepting what capitalism dishes out because there is nothing to be done in face of the iron law of its necessity, of its spontaneous forces. There is plenty of work to be done "to free the process of spontaneous growth from the obstacles and encumbrances that human folly has erected" (410). All will be for the best if we just stop worrying and learn to love the market and the glorious freedom it provides within a noncoercive order.

Obviously, Hayek's work is fully in tune with the traditional conservatives' emphasis on order, insistence that inequality is inevitable, and belief that deliberate action must prove futile at best and downright disastrous at worst. True, the unequal status quo defended by the laissez-faire conservative is not the unequal aristocratic society that the traditional conservative extolled. The laissez-faire philosophy was originally used by liberals in England to combat aristocratic power and wealth. But once the concentration of wealth and power moved toward a new capitalist class, liberals abandoned laissez-faire thinking. That's because greater equality, a wider distribution of power and effective freedom, is the liberal goal. Similarly, the defense of privilege, of actual existing inequalities, is central to conservatism; the adoption of laissez-faire thought as an argument for the necessity of inequality marks such thought as conservative from 1880 on. This reversal is not so confusing—or surprising—if we keep our eye on the ball of equality. (Additionally, I will remind my readers one last time, laissez-faire thinking was rare to nonexistent in American political thought before 1880.) As Steven Lukes puts it: "The left is defined by its commitment to what we may call the *principle of rectification* and the right by opposition to it. . . . [The left] makes the assumption that there are unjustified inequalities which those on the right see as sacred or inviolable or natural or inevitable," and the left calls for and acts toward their rectification.[33]

Oddly enough, given his obsession with coercion, Hayek (as does laissez-faire thinking in general) evidences the conservatives' blindness to power.

Once the state is out of the picture (compare with Marx's notion of the "withering away" of the state), the "spontaneous forces" of society operate frictionlessly. Those forces' complete transcendence of human control renders power of any human sort nugatory. Yet "human folly" does have the ability to muck things up. Hayek, like so many conservatives, forgets the lesson that Montesquieu taught and Madison learned so well: it takes power to check power. The system will not right itself, and it is naive to believe that everyone will play the game fairly and wait passively and accept peacefully its (in Hayek's view) inevitably unfair, inequitable, and incalculable results. The rules of the game, even if they arose spontaneously (surely an oversimplified version of how laws are written and evolve), will not maintain themselves. Power will always queer the pitch, a fact organicist conservatives of either the Burkean or laissez-faire variety consistently ignore.

So there is plenty for the traditional conservative to like in Hayek. But there is also one big stumbling block: the amoral pluralism of the marketplace. Modern market societies cannot "reward individuals according to commonly shared standards of merit or value" because "there *are* no such shared standards."[34] Any attempt to impose such standards counts as an unacceptable version of coercion. In Irving Kristol's words: "In the name of 'libertarianism,'" laissez-faire thinkers like Hayek and Milton Friedman refuse "to impose any prohibition or inhibition on the libertine tendencies of modern bourgeois society." Kristol goes on to scorn that other convenient version of "hidden hand" thinking, namely "the belief that private vices, freely exercised, will lead to public benefits." Hayek and Friedman have "too limited an imagination when it [comes] to vice." They do not recognize "that self-destructive nihilism [is] an authentic and permanent possibility that any society [has] to guard against."[35] Traditional conservatism has always distrusted and feared modern individualism, has always suspected that freedom might just be an honorific name for license, and contemporary writers like Kristol and Robert Bork, not to mention the religious right, have picked up on this theme. Liberals have been bemused by such conservatives' fervent belief that it is liberal permissiveness, not capitalism itself, that has severed the bonds that kept individualistic excesses in check. Somehow the gay person's desire to live with her partner in peace overshadows the behavior of the CEO who secures for himself a golden parachute while outsourcing the companies' jobs to sweatshops overseas and reneging on employees' pensions.[36] This blindness to capitalism as the great social solvent of our era means that today's social conservatives favor moral coercion of various (including legal) sorts but think that economic processes should be left alone.[37] The market's amoralism (any behavior or the selling of any commodity is justified solely in terms of profit, with no other applicable standard) rarely agitates, is peacefully accepted by, moral conservatives.

This should be the wedge that splinters the conservative coalition of the last thirty years apart. But it has not. Why? On one level, of course, the answer is a series of compromises and trade-offs. Everyone who votes Republican (just like everyone who votes Democratic) dislikes some of her party's views. And it is precisely the most committed who have no place else to go. It's either vote Republican or stay home; voting for the liberal party is unthinkable. Partisans will necessarily have to accept the party's shortcomings, inconsistencies, and various sail trimmings. But, I think, on another level there is a deeper consonance between traditional and laissez-faire conservatism than might at first appear. Hayek's claim (quoted above) that abandoning the quest for "social justice" will help us focus on "the indispensable environment in which the traditional moral values alone can flourish, namely personal freedom" provides a clue. What today's social conservatives and laissez-faire conservatives share is a concept of "individual responsibility." Margaret Thatcher was the most forceful politician in the voicing of this theme. The individual is responsible for his deeds and must face up to their consequences. The wealthy have earned their money and are thus entitled to it. The poor have failed to work hard or long enough and deserve their penury. All mitigations of responsibility are sophistications. Liberals are constantly making excuses for people.

Vulgar laissez-faire thinkers take the offensive at this point and argue that economic inequalities are actually a positive good, not a necessary evil. They reward precisely actions that society should reward: hard work, creative thinking, and (especially) risk-taking. The market and morality get run together (a confusion Hayek never makes, but that Max Weber tells us can be traced all the way back to the sixteenth-century origins of both Protestantism and capitalism). Without the "incentive" of greater rewards, hard work and risk would be avoided. As Ted Honderich points out, such thinking claims that humans will rarely be motivated by "intrinsic" reasons as contrasted to "external incentives."[38] There are, it seems, few things we do for their own sake or on our own initiative. And many of those last are bad, because conservatives are also big on "disincentives," from capital punishment on down, various punishments to discourage undesirable behavior. Carrots and sticks all the way around. Note that it is hardly consistent to put so much emphasis on "individual responsibility" while also portraying individuals as so susceptible to, so in need of, external pushes and pulls.

This focus on responsibility and on the proper rewards and punishments of individual behavior joins traditional and laissez-faire conservatives even as it marks a huge gulf in sensibility between them and liberals. There is nothing less here than a fundamental difference in the emotional and intellectual understanding of the word "justice." For conservatives, justice is not about equality at all; it is about people getting what they deserve. And if that sounds more than vaguely threatening, it is meant to. They didn't call Margaret Thatcher the "Iron Lady" for nothing.

Hayek, of course, is clear that the market is not just. He recognizes the deep inconsistency between claiming that the workings of the market are too incalculable, too complicated, to allow for purposive action to steer them while also claiming that there will be some direct connection between hard work and an appropriate reward. He sticks carefully to the insistence on the intractable law of unintended consequences. We can never be sure of getting what we aim for. Luck and various contingencies (what used to be called "fate" or "fortune") mean that market outcomes are not just or unjust. His conservative followers don't usually adopt Hayek's scrupulous amoralism. Whereas Hayek tells those at the bottom of the economic heap, "Don't take it personally; there's no one to blame," most conservatives send an altogether different message: "It's your fault that you are poor."[39] Vulgar laissez-faire thinking is a strange mixture of social Darwinism (it's a competitive jungle out there but the fittest will survive, even thrive), the Protestant work ethic (virtue, equated with hard work, will be rewarded), some half-baked psychology about incentives, and Hayek-like assertions that capitalism is a necessary condition of freedom. Assessing each of these ideas' flaws, or the fact that they do not hang together well, need not detain us here. The larger point is that, in this worldview, justice produces inequality, not equality. Some people are better—morally—than others, so justice will differentiate according to merit. Inequality is the sign that justice has been in operation. No wonder, then, that inequality hardly seems like an evil. It's a positive good for which one should long: people got what they deserved in a world where, all too often, people seem to be getting away with murder. Hayek, with his usual bracing clarity, articulates succinctly the view that justice calls for inequality:

> With regard to the fundamental immorality of all egalitarianism I
> will here point only to the fact that all our morals rest on the different
> esteem in which we hold people according to the manner in which
> they conduct themselves. While equality before the law . . . appears to
> me to be an essential condition of individual freedom, that different

treatment which is necessary in order to place people who are individually very different into the same material position seems to me
not only incompatible with personal freedom, but highly immoral. But
this is the kind of immorality towards which unlimited democracy is
moving.[40]

Moralistic conservatives desire dramas of differentiation, agons that
clearly separate the sheep from the goats. That they consistently confuse
economic success with other kinds of merit should hardly surprise us. That
they seem, on the whole, to have lost the sense that the market itself should
be held to standards external to and independent of it is more distressing.
Laissez-faire conservatism makes the market unanswerable to anything outside itself. But we have seen already, of course, this tendency in conservatives
to elevate something (be it traditional society, or the family, or the nation)
above question, beyond criticism. These thoughts about the conservative
understanding of justice suggest that the anxiety about order that motivates
placing some institutions beyond criticism may also go hand in hand with a
need to see the wayward punished. Their "sense of justice," as the saying goes,
demands punishment. An implacable, and righteous, and awe-inspiring judge
is required. There is something deeply satisfying in the assurance that justice
will be done, that a fundamental order will assert itself in the face of human
waywardness.

We have reached here such a fundamental divide between liberal and conservative sensibilities that it seems never the twain shall meet. I do think the
common ground in sensibility shared by social and laissez-faire conservatives goes a long way toward their creating a coalition across some fairly wide
divides in substantive matters. In the meantime, as has often been noted,
laissez-faire conservatism also resonates with some traditional themes of
American populism, particularly the pride in "rugged individualism," the
abiding suspicion of government, and the distrust of intellectual elites. Many
Americans resist explanations of individual behavior that give a large role to
systemic, social, or other transindividual factors. Shorn of its larger necessitarian framework in which deliberate action is futile, a simple championing of entrepreneurial freedom can look a lot like common sense to many
Americans. Recognizably liberal values like self-determination are trans-
ferred into conservative mainstays when used to underwrite an acceptance of
economic inequality and a push for more stringent punishment of criminals
and deviants.

Liberals, for better and worse, can only answer laissez-faire and individualistic conservatism with the insistence that things are just more complicated than that. Liberals hardly deny individual responsibility (despite conservative caricatures to the contrary) but do think that mitigating factors are realities that should be taken into account. There are times when forgiveness is preferable to "strict justice," and when we should attend to people's needs, as much as if not more than, their deserts.[41] Similarly, liberals accept that all societies in history and all in the conceivable future contain some inequalities, and that some inequalities might even be beneficial. But they also insist that degrees of inequality matter, that the burden of proof for the harmlessness or positive good of any particular inequality squarely falls on the side of inequality, and that positive steps can—and should—be taken to lessen unjustifiable inequalities. Claims that existing inequalities are inevitable or natural or necessary are unacceptable. Substantial arguments are required that show those inequalities are better than any possible alternative.

When managing to abandon laissez-faire group think about the evil of any action that addresses economic inequalities, conservatism does offer some strong arguments for the benefits of inequality, both as incentive and as stimulus to economic growth that has the potential to improve the lot of many (if the fruits of growth are widely distributed). As Rawls's maximin principle already acknowledges, finding the right balance between inequalities that maximize economic prosperity and policies for equitable distribution that minimize the poverty of the least well-off is not easy. Arguments about where and how to locate that balance are a key dimension of politics in contemporary liberal democracies. Different citizens and different factions will continue to try to move the current balance in their favor. The polity will continue to experiment with different trade-offs. Liberals will always jealously try to keep any faction from gaining inordinate power (especially disproportionate to their members' actual numbers in the polity) and to keep resisting the recurrent conservative desire to maintain—or even increase—existing inequalities. Conservatives will either insist that straightforward disaster will follow movement toward more equality or, more subtly, that increasing inequality will actually benefit everyone in society even more. After years of trying to deny that fact of increasing economic inequality in America, conservatives have (for the most part) mostly caved in (as recent extended attention to the statistical facts has been paid by the *Wall Street Journal* and the *Economist*, as well as the *New York Times*).[42] Not, of course, that our conservative political leaders have shown any inclination to address this rising inequality; they are too busy trying to repeal the estate tax that plagues the richest 1 percent of Americans.

4

NEOCONSERVATISM

No one would accuse neoconservatives of neglecting the workings of power. I take the "Defense Planning Guidance," prepared in 1992 (when Dick Cheney was secretary of defense) by Under Secretary of Defense for Policy Paul Wolfowitz, as the quintessential statement of neoconservative thought. With the decline of the Soviet Union, Wolfowitz "called for a U.S. military sufficiently powerful to prevent the emergence of any rival in any region of the world; he proposed to encourage the spread of democracy and open economic systems; he argued for the use of military force if necessary to prevent the proliferation of nuclear weapons and 'weapons of mass destruction'; and he suggested reliance on 'ad hoc assemblies' of nations rather than on the United Nations to cope with crises, with 'the United States . . . positioned to act independently when collective action cannot be orchestrated.'"[43] We find here the basic worldview underlying the policy of "preemptive" strikes that President George W. Bush announced in June 2002 at West Point and put into action with the invasion of Iraq in 2003.[44]

The most striking, most alarming, and most antiliberal feature of neoconservative thought is its scorn for traditional "balance of power" foreign policy, for the notion that international peace is best assured when nations do not feel threatened by or subject to another nation that holds disproportionate power. From 1648 until World War I, Montesquieu's insight about power being checked by power underwrote European foreign relations. Admittedly, imperialism allowed those same European nations to exercise unchecked power outside of Europe.[45] But in the wake of Napoleon's attempt to conquer Europe, not even Britain claimed or was allowed preeminence. In the twentieth century, when Germany and Russia aspired to domination, war (in dealing with Germany) and strategies of containment (in dealing with the Soviet Union) followed.[46] And in the aftermath of both wars with Germany, an effort was made to create international institutions that could mediate the relations between nations and contain even predominant powers within a structure of international law.

The neoconservatives explicitly reject the strategies of containment characteristic of 1945 to 1989 and the worth, effectiveness, or relevance of the United Nations. They see in the collapse of the Soviet Union a historical opportunity to achieve a Pax Americana to rival the supposed Pax Britannica of the nineteenth century. "Supposed" because the one hundred years (from

1815 to 1914) of peace enjoyed in Europe belies the constant battles (the 1857 Indian mutiny, the Zulu and Boer Wars in South Africa, the Opium War and Boxer Rebellion in China, the Sudanese conflicts of the 1880s) between imperialists and subject peoples during all that time. In Robert Sidelsky's words: "The fundamental contradiction at the heart of empires is that they promise peace but beget war. Their claim to be benevolent institutions is subverted by continuous conflict on frontiers and the revolt of subject peoples."[47]

Here we can identify a key difference between a neoconservative and a liberal foreign policy. The liberal—guided by the same insights that justify full-scale pluralism at home—insists that the means to peace, stability, and order are granting other peoples and other nations the freedom to live (and shape) their histories as they see fit. Increased freedom is not a source of chaos, but of order. Peoples who enjoy freedom have no call to jeopardize it by taking up arms. They have too much to lose in armed conflict. It is when one group or one nation deprives another of freedom, when order is imposed from without, that violence ensues. Successful imposition of order by a superior power is temporary at best. Such imposition will never be accepted as legitimate, and those subject to it will always struggle against it. The means of that struggle will, almost invariably, be "irregular" and hence earn the name of "terrorist." The overwhelming disparity of military might between the imposing power and those imposed upon has, from the Boer War and the Irish War for Independence, led to the invention and development of a whole set of tactics designed to disrupt that imbalance. The current situation in Iraq only reinforces a lesson imparted in Ireland, Algeria, and Vietnam in the twentieth century: the maintenance of imposed power is bloody; it calls forth indiscriminate violence on both sides (with a concomitant public relations battle by each side to paint the other as having gone beyond the pale); and the task is rarely completed. In short, a mission undertaken in the name of "order" and "peace" generates chaos and war.

Liberals do not deny that the use of force is sometimes necessary. But they believe that unilateral force, the imposition of one nation's will upon another, will never be accepted as legitimate and thus will initiate a cycle of violence just about impossible to stop. Even admitting all of their imperfections, war crimes trials and/or peace and reconciliation commissions are important because they attempt to import legitimacy into the transfer of power from a former to the present regime—a transfer that, as in the case of Germany and Japan in 1945, was achieved by force. The trials, if accepted as legitimate by the subjects of those former regimes (never a certainty), serve to delegitimize their former rulers and prepare them to accept the legitimacy of the new order. Elections, of course, are also crucial in this transition. The problem in Iraq, then, is not the means (the trial of Saddam, the various elections) being used to establish the new regime and its legitimacy. Rather, it is the fact that the original violence was unilateral. When the imposition of force is recognizably the product of the collective action of many nations, it is much more likely to be accepted by the citizens of the single nation that is subjected.

It would be foolish to claim that internationalism offers a fail-safe solution to the problem of war. Nothing in human history so far has proved such a solution. But that failure hardly means that we should not keep trying to find ways to combat the evil of war, and it does mean that we should be open to trying new solutions, and to the lessons that history can impart. Just as laissez-faire conservatives feel compelled to rail against any suggestion and all evidence that Sweden and France might be viable alternatives to a fully neoliberal economic order, neoconservatives invariably speak of "the bankruptcy of their [liberals] international vision."[48] In Robert Kagan's words: "Despite the American role in inventing the United Nations and drafting the UN Charter, . . . the United States has never fully accepted the UN's legitimacy, and least of all the UN Charter's doctrine of the inviolable sovereign equality of all nations. The United States has always been acutely jealous of its own sovereignty."[49] For the neoconservatives, talk of legitimacy and of power either gathered in multinational institutions or distributed among the nations of the world is a formula for disaster, a naive underestimation of the evil lodged in the hearts of our enemies. (That international and multilateral action has had some notable successes—South Africa and the first Gulf War among them—and some semisuccesses—the various interventions in the former Yugoslavia—hardly stops neoconservative critics, even though it is difficult to point to any unambiguous triumphs for unilateral action since 1945.)[50] Kant's dream of "perpetual peace" through an enlightened internationalism provides an important ideal. In another one of those reversals between the left and the right that makes contemporary politics so confusing, neoconservatives have embraced liberal (and Kantian) universalism, especially the language of human rights, as exactly the way to legitimate their unilateral exercises of power. But as Robert D. Kaplan explains when outlining the importance of Kant to neoconservatives, "unlike Hobbes, Machiavelli, Thucydides, and Sun-Tzu, Kant provides little practical advice for dealing with a world governed by passion, irrationality, and periodic evil."[51] The recalcitrance of humans means that Kantian peace and Kantian rights must be achieved through Hobbesian force. Only a supreme power, not a pluralism of multiple powers in balance nor the cooperative, collective action of multiple powers, can secure peace or order (not to mention justice, a word rarely on neoconservatives' lips).

The neocons are fond of telling us that if American liberals and Europeans generally would just "face up to reality," they would recognize "that, in fact, the only successful American foreign policy on offer is a neoconservative one."[52] This reality is based on the fact that resentment against America, and various plots against it by evildoers, is inevitable. "Those who suggest that these international resentments [against the United States] could somehow be eliminated by a more restrained American foreign policy are deluding themselves. . . . Unless the United States is prepared to shed its real power and influence, allowing other nations genuinely to achieve a position of relative parity on the world stage, would-be challengers of the international order—as well as those merely resentful at the disparity of power—will still have much to resent."[53] Since parity is unthinkable, the United States has to suck it up, expect to be disliked, and employ a firm hand against those who resent its preeminence and seek to disrupt the order that U.S. power secures. Robert Kaplan is more explicit about the details of that order: it is the economic order of globalization and a political order that favors stability over democracy. We must expect constant conflicts because people will always struggle for political freedom and better economic conditions. "Political freedom itself has often unleashed the violence that liberal societies abhor. There is nothing more volatile and more in need of disciplined, enlightened direction than vast populations of underpaid, underemployed, and badly educated workers divided by ethnicity and beliefs. Peacemaking, in particular, will become increasingly difficult. That is because successful peace talks require the centralization of power. . . . Global capitalism will contribute to this peril [of endless conflict], smashing traditions and dynamically spawning new ones. The benefits of capitalism are not distributed equally, so the more dynamic the capitalist expansion, the more unequal the distribution of wealth that usually results." The "realist," then, should expect that "the evils of the twenty-first century" will "arise from populist movements, taking advantage of democratization" and "fueled by social economic tensions, aggravated often by population growth and resource scarcity in an increasingly urbanized planet."[54] Since, apparently, these problems are intractable, the proper response is to keep the lid on things as best as possible through an imposed peace. For Kaplan, as for Kagan and Kristol, there is no alternative to the United States sticking to its role as Hobbesian policeman, manfully shouldering the burden and accepting that its work will not be appreciated by the subject peoples who benefit from it.

I have deliberately echoed Rudyard Kipling's famous poem about the white man's burden in the last sentence because the neoconservatives not only appear determined to assume the mantle of British imperialism, but they also appear equally doomed to repeat every one of its plaintive self-understandings.[55] As Joseph Conrad told us in *Heart of Darkness*, imperialism, "which mostly means . . . taking [the earth] away from those who have a different complexion or slightly flatter noses than ourselves, is not a pretty thing when you look into it. What redeems it is the idea only." But Conrad's tale only shows us how that "idea" serves to justify even greater violence and more complete subjugation than exhibited by past conquerors who grabbed "what they could get for the sake of what was to be got."[56]

Like the British before them, the neoconservative purveyors of American power console themselves with their awareness of their benevolent intentions and the assurance that enlightened non-Americans know they have nothing to fear from us:

> As a practical matter . . . it will be very difficult for other nations to gang up on the United States precisely because it is so powerful. But the unwillingness of other powers to gang up on the United States also has something to do with the fact that it does not pursue a narrow, selfish definition of its national interest, but generously finds its interests in a benevolent international order. In other words, it is precisely because American foreign policy is infused with an unusually high degree of morality that other nations find they have less to fear from its otherwise daunting power.[57]

One problem is that other nations *do* fear American power. But the neocons' sublime assurance in American righteousness ensures that the message cannot get through. Told (during a European visit) that "most [Europeans] consider the United States the biggest threat to global stability," President Bush "responded: 'That's absurd. . . . We'll defend ourselves, but at the same time, we're actively working with our partners to spread peace and democracy. So whoever says that is—it's an absurd statement.'"[58]

Liberals believe that no country should be the judge of its own case. That's why, imperfect though they surely are, liberals want to develop and strengthen international institutions. One nation's insistence on its good intentions is hardly enough. It is far better to create an international order in which nations can be restrained (before the fact) and held accountable (after the fact) than to leave all conflicts to the battlefield. In an increasingly interdependent and interconnected world, every step toward the creation of an international rule of law is progress toward a laudable goal. International law, with functioning international courts, can provide a check to national power, even as the continued existence of nations will serve as a limitation on international power. As a matter of current fact, international institutions are hardly balanced in power with nations; the world is still very much in the process of trying to create this "check" on nations. But conservatives in the United States have succeeded in keeping our government from cooperating in this effort, most notably in the American refusal to accept the jurisdiction of the International Court of Justice. They have steadfastly adopted the point of view advocated by Irving Kristol: "World government is a terrible idea since it can lead to world tyranny. International institutions that point to an ultimate world government should be regarded with the deepest suspicion."[59] No matter that almost all the power currently resides in nation-states; the tyranny we have to fear is from anything that might check that national power. The basic liberal strategy of proliferating sites of power, of checking one power with another, runs headlong into the neoconservative insistence on consolidating power, its Hobbesian view that only a solitary, overarching, and superior power can quell chaos. Any dilution of that power, any delegation or alienation of its power to other institutions (whether international or not), will be fiercely resisted by the conservative.

Frank neoconservatives like Robert Kaplan and Niall Ferguson recognize that they are proposing imperialism as the alternative to liberal internationalism. Yet both Kaplan and Ferguson also understand that imperialism runs so counter to America's liberal tradition that it must, for the most part, remain a foreign policy that dare not speak its name. Forthright, fact-facing, neoconservatives will, of course, call a spade a spade among themselves. But, as Leo Strauss taught them at the University of Chicago years ago, what the elites can say among themselves is entirely different from what they can say to the masses.[60] Not in front of the children, please. While Ferguson, the Brit, laments that Americans cannot just openly shoulder the white man's burden, Kaplan, the American, tells us that "only through stealth and anxious foresight" can the United States continue to pursue the "imperial reality [that] already dominates our foreign policy," but must be disavowed in light of "our anti-imperial traditions, and . . . the fact that imperialism is delegitimized in public discourse."[61] The public, not surprisingly, has no taste for imperialism, not just its antidemocratic impositions of power on nonconsenting foreign populations, but also its need for endless occupations of foreign lands by American troops. Even as it resists any "timetable" for the withdrawal of U.S. forces from Iraq, the Bush administration keeps dodging the issue of permanent bases there even as it builds them. But, in Irwin Stelzer's words: "Imperialists, after all, don't spend a lot of time looking for 'exit strategies.'"[62]

This belief in the need for secrecy, added to the conviction that power must be concentrated in one place, has, I believe, precipitated a constitutional crisis in the United States. The Bush administration, justifying all of its actions by an appeal to "national security," has kept as many of those actions as it can secret and has scorned all limitations to executive power by other branches of government or by international law. The cornerstone of the administration's consolidation of power has been its continued insistence that the president, as commander in chief, "has the plenary Constitutional power to take such military actions as he deems necessary and appropriate to respond to the terrorist attacks" of September 11, 2001.[63] This interpretation of the president's constitutional powers was offered in an internal memo by an administration lawyer and was closely followed by memos that "sanctioned torture when the President deems it necessary" and the establishment of the category of "enemy combatant" so that people captured by American forces in Afghanistan would be held and treated outside the Geneva Conventions (to which the United States is a signatory) pertaining to prisoners of war. Notably, "most of these decisions, according to many Administration officials who were involved in the process, were made in secrecy, and the customary interagency debate and vetting procedures were side-stepped."[64] Similarly, the administration's sidestepping of the Foreign Intelligence Surveillance Act (FISA) court procedures for conducting wiretaps was kept entirely secret; the administration even succeeded in keeping the *New York Times* from making the wiretapping program public for over a year. The administration's defense of the wiretapping relied, once again, on the insistence that the president, during time of war, has unlimited power to act as he deems necessary for national security.[65]

The numerous ways that the Bush administration has violated in letter and spirit the checks and balances system so central to the rule of law in our society are totally consistent with its foreign policy: no checks or balances to American power abroad, no checks or balances to executive power at home. When, in *Hamdan v. Rumsfeld*, the U.S. Supreme Court, "in a withering opinion . . . declared unlawful the Bush administration's military tribunals, an alternative legal system established to prosecute enemy prisoners without granting them traditional rights," conservatives howled in protest.[66] The *Na-*

tional Review called the decision "an abomination" and the *Wall Street Journal*, in keeping with the neocons' Hobbesian logic, told us only that "the executive branch can act with [the] speed and decisiveness" needed "to act with energy and dispatch against our enemies. . . . A committee of 535 [i.e., Congress] simply cannot." And lest we forget that the Supreme Court's decision in this case was "liberal," and most decidedly not conservative, the *Journal* reminds us that a "single liberal retirement from the Court would put *Hamdan*'s reasoning in jeopardy."[67] For liberals, the *Hamdan* ruling is a ray of hope, the first significant resistance offered to an executive "power grab" that many (including myself) believe has precipitated a constitutional crisis to which Congress has resolutely turned a blind eye.[68] Just prior to the 2006 elections, that same Congress passed laws allowing the executive branch to torture and to suspend habeas corpus for its "detainees."[69] It remains to be seen whether the courts or the Democratically controlled Congress that assumed power in 2007 will do anything to check this placement of the executive above the law of the land.

How is neoconservatism a recognizable variant of conservatism as I have been describing it? The similarities are not hard to find. Neoconservatives have no truck with equality—and thus (by default as it were) must adopt the traditional conservative line that inequality is not just benevolent, but indeed the only way to secure the blessings of peace, stability, and prosperity. Neoconservatives push that paternalistic view to its extreme when they act in secrecy, convinced that the unenlightened many will prove (like all those caviling Europeans and ungrateful Iraqis) unappreciative of the things being done for their benefit. Heroic facers of reality, the neocons have the courage and fortitude to do what needs to be done when most would shy away from getting their hands dirty. No wonder they find Machiavelli so inspiring!

Of course, since they believe in the efficacy, even the necessity, of a centralized, overarching power, neoconservatives do not favor the minimal state advocated by laissez-faire conservatives. Irving Kristol makes this point straightforwardly: "Neocons do not feel the kind of alarm or anxiety about the growth of the State in the past century, seeing it as natural, indeed inevitable." In fact, this attitude toward the state "unite[s] neocons with traditional conservatives. . . . They are united on issues conserving the quality of education, the relations of Church and State, the regulation of pornography, and the like, all of which they regard as proper candidates for the government's attention."[70] When considering the current Republican coalition among traditional, laissez-faire, and neoconservatives, Hannah Arendt's observation about "the contemptuous indifference of imperialist politicians to domestic issues" offers an important clue.[71] How else can one describe the Republican insistence that "deficits don't matter," thus opening the way to offering tax cuts to the laissez-faire and populist wings of the party while spending billions on foreign adventures? Kristol goes a step further. He reminds neoconservatives that many provisions of the "welfare state" are "enormously popular" and basically suggests that they should throw in the towel on fighting them (except as regards such marginal—and hence vulnerable—figures like "welfare mothers.")[72] Bread and circuses. Tax cuts and a generous government at home to quiet the populace so as to concentrate, without undue interference from a restive demos, on the important stuff abroad. As various observers have noticed, for all their talk of patriotism, today's Republicans have carefully avoided asking for a single sacrifice from any segment of the American population apart from military personnel and their families.

Most crucially, however, neoconservatism evidences the conservative predilection for appeals to "necessity." And, although its favored term is "national security," we can recognize that it's the old conservative watchword of "order" that produces the necessities invoked to justify the state's actions. Those who object to such actions are either blind to reality or hypocrites who pretend that clean hands are possible in a dangerous world. The *Wall Street Journal* hit every one of these notes in an unsigned editorial justifying the secret prisons in Europe operated by the Central Intelligence Agency (CIA). Only "opportunism and political cowardice" can explain European leaders' "mock outrage" over America's treatment of detainees, including the "aggressive interrogation techniques" and "rough treatment" for which there are no "realistic options." "The broad reality, of course, is that European intelligence services have been helping the CIA in fighting terror. . . . The failure has come at the level of political leadership, where elected officials refuse to acknowledge such cooperation, or to defend its moral necessity. The danger here is less to America—which will continue to protect itself in any case—than it is to Europe. The phony outrage over American anti-terror practices will only make it harder for European governments to take the actions required to stop terror on their soil."[73]

Recall Russell Kirk's first plank of conservatism: "Conservatives generally believe that there exists a transcendent moral order, to which we ought to try to conform the ways of society."[74] Necessity is not the same as a transcendent moral order (although note the *Wall Street Journal*'s use of the term "moral necessity"), but it also establishes an external reality to which the rule of law can and should be subordinated. In discussing the right-wing governmental forms of imperialism, Hannah Arendt calls our attention to the moment when the "nation" supercedes the "state" in the nation-states of the modern era. The liberal state is, as we have seen, an interwoven and differentiated (separate branches of government) legal framework that jealously guards the law's independence from the demands of morality, the majority, powerful minorities, and (to put it in abstract terms) substantive visions of the good. To allow a single vision of what is morally required or of what is necessary to trump the existing plural interpretations (evidenced in the fact that citizens of the nation disagree about these things) of our current situation and the best ways to respond to it is the road to tyranny. There are legal mechanisms for reaching decisions in the face of that plurality—mechanisms that call for open public debate and various kinds of votes, as well as proper judicial oversight. Policies made in secret in the name of national security are fundamentally illiberal; they are direct attacks upon the rule of law.

It is not simply the pressure of difficult times that pushes neoconservatives in that direction. Conservative thought in all its variants appeals to necessities that trump political action taken within the established legal forms of liberal polities. I do not deny that some conservative thinkers (like Hume, Burke, and Oakeshott) are among the most eloquent defenders of the rule of law in the Western political tradition. But it is also noticeable that no American conservative thinker is intimately associated with that kind of commitment to the rule of law—and that since World War II it has been Republicans from Joseph McCarthy to Richard Nixon to George W. Bush and Dick Cheney who have repeatedly discounted civil liberties (and, at times, worse) in the name of national security.[75] Maybe the best way to make this point is to say that conservative thinkers have a deep tendency to think monologically: one supreme power, one overriding necessity, one set of moral truths, and homogeneous cultures. Conservatives are always struggling to bring strays back into the fold, always aiming to incorporate the many under the rule of the one, whether that one be the market, a certain moral vision, national security, or true patriotism. Liberals, on the other hand, think pluralistically: there are many laws, many institutions, many ways to live a life, many nations, and many cultures. What is needed are ways of peacefully coexisting, ways of distributing power and the means to life that prevent the rule of the one. Necessity is just another name for yet another pretender to the throne, a tyrannical overarching notion to which all are expected to bow. The rule of law exists to check all such pretenders, no matter what name they bear.

5
THE NONLIBERAL LEFT

In my corner of the academic universe (a corner called "literary theory," or simply "theory"), the nonliberal left has considerable, albeit diminishing, clout. (For simplicity's sake, I will mean the nonliberal left when I use the term "the left" throughout the rest of this section.) In general, a liberal polity is much better off if it must respond to challenges from both the left and the right. Conservatives push liberals to consider the ongoing reality and possible benefits of inequality, of nationalistic patriotism, and of military action. In response, liberals must articulate the costs of all three and offer ways to either temper those realities or establish preferable alternatives.

The left pushes liberals to recognize systemic inequalities that resist local remedies and ad hoc redress. Nonliberal leftists persistently identify whole groups of citizens who do not partake of the political freedoms and material well-being enjoyed by the privileged in American society. It is hardly a coincidence that the most sweeping reforms of the American political system occurred between 1890 and 1920, when the left was at its strongest in American history.[76] Direct election of U.S. senators, the enfranchisement of women, a graduated income tax, recall of elected officials, and the ballot initiative were reforms enacted by Progressive liberals who had to attend to pressure from a sizable left. It is no accident that American conservatives, from the Pullman and Homestead strikes in the 1890s, through the Palmer raids of 1919, up to Joseph McCarthy and J. Edgar Hoover's FBI from 1950 to 1970, devoted much energy to smashing the American left. That the conservatives have largely succeeded in this effort is one cause (among others) for the steady drift of American politics rightward since 1975.[77]

In my view, then, the left has been, in most although not all cases, a salutary presence in American politics and history. It has supplied fervent activists who have pushed a liberal polity toward a fuller realization of its stated ideals. The left's central role in trade unions won American workers the eight-hour day, the five-day workweek, pension plans, health and safety regulations, health care benefits, and regular vacations—gains for which almost every American has reason to be grateful. That so many of these hard-won gains are currently threatened is a result of the left's decline.

All that said, I do not think the left has an intellectually coherent or politically persuasive alternative to liberalism to offer at the current time. I have made this argument at length elsewhere and will not repeat it here.[78] Basically, my position is that the left makes sense when it calls liberalism to account for failing to live up to its ideals, but when leftists claim either that liberalism has the wrong ideals or that liberalism *must* inevitably betray its ideals, I think they go astray. My brief comments here will clarify why I hold this view.

One traditional leftist position (the one derived from Marx) was that true freedom was impossible in a capitalistic society or, even more broadly, in any society that permitted and protected private property. Undoubtedly, the development of the notion of "effective freedom" in liberal thought was a response to these leftist critiques. Some conservatives hold the exact opposite view: that capitalism is not just necessary for political and other freedoms but will, given time, actually produce those freedoms. The liberal will respond to arguments of this sort, either from the left or the right, that capitalism is not one single thing and it does not have inevitable consequences. Capitalism comes in various forms and can be politically and legally regulated in various ways—and these differences make a difference by leading to different outcomes. It is just empirically untrue that capitalism must be such and such—or that it must produce this one particular kind of political and social order. To live in the United States, Japan, Singapore, and Norway today are very different experiences, yet each country has a capitalist economy. In short, much traditional leftist thought was as necessitarian as much conservative thought is. Leftists dealt in big, underspecified abstractions—capitalism, socialism, the working class, private property—that proved ham-handed conceptual tools for understanding complex on-the-ground social relations. Leftists also claimed that history had only one plot. They liked the word "inevitable" as much as conservatives do. And because liberalism tolerates capitalism, these leftists concluded that liberal polities inevitably cannot deliver effective freedom to their citizens. Thus, liberalism—lock, stock, and barrel—had to go, replaced by something completely different.

I describe that form of leftist thought in the past tense because, in fact, it is pretty much dead. Hard-core leftist advocates for the abolition of private property are few and far between today. The cultural left rarely mentions economics these days beyond calling attention to the very real miseries inflicted by globalization—and certainly does not call for a socialist future. (By the "cultural left" I mean professionals in the arts and humanities who, partly as a matter of style, but mainly out of political and intellectual conviction, constitute the vast majority of the contemporary nonliberal left in the United States. A noncultural [i.e., populist or working-class] left barely exists in the United States, although it does exist in other parts of the world.) My sense is that the left, once the Marxist account of liberalism is abandoned, no longer possesses an intellectual or political case against liberalism, although it definitely keeps trying to find one and constantly insists that it is not liberal (anything but that!). The contemporary left, it seems to me, is just the left wing of liberalism, advocating the "social democracy" model of the most progressive European liberal democracies. I do not see anything in liberalism's principles and values that renders it incompatible with social democracy. In lieu of a compelling argument that liberalism cannot deliver social democracy and in the absence of offering any political or economic alternative to social democracy, I don't see how the contemporary left can be anything but liberalism's left wing, despite its own self-understanding.

Undoubtedly, some leftists would claim that the last paragraph misses some essential difference between the left and liberals on economic concerns. It is not just a matter of intraliberal fighting over how radically to redistribute resources and to regulate capitalism within contemporary societies, but also a question of some fundamentally different way of thinking about, of conceptually grasping, these issues. Generally speaking, I believe that the left is way too fond of this kind of transcendental (in the Kantian meaning of the term) thinking. Which is to say: the left consistently overvalues theory. Somehow, as the history of the left all too amply demonstrates, leftists often place a high premium on getting the terms of analysis, of understanding, right. There's this idea that "radical" change comes from digging beneath the surface, in an intellectual exercise known as "critique," to find the enabling conditions of this or that social phenomenon. And it is only by attacking the problem at that level, in altering the underlying "form," that real change can occur. Action on the surface, mere "reform" as contrasted to revolutionary transformation, is superficial. Most people are dazzled by surfaces and hence continually misunderstand the "real" conditions that shape political and social questions. Hence the continual importance of the notion of "ideology" in leftist thought, a concept deployed to explain how most people get it so wrong while the leftist intellectual is getting it right.

I must admit that I find all of this leftist theorizing too subtle by half. I find the intellectual pyrotechnics of critique dazzling in and of themselves. (I guess that means I aestheticize them and thus read Ernesto Laclau or Judith Butler much as I read Proust.) But I do not believe that some new analysis is going to unlock the door to utopia. I think we've got the fundamental terms basically right. We face problems stemming from the unequal distribution of power, resources, and access to various institutions. Renaming the problems—or convincing us that the real problems lie elsewhere—will not get us far in solving them. Building the political power to effect change—and making changes that increase effective freedom instead of increasing existing inequalities—is the hard work, especially because there are powerful opponents to those liberal goals. In short, I think that intellectual clarity about the problems and about possible solutions to them is very, very important—and this book strives to accomplish that intellectual task. But I do not think that we are still in the intellectual dark and that some startlingly original and hitherto unsuspected analysis of contemporary society is needed before true progress can be made politically. That said, it is also true that conditions change, and leftist intellectuals are much to be commended for calling attention to the shifts in capitalistic practice that we now call "globalization." That exploitation and threats to effective freedom are taking new forms needs to be understood, but the battle against these new dangers still requires the liberal framework of a concern with inequality.

Many of today's leftist intellectuals have, in fact, little to say about economic matters, focusing instead on issues broadly construed as "cultural." Adapting arguments that originally stem from the romantic reaction to the Enlightenment, the left claims that Kantian reason, often tied to universalist notions of human rights, fails to provide an appropriate recognition of "difference" and thus excludes, or condemns to silence, the cherished identities of marginalized persons or groups.[79] Without tracing the intricacies (and they get very intricate indeed) of these contemporary leftist versions of traditionally conservative arguments, I take them as crucial reminders to liberal regimes to live up to their promise to extend full freedom to all citizens, which means understanding that various ways of life possess traditions and values that the state should respect in every possible way.

Often, these arguments about cultural identities and the ways of life in which they are embedded insist that liberalism, because of some deep formal defect, must always and inevitably exclude some members of the polity. Hence, liberalism is a hypocritical fraud. The problem is that this more radical, liberalism-is-a-fraud left tends to accept the tragic position that all polities inevitably exclude. So if liberalism is guilty of a crime that all must commit, it is not clear what the political upshot of the critique is. The left needs to at least indicate markers of improvement and then to prove that liberalism, everywhen and everywhere, must inevitably resist improvement in that direction, in contrast to another political philosophy or actual polity that could do better. But all we get is the broad-stroke accusation. And, it seems to me, that accusation derives its bite from an acceptance of basic liberal values. Exclusion doesn't trouble the right at all because it insists that some people deserve to be excluded, have not earned the right to be included.

These leftist versions of necessitarian thinking—liberalism *must* fail to deliver effective freedom to all—evidences the all-or-nothing refusal to think in degrees (and thus to acknowledge progress that still falls short of perfection) we found in Hayek's insistence that "social justice is a mirage." Leftists also display their own version of conservative mysticism. Where conservatives point to mysterious processes (the organic society or the free market) too complex for human understanding and not susceptible to human control, the cultural left invokes notions of sublimity or the ineffable to characterize those "differences" that exceed any and all efforts to represent them either verbally or politically. Liberalism, they protest, assumes "communicability" across cultural divides and aims to progress toward justice through the negotiations and interactions that such communication makes possible.[80] The left claims that there are incommensurabilities and incomprehensions that defeat all efforts at communication—and undermine the justice of any agreements reached. Once again, this view tends toward the tragic conclusion that injustice is inevitable, while refusing to question whether liberalism is better or worse than other forms of politics in terms of the *degree* of justice it does and/or can achieve—or the degree of injustice it can manage to prevent.

If the point is simply that we should never smugly assume that we can or have reached the ne plus ultra of justice, then the left is playing its historic and salutary role of keeping liberalism on its toes. But, often enough, the suggestion seems to be that liberalism fails miserably in respect to justice because it has a naive faith in communicability. Some unheard cry of pain, lurking out beyond the realm of the representable, should continually trouble our consciences. Yet no alternative to liberalism's attempt to attend to all, to give all a place at the table, is suggested, just a resolute refusal to accept any negotiated agreement as acceptable because it must have excluded something. Once again, only liberals are likely to be troubled by and feel answerable to such critiques, which suggests the left's continuity with the very liberalism it disavows. Conservatives, even in more mundane and direct cases such as Native American complaints about the mascots and nicknames of sports teams, insist there is no harm meant or actually done and thus indignantly resist all calls for change.

In sum, with the collapse of a credible Marxist alternative, the left (in my view) has mostly criticized liberalism for its failure to promote liberal ideals vigorously enough. Leftists who are determined, for whatever reasons, not to be liberals have salted that criticism with the necessitarian claim that liberalism (because of some fundamentally formal—and fatal—flaw that they identify) cannot possibly live up to its ideals. But these leftists, because they lack any plausible alternative to liberalism, either embrace a tragic view of endless injustice or take refuge in the more pleasant land of endless (and, dare I add, self-righteous) critique.

My position, I hope, is clear. I think that liberalism is the sine non qua of political decency in our time. Only where the liberal rule of law, civil liberties, and political equality are firmly established and maintained do citizens (as the past three hundred years amply prove) have any chance to avoid grievous harm at the hand of states, armed groups, and economic exploiters. That such a small percentage of the world's population over that period has enjoyed these protections makes liberalism all the more precious. The left has traditionally played an admirable role in goading liberal politicians to extend their protection to more and more citizens. But where the left has contributed to the destruction of existing liberal regimes or the prevention of their development, the results have been catastrophic. Today, as in the past, the left plays with fire when it encourages contempt for liberalism and/or advocates its collapse. Yes, the liberal polity should move further in the direction of social justice. That movement, however, is only possible on the shoulders of the gains already made in the very real protections against harm already in place in liberal polities.

The threat to liberalism in the United States today does not come from the left, but from the right. That's why I spend so little time attending to the left in this book. The leftist critique of liberalism is mostly an intramural academic spat, largely irrelevant to the polity as a whole. I deplore the tone of that catfight for various reasons, but primarily because it distracts liberals and leftists alike from the real threat on the right.[81] It will add a sad chapter to the history of intellectuals' ivory tower–induced blindness if the right succeeds in seriously and permanently damaging American liberalism while liberals and the left fight each other in the learned journals. In the meantime, the left's articulation of its own version of liberalism's "bankruptcy" only adds to the confusion already engendered by the attacks on liberalism made by the Ann Coulters and Rush Limbaughs of the current American scene. Both intellectually and politically, the left would be acting much more responsibly if it examined its own ideals carefully and considered just how different they really are from liberalism's ideals. No doubt, some leftists will conclude that the differences are huge and that they will continue to work against a liberalism more endangered from the right than from their own attacks. But I venture to guess that many more leftists would recognize that their differences from liberalism are more a matter of degree (how much state regulation, how much redistribution of resources) and of tactics than of principles and values.

BOOK THREE

Historical Interlude

1
TOWARD STATE-ACTION LIBERALISM

Liberalism, I have argued, is particularly sensitive to accumulated power and works to check such power in the name of liberty and effective freedom. Liberalism's evolution is partly a question of how its basic commitments logically entail certain ancillary commitments. But that evolution is much more a historical story about the interaction of liberalism with the modern forces of nationalism and capitalism, as well as its ongoing relationship to the diversity of beliefs and ways of life in pluralistic societies. Liberals, unlike leftists, have never thought that stripping the market or the churches of all power was a solution to the ways that wealth and religion are potential sources of tyranny. Unlike conservatives, liberals have never believed that unregulated markets or established religions could secure the good. Unlike nationalists of left or right, liberalism has never elevated the state to an unassailable position as the obvious instrument of the people's will. And unlike libertarians, liberals have never imagined that self-sufficient individuals living in a fantasized "state of nature" would be paradise regained. Liberalism has always understood humans as existing within an array of powers, with the greatest chance for peace and happiness when those powers check and balance one another. Liberals aim for a distribution of power *among* the state, the economy, religion, individuals, the law, and the people, whereas other political positions favor empowering one of these entities *above* the others.

"Modern liberalism" refers to the understanding that there are social and economic concentrations of power that are as threatening to liberty as political concentrations of power—and that political arrangements and policies must attend to all such concentrations. State-action liberalism was born as a response to the ample proof provided by the nineteenth century that laissez-faire capitalism does not produce the best of all possible worlds.[1] An unregulated market yields brutal working conditions, subsistence or less-than-subsistence wages, unhealthy cities, no provisions for the unemployed or elderly, child labor, adulterated goods, and environmental devastation. The pivotal figure in liberalism's intellectual history is John Stuart Mill. Raised as a laissez-faire liberal, Mill remained a staunch individualist throughout his life. His *On Liberty* (1859) remains one of the strongest defenses of individual liberty ever written. But Mill came to realize that *effective* liberty was destroyed by laissez-faire policies, not protected by them.[2] The individual's liberty is meaningless if she hasn't got enough food to keep herself or those dear to her alive. In actual practice, laissez-faire liberalism provides liberty for the few and degradation through enslavement to necessity for the many. Mill's liberal commitments to a liberty that could actually be lived and to (as far as practically possible) an equal provision of liberty to all citizens led him to state-action liberalism. Although it remains important to provide checks to state power, it is also necessary to use the state to check the power of nonstate entities, especially, although not solely, economic ones. If capitalism tends to produce large economic conglomerates, then the state will also need to be fairly large to counterbalance them.

Thus, paradoxically, liberalism coincides historically after 1850 with the growth of the state. Today's conservatives want to loosen governmental oversight or regulation of commercial enterprise, which it polemically deems "private" or "free." They insist that an unregulated market's results are always better than anything that a mix of market and state (a check-and-balance arrangement) could achieve. State-action liberalism denies that assertion, taking history as its primary evidence, but also pointing to the ongoing and constant efforts of businesses to act in ways that would harm the liberty and lives of various members of society. Modern liberalism acknowledges that the absolutely perfect balance between market and state is difficult to discern and to achieve. We will be constantly experimenting, constantly adjusting, to get the best results. History offers no evidence that either laissez-faire or command economies offer real liberty—a freedom that can actually be lived—to citizens who live within the polities that pursue such policies. Simpleminded utopias of both the left and the right, ones that imagine pure unanimity or that place all power in one place—be it the state or the market—must be resolutely resisted in favor of multiplied powers, of constant vigilance, of numerous checks and balances throughout the polity. Accumulated power in the hands of corporations or the wealthy is as detrimental to freedom as accumulated power in the hands of the state or a political party.

If Mill is the poster child for liberalism's intellectual development, we must look to more concrete—and more complex—historical causes for the changes in liberalism in America since 1787. Book Three offers a highly selective account of that history. I take up only three of the many historical pressures to which liberalism has responded: war, the market economy, and racial/sexual discrimination. My aim is to offer some sense of how the liberal principles and values articulated in Book One interact with actual social circumstances. In each instance, we can see how Americans, throughout their history, have struggled to develop ways of deploying state action that addresses the exigencies of social needs while preserving liberty.

2

THE NATIONAL SECURITY STATE

In England the Napoleonic wars and in America the Civil War spurred massive state action in procurement, in the first development of large civilian armies, in the treatment of sick and wounded soldiers, and in the pensioning of deactivated soldiers after the conflict. Each successive war contributed to the development of a national security state and of the "military-industrial complex" (Dwight D. Eisenhower's memorable phrase) required to sustain it. Especially in the aftermath of World War II, the growth of the defense department and the "intelligence community" has created a government within the government that has altered the fundamental character of the American state and of American democracy. Today's conservative fulminations against "big government" ring hollow because these conservatives are committed to a massive and constantly maintained defense establishment. The costs of defense and of war are always huge. (See Appendix, item 5.) Once the state is on a wartime footing, it becomes a major player in the economy, both as a market for those who produce war materials and as a taxer to pay for its war or as a borrower to defer such payment. James Madison's 1795 statement about the dangers of war ring with a special resonance today:

> Of all the enemies of true liberty, war is, perhaps, the most to be dreaded, because it comprises and develops the germ of every other. War is the parent of armies; from these proceed debt and taxes; and armies, and debts, and taxes are the known instruments for bringing the many under the domination of the few. In war, too, the discretionary power of the Executive is extended; its influence in dealing out offices, honors and emoluments is multiplied; and all the means of

seducing the minds, are added to those of subduing the force, of the people. The same malignant aspect in republicanism may be traced in the inequality of fortunes and the opportunities of fraud, growing out of a state of war, and in the degeneracy of manner and of morals, engendered in both. No nation can preserve its freedom in the midst of continual warfare.[3]

The war-oriented state always poses a threat to civil liberties. From the Alien and Sedition Acts of 1798 to Abraham Lincoln's suspension of habeas corpus to the detention of Japanese citizens during World War II and on to more recent abuses, every single American war has produced significant restrictions on freedoms of speech, association, and dissent.[4] The national security state is not the absolutist state our founding fathers were trying to protect against, but it resembles the absolutist state insofar as it consistently subordinates individual liberty to pursue one's own distinctive course in life to the needs of the state.

War and liberalism do not mix. Neither does a government that is permanently on a war footing even if not actually at war. This is not to say that war is not sometimes a horrible, but an inescapable, necessity. But it is to say that we shouldn't fool ourselves and think that we can have war and liberty both. Liberty is put on hold while war is waged. When today's conservatives aim to expand the war state and declare an unending state of war in the battle against terrorism, they work against not only the historical direction in which liberalism has evolved, but also against the fundamental individual liberties that liberalism cherishes. The conservatives' claims to be against big government are belied by their continually augmenting the government's powers over all those who are deemed obstacles to the single-minded purposes of the security-obsessed government.

Regardless of what they may claim—or even think—that they are doing, conservatives have increased both the size and the power of the federal government, have undermined the standing and autonomy of all other social and political associations (those crucial bulwarks against tyranny in modern societies), and have been consistently intolerant of dissent and pluralism (the very signs of actual individual liberty). The conservatives take the self-evidence and righteousness of the cause—patriotism or the individual's right to pursue prosperity—to justify an impatience with, even contempt of, the law as fussy, technical, bureaucratic nitpicking, an impediment to taking forceful action. Life is a battle—whether against terrorists or in their Darwinian, survival-of-the-fittest vision of capitalism—and the last thing the strong man needs is to be hampered by a bunch of rules and regulations. The Geneva Conventions are "quaint" when there is a war to be waged.[5]

For liberalism, war is always a disaster. It is a disaster that, unfortunately, cannot always be avoided. But the liberal recognizes that everything liberalism values—starting with individual liberty—is suspended during wartime. So the liberal is slow to go to war (always searching out every possible alternative) and determined to restore the full conditions of peace once the war is over. Nothing in this stance implies that the liberal is less able to wage war fiercely when war is necessary. But the liberal will always be a reluctant warrior—and has become more reluctant as the horror of war has intensified so dramatically over the past one hundred years because of the weapons the human race has developed. To actually serve in a modern war is not an experience that generates any enthusiasm for warfare. Liberals insist that the conditions of modern warfare make the notion of a "test" of individual courage or of national fortitude nonsensical, while war destroys the very things—individual liberty, domestic felicity, and everyday social life—in the name of which it is waged. War has provided throughout American history the occasion for the most extreme—and unchecked—growth in the national state's power. A liberalism true to its fundamental insights about the nature of power will work to check the powers of the national security state by employing various oversight mechanisms, by resisting secrecy at every turn, and by protecting civil liberties.

3
MARKET INTERVENTIONS

From the earliest days of the republic, the U.S. government has actively worked to support commerce. In Ron Chernow's words, "[Alexander] Hamilton . . . promoted a forward-looking agenda of a modern nation-state with a market economy and an affirmative view of central government."[6] The American state was never imagined as a bystander in economic affairs. At stake, instead, was which economic agents the state's actions were going to benefit. Both sides to the conflict appealed to the "general welfare" clause of the Constitution to justify the state actions they wished to take. Historically, the state's first interventions against the interests of employers and manufacturers were undertaken in the name of public health.[7]

The need for state action to ensure public health rests in three key problems that arise when markets operate without governmentally imposed constraints. The first problem stems from the fact that the market can only function optimally, producing the beneficial effects for all that "classical economic theory" claims it will, if buyers as well as sellers possess complete and completely accurate information. In that case, the seller who provides adulterated bread, rotten beef, false medicines, and cars with exploding gas tanks will only profit for a short time. Informed consumers will stop buying from that producer. In large economies, however, sellers can move from locale to locale—and from one type of merchandise to another—fairly easily. Plus the effects of faulty products may not reveal themselves immediately, but only over fairly long periods of time. (Think of carcinogens.) Producers can take advantage of such time lags as well as the opportunity of finding new markets of consumers unfamiliar with the past performance of the seller. The market, in other words, does not provide a heavy enough penalty for fraud. An effective check is missing.[8]

The second problem is that there are often harmful by-products of manufacturing processes—waste materials that the producer never brings to market but that still can pose health risks to others. There is no economic incentive to spend money to prevent the creation of such by-products or to minimize the harm they can do if their creation is unavoidable. The environmental consequences of modern production techniques call forth governmental regulation.

The third problem is that, despite what market enthusiasts claim, markets do not respond to every need. Sanitation in the new cities that grew up around factories offers a classic instance. The demoralized and underpaid inhabitants of such places could not or would not pay enough for sanitation to make it worth any entrepreneur's trouble. This failure was partly a function of ignorance of the deleterious effects of unsanitary living conditions, partly an effect of poverty, and partly an illustration of the well-known human tendency to discount future consequences in relation to present needs and desires. (Every time someone smokes a cigarette or the government increases the deficit we see that tendency in action.)

In short, the dangers to public health—dangers that carry economic and health costs that are not solely borne by those who produce the dangers or even by those who engage in economic transactions with those producers—pushed the nineteenth-century state toward the creation of public health agencies and public sewer systems, the regulation of manufacturing processes (environmental protections), the inspection of manufactured goods (food and drug administrations), and the development of liability laws. Contemporary conservatives chafe at such governmental interventions—and continually try to roll them back. But they hardly dare suggest that the Environmental Protection Agency, Food and Drug Administration, or National Institutes of Health be abolished altogether (even if in their wildest dreams they would love to accomplish just that). The general acceptance of the need for such agencies is too wide to admit a full-scale return to the golden days of the 1840s. Our contemporary reality is liberal insofar as such interventions are established beyond the possibility of abolishment—and thus our political fights are about the appropriate scale of intervention, not about whether there should be any intervention at all.

In the first thirty-five years of the twentieth century, the U.S. government also stepped in to regulate working conditions for America's laborers.[9] State action here rests on a direct appeal to core liberal principles. Economic power is not the only, but it is certainly a crucial instance of, social power accumulated apart from the state. Political liberty is worth little if inequities in nonpolitical power deprive citizens of the ability to exercise that freedom. Leisure time, good health, and some disposable income beyond that required to provide for the necessities of life are required for the actual enjoyment of liberty. Liberal philosopher John Rawls adds "self-respect" to this package of "primary goods" required to make liberty meaningful. Working conditions or social prejudices that degrade the individual's sense of self-worth, his conviction that he is an equal living among other equals, render liberty empty.[10]

Just as humans have a tendency toward politically devised tyranny, they have a tendency toward economically devised exploitation. All of the evidence suggests that some humans, in pursuit of wealth, will deliberately and callously (without, it appears, much regret and, in some cases, with some pride in their fortitude) immiserate their fellow human beings. At its most extreme—an extreme that occurs all the time—they will exploit others to the point of causing their death. Poverty, illness, physical harm, and virtual or actual slavery are all too common by-products of working for another. Liberalism, as always, is drawn to create legal and political expedients designed to prevent such abuses—and such deprivations of individual liberty.

In today's world, liberal polities have made great strides in preventing the worst abuses of their citizen-workers. But that has led to the displacement of those abuses onto noncitizen-workers in the West and onto non-Western workers elsewhere in the world. Hypocrisy is the tribute vice pays to virtue. Here again we can see how fully liberalism has triumphed in today's world insofar as few employers openly display how badly they treat their employees. Instead, the actual working conditions—and the shapes of the lives those working under those conditions actually get to live—are carefully hidden. Western consumers remain blissfully unaware of the suffering that produced the shirt on their back—and even the exploiters themselves are carefully distanced from the suffering their business practices produce. Willfully ignorant, most Westerners don't know—and generally don't want to know—how and by whom and under what conditions the goods they buy were produced. Everything that Western liberalism slowly but surely eradicated in the West between 1850 and 1950—slavery, child labor, seventy-hour workweeks, company towns that kept workers in constant debt to employers for rent and food, subsistence wages, and unsafe and unhealthy working environments—still exists in other parts of the globe.[11]

To equate globalization—which facilitates this displacement of the worst features of capitalism from the West to the non-West—with "liberalization" is to ignore how resolutely Western liberalism has fought exactly those features of capitalism. We have seen that there is some historical justification for associating liberalism with unregulated markets, but the political liberalism that forefronts the protection of freedom from tyranny long ago took the logical step of recognizing that its core commitments required using state power to curtail economic exploitation. It is contemporary conservatism (or, if you will, neoliberalism) that has, again and again, refused to work for extending the benefits that Western workers have gained (only after a long historical struggle) to workers in the rest of the world. And it is those same conservatives who have tried, by pleading the "necessities" imposed by global economic conditions, to roll back the gains Western workers have made. They insist that the European social democracies will soon have to scale down the generous pensions, unemployment benefits, and vacations currently on offer—and they look for ways to reduce or completely restructure Social Security and Medicare benefits in the United States.

Contemporary conservatives use globalization as the stick by which they will reverse the gains made by American workers over the past one hundred years.[12] From 1950 to 1973 (the first oil crisis) was the golden era of modern liberalism in terms of employer-employee relationships. During that period, which is sometimes called the "post-war compromise" or (more misleadingly) the "welfare state compromise," relations between corporate power and labor power (mostly instituted in the large labor unions that were poised against large corporations) were fairly balanced, with the government working to keep either side from gaining too much of an upper hand.[13] Not surprisingly, that period saw the rise of a large middle class and the least extreme distribution of wealth in American history. (See Appendix, item 6.) But this balance of power was never stable; both sides were constantly jockeying for advantage. Such jockeying should be expected—and is legitimate. Even during the time of the "compromise," each contract was contested, and the results never fully satisfied either side. Neither side, however, was in a position to dictate terms to the other. Liberalism, with its commitment to equality and fear of tyranny, will work to see that the balance is not strongly tilted in one direction or another. And that is why liberals, almost universally, think that America has gone in the wrong direction since 1973. Ruthless capitalism has made a comeback and workers have lost ground, as is evident not only in every statistical measure of income and wealth distribution, but also in the loss of job security and in the erosion of union power. (See Appendix, item 7.) The state, far from helping the disempowered workers, has consistently aided the corporate seizure of power.[14] President Ronald Reagan's destruction of the air traffic controllers' union in 1981 announced the commencement of government working predominantly on the side of employers.

Liberals, I believe, should neither denigrate nor over-romanticize the real achievements of the New Deal and of the postwar compromise in the United States, just as they should be careful in assessing the triumphs and strains of the rather different Scandinavian model and of the yet different arrangements in Germany and France. Sticking to the United States, liberals will point out that strong unions, protected by various legal safeguards, got American workers the best overall deal they have ever gotten in American history. The South did worst during this period because union solidarity and decent schooling were sacrificed to poisonous race relations. Moreover, we should always remember that the New Deal was not extended to African Americans, since Roosevelt kept the loyalty of the Southern Democrats by doing nothing to upset Jim Crow. It was Harry S. Truman's decision to integrate the military in 1948 that began the Democratic Party's honorable break from its Southern members in the name of civil rights.[15]

Partly because blacks were kept out of it, the postwar compromise was not just a government-mandated peace.[16] It was certainly not some kind of "natural" equilibrium between competing forces. As our founding fathers knew, all balances of power are political achievements and are always threatened. They do not happen by themselves, and they cannot be maintained except by constant vigilance, adjustments, compromises, and negotiations. All the parties have to be talking to one another all the time, and they must have some minimal sense of being compatriots, of being in the same boat, of sharing (as quoted from Brian Barry earlier) a "common fate." The relatively halcyon days of the postwar compromise relied partly on a strong sense of fellow feeling, a strong commitment to the well-being of the citizens with whom one shared the nation and the goods it tried to provide and preserve. The shared traumas of the Great Depression and of World War II generated a sense that everyone deserved a piece of the postwar prosperity. Corporations thought of themselves as civic leaders, providing stable jobs and sponsoring various civic amenities (from parks to philharmonic orchestras). The notion that corporate leadership's only responsibility was to shareholders did not emerge until the first wave of hostile takeovers in the late 1970s and early 1980s. Once the "buy-out" of "under-valued" companies became common, any corporation that was not single-mindedly maximizing profits was vulnerable. Loyalty to employees or to a certain locale became an unaffordable luxury. A new round of ruthless capitalism—symbolized most fully by "capital flight," "downsizing," and "outsourcing"—had arrived by the 1980s and has continued unabated since then.[17] The Europeans have struggled in this new economic environment to maintain some balance between employers and employees—with some success. In America, there has barely been any effort made in that direction. The government has abandoned workers to the vagaries of a now global labor market—when it hasn't outright aided the corporate escape from any responsibility to its employees. The result has been the growing divide between the haves and have-nots in American society, the emptying out of the middle class. The gap is best symbolized by the huge salaries now given corporate executives as rewards for cutting payrolls and/ or workers' benefits. (See Appendix, item 8.) When all humane ties—and any continuity over a life span—are banished from the workplace, it is no surprise that churches become a last remaining refuge for social companionship and compassion in a world grown brutal.[18]

Conservatism's hostility to labor's legitimate claims to participate in America's prosperity marks its clearest difference from modern liberalism.[19] Only paleoconservatives can claim that we would all be better off if there was no governmental regulation of labor conditions. We tried that in the 1870s and 1880s, and there can be no going back to total laissez-faire. But contemporary conservatives try to minimize and undermine the power of labor and the extent of governmental oversight of employment conditions under the guise of promoting a total prosperity that will benefit all. Since the facts are in—and they clearly indicate that American workers have lost ground economically since 1970—liberals are entitled to their skepticism that conservatives have more than the welfare of the richest 15 percent at heart. (See Appendix, items 6–7.) The liberal commitment to minimizing tyranny and maximizing real, effective liberty means that liberals will favor placing the government's power on the side of those least well off. We know for a historical fact that an unregulated market will allow power to accumulate in the hands of a very few. So most regulation of the market will be against the interests of that few. Is it possible for regulation to go too far, to tilt the balance of power too much in the workers' favor? Theoretically, yes. And I guess you could describe the communist experiment in the Soviet Union and China that way, although I think that would be a highly inaccurate description because power in those societies went to the party, not to the workers. In any case, liberalism does not espouse eliminating any class of citizens. But it does, in its modern instantiation, identify a floor (recently this has come to be called a "living wage" to distinguish it from the current "minimum wage," which is substantially too little to actually live on). And it does work to make the negotiations within the market that partly determine economic outcomes like income a meeting between parties that possess fairly equal political and social power. It is bad enough that prevailing economic and social conditions (including globalization and immigration) have seriously weakened workers' leverage in the contemporary U.S. labor market, but it is outrageous that corporate power has found an ally in a conservative movement that places the state's power on the side of employers at that same historical juncture. Under these conditions, the worry that the balance could swing too far in the other direction, giving workers too much power, is a highly theoretical worry indeed.

The welfare state was a long time in coming—and may currently be in the course of going.[20] When full-fledged democracy (i.e., universal adult suffrage) finally arrived in Europe and the United States, most observers (both left and right) thought that some form of socialism was inevitable. The demos, once it had power, would raid not just the public treasury but also private wealth (via taxes) and distribute the spoils to itself. That such did not happen confounded both left and right. Historical experience indicates that only the wealthy have the gall and the greed to expect huge government handouts. The less well-off, it turns out, want protection from the more wild swings of the capitalist business cycle and from existential circumstances (disability, poor health, and age primarily). In other words, the demos desires the state to relieve poverty. The immediate cause of the first state efforts to relieve such poverty was economic fluctuation, the cyclic nature of modern economies. The periodic depressions (1857, 1873, 1893) of the nineteenth century culminated in the whopper of the 1930s. In response, democratic governments made monetary policy a function of the state, created job programs for the unemployed, and established a safety net for those impoverished by economic downturns. There were also, in Europe especially but also in the United States, state takeovers of some basic services, especially transportation and utilities.

The fate of socialism in the various Western democracies is a complicated story, one that need not detain us here.[21] Sticking to the United States, it is fair to say that a liberal ethos of "fairness," understood to function at an individual level, prevented the electoral triumph of socialism even in its strongest pre–New Deal days. The American movement toward a welfare state was strongly underwritten by notions of "merit." Depressions called for governmental relief efforts because those in need were destitute through no fault of their own. They were perfectly willing to work if work was to be had. The success of Social Security in the United States is tied to a similar logic: no one who has worked throughout their lifetime should live in poverty once too old to work. A more generous notion that poverty should be eliminated in a country that is so wealthy has rarely gotten much more than a toehold in the United States. A standing welfare program, available in good times and bad for people of working age, has always been less popular with the demos than Social Security and unemployment insurance. The work ethic—that no one should get something for nothing—combined with a fundamental individualistic desire to avoid dependence on the government remains strong in America. Nevertheless, the spectacle of poverty amid plenty, coupled with the economic cycles of boom and bust, has spawned an American state that is involved, to some extent, in providing welfare to the most needy and security to those who have worked long and hard. The state is expected to cushion the blows dealt out by an economy that has shown itself willing to use people so long as it can extract value from them and then discard them without a thought about their economic needs once they are no longer useful.

An excellent example of the American tendency to tie benefits to work is the way we have arranged health care in this country. After World War II, when most European nations established national health care systems, the United States assigned the provision of health insurance to the employer.[22] That move was a key part of the postwar cooperative pact between business and labor that lasted into the 1970s. Of course, any comprehensive entitlement program in the United States is always complicated by federalism. Both welfare and Medicare (although not Social Security) are administered at the state, not the national, level, as are other governmental functions like education, mass transit, road construction and maintenance, and utilities (almost always water and often electricity). But when Harry Truman took up the question of health care after World War II, the decision was made to not only leave the health care delivery system entirely private, but also to keep health insurance itself entirely private, with employers supplying health insurance as a part of employment packages. Like most everything else in the postwar period, this arrangement worked fairly well for approximately twenty-five years. But the strains were already showing by the mid-1970s, leading Jimmy Carter to call for national health insurance as part of his 1976 campaign for the presidency. Ever since, Democrats have clamored for health care reform and Republicans have blocked every reform effort when the Democrats are in power and have studiously ignored the problem when they are in power. The conservative position, apparently, is that the government's growing involvement in providing health care for the elderly and the indigent is unfortunate, but it can't be rolled back wholesale because voters (especially senior citizens) have come to expect it. But conservatives will make any cuts to services that they can get away with, while generating yearly budget crises in the states and growing deficits on the federal level by refusing to come to terms with rising medical costs. Any attempt to examine and then improve existing arrangements—attempts that might even lower costs—are anathema because that would admit that government has a real, legitimate, and (God forbid) positive role to play in an activity the Republicans want to maintain is "private" and best left to untrammeled market mechanisms. So what we get instead are piecemeal and uncoordinated programs that mix the public and the private in byzantine and costly ways because we are not allowed to openly acknowledge that government is deeply involved and will remain deeply involved in bearing some of the costs of health care for American citizens.

In sum, for better and for worse, the government's involvement in the nation's economy has, over the course of the past 150 years, grown tremendously to include oversight of monetary policy, negotiation and management of trade relations with other nations, regulation of manufacturing processes in the interests of public health, regulation of the terms of employment to offset the power differential between employers and employees, and direct provision of economic benefits to those the free market would leave destitute. In the past 40 years, however, the right has resisted that involvement on every front. Few citizens in modern democracies would advocate a complete withdrawal of government from all of these interventions. Even the most radical conservatives usually only recommend rolling back various "liberal" programs rather than abolishing them altogether. Those conservatives may actually desire a return to the 1880s, when men were men and robber barons could really rob to their heart's content, but they are unlikely to carry the majority with them. Characterization of governmental regulation of various economic interactions as "liberal" is justified by such regulation being aimed at rectifying power inequities. While conservatives can wax eloquent on the liberal theme of excessive government power, they fail to recognize that there are other forms of power within a society and that a full-bore liberalism is as committed to restraining nongovernmental tyranny as it is to combating the governmental variety.

Contemporary democratic politics in much of the world (not just in the United States and Europe, but also in Latin America, although not so much in Asia) centers around just how and where to strike the balance between state action and the free market. To what extent should the market's tendency to differentiate rather sharply between winners and losers be softened by the state's redistribution of wealth downward (in the most radical and direct schemes) or by the state's ensuring a certain minimum set of goods for all?

Liberalism as a political philosophy fully acknowledges that some balance between state action and the market's action must be struck. It accepts neither the extreme of laissez-faire capitalism nor that of a command economy. Things are not that simple. Where and how to strike the balance is never obvious—and any current arrangement will have to be renegotiated and revised in the future. Liberalism—in its most general sense—has two fundamental stakes when it provides the framework within which this day-to-day political jostling takes place: to maintain equality among the competing groups, and to contain conflict to the political processes of argument, deliberation, legislation, and court proceedings. Since the contestants will often be tempted to leverage their nonpolitical power—generally economic, but also possibly social, racial, or educational—to gain advantage, liberalism is not best described as neutral. It is, rather, committed to protecting the weaker party in any negotiation or debate, ever conscious of how easily inequality establishes and then perpetuates itself.

Modern liberalism contrasts with the individualistic and laissez-faire positions now embraced by self-described conservatives in insisting that much in modern economies lies far beyond the individual's control. It seems merely vindictive to blame the unemployed worker whose job has moved overseas—not to mention one who has lost his job and his pension to corporate malfeasance. The economic inequalities and the periodic downturns of capitalism place large numbers of people at risk in ways that they neither deserve nor can prevent.

4
DISCRIMINATION

Economic relations are hardly the only site of social interaction where power can accumulate. Liberalism's fundamental commitment to the notion of equality means that it works to resist the tendency to use various bodily differences (skin color, gender, age, etc.) and various social differences (accent, relative sophistication, family origins) to favor the accumulation of power by some groups and to underwrite the disempowerment of other groups. In the United States, racial discrimination against all those deemed "nonwhite," including African Americans, Native Americans, and Asian Americans, has a long, unsavory history. As a result of the civil rights movement of the 1950s and 1960s, no one in American public life openly defends differential treatment of different racial groups. To that extent, the liberal ideal of complete political and legal equality has won the day. The myth of "separate but equal" has been fully exposed as the fraud it always was. The state, it is now accepted, has the legitimate and important function of protecting its citizens from all forms of discrimination.

Yet there remains resistance to equality—and to the state actions that seek to secure it—on any number of fronts, from the failure in the 1970s to pass the "equal rights amendment" that addressed sexual equality to the current opposition to laws that protect homosexuals from discrimination. Antiliberals must be dragged, kicking and screaming, toward acceptance of each extension of equality to a disadvantaged group. For the most part, contemporary conservatives have not attempted to roll back through legislation any achieved equalities. But they have tried to chip away at the edges of those achievements through the courts, have been less than zealous in their use of the executive branch to enforce civil rights legislation, and have consistently resisted every effort—no matter on what group's behalf—to extend equality.[23] Their tactics of resistance vary—from denying that there is a problem to predicting dire social consequences (unisex bathrooms! the collapse of the nuclear family! the destruction of military morale!) if the proposed equal treatment is instituted. In short, here as elsewhere, conservatives have shown themselves the allies of entrenched privilege.

State action to prevent discrimination raises some very complex—and important—issues. For starters, civil rights has joined with national defense in American history as (arguably) the two most important factors in the relative growth of Washington's power vis à vis the states. Federalism, as instituted in America by the founders, follows the basic liberal idea of proliferating sites of power by creating what we nowadays call "the federal government" and the individual states. American history is a long march toward increased centralization of governmental power in Washington in conjunction with a steady decline in the power of the states. "The state," as I have been using that term thus far, encompasses both the federal and state governments. But it is not a matter of indifference that "the state" in the American system is divided into separate entities that, in theory at least, have their own jurisdictions, their own fields of action, their own responsibilities, and their own autonomous powers to act in relation to those jurisdictions, fields, and responsibilities.

National defense might seem an obvious responsibility of the federal government. But the founders well knew that concentrations of power are often enabled by a monopoly of military might. Therefore, they ensured the existence of state militias in the Second Amendment, which is so often misread as providing a personal right to bear arms. The complete absorption of these militias, now renamed the National Guard, into the national army has been completed by their wholesale use to meet the army's human resource needs in both the first and the second Persian Gulf Wars. As recently as the Vietnam War, there was a firm wall between the Guard and the army, as George W. Bush will recall. The different state Guards were under the direction of the governor of the state, not at the beck and call of the national government.

When we remember that the first massive growth of the federal government in response to the need to wage war was the American Civil War, we can be pardoned the slight exaggeration of saying that the quagmire of America's tangled race relations has been the single greatest cause of the federal government's growth. The issue of states' rights—over which the Civil War was fought—came to a boil because some states sought to perpetuate slavery at the same time as other states had outlawed it. The Civil War established that the federal government had the final word on various matters, especially those regarding the equal treatment of all citizens. After the conflict, the federal government tried fitfully to act on this newly declared power and to ensure the equality of the newly freed slaves. But the feds finally gave up. They refused too many times to call in federal troops to quell the white paramilitary groups that terrorized blacks who tried to act on their freedom. By the 1880s, the federal government withdrew from the South entirely, acquiescing in Jim Crow laws, which spread to non-Southern states and were eventually upheld by federal court decisions like *Plessy v. Ferguson* (1896). Washington also refused to combat the racial terrorism of lynching. The South appeared to have won by social intransigence and periodic violence what it had lost in the war. Short of slavery, any inequality between blacks and whites was acceptable, and states' rights, now synonymous with legally established and enforced discrimination, were back in the driver's seat.[24]

This situation posed a crisis for liberalism. To some extent, two liberal ideals could be seen as clashing here: the ideal of equality with the ideal of multiple sites of power. But this dilemma, at least as posed by this particular case, is only apparent, not real. No power, whether legally established or not, has the legitimate authority under our Constitution to treat citizens unequally. Jim Crow could only manage to exist under the legal cover of the Supreme Court decisions that declared segregation legitimate. Once *Brown v. Board of Education* (1954) explicitly repudiated the notion of "separate but equal," the states had no right to legally segregate the races. President Eisenhower's decision to send troops to enforce the *Brown* ruling in Little Rock reversed eighty years of federal dithering in the face of explicit denials of African Americans' right to "equal treatment under the law."

Liberals believe that Eisenhower made the right decision—and can only wish that President Ulysses S. Grant had taken similar action at certain key moments in the 1870s. Ensuring the freedom of all citizens is so fundamental a liberal commitment that it must override the rights of any social or political entity that acts to deny that freedom to some citizens. That's a no-brainer. No one in a liberal polity holds power legitimately—or is entitled to that power—if he or she uses it to deprive others of freedom. But liberals can be very sorry that it came to that in American history, necessitating both the massive suffering of the Civil War and the tremendous sacrifices made by African Americans before the federal government finally (and even then reluctantly) saw fit to intervene on their behalf. And liberals can be sorry that such strong action by the federal government proved the only possible course of action. The result was the centralization of power—and power, once accumulated, is extremely hard to disperse. The centralization of power—whether it rests in the hands of the federal government or in those of the wealthy or in those of one racial group—always bodes ill for the polity. Such concentrations generate abuses (power corrupts) and conflict (on the part of those who resist those abuses). American racism, unfortunately, necessitated the undermining of American federalism.

We should also remember that federalism has been progressive as well as racist in American history. States pioneered almost all of the legislation that improved working conditions, just as various states outlawed slavery long before the federal government was ready to do so. Today the states are in the forefront of environmental controls on automobile emissions and on curbing fraudulent corporate practices (especially in the financial sector). Liberal experimentation—the willingness to try out a policy and see if it delivers the intended benefits—is enhanced in a system that gives individual states lots of leeway. The tendency over the past fifty years—in everything from education to welfare to environmental and business regulation—has been toward standardization, with the federal government mandating and/or restricting what states can do.

Here, as elsewhere, liberalism eschews any simple solution or formula. Neither states' rights nor the central government's dictates are absolute. The rule of thumb, it seems to me, should be a presumption in favor of the individual state's independence except where its actions violate individual liberties that are guaranteed by the Constitution or encroach on activities specifically reserved for the federal government by the Constitution. What I am suggesting is that we have, throughout much of American history, managed to get the worst deal possible in sorting out the respective powers of the federal government and the states. Washington has shown itself too often irresolute in intervening to stop fundamental abuses of citizens by individual states while also demonstrating a continual inclination to interfere in state activities that it would do better to leave to the states' discretion. Today, federalism is close to nonexistent, with all of the public's focus on the national government and with that government gobbling up the lion's share of tax revenues. The states, left scrambling to pay the bills for education, health care, roads, mass transit, and the criminal justice system, have no room to maneuver. Meanwhile, the federal government blithely runs up massive deficits as it pursues costly experiments like a missile defense system and tax cuts. We are, quite literally, paying the price for the imbalance between the federal government's power and the power of the individual states.

To avoid misunderstandings, let me be clear. A reinvigorated federalism is usually a rallying cry for conservatives today, not for liberals. My argument here is that federalism accords with a fundamental liberal belief that proliferating sites of power is an excellent safeguard against tyranny. Therefore, the decline of federalism, while completely understandable given the history of racial discrimination in America, is not an unmixed blessing. That some conservatives pine for states' rights to weasel out from under the demands of equality does not discredit the notion of states' rights altogether. Good political arrangements are always capable of being used for bad ends.

The vicissitudes of the long American struggle, still ongoing, to tame the demons of racism also redound to the contemporary problems of the public sphere. I have described already (in Book One's section on "pluralism") liberalism's interest in securing and maintaining public spaces where the diverse citizenry of the modern polity can meet and interact. To that end, the liberal injunction against discrimination has been interpreted broadly so as to encompass employment, membership in various civic organizations, and admission to private universities as well as access to public places of commerce (such as restaurants and department stores) and public facilities (everything from parks to museums). The injunction against discrimination clashes, to some extent, with the traditional liberal freedom of association. Traditionally, liberalism focused more on forced association—and was thus at pains to guarantee each individual's liberty to leave any group that she or he no longer wished to be associated with. Ideally, individuals in a liberal polity would associate themselves with a number of different groups, moving relatively easily from one to the other, and not offering prime or sole allegiance to just one. The public sphere, to some extent, is comprised of these overlapping groups, connected to one another partly by the fact that the same individuals belong to them. But a growing awareness of the evils and effects of racism made it clear that associations can abuse power (the social power that a group can hold over and above an individual) by excluding as well as by forcibly including. To exit rights liberalism was moved, by the logic of the affront to equality, to add rights of joining. And the liberal tendency has been, as always, to place the burden of proof on the more powerful. Unless there are special justifying circumstances, all groups are required to admit all citizens as possible members. Groups (and employers) can have entrance requirements in terms of the group's specific needs and purposes, but groups cannot discriminate on the basis of preexisting individual characteristics such as race, sex, religious affiliation, age, and so forth.

The actual impact on the ground of the more aggressive enactment and enforcement of antidiscrimination laws over the past fifty years has been highly complex—and far from a happy ending to the unhappy history of American racism. As already discussed, liberalism's strong interest in a vibrant, open, and diverse public sphere provides another reason to prevent discrimination. Ideally, entrants into the public sphere should not have to check their distinctive identities at the door—and all identities should have equal access and an equal ability to speak up and to be heard. That's why it is hardly "free speech" when it costs so much that only the wealthy get to say anything. Private financing of political campaigns is discriminatory. The commons is the place where a plural society experiences and lives its plurality.

In the post–civil rights era, however, there has been an increasing emptying of the commons. Most crudely put, blacks were admitted to the public sphere and whites fled it. White flight—especially from the cities and from the public schools—was followed by niche capitalism and niche (special interest) politics, the carving up of the demos into separate, distinguished groups that have increasingly little to do with one another. The disaggregation of American society occurs from both the left and the right. The leftist version is called "identity politics" and, at its most extreme, preaches various versions of separatism. The right's version comes in a wider variety of forms, from gated communities to right-wing militias to anti-immigration groups to sectarianism. Even more alarming than these various splinter groups of both the left and the right is the general trend toward "privatization," toward moving more and more activities and interactions from the public sphere to private ones. Housing and schooling are the two primary examples of privatization, but cell phones, suburban sprawl, and the decline of civic organizations are others.[25] I want to be careful here because American liberalism has always recognized that maintaining a vital public sphere is difficult in a country where freedom has so often been understood as being left alone to do what one wants. John Dewey wrote one of his best books, *The Public and Its Problems*, in 1927 to bemoan the state of the American public sphere. So we are talking about a perennial problem in American politics. Liberalism is always struggling against power's desire to exclude, to consolidate, to have it all its own way. Establishing and maintaining a vital public sphere is never easy.

Today's version of this perennial problem gives us a society where money talks more than it has at any point since the Gilded Age, where the gap between the rich and the poor is growing, where actual interactions between the rich and the poor are at a minimum, and where income disparities track along ethnic and racial lines. (See Appendix, items 2, 4, 6–7.) As many observers have noted, America has succeeded in integrating public places to a fairly large extent since the end of Jim Crow. Job sites and universities are integrated to a lesser (but still significant) extent. But schools below the university level and private spaces are (especially in cities) often barely integrated at all.[26] In many places, particularly urban sites and urban public schools, whites have simply ceded the public sphere to blacks and want nothing further to do with it.

This dynamic has been heightened by low-level hostility (now, in some quarters, growing) to new immigrants, many of whom are also considered (in the folk categorization of these things) "nonwhite." Pushed both by leftist urges to maintain cultural identities and by rightist suspicion, there is widespread anxiety about how this new wave of immigrants will assume their place within American society. Will these immigrants—like those from the last great period of immigration from 1880 to 1915—follow the pattern that sees second and third generations adopt full-fledged American identities, even if they are flavored by some sense of ethnic or national or racial "roots"? Or will our new immigrants retain their pre-American identities more fully and be less integrated into American society as a whole? The jury is still out on this question, but early returns indicate that the pattern will be more similar to what happened in the first part of the twentieth century than not.[27]

Many contemporary conservative politicians have played on fears of various other groups to win votes among the white majority. To stir up the voters' passions through the high-pitched identification and denunciation of enemies internal and external is to play with fire. A siege mentality—or one that distinguishes between the saved who deserve the benefits society can offer and the reprobates who should be cast out—turns the differences of opinion, religion, sexual preference, culture, ethnicity, and race that are inevitable in a plural polity into so many threats that must be contained and neutralized. In supporting a privatization that allows the well-off to opt out of public spaces while also demonizing various portions of the population (gays, welfare mothers, abortion-supporting atheists, and liberals), conservatives are actively destroying the public sphere without, it seems to me, a clear sense of just how dependent civil peace and freedom are on that sphere's existence. As discussed further in Book Four, on "Democracy," a public sphere that acknowledges the equal right of all citizens to appear and that encourages them all to (minimally) acknowledge and (ideally) to interact more fully with each other is essential to healthy democracy.

But the aftermath of the civil rights movement has also taught us that just because you build a public space, that doesn't mean they will come. Often, commercial culture or, more generally, the bourgeois mind-set is blamed for the disinterest of many modern citizens in the public sphere. Work and family take up the vast majority of people's time, energy, attention, and devotion. Citizens are disengaged and voters are "apathetic."

Yet many more people have the disposable income and leisure time required to participate in public activities today than was true in an aristocratic society in which the great strove for honor and the vast majority struggled desperately for material necessities. Does a commercial culture offer the substitute of shopping for public engagement? Yes. But aristocratic cultures offered the substitutes of fox hunting, drinking, and whoring for the pursuit of worldly honor. Politics is never going to attract everyone. By any absolute measure, more people are engaged in public activities in a modern bourgeois democracy than in any previous societies, simply because large numbers were excluded from such activities in those societies. Does that mean all is for the best in our current situation? Hardly. The entry costs for public engagement are way too high—and getting higher all the time. To develop the citizenry's sense of involvement, especially if it would prove an antidote to frenetic consumerism, would, at the very least, have tremendous environmental benefits and, at best, foster a robust democratic culture.

But you cannot create such cultural transformations by fiat. To put the point in the sharp terms that express the hard lesson the civil rights movement has imparted: you cannot outlaw racism. Liberalism, you will recall, is a response to cultural pluralism. It does not offer a way to achieve cultural cohesion; in fact, it not only doubts that cohesion is possible to attain without a great cost in human suffering, but it also denies that such cohesion is a good to which we should aspire. That does not mean liberals cannot argue passionately that some cultural habits and practices (such as racism) are wrong. Furthermore, as this section has been at pains to explain, the law in liberal polities must actively strive to prevent harmful actions that follow from those cultural habits and practices. But the work of transforming culture (habits, attitude, practices, values) is not legal work; it is rhetorical work done by citizens in the public sphere. For the most part, those citizens are not state-sponsored and they do not have the force of law behind their work. If racism is extirpated from American culture, it will not be because racism has been outlawed, but because the cultural work of transforming attitudes has been done in civil society.

Such cultural work takes a long time. Stateways cannot change folkways, but that neither means that folkways can't be changed nor that stateways are entirely irrelevant to folkways. Legally barring discrimination doesn't keep people from discriminating in their hearts. But getting rid of legal discrimination was a necessary and big step forward. Call me a deluded optimist, but I think it is way too early—and way, way too easy—to call the American attempt to achieve racial integration a failure. Beliefs, prejudices, and fears are somewhat amenable to persuasion, but they are much more likely to change as a result of experience. If people simply have more and more interactions across racial lines—from the simplest, most casual encounters while waiting for a bus to the more extended experiences of being on sports teams or work teams together—they will begin to think of these racial others in more nuanced and differentiated ways.[28] Actually doing things with people of other races will lead to the point where their presence, their inclusion, their importance in my world will become second nature, just part of the landscape. Are we there yet? No. How long will it take? I don't know. But I do believe that real progress to that end has been made in my lifetime.[29]

The importance of integration as a lived reality stems directly from the fact that laws cannot do all the work in providing the goods for which liberalism aims. Just as you cannot eliminate racism by outlawing it, you cannot get employers to treat employees decently solely by legal means. Again, this is not to deny that the law is necessary and crucial. But it is not sufficient. For starters, there needs to be voluntary compliance with legal strictures against discrimination and mistreating employees. The law can't be everywhere at once. But even more importantly, only a sense of responsibility to and fellow feeling with other members of the polity will generate social relations that attend to the others' needs. Society is in bad shape when citizens' relationships to one another reflect only a legalistic sense of each other's "rights." To attenuate our responsibility to others to a legal requirement is to disengage from a full entanglement with the lives of our compatriots. The polity can thrive only when we feel that we are in this together, creating by our efforts a society within which each person can, in her own distinctive way, flourish. Just as Hume stressed the way that we each internalize the importance of keeping one's promises, the best polity is one in which each individual takes it personally, feels ashamed, when the needs of any individual are ignored, neglected, or denied. Cultivating such a sensibility is the cultural work to which liberals must attend.

Every effort—rhetorical or practical—to destroy that sense of responsibility to others, to single out some individuals or groups as unworthy of regard or as threats to my well-being, legitimates discrimination. Every act of disengagement, of withdrawal from spaces where I would encounter the full range of others who live within this country's borders, delays the achievement of a polity in which the capabilities of each individual are fostered by the lived conviction that I have a stake in the success of all. That individual achievement need not be a zero-sum game is something that the lucky among us have experienced in familial relations, in friendships, and as participants in various collaborative enterprises. Here, as elsewhere, liberalism calls for the proliferation of sites where such experiences can be had. The Republican Party, especially recently, has all too often attempted to substitute an abstract patriotism, focused on identifying threats to "our way of life," for a commons in which individuals actually encounter and interact with other Americans in all their diversity. The Americans who live in cities, who have the most concrete experience of pluralism, are the ones most likely to be liberals, to affirm that a diverse public sphere enriches life, to take pride in the fact that America once again, as it has throughout its history, is offering an opportunity to enjoy the benefits of freedom to a whole new set of immigrants. To rend the social fabric by starting and fanning the flames of "culture wars" is to aid the economic forces that are already seeking ways to segregate the winners from the losers, and is to facilitate the exploitation of marginalized groups that find their claims on us and the polity can thus be more easily ignored. Discrimination is a social wrong that almost invariably has economic consequences. The liberal state must act to counteract it as far as legal means allow, while liberals must be active in the public sphere to foster the multiple interactions across differences needed to overcome the cultural attitudes that underwrite discrimination.

5
THE LIBERAL CREDO

Liberalism often looks downright Aristotelian in its search for a golden mean between the extremes of laissez-faire and direct rule from above. Less grandly, liberals can be viewed as wishy-washy, as drunkenly weaving between letting things be and favoring legal or state intervention. But the liberal position makes more sense once we adopt the goal of "effective freedom." Liberals recognize how many forces are arrayed within modern complex societies. The simplicities of laissez-faire and of state command do not actually enhance the capacity of individuals to live the lives they choose for themselves. More complex balancing of various forces is required to achieve that end. And the exact balances struck will need to be continually readjusted as situations change and as various forces work within the current balance to gain an advantage. Competition and conflict, like racial prejudice and alcohol abuse, are never going to disappear. Liberalism's task is to keep such competition and conflict within bounds, to keep it from spilling over into violence or into tyranny. How and where to strike the balance, how and where to locate the checks on each source of power, is the stuff of politics in a liberal polity. We can expect an ongoing contest over the best ways to protect individual freedom.

Once we accept this desire to keep various social forces in balance in order to provide "effective freedom" and maintain (or create) an equality that makes domination impossible, modern liberalism is easily recognized as continuous with the liberalism of the founders. We can trace a fairly direct path from Madison and Jefferson to Tocqueville and then onto Dewey. As we have seen, Madison in the 1790s came to worry about inequities of wealth as threats to liberty. Tocqueville explains how a concern with tyranny and freedom leads to an emphasis on equality:

> It is possible to imagine an extreme point at which freedom and equality would meet and blend. Let us suppose that all the people take a part in the government, and that each of them has an equal right to do so. Then, no one is different from his fellows, and nobody can wield tyrannical power; men will be perfectly free because they are entirely equal; and they will be perfectly equal, because they are entirely free. Democratic peoples are tending toward that ideal.[30]

Ninety years later, Dewey would make the link between equality and freedom in a vocabulary that anticipates the "capabilities approach" of liberal thinkers in the final decades of the twentieth century:

> One person is morally equal to others when he has the same opportunity for developing his capacities and playing his part that others have, although his capacities are quite unlike theirs. . . . All special privilege narrows the outlook of those who possess it, as well as limits the possibilities of those not having it. A very considerable portion of what is regarded as the inherent selfishness of mankind is the product of an inequitable distribution of power—inequitable because it shuts out some from the conditions which evoke and direct their capacities, while it produces a one-sided growth in those who have privilege.[31]

If we focus on the substantive goods the founders strove to achieve—stability, peace, and effective freedom for all—instead of the substantive positions they might have taken on this or that topic, the continuity of today's liberalism with that of the founders rests on a continued commitment to those goods, a continued conviction that pluralism is an ineluctable characteristic of modern societies, and a fierce attachment to the belief that justice demands the equal treatment of all. Liberalism aims to produce a just world in which we would be proud to live: a world in which all have effective freedom, and in which one individual's freedom is not secured at the price of another's.

BOOK FOUR

Democracy

1

DEMOCRACY AND LEGITIMACY

In today's world, democracy is beyond criticism. It is the only form of government recognized as legitimate even while liberalism is scorned from right and left. Yet the rhetoric of democracy often masks deeply undemocratic practices in sitting governments and among social elites. Even among those who are sincerely democratic, the articulation of what democracy entails is neither precise nor demanding. It seems to be taken for granted that we all know what democracy looks like and what it is for. Democracy is presented as self-evident; we automatically know what counts as democratic or not, and the good of democracy is similarly self-evident.

What does democracy mean? The first—and often, it seems, the only—specific answer offered is "free and fair elections." Why are elections so crucial? They have become the standard mechanism through which the people express their opinions, their will, or their consent. This formula provides one crucial principle of democracy: ultimate authority rests in the people. Government only acquires and maintains legitimate authority over the governed if the people, as the source of authority, give that authority to the government and periodically reaffirm that giving.

Elections have become *the* sign of democracy because they offer, at minimal inconvenience, each citizen a voice. Each step further up the ladder of political involvement finds less and less people involved, since it takes time, energy, money, and commitment to become actively engaged. Even the minimal bother of casting a vote is not worth it to large percentages in many democracies. (Making registering to vote easier and either restoring election day as a holiday or extending voting over a four-day period that includes Saturday and Sunday are expedients worth trying to increase participation.) But even where voter turnout is low, elections are crucial because they signal the government's willingness to place itself on the block. Those currently holding power will only be granted a reprieve, the right to continue governing, if the people so desire.

The most fundamental principle of democracy, then, is that legitimate authority rests with the people. Madison's understanding of a "republic," as described in Federalist No. 39, is, to that extent, democratic: "We may define a republic to be, or at least bestow that name on, a government which derives all its powers directly or indirectly from the great body of the people; and is administered by persons holding their offices during pleasure, for a limited period, or during good behavior. . . . It is *sufficient* for such a government, that the persons administering it be appointed, either directly or indirectly, by the people; and that they hold their appointments by either of the tenures just specified."[1] Every government must claim authority over at least some actions of individuals. A liberal government will try to extend the range of the permissible as far as possible, but all governments will forbid some behavior and use force to restrain and/or punish those who engage in the forbidden behavior. What gives government the right to be coercive? Democracy's answer is that the people can only be bound to a government that they have created themselves, to which they periodically reaffirm their allegiance or their consent, and to which they appoint those who hold office.

Democracy recognizes the people as the source of authority for reasons both principled and prudential. The principle, most memorably articulated by Kant, is that people are not free unless they are obeying laws of their own devising or, at least, laws to which they consent without coercion even if they did not write them. The English political writer Richard Price stated the basic principle quite clearly in 1776 in his *Observations on Civil Liberty*, a text familiar to many of America's founding fathers. "Civil Liberty," Price writes, "is the power of a Civil Society to govern itself by its own discretion; or by laws of its own making."[2] Freedom is a fundamental good. There have been, of course, many elaborate ways of defining freedom offered by various philosophers and political theorists. The liberal democrat insists that freedom is a simple concept—and that all attempts to complicate it are snake oil, are ways of diminishing actual freedom. Self-determination is the key. An individual or a nation is free when it determines for itself the rules under which it lives, the goals for which it will aim, and the courses of action it will undertake to reach those goals. We have already seen that modern liberalism is committed to the additional proviso that freedom is not "real" unless it can be actualized, unless free individuals or nations have the capacity to act on their decisions and realize their aims. The liberal democrat has a principled commitment to freedom as a good in and of itself, as something that government exists to enable and preserve. Thus, democratic government exists in service of the people's authority, of their self-determining rule of themselves. Abraham Lincoln captured this fundamental principle of democracy when he spoke of "government of, by, and for the people."

The prudential argument for the people's authority rests simply on the observation that modern people cherish their freedom, resent highly any effort to lessen it, and are far more likely to adhere to laws of their own making than to laws imposed on them. The stability of democracies, as contrasted to other forms of government in the modern world (the same was not true in ancient times), surely reflects the refusal of modern peoples to accept the legitimacy of any state or legal authority that tries to insulate itself from periodically seeking the people's endorsement at the polls. Of course, particular democracies today can be highly vulnerable and thus unstable. But the various forms of authoritarian regimes that usurp democracy in various parts of the world can never achieve full legitimacy in the eyes of their own people or in the eyes of the international community. That's why such countries almost invariably call themselves democracies and stage elections (albeit rigged and fraudulent ones). They are trying to gain the stability that only legitimate democracies enjoy under modern conditions—and they are paying homage to, even as they try to subvert, the widespread acceptance of the principle that a free people exercises its own authority over itself through its government and its laws. Today, no competing principle has much credibility or standing, even though many people have little or no commitment to the democratic principle.

There is, however, a different way to understand democracy, one that does not focus on the people's authority. This second way can be called the pragmatic account of democracy, because it is in the spirit of the American pragmatist philosophers William James and John Dewey and because it focuses on the practical difficulties of governing dynamic and diverse modern societies. I don't think, ultimately, that this second account contradicts the principle of the people's authority. But it does attend to different matters—and points us toward various crucial features of democracy, features that an exclusive focus on the "the people" and on elections would lead us to miss.

Pragmatist or pluralist democrats recognize that the consent of the people is crucial for legitimacy, stability, and civil peace. But they refuse to assume that the abstraction of "the people" makes much sense. The pragmatist calls our attention to the marvelous—and somewhat mysterious—fact that elections have winners and losers and yet do not, in a well-functioning democracy, foment civil strife. The great accomplishment of democracy according to this account is that it provides decision-making procedures for crafting legislation, making policy, choosing courses of action, and filling governmental posts in societies where there is deep disagreement over what should be done and who should hold office. Yet if the procedures are followed, the losing side accepts the result as legitimate and voluntarily complies with a law or a decision or an electoral result that it strove mightily to prevent.[3] Democracy's alchemy provides a way to transform conflict into peaceful acquiescence.

There is no need to romanticize this feat. The acquiescence may be grudging, and the losing side will, if passionate enough, continue to plot and scheme how it can best win the next election or the next legislative battle. We are not talking about the lion lying down with the lamb. But the fact remains that democracy offers procedures—most usually, through a vote after a period of debate and deliberation—for closing contention and coming to a decision in cases where there are deep disagreements and multiple opinions. And, for the most part, all sides to the conflict agree to and in fact do abide by the decision reached. How does that happen? Humans are not notably good losers; indeed, they have manifested strong tendencies to do everything and anything—up to and including the use of violence—to get their own way. Democracy, viewed in this pragmatic way, appears an astounding and invaluable means for keeping conflict from generating endless irresolution on the one hand and from fostering violence on the other. A neat trick, to say the least. A nice form of government, if you can get it.

The rule of law plays a crucial role in this accomplishment. Democracies are dependent on a strong sense of what counts as "legitimate" procedures for decision-making.[4] That's why "irregularities" (the understated term used these days) in elections or in legislative bodies are so debilitating. If the political contestants do not have an equal chance to make their case and the decision-making procedures are not followed fairly, then the loser will deem the outcome illegitimate and refuse to accept his obligation to abide by it. As we saw with the impeachment of Bill Clinton and the presidential election of 2000, there is a strong sense for preserving the democratic system in this country. A majority of the public turned its back on the Republican Congress that tried to unseat a duly elected president, while the public as a whole also accepted the flawed denouement of the 2000 election because the alternatives all seemed worse. Democracy, to a large extent, rests on there being peaceful transitions of power from one party to another and on the party in power being accepted as legitimate governor by the vast majority of the people, whether they voted for that party or not.

We reach here a rather different understanding of democracy, one that focuses less on majority rule or the consent of the governed and more on the way in which democracy gives all factions in a pluralistic society a stake in maintaining the electoral and decision-making procedures. How can we characterize that stake? For starters, there is the stability and peace that democracy can provide. We would expect most citizens to desire stability and peace if (and this is a big *if*) they live in a nation in which most of them have a modicum of economic prosperity and some property. Citizens are less likely to take to the streets (or to the mountains as guerrillas) if they have comfortable and fulfilling lives under the present arrangement. Admittedly, there is no simple formula here. The historical evidence suggests that a sense that I am ruled by "foreigners" or that my living conditions are "unjust" more than the brute fact of poverty moves people to rebellion.[5] Democratic government, then, does not exist in a vacuum. It rests on a society in which people have good reasons to want to preserve the tenor and texture of daily life, from their economic interactions to their familial bonds to their various ways of associating with other citizens. People will support democracy precisely as a way to avoid violent political conflict when they enjoy a social existence whose basic conditions and goods are not greatly altered—or threatened—by changes in government.

Such a statement suggests that democracy is rarely extreme—and perhaps not well suited to extremism.[6] I think that is probably the case. Here's why: The key to democracy, pragmatically understood, is that any faction or party must be willing to surrender power to its opponents if they lose an election. I'll go further. A party or faction is not democratic if it denies the legitimate right of its opponents to serve as the nation's governors. I think the most crucial test of democracy, the best sign that a country has now become a democracy, is whether or not it has managed at least two peaceful transitions of power from one party to its opponents. Having an election proves just about nothing. Having an election in which the party in power loses and peacefully accepts the result is when you can begin to claim—or hope for—success in establishing a democracy that has a decent prospect of surviving. Extremists are rarely willing to grant their opponents' legitimate right to rule. More usually the extremist insists that his opponents are enemies of the people or of the state—insists that "they" cannot be trusted and may even need to be purged from the body politic. Democracy works by being inclusive, not exclusive. By granting everyone's legitimate participation in the system of political contention, it keeps all of society's members in the game. They all have a reason to keep competing because they all have a chance of winning and of gaining political power as a result of their victory. Any social faction excluded from such a chance has no incentive to accept the result of an election that goes against it or to work within the peaceful channels of political wrangling, debate, and elections.

In other words, democracy prevents violent political conflict by assuring the losing party that all defeats are only temporary. One reason why democracies are inefficient and can be so infuriating is that nothing (it sometimes seems) is ever decided once and for all. Any issue about which a democratic society is deeply divided will almost inevitably come up for a vote again and again. The losers will make their defeat on this or that issue part of their appeal to the voters in the next election and will then reintroduce the issue in subsequent legislative sessions. Few defeats are simply accepted as final; the defeat is accepted temporarily—and thus not understood as an unmitigated disaster justifying outright rebellion. (In the United States, we have developed a weird—and not altogether benign—version of this response to legislative defeat. Today, the losers often appeal the law in the courts, in multiple venues and in multiple variants. So we are condemned, again and again, to judicial honings of separation of church and state, disability rights, and countless other contentious issues.) Some issues, of course, finally die. Legal segregation in public places now appears firmly a thing of the past; there is no longer a significant minority fighting that battle. Social consensus is achieved on some fronts over time; but the pluralist, of course, claims that consensus, which is always possible, should not be expected on every front at the same time.[7]

This focus on democracy as a means for the peaceful transition of power has some highly significant consequences, ones too rarely understood or discussed in current invocations of the glory of democracy. Most crucial is that the chances for democracy are very poor in any country where there is likely to be a permanent majority. Another way to say this is that every democracy, to remain viable, needs swing voters. If voters, for whatever reason, have an unchangeable loyalty to one party, then the same party (or group of parties in a multiparty, as contrasted to a two-party, system) will keep winning every election. Obviously, this situation is most dire in countries where parties represent a particular ethnic group or a particular region or some other particular "identity." If the voters choose that party irrespective of its actual performance in office, but simply because it is "us" and not "them," democracy is pretty much a nonstarter. The identities, groups, and factions that are on the permanent outs in such a situation have no stake in the democratic system. Even if, in theory, their legitimate right to rule is granted, in practice they will never get to exercise that right. For this reason, in many divided societies—Switzerland and Belgium are two examples—the democratic electoral system is set up in such a way that permanent power-sharing among the different groups is guaranteed. Here, there are not clear winners or losers (as in the United States or Britain) because the possible swings in power are limited by statute.[7]

The United States, I believe, is very lucky that identity markers of race, ethnicity, religion, gender, region, and class have never become full-scale determinants of how people vote. Of course, there are tendencies, but few of these identity markers predict how the vast majority (say 80 percent) of the people in a particular group will vote. There are two significant exceptions to this rule in American politics—and they are historically yoked to one another. The South has almost always voted as a bloc in national elections, and African Americans (once they secured the right to vote and, of course, only much later the actual ability to exercise that right in many parts of the country) have overwhelmingly voted for the party that the South did not support. The South's voting as a bloc has given it a disproportionate influence throughout American history—and one that has seldom been used for liberal ends. Yes, the New Deal was enabled in part by the South's solid support for FDR, but the price for that support was the neglect of the civil rights of African Americans.

Swing voters are crucial because they keep the governing party in line. Opposition parties have an interest in keeping the public informed about the missteps and misdeeds of the party in power. In other words, the opposition is as instrumentally central to publicity as a free press. And publicity is an important safeguard—not the only one, but a vital one—against governmental abuse of power. But the publicity only makes a difference if a fairly large proportion of the public changes which party it votes for in relation to the party's performance in power. Once you get a polarized polity, one in which most voters would never support the other party under any circumstances, the fluidity required for a functioning democracy begins to evaporate.

Democracy, in short, cannot survive with one-party rule. There's a paradox here, since each of the rival parties can be expected to do everything it can to become the dominant party and to maintain that dominance once achieved. But, in fact, disaster will follow if any of the parties ever actually succeeds in that aim. Once you create a minority that is permanently on the outside, its members will be tempted to secede. Why stay in a system where it is inevitable that they will lose every time? Civil peace will yield to civil war.

Democracy is a competition in which you cooperate with your partner even as you try to beat him. Think of a tennis match. You want to beat your opponent, but you also depend on him to have the match at all, and you can only expect to get to play with him again if you, like him, follow the rules of the game. Political parties that subvert the process or use dirty tricks or steal elections are undermining their own chance to rule in peace; similarly, parties that stigmatize their opponents as unfit to rule are encouraging their opponent to quit the game and take up the conflict in a different register. Those who worry about the increased partisanship in contemporary American politics have good reason to be concerned. It is not clear that the public as a whole is as polarized as the political class itself.[9] But there is no doubt that political partisans—especially on the right—have encouraged the notion that certain governmental actions and policies are illegitimate and that any and all means to prevent certain groups from having power are justified. It has not, of course, come to armed rebellion in America—and the vogue for rightist paramilitaries seems to have faded while we have a conservative president. But our democracy is frayed. Many on both sides of the political fence no longer trust the other side to follow the legitimate procedures or refrain from undermining or disobeying the results (laws, regulations, policies) of those procedures. The causes of this fraying are multiple and complex—too various and complicated to unpack here.[10] But the siege mentality of the younger Bush presidency—its hypersensitivity to criticism, its vetting crowds for presidential appearances to ensure that only supporters are admitted, its strong attacks on all opponents, and its characteristic tone of aggression tinged with defensiveness—indicates the extent to which those in power now feel as if their right to hold power is continually being questioned.

When Newt Gingrich says "The left at its core understands in a way Grant understood after Shiloh that this is a civil war, that only one side will prevail, and that the other side will be relegated to history," he threatens our democracy. If political antagonists become convinced that the other side is out to obliterate them, and if there is no longer understanding or tolerance of the notion of a "loyal opposition," the contending parties have no reason to trust their opponents and will come to believe that any and all means of winning are justified by the perfidy of their opposites. In terms of the most effective way to win elections and to stay in office once the election is won, there are two basic strategies. The first is to move toward the center and try to be as inclusive as possible in rhetoric and policy. The other is to try to build a majority on only one side of the political spectrum. This second strategy almost always requires demonizing some portion of the population, thus mobilizing a majority in the face of a threat to their way of life, or values, or prerogatives. Various parties—from the Know-Nothings and abolitionists in the 1850s to the white supremacists and states' rights populists of the twentieth-century South—have pursued such strategies during American history. In each case, some group was designated as unfit to claim full citizenship rights in the polity or to hold political power.

I worry that we somehow have come to the complacent belief that "it can't happen here." We seem to think that our current divisive political landscape is somehow a game, a form of entertainment. So, for example, the various vituperative right-wing talk radio hosts were shocked that anyone would link their shows to the Oklahoma City bombings. In a similar way, we seem to think that the social fabric of an America where diverse peoples mingle in public daily is somehow disconnected from our politics. A civil politics depends on accepting that your opponents have the good of America—as they understand it—at heart. Attacking your opponents as enemies of the good may be an extremely effective campaign tactic, but it undermines the very conditions that make democracy—and the peace and stability it affords us—possible. Here's how Gingrich concluded his remarks: "While we are lucky in this country, that our civil wars are fought at the ballot box, not on the battlefields, nonetheless this is a civil war."[11] Yet it is not "luck" that keeps us off the battlefield. Our peace is the result of the ways in which we interact with other citizens, most crucially the ways in which we respect each one of them as having the equal right to put forward their vision of what the country can and should be. We are playing with fire when we begin to denigrate some Americans as nonpatriots, as traitors, or as threats who must be eliminated. In a well-functioning democracy, each political party acts as a corrective to the blindnesses and crotchets of the other parties. The nation as a whole benefits from electoral and political competition. Monopolies—also known as one-party rule—are as disastrous politically as they are economically.

There is much in our current political climate to suggest that we, as a nation, have lost this understanding of how a democracy functions—and have lost a salutary awareness of how fragile democracy is. Democracy is a political system that locks us into continual dialogue and interaction with citizens who do not hold our own political views in every instance. We will argue with those citizens—and we will hold votes to reach decisions when we cannot come to an agreement. But if we treat their views and their arguments with disdain, if we don't listen to them and then begin to devise ways to keep them from speaking at all, we are placing our democratic union at risk.

A healthy democracy relies on open-ended political contestations, on procedures that give all of the contending parties an opportunity to make their case. This openness cannot be faked because it is the losers whose affirmation of the process is most crucial. Only if the losers believe they were given a full and fair shot at winning the debate and the subsequent vote will they willingly accept the decision, even though it went against them. It's not easy to fool these folks. They will know when they have only been paid lip service, or when they have been ignored altogether, or when they have been shut out by various procedural or parliamentary maneuvers. As with freedom of speech, it may seem counterintuitive to insist that vigorous debate, inclusiveness, and the acceptance that any faction could prove legitimate rulers of the polity would better promote stability than careful control over the expression of opinion and careful vetting of all contenders for power. But such is the case. Democracy rests on a faith that the people, if given the full freedom to make decisions, will choose the rulers and the policies that will best serve the nation as a whole. In Federalist No. 39, Madison expresses his reliance on the "genius of the people of America," on their commitment to "the fundamental principles of the revolution" and their "honorable determination, which animates every votary of freedom, to rest all our political experiments on the capacity of mankind for self-government" (209). Without that faith, democracy is doomed. Another way to state that faith is: A democrat will believe that the people are better than its politicians. A politician will look for immediate advantage and for ways to hold onto power and will often succumb to the temptation to demonize her opponents, but the people will know that their interest lies in having a vigorous opposition that keeps those in power in check. And the people will move their allegiance from one party to other parties in response to each party's behavior. Out of such fluidity comes the benefit of long-term social stability.

2

DELIBERATIVE DEMOCRACY

We are accustomed to the phrase "the democratic process." To what does it refer and why does allegiance to that process matter? Most broadly, the democratic process provides for a period of public debate and deliberation prior to the making of any decision—and provides a set of procedural rules for decision-making that grants all parties access to the debate and guarantees that all parties have an equal say in the final outcome.[12] All should feel that they were given an adequate opportunity to sway the final votes of the other participants. "Free and fair" elections entail the right of all citizens to contend for office, provide an open public square in which all positions can be aired, allow sufficient time for full publicity before the votes are cast, ensure all citizens the opportunity to vote, and give each vote exactly the same weight. Similar principles apply to the deliberative process in legislative bodies.

Pragmatically, a fair process keeps the losers on board, ready to accept the outcome as legitimate and willing to participate in the process again the next time. But various champions of democracy—most notably John Stuart Mill and John Dewey—have also insisted that the democratic process produces the best possible results. Their reasons for making this claim differ somewhat, but both men argue that collectively achieved decisions are better than those determined by a single individual and, crucially, that the more people involved the better. "Public reason" exercised at a variety of sites in the "public sphere" is the hallmark of democratic societies.

Mill regards this public debate as a "marketplace of ideas." Everyone who wishes to influence the final decision will bring to the forum his or her reasons for advocating one outcome over another. The result will be a plenitude of considerations and information that far exceeds anything any single individual could ever produce or conceive. The society as a whole has produced—through its interactions, through its debate—this knowledge and these thoughts. As with the economic marketplace, the range of products and the multiplicity of choices can be rather overwhelming. The din of the public square or the legislative debate or the electoral campaign can seem just cacophony. But the individual must judge for herself where she will take her stand, just as the individual consumer makes a decision about how she will spend her money.

Mill has no doubt that participation in the public square can be transformative. The individual will find his views changed by hearing the arguments and information put forward by others. Mill views that result positively.[13] Close-minded individuals, who cling desperately and stubbornly to their original views, are hardly praiseworthy. Democracies are dynamic and innovative precisely because they encourage frequent, raucous, and transformative interchanges among citizens. For Mill, the attempt to protect individuals from possible conversion by the articulated views of others is just another species of paternalism. So long as transformation is not coerced, but only a product of persuasion as contrasted to force, change is to be embraced not feared. Democracy entails trusting that the individual is fully capable of judging his own good, of making up his own mind. That one person's meat is another's poison, that one might deplore the other's decisions, is neither here nor there. We should expect such incredulity and distaste in a fully pluralistic society, but that does not mean I should protest his self-determination (at the end of the deliberative process) when I have no intention of foregoing my own.

Dewey's version of this process is, somewhat paradoxically, both darker and more optimistic than Mill's. Mill takes the analogy with the "marketplace" very seriously. He assumes, as classical economic theory inspired by Adam Smith usually does, a perfectly functioning market. In particular, Mill assumes that all the parties to a debate will play fair and that the individual who makes the final decision will be fully informed. Mill considers neither the deliberate misinformation that some advocates might spread nor the individual who, for good reasons or bad, does not pay enough attention to get all the relevant information. Mill believes that the marketplace of ideas, like the marketplace in classical economic theory, is self-correcting. Deceptive advertising that leads one to buy a faulty product cannot be sustained over the long term; the truth will out. Similarly, the lying politician can succeed only for a short time before he is found out and rejected by the voters. The mechanism can only self-correct if there really is complete freedom for competitors to operate. When economic or political winners in the first round use their victory to consolidate their position and limit access to their opponents, the chances for self-correction diminish. Mill's position appears naive given what history has wrought in the 150 years since he wrote his books. Manipulation of information and opinion has become a fine art—in many ways exactly because democracy's reliance on deliberation has made the stakes of these processes so high. Both the economic marketplace and the marketplace of ideas rely on norms of truth-telling and openness to competition that must be legally enforced; fair advertising and nonmonopoly will not automatically appear on their own, either in economics or in politics. Nevertheless, Mill's overly idealistic account provides a strong standard that allows us to insist that all efforts to distort, withhold, or exclude relevant information are antidemocratic.[14] Given the very high standard Mill sets, we might reasonably conclude that democracy is an ideal for which we strive, but which we will most likely never fully reach.

Dewey takes a different tack. He frankly acknowledges that the different parties in a political contest, just like the different parties in an economic transaction, have competing interests. We should not expect perfect information utterly uninflected by beliefs and opinions from anyone. That just isn't going to happen in this world. Experts and professionals, even when not expressly partisan, will have their own "professional deformation," their own allegiance to their guild and to the habitual ways their discipline frames questions and gathers data. All information is tainted in one way or another—and part of the process of judgment is assessing information and opinions in relation to their sources. Mill, according to Dewey, underestimates how complex judgment is. Mill also imagines an individual with world enough and time to become fully informed. But how many people are really like that?

Dewey argues, instead, that the democratic process provides for the exercise of "collective intelligence" (his term for what I have called "public reason"). Each individual will make *some* judgment—insofar as he votes. (Of course, some people opt out altogether by not voting.) Each of these votes will be based on some notion of the right way to choose, even if we can always criticize the bases of that notion, and even if that notion is based on scanty information. The chances of any particular voter making a faulty judgment are fairly high. But the chances of the whole community making a poor judgment are much less. The aggregate of choices makes the collective decision more reasonable than any one choice within it.[15]

Can the collective still judge poorly? Of course. Can the majority have been fooled by misinformation and manipulation by partisans? Yes. Dewey's position, no less than Mill's, indicates how much democracy relies on a "fair" process—and thus provides a justification for a democratic polity's strongly regulating for fairness.[16] But Dewey insists not only that, as judges, we are capable of "discounting" some claims in relation to their sources, but also that, to recall Lincoln's formula, it is awfully difficult to fool all of the people all of the time. In today's America, our problem is better characterized as excessive discounting, rather than naïveté. No information seems trustworthy in our heightened partisanship; many citizens seem unswayable because they simply do not credit facts that would put their worldview into question.[17]

Dewey, although for slightly different reasons than Mill, also believes that the democratic process, in its dynamism, is self-correcting. You might succeed in fooling all of the people (or a majority) this time, but subsequent events and consequences will reveal your dissembling. Because there are multiple occasions for judgment and because people learn from their mistakes, the demos will not continue indefinitely making and then acting on decisions that do not fit the facts because such actions will not produce the desired results. There is a feedback loop—one that includes elections and public debate as well as the outcomes of decisions made and implemented. The democratic process is, in Dewey's view, fallible, but it is less fallible than the individual simply judging on her own. That's why we should have frequent opportunities to make decisions—and to revisit past decisions. Persistence in error is the only true irrationality. Making mistakes is part and parcel of our regularly falling short of perfection.

The deliberative democratic process has one further consequence that neither Mill nor Dewey considers. In legislative bodies or in town meetings, deliberative democracy involves the face-to-face interaction of all parties to a dispute, with each given the chance to articulate his or her reasons for favoring one course of action over another. At a minimum, the process accords each party recognition as a legitimate player, as someone who is entitled to a place at the table when a decision is being made. In many situations, it is hard to extend that recognition without feeling moved to back it up with substantive concessions. Although it sounds strange—or even Pollyannaish—to say so in today's poisoned political climate, the democratic process often fosters compromise.[18] It is difficult in face-to-face encounters with people acknowledged as one's fellow citizens and neighbors to ignore and/or reject their views and desires altogether. If you are going to deny them outright, it is much more courageous and forthright to do so to their face. This pressure toward compromise, toward inclusiveness (so that all parties get some of what they want), suggests once again that democracy attends to maintaining a community even as it makes specific decisions. A process in which as many people as possible feel respected and feel like they can truly influence the outcome underwrites civility among disputants now and in the future. Extreme partisanship, which scorns compromise as weakness (or, even worse, as giving in to an enemy whose views are outside the pale of the acceptable), will often go hand in hand with efforts to limit input in the crafting of policy and the making of decisions. Such efforts, even when they do not violate the letter of the law, run counter to the spirit of democracy.

Of course, partisanship encourages all kinds of stratagems to exclude participation at all stages of democratic deliberation. Imagine, if I may indulge a utopian fantasy for a moment, how different our elections would feel if debating candidates engaged in a discussion, a genuine give-and-take, about how to address the complex problems that face the polity. Here are two people who want to improve the nation (or the state or the county), who are interested in discovering the best way that can be done and who are using the electoral process to aid in the process of that discovery. That such serious and respectful debates appear a risible fantasy only tells us how far we have strayed from ideals of democratic deliberation. We laugh at what shames us, at what reminds us of how resistant we actually are to living by ideals we also claim to find admirable.

Deliberative democracy, then, is a collective process, one that increases the interaction of citizens with one another. Yet it retains a crucial individual element since it honors—and stresses the dignity of—each individual as the ultimate judge for him- or herself of what it is right to do. We fall short of full democracy if the deliberative process is short-circuited to prevent universal participation or if each participant's judgment is not counted equally. The process needs to be safeguarded not only against exclusion but also against excessive distortion by partisans who purvey false information or otherwise manipulate the discussion.

How often, in what locales, and with what participants should democratic deliberation occur? An advocate of democracy like John Dewey calls for introducing democratic procedures in all kinds of places—most notably the workplace—where it is currently deemed inappropriate. Dewey's reasons are that people should have a voice in decisions that materially affect them and that, since collective decisions are more intelligent than unilateral ones, the more we use democratic deliberation, the better off we will be. Democracy builds communities through the experience of working together to make good decisions, and it gives the parties to those decisions a stake in working together to implement them, to demonstrate that they were right.

Such a view counters the economic orthodoxy that claims that the best results for a society come from competition. Democracy can be a process that encompasses competition within a wider cooperative framework. Yes, it is crucial that competing viewpoints clash in the debate, but the wider context is the good of society, the maintenance of civil peace, and the fostering of a commitment by as large a plurality as possible to the decisions the process yields. Democracy counters the individualism of the economic sphere by engaging citizens in this deliberative interaction with others and providing those citizens with a stake in the well-being of the whole society. Advocates of democracy believe that introducing the deliberative process into the workplace would increase employers' and employees' loyalty to one another and their ability to work efficiently together.

Certainly, we should recognize that it will be difficult to sustain a vibrant democratic society if citizens never have the experience of full participation in democratic deliberation. Elections are a poor substitute because they involve so little face-to-face exchange with citizens who hold contrasting or opposing views. Elections under contemporary conditions are much too abstract—or virtual. Most crucially, they neither involve nor model the potential transformations of actual deliberative interchanges. A process in which no one ever changes their mind, ever comes to view things differently through exposure to new information or the views of others, is not simply impoverished, but also dangerous to the long-range health of the polity. So once again we are brought to the view that elections are necessary, but not sufficient, for full democracy. They are not rich enough experiences to foster a democratic citizenry, one that is jealous of its authority as the ultimate source of power yet adept in the give-and-take of debate with fellow citizens whom it honors by trying to persuade even while remaining open to being persuaded. Decentralization, the proliferation of sites of power so crucial to liberalism, is also important democratically since it affords citizens the hands-on experience of participation in democratic processes of deliberation and decision-making, and in the implementation of those decisions.

All that said, sheer practicality necessitates delegation.[19] No one can participate in all of the decision-making processes that culminate in decisions that effect her. As Oscar Wilde famously quipped, the problem with democracy is too many meetings. Everyone loves to complain about meetings, but they are, in fact, productive and even interesting when one has real input and when a group is thinking creatively together. Everyone should have that experience—and fairly regularly—in a democracy. But, just as obviously, meetings are time-consuming, not terribly efficient (although the superiority of the end product can justify the extra time needed), and not the be-all and end-all of existence. Meetings are currently—and should remain—a primary way that decisions get made, involved parties are kept in the loop, and things get done. But practical considerations mean that it will be representatives of various parties who will attend those meetings, not every single person with an interest in the matter.

Rousseau was adamantly against representative democracy because he insisted that we cannot guarantee against a slippage between the wishes of the demos as a whole and the actions taken by the representative. And, of course, he is right. But even if we are reconciled to the necessity of representation—and aware of the imperfections that the tension between the representative's accountability to those he represents and his semiautonomy reveal—various additional problems concerning the relation of representation to democracy arise. One key issue is who will represent whom? Or, to put it another way, to what extent will our gathering of representatives actually be representative of the full diversity of opinions, values, desires, and interests in a pluralistic society? Once we move from a thin notion of democracy that relies solely on information-poor elections to a full-bodied commitment to deliberative processes, inclusion of all viewpoints becomes much more important. When the popular vote is not the actual point of decision-making, but only the election of representatives who will engage in the deliberative work of crafting legislation and policy, the stabilizing benefits of deliberation can be achieved only if all groups believe that they are fairly included.

These considerations mean that every democracy must make crucial decisions about how to organize representation. In the United States, representation until the late 1970s (approximately) was solely geographic. The Constitution accepted the existing boundaries between the colonies when forming the states of the new nation and in "the great compromise" gave the less populous states equal representation in the Senate.[20] The basis for representation in the House of Representatives is almost completely unspecified in the Constitution. Beyond stating that the number of representatives "shall not exceed one for every Thirty Thousand people" and that each state will have at least one representative, the establishment of districts and of election procedures is left to "each State by the Legislature thereof," although "the Congress may at any time by Law make or alter such Regulations" (Article I, Sections 2, 4).

This constitutional silence has allowed the gerrymandering of districts throughout American history. The practice is now so widespread that, by 2002, less than 15 percent of the seats in the House were actually competitive. (See Appendix, item 10.) The two major parties have colluded in this effort and are equally to blame. There is good evidence that the growing partisanship in Washington has little to do with the general public's beliefs and sentiments, but reflects instead the obsessions and interests of politicians who need not consider the voters' preferences because they are in no danger of losing the next election.[21] Politicians with safe seats are concerned with keeping big donors happy and with milking passionately engaged special interests for money. Such funds are then parceled out to vassals in order to build the politicians' power. The politician who plays this game doesn't need the money for his own campaigns, which are not seriously contested, and he is no longer accountable to the majority of citizens who do not donate money to political campaigns.

This use of money to consolidate power works hand in glove with organizing representation solely along geographic lines to encourage pork barrel spending. Since the member of Congress is only answerable to the voters in her own district, she would be cutting her own throat if she did not aggressively try to funnel as many federal dollars as possible to that district. The recent surge in "ear marks" combines the increasing power of money—and of the lobbyists who provide it—with the more traditional practice of bringing the pork home to a district. Lobbyists usually start with the representative in whose district the company and/or project is located. (See Appendix, item 10.) There is no incentive for weighing the national good—or even the actual good of the funded project—against the imperative to garner more than one's share of the pie. High-minded politicians in such a system have short careers. Combine this system with gerrymandering and the feeding frenzy is on. Politicians will compete to see who can most successfully raid the national treasury.

In short, geographic representation, like anything else, needs to be checked and balanced. Multiple, cross-cutting types of representation would not only yield better results, but also be more democratic. The key in any representational system is to provide for a constant flow of information between those in office (whether in a governmental, bureaucratic, or corporate structure) and those further down the ladder. Most representational systems try to achieve this end by a combination of elections (understood as messages sent from the electorate to its representatives) and a diverse group of representatives. The American system has tended not to place much stress on the diversity (apart from geographic diversity) of its representatives.

I will not rehearse here the various methods by which elections and redistricting could be organized to multiply the kinds of representation—and hence the groups of people represented. There is a large literature on this topic and a plethora of practical experience since so many different systems are currently practiced in various countries throughout the world.[22] For now, it suffices to note that many different systems are still worthy of the label "democratic"—and that schemes that aim toward power-sharing and the increased distribution of power among various "factions" in the population attend to the basic liberal commitment to resist the accumulation of power through its multiplication. To linger any further on alternatives to the current arrangements in the United States seems futile because it is unlikely there will be any change in those arrangements in the foreseeable future.

3
DEMOCRACY AND EQUALITY

Democracy holds that power should be vested in the people and fluid between various parties. Decisions should follow from publicly conducted debates and fully inclusive voting. Thus, democracy, as much if not more than liberalism, has a strong stake in equality and in resisting the accumulation and ossification of power.

The best expedient for maintaining representatives on a par with those they represent is to make sure that they are truly accountable to the people. The first and most obvious step is to ensure that politicians really are susceptible to losing elections. Fully contested elections require nongerrymandered districts, but also working against the advantages of incumbency. Experiments with term limits have barely been tried; somehow their proponents seem to lose their taste for them once in office. We do, of course, have term limits for the president (and for governors in some states), and they seem to work pretty well. Short of term limits, there are various ways to level the contest between incumbent and challenger. The most obvious would be strict—and strictly enforced—campaign spending limits. Various reform efforts over the past forty years that attend to the *source* of money have not only failed, but also attack the problem at the wrong end. We cannot keep big money out of politics—and keep officeholders from becoming full-time fund-raisers—until we put a ceiling on the cost of campaigns. Fully effective reform may require public financing of campaigns; short of that, only spending limits will work.[23] In any case, it is tragic—and a travesty—that appeals to "free speech" have trumped effective campaign finance reform in the United States. The monetary barriers to running for office have become ludicrously high (only millionaires need apply), while information is disseminated only by the partisan and the well-heeled.[24] An election should be a deliberative interchange among the whole citizenry about who should lead the nation into what future. Instead, our system succeeds in shutting out the vast majority of potential participants in the debate and in making sure that only the most biased voices will be heard. It would have been hard to intentionally design a worse procedure—one that more completely marginalizes most voters and produces greater inequities between various citizens' ability to influence representatives.

Ways of increasing voter participation—in deliberative assemblies as well as in casting a ballot—would also help.[25] The United States has a long history of discouraging—or outright preventing—certain people from voting. Although the worst abuses of the past are mostly gone, various mechanisms linger that make it unnecessarily difficult to vote. Similarly, many states and other jurisdictions make it difficult to run for office, thus giving the two major parties an unjustifiable advantage. Once more entrenched power rears its ugly head. Our elections are information-poor partly because that is in the nature of elections, but also partly because the powers-that-be game the system to insulate themselves from unwanted results, even as the fact that speech during campaigns is almost all bought shuts out many voices. We learn almost nothing about the citizenry and its hopes, fears, and wishes. What little we do learn comes from "opinion polls" that are sometimes collected by partisans (the infamous "push polls") and always driven by the questioner's understanding of the issues, so that questions are framed in specific—and often highly unnuanced—ways. In short, having sitting officeholders in charge of drawing representatives' districts and of specifying some of the rules governing elections is a very bad idea.[26] It violates the founders' constant insistence that one should never be in a position to judge a case in which one is also an interested party. To allow such judgments, they believed, was the surest way to legitimate and to entrench abuses of power.

Equal access to the seats of power requires decoupling economic power from political influence. Traditionally, the great enemy of republics is corruption, and democracy seems no different in this regard. That great watchdog Rousseau insisted that the political equality for which democracies strive cannot coexist with substantial social or economic inequality.[27] Economic inequality, left to itself, increasingly widens the gap between rich and poor. Most of the historical evidence suggests that, far from a trickle-down effect, the tendency is for the rich to get richer and the poor poorer even at times (especially at times?) when the aggregate wealth of the nation is on the rise. Once the gap between economic haves and have-nots starts to widen, the fear of being left on the wrong side generates frantic activity to position oneself— and especially one's children—advantageously. People begin to use money freely to secure advantages—and then expect those advantages to bring a bigger payoff because they have been so dearly bought. The stampede to private schools and to prestigious "name" universities over the past thirty years illustrates this dynamic.[28] When the costs of being left behind are visibly higher, people will act in ways that heighten the very differentiation they fear.

It is no surprise, then, that high economic inequality breeds high corruption, with various players looking to secure an advantage through various political means. Government can skew the playing field in a number of ways, from direct payouts in the form of contracts to tax breaks to favorable regulations. When politicians need large sums of money for increasingly expensive campaigns (or to gain power by helping to finance the campaigns of other members of their party), they find perfect partners in citizens who want to profit economically from various governmental favors. Corruption denies equal access to the government and its representatives because only money talks.[29] Lobbyists, not citizens, have the government's ear. (See Appendix, item 10.) At the very least, a democracy should be ever vigilant that economic power does not translate easily or directly into political access and power.

Effective political equality requires that all citizens have equal access and an equal chance to influence the government. Clearly, that is not the case in contemporary America, which is why we urgently need ways to balance the power of money in politics. But civil society also provides a different—and vital—form of equality, a kind of equality often associated with dignity. If we understand public life in its widest sense, as encompassing all of our interactions with nonfamilial others, then a democratic culture is marked by the insistence that all parties to such interactions are equal. The "tone" (for lack of a better word) of American life is set by this assumption of equality. No one need apologize for who she is, and no one is entitled to "put on airs" because of who she is. Again, this is not to deny all of the tendencies to produce various kinds of social hierarchies. But there remains an almost instinctive and a fierce egalitarianism in American culture that is played out in our civil society, in our daily interactions with our compatriots. Some of the greatest rewards offered by our democratic culture reside in the experiences that engagement in civil society affords. The goal need not be some benefit we extract from the state; instead, it is what we achieve together without regard to the state that is the focus and the benefit. But it seems unlikely that we can expect to retain the benefits of equality in the public sphere at the same time that increasing economic inequality excludes some from full participation in that public sphere and affords some the means to sway the government toward policies that encourage further increases in inequality.

At the beginning of this book, I said that democracy without liberalism is not worth a damn. Only a fierce liberal commitment to equality along all its dimensions can yield a society in which democratic processes of elections and deliberations coexist with the ability of all citizens to engage in those processes and influence their outcomes. The commitment to equality entails a vision of a larger social good that will curb the selfish quest for personal advantage. Modern liberals deny that the competitive pursuit of self-interest, uncoupled from a concern with other citizens' well-being and dignity, can produce a just society. Certainly, a government that ignored the "general welfare" in favor of enabling the unbridled pursuit of personal interest would be stepping away from its most basic responsibilities. Democracy, in and of itself, does not provide the fully elaborated value of a justice that is intimately tied to equality. Modern liberalism articulates and recommends that robust version of justice—and continually calls contemporary democracies to account for failing to be completely just. Contemporary conservatism forthrightly disputes the liberal understanding of justice and increasingly boldly proposes an illiberal democracy in its stead. Our current choice between these two versions of democracy forms the burden of my conclusion.

Liberal versus Illiberal Democracy

The power of the state in democratic polities should always be balanced by the power resting in the demos, whereas the power of the state in a liberal polity should always be checked by the restraints enunciated in the Constitution. The people's power expresses itself through the direct pressure it places on the state; the Constitution's power is expressed through the rule of law institutionalized in the judicial system and in the procedures through which the law is administered, interpreted, and enforced. The tension in a liberal democracy resides in the fact that the state cannot be a direct expression of the people's will. Constitutional imperatives alone prevent pure majority rule. But it is important to realize that, especially in plural societies, it is simply inaccurate to identify any opinion as the people's will 'or the will of a majority. The range of opinions on any topic and the differences in the fervor with which a policy is endorsed render clear-cut assertions about what "the people want" oversimplifications. Similarly, any straightforward account of the state as the people's instrument belies the complexities both of the modern state and of the ways power is distributed and deployed in modern societies. The state is engaged in a wide variety of activities as it addresses the plural needs and desires of a diverse population. Just as the people do not speak with one voice, the state does not act univocally.

Politics is the daily attempt by various parties to capture at least part of the state's attention, to garner some of the state's help and/or resources in addressing certain needs or problems. Democracy allows the widest possible scope to that jostling for the state's attention, while liberalism provides the watchful eye that checks to see that power does not accumulate in one place or with one group—and that acts to restore balance if power so accumulates. A liberal democracy, then, is an arrangement of governmental functions and power that is based on the insistence that the government is "by and for" the people, which means *all* of the people. The liberal part comes in precisely to combat the ever-present threat that some faction of the people (be that faction a majority or simply a disproportionately powerful minority) will gain control of the government and will use that control to sever the connection of the government from all of the people. When government has been captured by a faction, we can expect that equality before the law and political equality will be eroded for particularly vulnerable and marginalized citizens. But even where legal equality and political equality remain in place, such equality is not sufficient from the liberal point of view if decoupled from power. The citizens who enjoy such equality must have the capability to actually influence the course of their own individual lives and the shape of the conditions under which those lives are lived. Equality is meaningless without access to the places where consequential social decisions are made and without the capacity to carry through with one's own personal decisions.

Modern liberalism, as I have argued, insists that only effective freedom is worth having and that only a commitment to equality across the various dimensions of legal, political, social, and economic wherewithal can provide effective freedom. Thus, the modern state must attend to the distribution of power and resources as well as to the protection of citizens against discriminatory practices. The mechanisms for attending to distribution are up for grabs and subject to constant adjustment in response to past results and to the ongoing dynamics of power and resource flows in complex societies. But modern societies that retain a liberal orientation will take the creation of multiple sites of power and multiple instances of economic sufficiency as substantive goals that justify state action whenever power and resources begin to coagulate. As a result, the relation between the state and business enterprises, or between the state and religious groups, and, more generally, between the state and any faction, will at times be cooperative, at times adversarial. The factions—with their distinct interests, goals, and perspectives—will often be pulling in different directions, and will have to clear out separate spheres of activity in some instances or, at other times, negotiate ways to coexist or even to work together. No formula can capture the wide variety of relationships to the state—or to other social actors—that a particular agent or a particular faction will devise. And that plasticity is crucial to the maintenance of equality. Once any particular arrangement becomes the rule, the distribution of power will harden and certain factions will begin to have a permanent advantage. Since power and resources tend to accumulate (them that's got shall get), a liberal polity must work extra hard to keep redistributing power and resources in order to maintain the balances in place and in play. If democratic processes and procedures threaten those balances, liberalism must act as a check on pure democracy.[1]

That democracy need not work against the liberal commitment to equality is evidenced by the fact that for much of the nineteenth century, as is most dramatically illustrated in Alexis de Tocqueville's work, "democracy" was the code word for "equality."[2] For Tocqueville, "democracy in America" did not primarily mean a certain form of government or a certain way of granting final authority to the people; rather, democracy meant a way of life, a new kind of society in which all of its members felt and lived the daily conviction that "I am the equal of all with whom I associate." I have argued that the liberalism of the eighteenth century already contained the seeds of this newfound value of equality. For that reason, liberalism and democracy can work together without much tension. The push toward democracy in the nineteenth century was in many ways a push to gain what liberalism had already promised. There was in 1840, as there still is today, the gap between the ideal and the reality. But there is a huge difference between a society for which equality is a primary goal and one that is oriented toward other ends.

What impressed Tocqueville most—and made him believe that America was a harbinger of the future—was not that Americans had an ideal of individual freedom that was underwritten by a commitment to equality; it was that Americans embodied that ideal. They were not so much striving to be free and equal as they were living out their conviction that they *were* free and equal. In short, democracy, as Tocqueville saw it, was a way of life, an ethos, as much as it was a politics. Even before anything we would acknowledge as a fully democratic politics was achieved, American society was democratic and individual Americans were living the kinds of lives only possible for selves confident of their freedom and equality. Tocqueville thought that democracy must triumph in America because its people would tolerate nothing else. These Americans were proud of (and thus somewhat touchy about) their deserving to sit down as equals with anyone who came to life's feast. They would never accept that any one or any institution merited a disproportionate power, but would always call for the redistribution of power—and the capacities that flow from it—back to the people.

Many a conservative in 2006 would say "Amen" to the above paragraph—and then go on to claim that our government has accumulated too much power while remaining silent about the vast economic power vested in astoundingly few hands in contemporary America. That same conservative, more likely than not, would also approve of our country's vast military might and of the various limitations in civil liberties underwritten by "security" concerns. And that same conservative, most likely, would either deny that the middle class is being emptied out as the gap between the haves and the have-nots in our nation grows, or accept (even praise) that widening divide as the just results of an economic system that rewards those who deserve it and penalizes those who fail to make the grade. More generally, I think a vision of the polity that can be accurately named "illiberal democracy" has emerged in our country over the past sixty years. Its hallmark is the consolidation of power, and its basic appeal is to the need to preserve America's "position in the world" and "economic prosperity" at home. In the public sphere, this vision is constantly justified by identification of "threats" (both internal and external) to what America possesses or, more vaguely, to America's "values" or its "way of life." Each of these threats—whether the Communists of Joseph McCarthy's nightmares, the "welfare queens" derided in the 1980s, the homosexuals who incense the Christian right, the terrorists who inspire the neoconservatives' foreign policy adventurism, the liberals whose relativism will sap our nation's strength, or recent immigrants—serves to legitimate placing more power in the hands of the haves while marginalizing the have-nots.[3] Instead of an openly pluralistic society in which all citizens are entitled to possess power, illiberal democracy plays the game of dividing between "us" and "them," always working to deny "their" legitimate claim as equal members of the polity.

It has always been the Achilles' heel of democracy that an unchecked majority could trample minorities. In America today, we have created a tremendous fear by placing the vast majority over the precipice of economic ruin— only a pink slip or a major medical emergency away from losing just about everything for which one has worked so hard.[4] Such vulnerability does not generally breed solidarity, but rather an "each man for himself" (*sauve-qui-peut*) mentality, a result reinforced by the fierce rhetoric of personal blame (as if not having medical insurance were a personal choice) prevalent in our culture. As economic inequality rises and thus fear increases (almost everyone sees people who have fallen off the boat into the flood waters), politicians who seem to offer ways for me to consolidate and protect what I have, even at the cost of others, are very appealing. An "us" versus "them" divide enters the polity. We don't want "our" tax money going to "them"; "they" are lazy, improvident, and undeserving of "our" support. I am entitled to what I have earned and need feel no compunction about my privileges or the less comfortable lives afforded to others. This basic strategy of dividing between the well-off and the rest moves from the macro to the micro level, from foreign and economic policies built on the assumption that Americans have a right to consume the lion's share of the world's resources (especially oil) to local zoning decisions that displace the responsibility for the waste a community produces onto some less well-off neighboring locale.

As I have insisted countless times throughout this book, power tends to accumulate, and we should always expect that various groups and persons within any society will work actively against equality.[5] But that only gives us all the more reason to utilize the political power vested in our constitutional government to work against those tendencies. Our democracy will cease to be liberal if the citizenry chooses to endorse governmental policies that aid and abet the accumulation of power in the national security state and in transnational corporations. If we as a nation choose salvation from hardship by off-loading those hardships onto demonized (or simply invisible) others in our midst and around the globe, we will have reneged on the ideals that have made America stand for a cherished experiment in human history.

Illiberal democracy often displays impatience with democratic procedures, with deliberations accessible to all, with legislative debates and compromises, and, at its most extreme, with the rule of law. From Napoleon III to Arnold Schwarzenegger, "strong" illiberal leaders have liked the plebiscite, which does an end run around established governmental procedures in order to go "directly to the people."[6] The problem with plebiscites is that they preclude deliberation and the revisions that deliberation might introduce in favor of an up or down vote on the issue at hand as framed by one party to the disagreement. Armed with the people's general approbation, the leader then attempts to bypass politics as usual in the name of some good that transcends the interests, concerns, and commitments of various participants in the debates and wranglings of everyday politics. The leader has become the appointed, and unquestionable, guardian of that transcendent good. Especially at times when that good, however defined, can be portrayed as imperiled, the leader understands himself as justified in ignoring—or, at least, taking fairly casually—the constituted checks and balances of liberal democracy. The rule of law and various oversight mechanisms are clumsy, inefficient, and too slow to deal adequately with the crisis at hand. Of course, war has been the most dire "state of emergency" that is used to justify suspending, or minimizing, attention to the forms and protocols of liberal democracy—which is precisely why understanding our nation as existing in an ongoing state of war is such a threat to everything our adherence to liberal democracy has secured for us.

More ordinary, especially when it comes to be cynically or resignedly accepted as "business as usual," is the power of money—and of the wealthy people who wield it—in our national and state governments. Jacob Hacker and Paul Pierson have recently argued that "the American political elite . . . is increasingly pulling American government away from its citizens." They have done so by manipulating the system to weaken the accountability of elected officials to the people. "The cords of accountability have weakened because the electoral map has sorted into safely Republican and Democratic districts. They have weakened because of rising incumbency advantage. They have weakened because of the growing importance of money in the electoral arena. They have weakened because of the growing inequality of resources and organization between the rich and the rest. And perhaps most overlooked, they have weakened because of the deliberate efforts of political elites to make it hard for Americans to know what they are up to—to manage and distort information in ways that greatly undermine the sway of ordinary voters."[7] An illiberal democracy that stages spectacular elections yet carries on its daily business far from citizen attention or oversight can prosper with a politics awash in money, but the results will hardly redound to the general welfare.

It is tempting at this point to assume the role of an Old Testament prophet and predict all sorts of dire consequences if Americans choose illiberal over liberal democracy as their future. In fact, I do believe that we will do significant harm to ourselves as well as to others if we follow the illiberal course. At the very least, America will become increasingly isolated, increasingly a pariah in the world, only heeded because of its might while resisted in every possible way by non-Americans who resent our abrogation of the world's goods and our pushing for a global economic order that serves our needs alone. A fractious world will become more fractious still. I also believe that, eventually, such conflicts will flare domestically. But when "eventually" will arrive is very hard to tell—and maybe it will never come. The slow erosion of economic equality in this country (the emptying out of the middle class, which has now divided into a professional middle class—doing just fine, thank you, so long as the members keep their jobs—and a nonunionized lower middle class with few benefits and less job security) has thus far met with only tepid resistance even as it has turned the general public mood ugly. The straw that breaks the camel's back may never make its appearance. Power has multiple ways to maintain the inequalities that it establishes, so maybe America will just drift, almost imperceptibly to the demos, toward conditions we currently think of as Brazilian. (See Appendix, item 7.)

Similarly, it's hard to know just how and when our current financial and environmental overdrafts will come due. Part of our *sauve-qui-peut* illiberalism entails displacing the cost of our current extravagances onto future occupants of the earth as well as onto the least fortunate among its current occupants. When will those IOUs come due—and with what consequences? An illiberalism bent on consolidating and enjoying its own gains doesn't even ask that question, no less try to answer it.

With all these uncertainties, and with an acknowledgment that accumulated power often successfully entrenches itself, I do not rely on apocalyptic scenarios of dire consequences. Such warnings are always the stock-in-trade of those who disagree with the way the world is currently going. My case rests instead on our ideals for ourselves as Americans, as a nation. It is no accident that current-day conservatives cannot openly espouse wide inequalities even as they pursue policies to produce them. Conservatives have to offer their "voodoo" economics to explain why giving more money to the rich actually benefits the poor, just as they have to disguise extended exploitation of the environment under the labels of "the Clear Skies Act" and the "Healthy Forests Initiative."[8] If we wish to live in a nation that we can be proud of, a nation that is true to its stated ideals of liberty and equality, we cannot stand by and watch state power and economic power (sometimes in cahoots, sometimes acting separately) undermine the capacity of individuals to live full, satisfying, self-designed, and self-chosen lives in the company of others whose well-being, affection, and recognition are central to the individuals' well-being. Instead, we must use politics—and the state—as tools for the maintenance of civil peace and of an effective freedom underwritten by equality. A balance of power does not occur by itself; some state action is necessary, even while the state itself remains one place where power may accumulate. Society will always be a dynamic interplay among groups and forces angling for advantage. Neither the state nor commercial enterprises are simple angels or pure devils on this scene. Eternal vigilance and endless adjustments are required. But the rewards of effective freedom for all and of a national life that matches our ideals are well worth the effort.

I am an English professor, not someone who teaches American history or American politics. I wrote this book as a concerned citizen, and it presents some of what I think an "education in civics" should include. America is in danger of losing touch with what its liberal democracy has striven to be over the past 230 some years. But, maybe because I read and teach novels as much as I read political treatises, I sometimes worry that the portrait of our nation, its ideals, its potential, and its history, offered in this book is hopelessly "thin." What has been left out of this civics lesson—and what I sincerely believe must be part of every such lesson—are the struggles on the ground throughout our history, the passionate endeavors by various social actors to gain power, money, and influence or, conversely, to insist upon and wrest from entrenched privilege a modicum of equalities previously denied. The most ambitious American novels of the past fifty years—by writers like Don DeLillo, E. L. Doctorow, Toni Morrison, and Edward Jones—present a far messier picture of our history and our social life, where the various actors are far too immersed in the daily struggle to survive to be much motivated by the high ideals articulated in this book. Yet, even while in constant danger of being overwhelmed by the difficult situations in which they find themselves, the characters in those novels generally retain that fierce American assertion of dignity that surfaces in the conviction that "I am as good, as worthy, as any one else who walks the earth, and I will assert that fact in the teeth of every effort to insist that I do not belong here, that I have no legitimate claim upon this society or this nation."

When I consider the tales of those struggles and think about how slow—and how painfully won—has been the progress in American history toward equality (a progress that is currently being reversed), I sometimes think it a miracle that liberal sensibilities and a liberal political order have ever found even a foothold in this world. Measured against the passionate pursuit of advantage, the rule of law and the commitment to equality that motivates the self-abnegating refusal to make an exception of oneself seem highly unlikely human achievements. Certainly the novelists I have just mentioned are, on the whole, pessimistic about actual or potential justice being done in American society, even while they are each strongly motivated to speak out indignantly against the injustices they perceive.

Given the passionate search for advantage and the ever-present tendency of power to sweep all before it, the restraint of the founders (victors in a bloody revolution and comfortably situated at the top of society), along with their determination to place the law above men and to provide an institutional framework for freedom and equality (rather than for privilege and hierarchy), can also strike us as a miracle, even when we take into account their failures (most notably, their bowing to the reality of an established practice of slavery that they could not see their way to abolishing). The republic they instituted has been transformed, through good times and bad, through struggle and slowly forged agreements, into the liberal democracy that today stands in peril. Our liberal democracy—embattled, fragile, never completely secure, but nonetheless real, at times effective, and always an embodiment of cherished hopes and values—will continue to exist only so long as our actions reproduce it. Liberal democracy is never fully achieved, but it stands for what we aspire to be as a nation, and it provides a measure of how far we have come at any given moment and of how far we have fallen short of our best vision of ourselves. Much of what we most cherish in this world—peace, freedom, and the ability to live an undisturbed life in the company of those we love—depends on a liberal order that recognizes the equal claim of others to those exact goods and thus works to secure those goods for them as well as for oneself. The miracle of liberalism depends on our continuing to foster the sensibility that underwrites it and the political expedients that make it possible in a world where many passionately pursue illiberal visions.

APPENDIX Relevant Facts and Figures

1. RACIAL INEQUALITY

A. Differential Outcomes for Whites and Blacks in the Criminal Justice System

"Cases involving white murder victims are more likely than those with black victims to terminate in a death sentence. Since the reinstatement of the death penalty in 1976, only 13 percent of all capital cases have involved black victims, yet about half of all murder victims are nonwhite."

SOURCE: Marvin D. Free Jr., "Race and Presentencing Decisions," in *Racial Issues in Criminal Justice: The Case of African Americans*, ed. Free (Westport, Conn.: Praeger, 2003), 145.

"Once in prison, African Americans remain incarcerated longer than whites. . . . Non-Hispanic African Americans average three months longer in prison than non-Hispanic whites for discretionary parole releases. The largest racial disparity appears in forcible rape, in which non-Hispanic African Americans average 42 months longer than their non-Hispanic white counterparts. For mandatory parole releases, there is an average 7-month differential favoring non-Hispanic whites."

SOURCE: Marvin D. Free Jr., "Race and Criminal Justice in the United States: Some Introductory Remarks," in *Racial Issues in Criminal Justice: The Case of African Americans*, ed. Free (Westport, Conn.: Praeger, 2003), 3.

2. ECONOMIC INEQUALITIES IN RELATION TO ETHNIC AND GENDER DIFFERENCES

A. Earnings of Women Compared to Those of Men

In 2004, women (working full-time, year-round) earned, on average, 77 cents for every dollar earned by men. In 1960, women earned 61 cents for every dollar earned by men.

SOURCE: U.S. Census Bureau, "Income, Poverty, and Health Insurance Coverage in the U.S.: 2004" (report issued August 2005), <http://www.census.gov/hhes/www/img/incpov04/fig12.jpg>.

B. Recent Data on Gender Pay Gap

"The disparity in median hourly pay between men and women narrowed to 18.3% in August [2006] from 21.5% five years earlier, according to recently released census figures. . . . The wage differential was the smallest since the Department of Labor began tracking it 33 years ago, when it was 36.9%. . . . The difference between men's and women's median annual earnings shrank between 2000 and 2005 from 26.3% to 23%, or 77 cents on each dollar earned by men. . . . However—as the economy expanded, profits rose and unemployment fell—men's hourly wages declined a total of 2% from 2000 to 2005 while women's rose 3%, census records show. Women's gains were barely enough to keep up with inflation. 'Wages generally have been depressed, but men's wages have been more depressed,' said Michele Leber, chair of the National Committee on Pay Equity, who called the trend 'discouraging.'"

SOURCE: Molly Hennessy-Fiske, "Gender Pay Gap Narrows—For Unexpected Reasons," *Los Angeles Times*, December 3, 2006, <http://latimes.com/news/nationworld/nation/la-na-wagegap3dec03,0,656909.full.story?coll=la-home-nation>.

C. Median Household Income by Race, 2004

Asian: $57,500
White, non-Hispanic: $49,000
Hispanic: $34,200
Black: $30,100

SOURCE: U.S. Census Bureau, "Income, Poverty, and Health Insurance Coverage in the U.S.: 2004" (report issued August 2005), <http://www.census.gov/hhes/www/img/incpov04/fig07.jpg>.

D. Historical Trends in Family Incomes (Not Adjusted for Inflation) for Whites and African Americans

Median Family Income for Whites
2001: $54,067
1984: $27,686
1968: $8,937
1960: $5,835
1954: $4,613

Median Family Income for Blacks (Percentage of White Median)
2001: $33,598 (58)
1984: $15,431 (56)
1968: $5,360 (59)
1960: $3,230 (55)
1954: $2,416 (52)

SOURCE: U.S. Census Bureau, "Historical Income Tables—Families," <http://www.census.gov/hhes/income/histinc/f05.html>.

3. MINIMUM WAGE AND UNION MEMBERSHIP

A. Minimum Wage

1997–2004: $5.15
1996: $4.75
1991–95: $4.25
1990: $3.80

SOURCE: *Statistical Abstract of the United States*, 124th ed. (Washington, D.C.: U.S. Census Bureau, 2004), table 626.

B. Minimum Wage and Poverty

"The minimum wage—the lowest amount that employers are allowed to pay most workers, now [2005] $5.15 an hour—is not adjusted for inflation. Its value therefore declines over time unless Congress and the President agree to raise it, and for many years they routinely did. The minimum wage, however, has not been raised since 1996. Today, a full-time minimum wage worker makes $10,712 per year, well below the poverty line for a family. Indeed, the minimum wage would have had to be raised to $8.49 in 2004 to equal the purchasing power it had in 1964. David Lee, an economist at the University of California at Berkeley, has concluded that failure to increase the minimum wage accounts for about half the increase in the disparity between average wages and the wages of workers in the bottom tenth of wage distribution."

SOURCE: Jacob S. Hacker and Paul Pierson, *Off-Center: The Republican Revolution and the Erosion of American Democracy* (New Haven: Yale University Press, 2005), 101.

Poverty thresholds for 2004 were $9,827 for one person under 65, $12,714 for two persons under 65, and $19,307 for a four-person family.

SOURCE: U.S. Census Bureau, <http://www.census.gov/hhes/www/poverty/threshld/thresh04.html>.

C. Union Membership

1983: 16.5% of private sector employees; 2003: 8.2% of private sector employees
1983: 36.7% of public employees; 2003: 37.2% of public employees

SOURCE: *Statistical Abstract of the United States*, 124th ed. (Washington, D.C.: U.S. Census Bureau, 2004), table 638.

4. SCHOOL SEGREGATION

A. *Percentage of Southern Black Students in Majority White Schools, 1954–2000 (various years)*

1954: 0
1965: 2
1969: 15
1971: 35
1990: 45
1993: 40
1996: 35
2000: 32

SOURCE: John Charles Boger and Gary Orfield, eds., Introduction to *School Resegregation: Must the South Turn Back?* (Chapel Hill: University of North Carolina Press, 2005), 8.

B. *Reasons for Resegregation*

"Levels of school desegregation for black and white students increased—in spite of the shrinking white majority—until the 1990s, when such levels went into a period of continual decline, a sudden change that corresponded to no sudden demographic change. . . . As research by Sean E. Reardon and John T. Yun [included in the volume being quoted here] shows, residential segregation declined in the region as school segregation rose, indicating that a key problem was the declining role of school assignment plans, which had made schools substantially less segregated than neighborhoods. The resegregation of the South has clearly been related to court decisions. . . . The reversal in the South was clearly related to a 1991 Supreme Court decision, *Board of Education of Oklahoma City v. Dowell*, that authorized federal courts to end desegregation plans. In a stunning reversal of earlier expectations, the Court adopted the basic ideas put forward by President Reagan's Justice Department—that desegregation was a temporary rather than a permanent goal for schools and that courts could dissolve existing orders and permit the restoration of segregated neighborhood schools as long as the school districts said that they made these changes for educational rather than racial reasons."

SOURCE: John Charles Boger and Gary Orfield, eds., Introduction to *School Resegregation: Must the South Turn Back?* (Chapel Hill: University of North Carolina Press, 2005), 9–11.

5. MILITARY SPENDING

A. *Expenditure by Country, 2002*

United States: $399.1 billion
Russia: $65.0 billion
China: $47.0 billion
Japan: $42.5 billion
United Kingdom: $38.4 billion

SOURCE: *Statistical Abstract of the United States*, 124th ed. (Washington, D.C.: U.S. Census Bureau, 2004), table 1384.

B. *World Military Spending and the United States*

"World military expenditure in 2005 is estimated at $1,118 [billion] dollars, [which] corresponds to 2.5 percent of world GDP or an average spending of $173 per capita; 2005 expenditures represent a real terms increase of 3.4 percent since 2004, and of 34 percent over the ten year period 1996–2005; the USA [is] responsible for about 80 percent of the increase in 2005; . . . The USA is responsible for 48 percent of the world total, distantly followed by the UK, France, Japan and China with 4–5 percent each."

SOURCE: Anup Shah, "World Military Spending," <http://www.globalissues.org/Geopolitics/ArmsTrade/Spending.asp?p=1>.

6. WEALTH DISTRIBUTION AND THE MIDDLE CLASS

A. *Distribution of Wealth over Time*

"The growing divergence evident in income distribution is even starker in wealth distribution. Equalizing trends during the 1930s through the 1970s reversed sharply in the 1980s. The gap between haves and have-nots is greater now—at the start of the twenty-first century—than at any time since 1929. . . . Wealth inequality in the United States was at a seventy-year high in 1998 . . ., with the top 1 percent of wealth holders controlling 38 percent of total household wealth. If we focus more narrowly, on financial wealth [i.e. excluding the value of people's homes], the richest 1 percent of households owned 47 percent of the total. . . . The rise in wealth inequality from 1983 to 1998 (a period for which there is comparable household survey information) is particularly striking. The share of the top 1 percent holders rose by 5 percent. The wealth of the bottom 40 percent showed an absolute decline. Almost all the absolute gains in real wealth accrued to the top 20 percent of wealth holders."

SOURCE: Edward N. Wolff, *Top-Heavy: The Increasing Inequality of Wealth in America and What Can Be Done about It* (New York: New Press, 2002), 2, 8–9.

B. The Growing Gap between the Upper Middle Class and the Rest of the Middle Class

"Despite the tremendous overall economic growth of the 1980s and 1990s and the low unemployment rates of the late 1990s, the gaps between high-income and low- and middle-income families are historically wide. . . . In all but five states, income inequality has increased over the past 20 years; prior to the late 1970s, economic growth in the United States was more evenly shared. . . . In 43 states, the average income of families in the middle of the distribution remained the same or rose over the 20-year study period [1979–99], but did not keep pace with increases in the average income of families in the top 20 percent of the distribution. In eight of these states, incomes in the middle fifth grew less than 10 percent while the top fifth grew by more than 20 percent. In one additional state—Wyoming—incomes in the middle fifth declined while the top fifth grew. In West Virginia, for example, the average income of the middle fifth of families increased five percent, or by $1,640. The richest fifth of families in West Virginia, however, saw their incomes increase by $27,870 on average, an increase of 37 percent. . . . In the late 1970s, there was not a single state where the average income of families in the top fifth of the distribution was as much as 2.7 times as great as the average income of families in the middle fifth. By the late 1990s, there were 30 states where the gap was this wide."

SOURCE: "Despite Past Boom Times, Income Gaps Have Widened in 45 States over the Past Twenty Years," Economic Policy Institute and Center on Budget and Policy Priorities, press release, April 23, 2002, <http://www.cbpp/4-23-02sfp-pr.htm>.

C. Wealth Distribution in the United States, 1998

Top 0.5% has 25.6% of total
Next 0.5% has 8.4% of total
Next 4% has 23.4% of total
Next 5% has 11.4% of total
Next 10% has 12.8% of total
Final 80% has 18.5% of total

In other words, the top 20% owns 81.6% of America's wealth, leaving 18.6% for the remaining 80%.

SOURCE: <http://tiger.berkeley.edu/sohrab/politics/wealthdist.html>.

D. Income Distribution in the United States, 2000

Richest quintile: 50%
Fourth quintile: 23%
Third quintile: 15%
Second quintile: 9%
Poorest quintile: 4%

In other words, less than 30% of the income each year goes to 60% of the people.

SOURCE: U.S. Census Bureau, cited in Dennis Gilbert, *The American Class Structure* (Belmont, Calif.: Wadsworth, 2003), 94.

7. RUTHLESS CAPITALISM REDUX:
FALLING REAL WAGES, RISING PROFITS AND POVERTY,
AND GROWING ECONOMIC INEQUALITY

A. Poverty Levels

"The poverty rate rose from 11.3% in 2000 to 12.7% in 2004. The number of people living in poverty has increased by 5.4 million since 2000. More children are living in poverty: the child poverty rate increased from 16.2% in 2000 to 17.8% in 2004."

SOURCE: Lawrence Mishel and Ross Eisenbrey, "What's Wrong with the Economy?," Economic Policy Institute, December 21, 2005, <http://www.epi.org/content.cfm/pm110>.

B. Profits Up, Average Family Income Down

"Inflation adjusted hourly and weekly wages are still below where they were at the start of the recovery in November 2001. Yet, productivity—the growth of the economic pie—is up by 13.5%. Wage growth has been shortchanged because 35% of the growth of total income in the corporate sector has been distributed as corporate profits, far more than the 22% of previous periods. Consequently, median household income (inflation-adjusted) has fallen five years in a row and is 4% lower in 2004 than in 1999, falling from $46,129 to $44,389."

SOURCE: Lawrence Mishel and Ross Eisenbrey, "What's Wrong with the Economy?," Economic Policy Institute, December 21, 2005, <http://www.epi.org/content.cfm/pm110>.

"The median income of American households rose by an inflation-adjusted 1.1% last year after falling five years in a row, the Census Bureau said in its annual report on the well-being of Americans. But the gap between the best-off and worst-off Americans widened last year, continuing a trend that dates to the early 1970s with a pause in the late 1990s. The top fifth of American households claimed 50.4% of all income last year, the largest slice since the Census Bureau started tracking the data in 1967. . . . Although the overall economy has grown 11.7% since the recessionary year of 2001, the income of the median household is down 0.5% in that period. Moreover, earnings for full-time workers employed year-round dropped last year. The median man's earnings declined 1.8% . . . and the median woman's earnings dropped 1.3%."

SOURCE: Robert Guy Matthews, "Median Household Income Rises 1.1%," *Wall Street Journal*, August 30, 2006.

In a subsequent article that worries about rising labor costs, the *Journal* tells us that "profit margins are at a 40-year high."

SOURCE: Greg Ip, "Puzzling Economic Data Are Explained, Bringing Some Welcome News on Inflation," *Wall Street Journal*, September 18, 2006.

C. Distribution of Household Income in 2004 and Changes since 1995

Lowest quintile: 3.4%; change since 1995: -8.5%
Second quintile: 8.7%; change since 1995: -4.5%
Third quintile: 14.7%; change since 1995: -3.2%
Fourth quintile: 23.2%; change since 1995: 0
Fifth quintile: 50.1%; change since 1995: +2.9%

SOURCE: U.S. Census Bureau, "News Conference on 2004 Income, Poverty, and Health Insurance Estimates from the Current Population Survey," figure 11, <http://www.census.gov/hhes/www/img/incpov04/fig11.jpg>.

D. Rising Profits Not Going to Workers

"Commerce Department data on national income trends released on August 27 [2004] point toward troubling developments in the current economic recovery. Of greatest concern, wage and salary growth for workers has been exceptionally poor while corporate profits have enjoyed unusually high gains. . . . The share of income growth, after adjusting for inflation, that has gone to wages and salaries has been only about one-third as much as has gone to corporate profits. This contrasts sharply with other recoveries since the end of World War II; during the other recoveries, the share of income growth that went to wages and salaries averaged *more than twice* as much as the share going to corporate profits."

The report then provides a table that indicates that 15% of the current economic recovery's "national real income growth" is going to wages and salaries, while 47% is going to corporate profits. The average for other post–World War II recoveries is 49% going to wages and salaries and 21% going to corporate profits.

Tracking out historical trends, the same report also tells us: "The share of national income that consists of wages and salaries [as indicated by Commerce Department data] was at the lowest level ever recorded, with data available back to 1929," whereas "after-tax corporate profits comprise the largest share of national income in 75 years. . . . High pre-tax corporate profits and low corporate income taxes have resulted in after-tax corporate profits in the first half of 2004 that represent a larger share of national income than in any year since 1929."

SOURCE: David Kamin and Isaac Shapiro, "An Uneven Recovery: New Government Data Show Corporate Profits Enjoying Unusually Large Gains, while Workers' Incomes Lag Behind," Center for Budget and Policy Priorities, September 3, 2004, <http://www.cbpp.org/9-3-04ui.htm>.

E. Inequality of National Income Distribution in Various Nations

These figures represent the share of the poorest quintile in the national income:
Japan: 10.6%
Czech Republic: 10.3%
Finland: 10.1%
Korea: 9.7%
Norway: 9.7%
Sweden: 9.1%
India: 8.1%
France: 7.2%
United Kingdom: 6.1%
China: 5.9%
Ecuador: 5.4%
United States: 5.2%
Peru: 4.4%
Mexico: 3.4%
Brazil: 2.2%
South Africa: 2.0%

SOURCE: *2003 World Bank Atlas* (Washington, D.C.: Development Data Group, World Bank, 2003), 56–57.

F. Declining Social Mobility

"There is little doubt that the American social ladder is getting higher. In 1980–2002 the share of total income earned by the top 0.1% of earners more than doubled. But there is also growing evidence that the ladder is getting stickier: that intergenerational mobility is no longer increasing, as it did during the post-war boom, and may well be decreasing. This is hardly the first time that America has threatened to calcify into a class society. In the Gilded Age, in the late 19th and early 20th centuries, the robber barons looked like turning into an English upper class. But this time round it could be much harder to restore the American ideal of equality of opportunity. The reason for this lies in the paradox at the heart of the new meritocracy. These days the biggest determinant of how far you go in life is how far you go in education. The gap in income between the college-educated and the non-college-educated rose from 31% in 1979 to 66% in 1997. But access to college is increasingly determined by social class. The proportion of students from upper-income families at the country's elite colleges is growing once again, having declined dramatically after the second world war. Only 3% of students in the most selective universities come from the bottom income quartile, and only 10% come from the bottom half of the income scale."

SOURCE: "Minding the Gap," *Economist*, June 11, 2005, 50.

G. Declining Benefits and Increased Financial Insecurity

"American workers do, though, have plenty of other reasons for feeling anxious. Although the way companies hire and fire has not changed much, there have been tremendous changes in the kinds of risk that individual workers have to bear. Corporations have scaled back benefits, most notably health coverage and pensions. The percentage of companies that offer health benefits to their employees has dropped thirteen percent in the past five years, and even employees who are covered now generally pay more of their own costs. With pensions, the shift has been fundamental: defined-benefit plans, in which companies guarantee a set payout to employees, have been gradually replaced with defined-contribution plans, like 401(k)s. . . . With a defined-benefit plan, the company assumes the risk of investing assets, absorbing the impact of market downturns, but with a 401(k) it is entirely up to the employee to prosper or plummet. Compounding these problems is the fact that the workforce has become increasingly stratified. Companies now tie compensation more closely to performance, so that people at the top take home much more, relative to their colleagues, than did the high-fliers of thirty-five years ago. Meanwhile, the risk exposure of anyone unfortunate enough to lose a job has soared. People who are unemployed stay unemployed, on average, about fifty per cent longer now than they did in the seventies, and only about half as many receive unemployment insurance as did so in 1947. Furthermore, the explosion in health-care costs means that the consequences of forfeiting company health insurance are graver than ever. So even though incomes have risen over the past three decades, they fluctuate much more than they once did. Economists estimate that income volatility is about twice what it was in the early seventies. Some of these changes make good business sense. But cumulatively they add up to what Jacob Hacker, a political scientist at Yale, calls 'the great risk shift.' The underlying problem is that workers are not being compensated with higher wages for taking on all this new risk. Real wages for the eighty percent of Americans whom the government labels 'production and nonsupervisory workers' have actually fallen since 2001, and, even after a burst of growth in the late nineties, the average household income is only slightly above where it was in 1973. This, and not rates of lifetime employment, is the true difference between employment today and in the sixties. Back then, real wages grew steadily year after year, rising roughly in tandem with productivity. Today, real wages are stagnant, and most of the economy's gains in productivity are going to shareholders or to people at the top of the corporate pyramid. More risk, less reward: now, that's something to worry about."

SOURCE: James Surowiecki, "Lifers," *New Yorker*, January 16, 2006, 29.

8. CEO SALARIES

A. As Percentages of Average Employee's Wages in Various Countries

United States: 531:1
Brazil: 57:1
Mexico: 45:1
United Kingdom: 25:1
France: 16:1
Germany: 11:1
Japan: 10:1

SOURCE: Gretchen Morgensen, "Explaining (or Not) Why the Boss Is Paid So Much," *New York Times*, January 25, 2004.

United States: 475:1
United Kingdom: 22:1
South Africa: 21:1
Canada: 20:1
France: 15:1
Japan: 11:1

SOURCE: "Are CEOs Worth Their Weight in Gold?," *Wall Street Journal*, January 21–22, 2006.

B. Growth in U.S. Executive Compensation, 1993–2004

"CEO Compensation packages" grew over 100% (adjusted for inflation) from 1993 to 2004, while compensation packages for the top five executives grew nearly 90%. "The ratio of aggregate top-five compensation to the aggregate earnings of these firms increased from 5 percent in 1993–95 to about 10 percent in 2001–03."

SOURCE: Lucian Bebchuk and Yaniv Grinstein, "The Growth of Executive Pay," *Oxford Review of Economic Policy* 21, no. 2 (2005): 283–303.

9. HEALTH CARE STATISTICS

A. Numbers of Uninsured

"In 2003 45 million Americans, more than one out of every six people, had no health insurance. That number, as large as it is, tells an incomplete and potentially misleading story, because many more people are uninsured for some period over any two-year time span. In 2002 and 2003 nearly 82 million people—one out of every three Americans—went without health insurance for all or part of the two years. Most were average people in working families. Nearly eight out of ten were working, and another 6 percent were looking for work. Only 15 percent were not in the labor force, in most cases because they were disabled, chronically ill, or family caregivers."

SOURCE: Jill Quadagno, *One Nation, Uninsured* (New York: Oxford University Press, 2005), 3.

B. Health Care Costs and Outcomes in the United States

"The United States continues to spend significantly more on health care than any country in the world. In 2002, Americans spent 53 percent per capita more than the next highest country, Switzerland, and 140 percent above the median industrialized country. The study's authors analyzed whether two possible reasons—supply constraints and malpractice litigation—could explain the difference in health care costs. They found that neither factor accounted for a large portion of the U.S. spending differential . . . U.S. citizens spent $4,267 per capita on health care. The country with the next highest per capita expenditure, Switzerland, spent $3,366 per capita. The median OECD country [a group of 30 industrialized nations] spent $2,193 per capita."

SOURCE: "U.S. Still Spends More on Health Care Than Any Other Country," Public Health News Center, Johns Hopkins Bloomberg School of Public Health, July 12, 2005, <http://www.jhsph.edu/publichealthnews/press_releases/2005/anderson_healthspending.html>.

"The reason why we spend so much more money on health care in the United States than they do in other industrialized countries is because we spend 2 to 2.5 times more for the same services offered in other countries.

"Q: If we are paying more for health care than other countries, are we healthier?

"A: The short answer is, no. We originally looked at data on life expectancy and infant mortality among industrialized countries. It showed that the United States had lower rates of life expectancy and higher infant mortality rates than other industrialized countries. However, we know that life expectancy and infant mortality were primarily determined by other factors other than medical costs. We then focused our research on a series of indicators that were related to what health care actually provides. For instance, if you were a woman diagnosed with breast cancer, what is your prognosis over five years? What we found was that people in the United States did not do significantly better on most indicators compared to people in Canada, Australia, New Zealand, and England. Overall, although we are spending 2.5 times more for health care, our health outcomes are no better, and in some cases worse, than other industrialized countries. . . .

"Q: So why are we paying more?

"A: The simplest answer is that we just pay more for comparable services. I wouldn't mind paying more if I got better service, but we don't. . . .

"Q: Do other countries spend more tax dollars on health care?

"A: Surprisingly, the U.S. ranks third in relation to other industrialized countries when it comes to spending federal dollars on health care, even though our federal spending only covers 25 percent of the population. Other countries manage to cover a much larger percentage of their populations with their tax dollars. The reason is that they pay much lower prices."

SOURCE: "It's the Prices, Stupid: An Interview with Gerald Anderson," Public Health News Center, Johns Hopkins University Bloomberg School of Public Health, August 24, 2005, <http://www.jhsph.edu/publichealthnews/articles/2005/anderson_prices/html>.

10. CAMPAIGN COSTS, GERRYMANDERING, AND THE
RISING ROLE OF MONEY IN POLITICS

A. *Rising Campaign Costs*

"Since first being systematically compiled in the 1970s, campaign expenditures have risen substantially, even exceeding the overall rise in the cost of living. Campaign finance authority Herbert Alexander estimated that $540 million was spent on all elections in the US in 1976, rising to some $3.9 billion in 2000. Early indications are that spending in 2004 greatly exceeded that level. Aggregate costs of House and Senate campaigns increased eightfold between 1976 and 2000, from $115.5 million to $1.007 billion, while the cost of living rose threefold; the 2002 elections, however, recorded a drop in overall spending, to $936 million. Campaign costs for average winning candidates, a useful measure of the real cost of seeking office, show an increase in the House from $87,000 in 1976 to $891,000 in 2002; a winning Senate race went from $609,000 in 1976 to $4.9 million in 2002 (not adjusted for inflation)."

SOURCE: Joseph E. Cantor, "Campaign Financing," CRS Issue Brief for Congress, Congressional Research Service, Washington, D.C., CRS-2, 2005, <http://www.infousa.ru/government/1b87020.pdf>.

Presidential candidates spent a total of $671 million for the 2000 election but $1,230 million for the contest in 2004. Although there were only 76 competitive congressional seats in 2004, in contrast to 104 in 2000, total spending for congressional races in 2004 was $1,259 million, up from $1,007 million in 2000.

SOURCE: David B. Magleby, Anthony Corrado, and Kelly D. Patterson, eds., *Financing the 2004 Election* (Washington, D.C.: Brookings Institution Press, 2006), 71, 151.

B. *Gerrymandered Congressional Districts*

"In 2002, eighty-one incumbents [in the House of Representatives] ran unopposed by a major party candidate. 'There are now about four hundred [out of 435] safe seats in Congress,' Richard Pildes, a professor of law at NYU, said. 'The level of competitiveness has plummeted to the point where it is hard to describe the House as involving competitive elections at all these days. The House isn't just ossified; it's polarized, too. Members of the House answer only to primary voters, who represent the extreme partisan edge of both parties. As a result, collaboration and compromise between the parties have almost disappeared. . . .

"Even in states where voters were evenly divided, the Republicans used their advantage in the state capitols to transform their congressional delegations [after the 2000 census]. In Florida . . . the new district lines sent eighteen Republicans and seven Democrats to the House [in the 2002 elections]. In the Gore state of Michigan, which lost a seat in redistricting, the delegation went from 9–7 in favor of the Democrats to 9–6 in favor of the Republicans—even though Democratic congressional candidates received thirty-five thousand more votes than their Republican opponents in 2002.

[Democratic Party–controlled legislatures in California and Maryland have drawn districts that favor their party, as Toobin mentions elsewhere in his article.]

"One state that has gone its own way is Iowa, which turned redistricting over to a nonpartisan civil-service commission after the 2000 Census. Consequently, four of Iowa's five House races in 2002 were competitive, so a state with one percent of the seats in the House produced ten percent of the nation's close elections."

SOURCE: Jeffrey Toobin, "The Great Election Grab," *New Yorker*, December 8, 2003, 64–65, 80.

C. Noncompetitive Elections

"In 2002, only fifteen of 435 congressional races were decided by four percentage points or less. Of the fifty congressional incumbents who ran in California, not one lost, and all got at least 58 percent of the vote. . . . In 2004, just 2 percent of House incumbents and a single Senate incumbent . . . lost."

SOURCE: Stephen Macedo et al., *Democracy at Risk: How Political Choices Undermine Citizen Participation, and What We Can Do about It* (Washington, D.C.: Brookings Institution Press, 2005), 20.

D. Growth in Lobbying

"The expansion of lobbying began in the 1960s and has continued ever since. In the mid-1950s there were 5,000 registered lobbyists in Washington; they doubled by 1970, then doubled again by 1990. . . . In 1979 there were 117 health groups in Washington. By 1993, with President Clinton proposing sweeping changes in this area, that number had jumped sevenfold."

SOURCE: Fareed Zakaria, *The Future of Freedom: Illiberal Democracy at Home and Abroad* (New York: Norton, 2003), 173.

"The number of registered lobbyists in Washington has more than doubled since 2000 to more than 34,750 while the amount that lobbyists charge their new clients has increased by as much as 100 percent."

SOURCE: Jeffrey H. Birnbaum, "The Road to Riches Is Called K Street: Lobbying Firms Hire More, Pay More, Charge More to Influence Government," *Washington Post*, June 22, 2005.

NOTES

INTRODUCTION

1. Jacob S. Hacker, *The Great Risk Shift: The Assault on American Jobs, Families, Health Care, and Retirement and How You Can Fight Back* (New York: Oxford University Press, 2006). Hacker's important book documents the increasing volatility in income, the dramatic rise in bankruptcies, and the growing fear of being laid off from one's job as some of the evidence of this shift.

2. However, if the information at <http://www.bartleby.com/73/1073.html> is correct, the actual author is Wendell Phillips (1811–84), who in a speech given in Boston in 1852 said: "Eternal vigilance is the price of liberty—power is ever stealing from the many to the few," a sentiment that captures the spirit of liberalism as this book presents it.

3. John Dewey, *The Public and Its Problems* (1927; repr., Athens, Ohio: Swallow Press, 1980); John Rawls, *A Theory of Justice* (Cambridge: Harvard University Press, 1971); Martha Nussbaum, *Women and Human Development: The Capabilities Approach* (Cambridge: Cambridge University Press, 2000). See also Rawls's more reader-friendly presentation of his views in *Justice as Fairness: A Restatement* (Cambridge: Harvard University Press, 2001). My inclusion of FDR as a political philosopher will strike some readers as more odd. But Roosevelt's speeches lay out a wide-ranging and crucial version of "modern" American liberalism that has both shaped our nation's history and won wide acceptance among its people. See Franklin Delano Roosevelt, *Great Speeches*, ed. John Grafton (Mineola, N.Y.: Dover Thrift Editions, 1999). Cass R. Sunstein, *The Second Bill of Rights: FDR's Unfinished Revolution and Why We Need It More Than Ever* (New York: Basic Books, 2004), provides a convincing portrait of FDR as an important political thinker and visionary.

4. I take the term "essentially contestable" from David Wiggins, *Needs, Values, Truth: Essays in the Philosophy of Value*, 3rd ed. (Cambridge: Cambridge University Press, 1998), 314. Wiggins takes the term from W. B. Gallie's 1955 essay, "Essentially Contested Concepts," *Proceedings of the Aristotelian Society*, vol. 56.

5. Thomas Nagel, "Progressive but Not Liberal," *New York Review of Books*, May 25, 2006, 46.

6. Dewey, *The Public and Its Problems*, 134; Rawls, *A Theory of Justice*, 134.

7. Norberto Bobbio, *Left and Right* (Chicago: University of Chicago Press, 1996), 69.

BOOK ONE

1. Some radical Protestant sects, like the Levellers during the English Civil War, were democrats during the era when liberalism was just emerging. But democracy as a shaping influence on the form modern governments and political institutions actually

take comes historically after the influence of liberalism on those forms. Absolute precision in these matters is, of course, elusive. Locke and Kant did not call themselves liberal; the word "liberal" was first used to characterize a political position in 1820. So there is a certain anachronism in using the term to describe eighteenth-century thinkers and political figures. But the political stance that comes to be called "liberalism" is deeply indebted to Locke, Kant, and the American founders, and thus justifies the retrospective identification of the liberal elements in their thought.

2. Stanley Elkins and Eric McKitrick, *The Age of Federalism: The Early American Republic, 1788–1800* (New York: Oxford University Press, 1993), 451. Sean Wilentz, *The Rise of American Democracy: Jefferson to Lincoln* (New York: Norton, 2005), makes a similar assertion: "This book's simple title describes the historical arc of its subject. Important elements of democracy existed in the infant American republic of the 1780s, but the republic was not democratic. Nor, in the minds of those who governed it, was it supposed to be. A republic . . . was meant to secure the common good through the ministrations of the most worthy, enlightened men. A democracy . . . dangerously handed power to the impassioned, unenlightened masses. Democracy, the eminent Federalist political leader George Cabot wrote as late as 1804, was '*the government of the worst*.' Yet by the 1830s, as Alexis de Tocqueville learned, most Americans proclaimed that their country was a democracy as well as a republic" (xvii).

3. Garry Wills, *Explaining America* (Garden City, N.Y.: Doubleday, 1981), esp. 216–47, provides an extended discussion of Madison's reasons for preferring a republic to a democracy, a position explicitly stated in Federalist No. 10.

4. Louis Hartz, *The Liberal Tradition in America: An Interpretation of American Political Thought since the Revolution* (New York: Harcourt, Brace and World, 1955), assails "our modern confusion of Jeffersonian theory with European theories of laissez faire," warning that a failure to consider context leads to misunderstanding: "Words that look the same can be very misleading indeed" (100). Wilentz, *Rise of American Democracy*, writes: "Although he couched his proposals in the familiar Jeffersonian doctrines of limited government—themes that later readers, critics and admirers alike have sometimes confused for conservative laissez-faire—Van Buren, like Jackson, took them to mean that the government should not be enlarged to serve the interests of a privileged and ambitious few. 'It is not [government's] legitimate object,' he bluntly asserted, 'to make men rich.' Van Buren's conception of limited government did not preclude regulation for the public good" (459). Joyce Appleby's *Capitalism and a New Social Order: The Republican Vision of the 1790s* (New York: New York University Press, 1984) offers the most nuanced version of the thesis that Jefferson's political ideals lent themselves to the development of an economic sphere understood as "private," as outside the purview of the state.

5. In Jerry Z. Muller, ed., *Conservatism: An Anthology of Social and Political Thought from David Hume to the Present* (Princeton: Princeton University Press, 1997), Muller writes that "conservatism was recast in response to the more egalitarian and interventionist direction of liberalism and to the rise of socialism. It was the growing opposition to capitalism in late nineteenth-century America which called forth a new brand of American conservatism" (233).

6. Various writers on the founders have argued that they were republicans and neither democrats nor liberals. But I agree with Gordon S. Wood, *The Creation of the American Republic, 1776–1787* (Chapel Hill: University of North Carolina Press, 1998), that

"republicanism has come to seem to many scholars to be a more distinct and palpable body of thought than it was in fact" and that the founders' republicanism contained many basic commitments we now understand as liberal (vii–x).

7. Robert A. Dahl, *How Democratic Is the American Constitution?* (New Haven: Yale University Press, 2001), eloquently and concisely explains how and where the Constitution is not democratic, concluding that "the beliefs of Americans in the legitimacy of their constitution will remain, I think, in constant tension with their beliefs in the legitimacy of democracy" (39).

8. Russell Kirk, *The Portable Conservative Reader* (New York: Viking Press, 1982), xxv–xxvi.

9. David J. Siemers, *Ratifying the Republic: Antifederalists and Federalists in Constitutional Time* (Stanford, Calif.: Stanford University Press, 2002), 74–105, provides an excellent guide to the differences between Hamilton and Madison, especially that Hamilton believed power must reside in one, sovereign body whereas Madison thought power could be distributed between the states and the national government—and should be so distributed as a bulwark against tyranny.

10. James Madison, Federalist No. 47, quoted from *The Federalist* (New York: Barnes and Noble, 2006), 268. Subsequent references to the Federalist Papers come from this edition, with page numbers given parenthetically in the text.

11. Quoted from Siemers, *Ratifying the Republic*, 91.

12. Jefferson expresses this view in a letter to Madison dated September 6, 1789. Madison was less than thrilled with the idea, as his letter to Jefferson of February 4, 1790, makes clear. Both letters can be found in Susan Dunn, ed., *Something That Will Surprise the World: The Essential Writings of the Founding Fathers* (New York: Basic Books, 2006), 283–88, 392–95.

13. Steven Lukes, ed., *Power* (New York: New York University Press, 1986), 9–10.

14. Hamilton offers the most succinct statement of the expedient of "checks and balances" in Federalist No. 9, where he celebrates this development as one of the great discoveries of the "modern" age. "The regular distribution of power into distinct departments—the introduction of legislative balances [*sic*] and checks—the institution of courts composed of judges, holding their offices during good behavior—the representation of the people in the legislature by deputies of their own election—these are either wholly new discoveries or have made their principal process towards perfection in modern times" (47). Madison's most succinct statement on this subject is his short 1792 essay, "Government of the United States," which begins: "Power being found by universal experience liable to abuses, a distribution of it into separate departments, has become a first principle of free governments." Quoted from James Madison, *Writings* (New York: Library of America, 1999), 508.

15. Gary Wills, *James Madison* (New York: Henry Holt, 2002), argues that Madison's ideas of political freedom were derived from his prior commitment to the idea of religious freedom. "Madison's views on religious freedom are the inspiration for all that was best in his later political thought. . . . Some modern critics of Madison's separation of church from state think it is a 'secularist' position, one that somehow downgrades or disables religion. On the contrary, he observed the greater sincerity of religion practiced under conditions of freedom. This became a touchstone for him of the blessings of freedom in general. It was a religious insight before it was a political one" (18).

16. I will have much to say about "civil society" (aka "the public sphere") in this book. My two major sources are G. W. F. Hegel, *The Philosophy of Right*, trans. T. M. Knox (Oxford: Oxford University Press, 1967), and Jürgen Habermas, *Structural Transformation of the Public Sphere* (Cambridge: MIT Press, 1991). Overviews of the topic can be found in Jean L. Cohen and Anthony Arato, *Civil Society and Political Theory* (Cambridge: MIT Press, 1992), and John Keane, *Civil Society: Old Images, New Visions* (Stanford, Calif.: Stanford University Press, 1998). Useful collections that discuss "civil society" from a variety of perspectives are Craig Calhoun, ed., *Habermas and the Public Sphere* (Cambridge: MIT Press, 1992), and John Keane, ed., *Civil Society and the State: New European Perspectives* (London: Verso, 1988).

17. Isaiah Berlin, *Four Essays on Liberty* (New York: Oxford University Press, 1969), xl.

18. Albrecht Wellmer, "Models of Freedom in the Modern World," *Philosophical Forum* 21 (1989): 227–52, offers a clear overview of this distinction between "negative" and "positive" views of freedom. The crux is that once we accept that "human individuals are essentially *social* individuals," freedom is recognized as derived from and dependent on "the structures, institutions, practices, and traditions of a larger social whole" (228–29).

19. Hamilton clearly states that the Constitution is the supreme and "fundamental" law in the land precisely because it is the law that has been *directly* ratified by the people, who are the "superior" power. Thus both the legislative and judicial branches are subject to the Constitution—and that is why legislation passed by Congress must be subject to judicial review. Congress cannot decide for itself if its laws are constitutional, since it will not have the requisite impartiality. (No man should judge his own case.) Thus, the judiciary must perform the review. But both the judiciary and the legislature are subordinate to the Constitution. Here is the relevant passage, with the context being Hamilton's denial that judicial review somehow makes the judiciary superior to the legislature: "Nor does this conclusion [about the need for judicial review] by any means suppose a superiority of the judicial to the legislative power. It only supposes that the power of the people is superior to both; and that where the will of the legislature declared in its statutes, stands in opposition to that of the people declared in the constitution, the judges ought to be governed by the latter, rather than the former. They ought to regulate their decisions by the fundamental laws, rather than by those which are not fundamental" (Federalist No. 78: 430–31).

20. Siemers, *Ratifying the Republic*, 88.

21. In Federalist No. 44, Madison explains why it was important that the Constitution not aim for completeness. It is to provide a legal framework, not specified rules that aim to cover every case that might arise in the (unforeseeable and unpredictable) future. It would be "chimerical," he insists "to attempt . . . a compleat digest of laws on every subject to which the constitution relates; accommodated not only to the existing state of things, but to all possible changes which futurity might produce: For in every new application of a general power, the *particular* powers, which are the means of attaining the *object* of the general power, must always necessarily vary with that object; and be often properly varied whilst the object remains the same" (252).

22. It does not help matters that both "strict constructionists" and those who argue that the Constitution must adapt to changing circumstances can quote Madison to support their position. In his debates during the 1790s with Hamilton over the new

national government's financial policies, Madison reneged on his strong advocacy of a powerful national government and of an evolving Constitution and adopted positions that favored "states' rights" and "strict constructionism." Elkins and McKitrick, *Age of Federalism*, 231–35, tell this story particularly well, concluding with this observation: "Strict constructionism . . . is in a special sense the resort of persons under ideological strain. It represents a willingness to renounce a range of positive opportunities for action in return for a principle which will inhibit government from undertaking a range of things one does not approve of. It marks the point at which one prefers to see the Constitution not as a sanction for achieving one's own ends but as a protection against those designs of others which have come to be seen as usurping and corrupting" (234). The Constitution, like power itself, both enables and forbids. We can expect constant contention over what should be permitted or even purposively undertaken by the government and what actions the government should regulate or even prohibit. These conflicts will be adjudicated in the courts (they will also take place in the legislature) within the framework of a Constitution that is, in many cases, silent on the exact topic under consideration. Siemers, *Ratifying the Republic*, esp. 89–94, also places Madison's views about interpretation of the Constitution in the context of disputes with Hamilton's federalism—and concludes that Madison is never as inconsistent as some historians claim and always occupies a middle ground between "strict" and "loose" construction. See Wills, *Explaining America*, 48–54, for a contrasting argument that the Madison of the Federalist Papers is a "loose constructionist."

23. On October 19, 2005, political blogger Andrew Sullivan (<http://www.andrew-sullivan.com/>) wrote: "At the core of my compromise [on the question of abortion's legality] is an understanding that politics and morality are overlapping but separate spheres. That distinction between law and morality is at the heart of the liberal project; and attacking it is at the heart of the theo-conservative and hard left project. In that sense, I am a proud liberal." The conservative desire to collapse law and morality into one was articulated by Supreme Court Justice Antonin Scalia in his dissenting opinion in *Lawrence v. Texas* (No. 02–10, June 26, 2003): "The ancient proposition that a governing majority's belief that a certain sexual behavior is 'immoral and unacceptable' constitutes a rational basis for regulation" (<http://www.law.cornell.edu/supct/html/02-102.ZD.html>).

24. E. P. Thompson, *Whigs and Hunters* (New York: Pantheon Books, 1975), 258–69, offers a balanced account of just what the rule of law can—and cannot—accomplish.

25. Rick Fantasia and Kim Voss, *Hard Work: Remaking the American Labor Movement* (Berkeley: University of California Press, 2004), esp. chap. 2 (34–77), document the various ways that union organizing and activism are currently undermined by federal and local authorities' turning a blind eye to employers' retaliations against employees who are pro-union.

26. I am especially relying on Section V, "Of the Obligation of Promises," of Part Two of the Third Book, entitled "Of Morals," of Hume's *A Treatise of Human Nature*, ed. L. A. Selby-Bigge (Oxford: Clarendon Press, 1975), but all of Part Two of the Third Book is relevant. My understanding of Hume is particularly indebted to chap. 9 of David Bloor's *Wittgenstein, Rules, and Institutions* (London: Routledge, 1997).

27. Arendt discusses promises in both *The Human Condition* (Chicago: University of Chicago Press, 1958), 243–47, and *On Revolution* (New York: Penguin, 1977), 169–78. In *On Revolution*, she concludes that "the making and keeping of promises . . . in the

realm of politics, may well be the highest human faculty" (175) since it forms the basis of society. "[A] community is based on reciprocity and presupposes equality; its actual content is a promise, and its result is indeed a 'society,' or 'cosociation' in the old Roman sense of *societas*" (170).

28. Jerry Z. Muller, *Conservatism*, 4–9, distinguishes "conservative" from "orthodox" thinkers on the basis of a conservative reliance on an assertion of "historical utility" to justify existing social arrangements as contrasted to the orthodox argument that such arrangements reflect the will of God. Burke and Hume, in Muller's view, revere the established and traditional arrangements because they have worked and because people have developed a loyalty to those arrangements based on that past (and continuing) success. No theological scaffolding or grounding operates in their thought. In other words, Burke and Hume are thoroughly "humanist" and thus occupy a position eschewed by many self-described conservatives in contemporary America.

29. We can call these conservatives either "natural law" or theological conservatives. Antonin Scalia explicitly embraces this theological view when he writes, in "God's Justice and Ours," *First Things* 123 (May 2002): 17–23, that he accepts St. Paul's view "that government . . . derives its moral authority from God" (19). Interestingly, however, Scalia is careful to say in that essay that, where he is legally bound by the Constitution, his religious beliefs are irrelevant to his judicial decisions. So he does recognize the autonomy of humanly made law from the dictates of a morality derived from God. It is the "moral authority" of government that comes from God—and, presumably, there are other kinds of authority. Of course, many theocrats make no such fine distinctions. Hume's argument is presented precisely to explain the fact of "moral authority" without making any appeal to the divine. Burke, by way of contrast, really does not address the question of authority's origins; he simply calls upon us to respect established authority, and he praises religion for the role it plays in fostering obedience while remaining mostly silent about whether religion is "true" in any way.

30. My discussion of Hume here is indebted to Martin Hollis, *Reason in Action: Essays in the Philosophy of Social Science* (Cambridge: Cambridge University Press, 1996), esp. chap. 6.

31. Here's Madison in Federalist No. 10: "No man is allowed to be a judge in his own cause; because his interest would certainly bias his judgment, and, not improbably, corrupt his integrity" (54). Gary Wills, *Explaining America*, particularly emphasizes the persistent return in the Federalist Papers of the essential principle that no one serve as judge in a case to which he is a party. In other words, a key check on power is that all actions must be subject to being tried by an impartial arbiter; the legality—or the justice—or any action can never be decided by the agent herself.

32. For a succinct introduction to the notion of performatives, see J. L. Austin, "Performative Utterances," in *Philosophical Papers*, 3rd. ed. (Oxford: Clarendon Press, 1979), 233–52. Austin develops the ideal more fully in *How to Do Things with Words* (Cambridge: Harvard University Press, 1965).

33. Because of the upsurge in ethnic conflicts following the collapse of the Soviet Union, there has been tremendous interest in nationalism over the past twenty years. Craig Calhoun, *Nationalism* (Minneapolis: University of Minnesota Press, 1997), offers a good historical overview of the rise of nationalism since the eighteenth century and of the different forms it has taken. Anthony D. Smith, *Nationalism: Theory, Ideology,*

History (Cambridge, England: Polity Press, 2001), emphasizes the "sacred" character of national identities and the loyalties they engender. Margaret Canovan's superb *Nationhood and Political Theory* (Brookfield, Vt.: Edward Elgar, 1996) directly addresses the challenge nationalism poses to accounts of liberal democracy that take the unity of "the people" and its loyalty to the state for granted rather than recognizing them as contingent facts that need to be explained. Bernard Yack, "Popular Sovereignty and Nationalism," *Political Theory* 29, no. 4 (2001): 517–36, argues that "the people" comes into existence politically (at the moment of constituting the nation), and it is a mistake to think that nationhood and the people exist prior to that moment of political founding. But it is an understandable mistake because of the desire to posit a "prepolitical basis of political community" (524). Hence, Yack writes, we can explain the rise of nationalism in the modern era (i.e., from 1700 on) because it is only then that sovereignty is lodged in "the people" and, thus, only then that the people's loyalty to and bonds with one another become such a crucial issue.

34. Jon Elster, *The Cement of Society: A Study of Social Order* (Cambridge: Cambridge University Press, 1989), and Benedict Anderson, *Imagined Communities: Reflections on the Origin and Spread of Nationalism* (London: Verso, 1983), are excellent resources for considering the question of what holds multiethnic and multireligious societies together.

35. In *The Subjection of Women*, Mill writes: "For, what is the peculiar character of the modern world—the difference which chiefly distinguishes modern institutions, modern social ideas, modern life itself, from those of times long past? It is, that human beings are no longer born to their place in life, and chained down by an inexorable bond to the place they are born to, but are free to employ their faculties, and such favourable chances as offer, to achieve the lot which may appear to them most desirable." Quoted from J. S. Mill, *Three Essays* (Oxford: Oxford University Press, 1975), 445.

36. Not surprisingly, considering the current migration of peoples across the globe, there has been a lot of hard thinking about what citizenship means and how that legal category can function in relation to current realities. Will Kymlicka, *Politics in the Vernacular: Nationalism, Multiculturalism, and Citizenship* (Oxford: Oxford University Press, 2001), and Kymlicka and Wayne Norman, eds., *Citizenship in Diverse Societies*, (Oxford: Oxford University Press, 2000), offer good overviews of contemporary issues and of various views on those issues. Seyla Benhabib's *The Rights of Others: Aliens, Residents, and Citizens* (Cambridge: Cambridge University Press, 2004) is a passionate and cogent engagement with the topic.

37. Jürgen Habermas uses the term "constitutional patriotism" for this nonethnic, non-nationalistic bond to political institutions: "The political culture of a country crystallizes around its constitution. Each national culture develops a distinctive interpretation of those constitutional principles that are equally embodied in other republican constitutions—such as popular sovereignty and human rights—in light of its own national history. A 'constitutional patriotism' based on these interpretations can take the place originally occupied by nationalism." Habermas, *The Inclusion of the Other* (Cambridge: MIT Press, 1998), 118. Habermas is clearly trying to work the same ground that David Hollinger's *Post-Ethnic America* (New York: Basic Books, 1995) explores with the concept of "civic nationalism." My thinking on these matters has been clarified and influenced by my colleague Jeff Spinner-Halev's discussion of

the strengths and weaknesses of this kind of patriotism compared with more familiar nationalistic loyalties in his (yet unpublished) essay, "Democracy, Nationalism, and Power," and by chapters 4, 6, and 7 of Amanda Anderson's *The Way We Argue Now* (Princeton: Princeton University Press, 2006).

38. Hollinger, *Post-Ethnic America*, 133–34.

39. In his introduction to Nathan Hauser and Christian Kloesel, eds., *The Essential Peirce: Selected Philosophical Writings*, vol. 1: *1867–1893* (Bloomington: University of Indiana Press, 1992), Hauser describes Peirce's notion of "fallibilism" as "the thesis that no inquirer can ever claim with full assurance to have reached the truth, for new evidence or information may arise that will reverberate throughout one's system of beliefs affecting even those most entrenched" (xxii). On Popper, see John Gray, "The Liberalism of Karl Popper," *Liberalisms: Essays in Political Philosophy* (New York: Routledge, 1989), 10–27.

40. See Immanuel Kant, "Perpetual Peace: A Philosophical Sketch," in H. S. Reiss, ed., *Political Writings* (Cambridge: Cambridge University Press, 1991), 93–130, and John Rawls, *Justice as Fairness: A Restatement* (Cambridge: Harvard University Press, 2001), 8–9, for his notion of a "well-ordered society," along with his recognition that "the idea . . . is plainly a very considerable idealization," one that, "given the fact of reasonable pluralism," may well be "impossible" (9).

41. Similarly, Alexander Hamilton, in Federalist No. 76, writes: "The supposition of universal venality in human nature is little less an error in political reasoning than the supposition of universal rectitude. The institution of delegated power implies that there is a portion of virtue and honor among mankind, which may be a reasonable foundation of confidence" (421). Clearly, Madison and Hamilton refused to accept unidimensional descriptions of "human nature."

42. Edmund Burke and Michael Oakeshott, among conservative thinkers, argue that purposive political action is not trustworthy and thus should be avoided. Various apologists for the free market make similar claims about purposive action (beyond the level of individual decisions motivated by self-interest) in economic affairs.

43. William James, in *Pragmatism*, writes: "On the pragmatist side we have only one edition of the universe, unfinished, growing in all sorts of places, especially in the places where thinking beings are at work." This pragmatist notion "of 'reality,' as something resisting, yet malleable" allows for work, for action, to make a difference. The "pluralistic pragmatist," James concedes, will seem a "happy-go-lucky anarchistic sort of creature" to the philosopher attached to identifying the necessary as distinct from the possible. For such thinkers, "the phrase '*must be*' is ever on its lips. The bellyband of its universe must be tight." Quoted from *Writings, 1902–1910*, ed. Bruce Kuklick (New York: Library of America, 1987), 600. Because there are multiple ways to live a life, James emphasizes the "ideal" (the goal or vision) that underwrites one's choices among those possibilities. Life takes on "significance" for the individual insofar as it is pursued in the light of an ideal. See James, "What Makes a Life Significant," *Writings, 1878–1899*, ed. Gerald E. Myers (New York: Library of America, 1992), 861–80. For a fuller discussion of James's pragmatic pluralism, see my essay "Literature as Equipment for Living: A Pragmatist Project," *Soundings: An Interdisciplinary Journal* 86, nos. 1–2 (2003): 119–48.

44. John Dewey, *Reconstruction in Philosophy* (Mineola, N.Y.: Dover Publications, 2004), is interested in importing the experimental attitude he finds in the sciences

to our approach to social, political, and moral questions. The resistance to this reverence for the sciences is, needless to say, widespread. But it is worth hearing—and then thinking about—how Dewey understands the "intelligent" approach to nonscientific issues that are, of course, deeply important to us. He contrasts his approach to what we might think of as armchair thinking or "theory." He writes: "Reason, as a Kantian faculty that introduces generality and regularity into experience, strikes us more and more as superfluous—the unnecessary creation of men addicted to traditional formalism and to elaborate terminology. Concrete suggestions arising from past experiences, developed and matured in the light of the needs and efficiencies of the present, employed as aims and methods of specific reconstruction [of received truths, institutions, or practices], and tested by success or failure in accomplishing this task of adjustment, suffice. To such empirical suggestions used in constructive fashion for new ends the name intelligence is given. . . . Intelligence is not something possessed once for all. It is in constant process of forming, and its retention requires constant alertness in observing consequences, an open-minded will to learn and courage in re-adjustment" (95–97). An armchair theory about what "human nature" renders possible or impossible forecloses the case prematurely.

45. Berlin's *Four Essays on Liberty* offer the most important articulation of his "value pluralism." For useful engagements with Berlin's version of pluralism, see Steven Lukes, *Liberals and Cannibals: The Implications of Diversity* (London: Verso, 2003), esp. chaps. 1, 3, 7–8.

46. Hannah Arendt, *The Origins of Totalitarianism* (San Diego: Harcourt Brace, 1966), defines totalitarianism as the attempt to erase the "reality" of "plurality" and replace it with a "fiction" of sameness. Totalitarian governments attempt "to organize the infinite plurality and differentiation of human beings as if all of humanity were just one individual" (438).

47. See Thomas Edsall, *Building Red America: The New Conservative Coalition and the Drive for Permanent Power* (New York: Basic Books, 2006). Edsall provides a shorter account of Rove's strategy in his essay, "Karl Rove's Juggernaut," *New Republic*, September 25, 2006, <http://www.tnr.com/doc.mhtml?i=20060925&s=edsall092506>.

48. Madison, *Writings*, 517.

49. William A. Galston, "Liberalism and Public Morality," in *Liberals on Liberalism*, ed. Alfonso J. Damico (Totowa, N.J.: Rowman and Littlefield, 1986), 129–47, offers the most compelling version of this argument that I have read. He concludes that "the moral commitments of liberalism" to noncoercion and to the virtue of tolerance "influence—and in some cases circumscribe—the ability of individuals within a liberal society to engage fully in particular ways of life. If, to be wholly effective, a religious doctrine requires control over the totality of individual life, including the formative social and political environment, then the classic liberal demand that religion be practiced 'privately' amounts to a substantive restriction on the free exercise of that religion. The manifold blessings of liberal social orders come at a price, and we should not be surprised when those who are asked to pay grow restive" (144). Galston is careful to distinguish this claim from the false one that "the scope for diversity in liberal societies is no greater than in closed or theocratic communities" (144).

50. The term "pluralism" as first used in twentieth-century political science by Harold Laski and Robert Dahl (among many others) retained a sense fairly close to Madison's notion of "factions." The pluralists were interested in the continued vital-

ity of different groups within modern democratic societies and in the contention/ negotiation between those groups for power and resources. In more recent years, however, discussions of pluralism have been interested in much more various sources of diversity within modern polities, including sources that are associated with markers of "identity." The issue is still "factions," but with a greatly expanded understanding of the various forms factions take and the various ways they may interact, compete, conflict, cooperate, and communicate. For an excellent discussion of the movement from what could be called "modern" notions of pluralism to "postmodern" notions, see Gregor McLennan, *Pluralism* (Minneapolis: University of Minnesota Press, 1995). For a full-scale argument for pluralism working from postmodern assumptions, see William Connolly, *Pluralism* (Durham, N.C.: Duke University Press, 2005). William A. Galston, *Liberal Pluralism* (Cambridge: Cambridge University Press, 2002) and *The Practice of Liberal Pluralism* (Cambridge: Cambridge University Press, 2005), Nicholas Rescher, *Pluralism: Against the Demand for Consensus* (Oxford: Clarendon Press, 1995), and Richard E. Flathman, *Pluralism and Liberal Democracy* (Baltimore: The Johns Hopkins University Press, 2005), approach pluralism through a lens closer to my own. I have found Galston's work especially convincing and inspiring. For a strong argument against pluralism that insists that liberalism and pluralism are incompatible commitments, pulling in different directions, see Brian Barry, *Culture and Equality: An Egalitarian Critique of Multiculturalism* (Cambridge: Harvard University Press, 2001). My understanding of rights as political, not natural, underwrites my disagreement with Barry's position, as with the similar position taken by Martha Nussbaum (in her essay, "Human Functioning and Social Justice: In Defense of Aristotelian Essentialism," *Political Theory* 20, no. 2 [1992]) on these particular issues. In contrast to Barry and Nussbaum's universalism, Todd Gitlin's *The Twilight of Common Dreams: Why America Is Wracked by Culture Wars* (New York: Henry Holt, 1996) laments the loss of a unifying leftist vision, one that he thinks has been swamped by the "politics of difference" practiced by today's left.

51. John Locke's *A Letter concerning Toleration* (1689; repr., Indianapolis: Hackett Publishing, 1983) is still the founding text for liberal accounts of tolerance. David A. J. Richards, *Toleration and the Constitution* (Oxford: Oxford University Press, 1989), examines tolerance in the American constitutional context, whereas Michael Walzer, *On Toleration* (New Haven: Yale University Press, 1997), offers a more general reflection on tolerance's benefits. Perez Zagorin's *How the Idea of Tolerance Came to the West* (Princeton: Princeton University Press, 2003) traces the history of the rise of religious tolerance. For writers critical of liberal tolerance, see (from the left) Anna Elisabetta Galeotti, *Tolerance as Recognition* (Cambridge: Cambridge University Press, 2002), and Wendy Brown, *Regulating Aversion: Tolerance in the Age of Identity and Empire* (Princeton: Princeton University Press, 2006); and (from the right) Brad Stetson and Joseph G. Conti, *The Truth about Tolerance: Pluralism, Diversity, and the Culture Wars* (Downers Grove, Ill.: InterVarsity Press, 2005). For a succinct summary of such criticisms, see Stanley Fish, "The Trouble with Tolerance," *Chronicle of Higher Education: The Chronicle Review*, November 10, 2006, <http://chronicle.com/temp/reprint. php?id=f2281gdy909q6jfczpj22f7gtkg3cqft>.

52. Elkins and McKitrick, *Age of Federalism*, 290–91, offer us a signal instance of how the word "liberal" was associated with tolerance and a generous interpretation of

others' intentions in the Federalist period: "'How unfortunate,' [George] Washington wrote to Jefferson on August 23 [1792], '. . . whilst we are encompassed on all sides with avowed enemies and insidious friends, that internal dissensions should be harrowing and tearing our vitals.' Without 'more charity for the opinions and acts of one another,' he feared, the parts of government could not be kept together. 'My earnest wish, and my fondest hope therefore is, that instead of wounding suspicions and irritable charges, there may be liberal allowances—mutual forbearances—and temporising yieldings on *all sides*.'"

53. Part of the current decline of liberal values in the United States involves the "privatization" of public spaces and public goods. The increasing deregulation of the "public airwaves" and concentration of media outlets into a few megacorporations' hands offers one example. The abandonment of American downtowns and the growth in "gated communities" offers less public spaces for all to mingle. For excellent discussions of the threat to "civil society" posed by privatization, see Setha Low and Neil Smith, eds., *The Politics of Public Space* (New York: Routledge, 2006), and Si Kahn and Elizabeth Minnich, *The Fox in the Henhouse: How Privatization Threatens Democracy* (San Francisco: Berrett-Koehler Publishers, 2005).

54. Elkins and McKitrick, *Age of Federalism*, 451–61, offer a fascinating and convincing (at least to this reader) argument that civil society first emerged in America during the Federalist era, so that the passion among Americans for "voluntary associations" noted by Tocqueville when he visited in the 1830s was, they claim, almost completely unknown in this country before 1790. Thus, civil society arose precisely when Americans were establishing their way of making the Constitution a living document, one that is actually embodied in a set of political institutions and practices. Sean Wilentz, *Rise of American Democracy* (52–62), tells essentially the same story, but with a different emphasis, by focusing on the activities of the "democratic societies" that were active from 1792 to 1795.

55. Anderson, *Imagined Communities*, chap. 1.

56. Ashutosh Varshney, *Ethnic Conflict and Civil Life: Hindus and Muslims in India* (New Haven: Yale University Press, 2002), documents the extent to which intercommunal participation by Hindus and Muslims in particular locales correlates with lower levels of violence between the two ethnic groups. Interestingly, while Varshney does not completely dismiss casual, everyday encounters in the public square, he finds much stronger evidence for "the greater value of associational, as opposed to everyday, engagement" (281). "The key determinant of peace is *inter*communal civic life, not civic life per se" (282), and peace is even more likely where the different ethnic groups belong to and interact within what, following Tocqueville, we can characterize as "voluntary associations," that is, civic groups that are fairly formally constituted and have goals toward which the members work.

57. I take the term "public reason" from John Rawls, "The Idea of Public Reason," in *Deliberative Democracy: Essays on Reason and Politics*, ed. James Bohman and William Rehg (Cambridge: MIT Press, 1997), 93–141. I use the term rather differently than Rawls does; my understanding of it is much more rhetorical and much more expansive (not simply restricted to questions of the common or public good). But I want to activate Rawls's interest in the public giving of reasons. I have been greatly influenced by Robert B. Brandom's *Articulating Reasons: An Introduction to Inferentialism*

(Cambridge: Harvard University Press, 2000). Brandom describes his project as "a *rationalist* pragmatism [that] give[s] pride of place to practices of giving and asking for reasons" (11).

58. Kenneth Burke, *Attitudes toward History*, 2nd. ed. (Boston: Beacon Press, 1959), 341–42.

59. For good discussions of the concept of "recognition" and how it might be placed among other desires expressed by citizens in modern polities, see Charles Taylor et al., *Multiculturalism: Examining the Politics of Recognition*, ed. Amy Gutmann (Princeton: Princeton University Press, 1994); Nancy Fraser and Alex Honneth, *Redistribution or Recognition?: A Political-Philosophical Exchange* (London: Verso, 2003); and Robert R. Williams, *Hegel's Ethics of Recognition* (Berkeley: University of California Press, 1997). Patchen Markell's *Beyond Recognition* (Princeton: Princeton University Press, 2003) offers a dissenting view—that recognition is almost always attached to hierarchies that limit the possibilities of equality and justice.

60. Hannah Arendt, *The Human Condition* (Chicago: University of Chicago Press, 1958), contrasts "the sheltered life in the household" with "the merciless exposure of the *polis*" and concludes that the "courage" to venture into the public square is thus "one of the most elemental political attitudes," perhaps even "the political virtue par excellence" (35–36).

61. See my *Democracy's Children: Intellectuals and the Rise of Cultural Politics* (Ithaca: Cornell University Press, 2002), chap. 4.

62. Judith Shklar's "The Liberalism of Fear" (1989; repr. in Shaun P. Young, ed., *Political Liberalism: Variations on a Theme* (Albany: SUNY Press, 2004), 149–66) emphasizes the extent to which liberalism is a response to the threat of tyranny.

63. Franklin Delano Roosevelt, "Acceptance Speech at Democratic Party Convention, Philadelphia, June 27, 1936," in *Great Speeches*, ed. John Grafton (New York: Dover Publications, 1999), 49.

64. John Dewey, *Liberalism and Social Action* (1935; repr., New York: Capricorn Books, 1963), 57–58. Robert B. Westbrook, *John Dewey and American Democracy* (Ithaca: Cornell University Press, 1991), offers this account of Dewey's view: "Properly understood, Dewey argued, liberty was not just an abstract principle, but *power*, the 'effective power to do specific things.' . . . Equality was simply a demand for a distribution of liberty (power) which was conducive to the full development of the individuality of everyone in a society. . . . Equality was not opposed to liberty but was a democratic distribution of liberties. At the same time, 'the tragic breakdown of democracy is due to the fact that the identification of liberty with the maximum of unrestrained individualistic action in the economic sphere, under the institutions of capitalistic finance, is as fatal to the realization of liberty for all as it is to the realization of equality'" (435–36). Westbrook is quoting from Dewey's 1935 essay "Liberty and Social Control" and 1936 essay "Liberalism and Equality."

65. Shklar, "Liberalism of Fear," 149.

66. Sen's "capabilities approach" to understanding freedom and equality emphasizes the "capacity" of individuals to realize the ends they have freely chosen for themselves. His most nontechnical description of his views can be found in Sen, *Inequality Reexamined* (Cambridge: Harvard University Press, 1992). Martha Nussbaum's account in *Women and Human Development: The Capabilities Approach* (Cambridge: Cam-

bridge University Press, 2000) is more accessible for the noneconomist (like myself), and I have relied on it heavily.

67. Sen, *Inequality Reexamined*, 49.

68. Nussbaum, *Women and Human Development*, 70–71. Nussbaum goes on to provide a list (78–80) of those "core areas of human functioning." The list offers a sense of the "decent social minimum for a human life" but falls short of what would be needed for a fully "flourishing" life.

69. See ibid., 75. That alleviating extreme poverty is the first need is dramatized by the World Bank's estimate (in relation to the United Nation's Millennium Project to Reduce Poverty) that "half the world—nearly three billion people—live on less than $2 a day." Quoted from Anup Shah, "Causes of Poverty: Poverty Facts and Statistics," 1, <http://globalissues.org/TradeRelated/Facts.asp?p=1>. Shah offers detailed sources for—and interpretations of—this bald claim.

70. Roosevelt, *Great Speeches*, 48–49.

71. The information and quotations in this paragraph are from Ron Chernow, *Alexander Hamilton* (New York: Penguin Press, 2004), 210–16.

72. Wood, *Creation of the American Republic*, 89. Wood takes the view that slaveholders like Jefferson were only dimly aware of the Pandora's box their talk of equality opened up. But he is clear that the implications of that talk were almost immediately apparent to others—and seized on. "Few of the ideas developed in the controversy with England could be limited; they were in fact easily exploited in ways that had not been anticipated. By attempting to claim equality of rights for Americans against the English, 'without Respect to the Dignity of the Persons concerned,' even the most aristocratic of southern Whig planters, for example, were pushed into creating an egalitarian ideology that could and even as early as 1776 was being turned against themselves" (83).

73. Muller, *Conservatism*, 422. Robert Bork, *Slouching toward Gomarrah: Modern Liberalism and American Decline* (New York: Regan Books, 1996), solves this problem by telling us that Jefferson did not really mean what he said: "It was indeed stirring rhetoric, entirely appropriate for the purpose of rallying the colonists and justifying their rebellion to the world. But some caution is in order. The ringing phrases are hardly useful, indeed may be pernicious, if taken, as they commonly are, as a guide to action, governmental or private. Then the words press eventually toward extremes of liberty and the pursuit of happiness that court personal license and social disorder. The necessary qualifications assumed by Jefferson and the signers of the Declaration were not expressed in the document. It would rather have spoiled the effect to have added 'up to a point' or 'within reason' to Jefferson's resounding generalities" (57).

74. Tocqueville's doubts are reflected in the title of the chapter that begins his discussion of equality: "Why Democratic Nations Show a More and Enduring Ardent Love of Equality Than of Liberty." *Democracy in America*, trans. George Lawrence (New York: Harper and Row, 1966), vol. 2, pt. 2, chap. 1. Tocqueville's ambivalence comes from his worry that pursuit of equality brings various costs (mediocrity, for one) and, possibly, the impetus for a strong state. He thinks this latter danger can only be overcome by the existence of "voluntary associations" in a thriving civil society.

75. Along with Gordon S. Wood's (*Creation of the American Republic*) discussion of radical versions of equality during the Revolutionary period, see Charles Seller's *The*

Market Revolution: Jacksonian America, 1815–1846 (New York: Oxford University Press, 1991) for an account of popular agitation for social and economic equality during the pre–Civil War era.

76. For Madison's evolving views about political parties and, especially, the function of an "opposition party," see Richard Hofstadter, *The Idea of a Party System: The Rise of Legitimate Opposition in the United States, 1780–1840* (Berkeley: University of California Press, 1969), chap. 3.

77. Madison, "Parties," *Writings*, 504.

78. The particular cause of Madison's uneasiness was Hamilton's desire to repay the Revolutionary war debt at par. For Madison, there was a fundamental injustice in the fact that the soldiers who had fought the war and had taken government paper in exchange for their services had been forced to sell that debt for pennies on the dollar during the hard times following the end of the war. Now, eight to ten years later, men who had never worked for or suffered a day for the government would be making huge profits on the debt they had bought up as "speculators." Hamilton basically said that is the way financial markets operate—plus the government needs to honor its debt fully in order to establish its good credit. Madison found the fundamental unfairness of it—that the profit went to those who had possessed the economic wherewithal in the first place to wait the government out—outrageous. Thus Madison—with Jefferson as his ally—pushes the idea of equality in a liberal direction while Hamilton takes up the conservative position in American politics, which is to resist further movements to equality. I have rather oversimplified a very complex story here; I have been guided in my sense of how Madison's thoughts developed in the 1790s by Elkins and McKitrick's detailed account in *Age of Federalism*, esp. chaps. 3 and 7. Let me also add that I buy Elkins and McKitrick's assertion (also found in Wills's *Explaining America*) that there were no significant differences between Hamilton and Madison's viewpoints when they wrote the Federalist Papers. The differences only arose later and, I think, can be most plausibly traced to their fundamentally opposed views of economic inequality.

79. Wilentz, *Rise of American Democracy*, 76.

80. Quoted from <http://globalissues.org/TradeRelated/Facts.asp?p=1>, where the source is identified as the *New York Times*, in its Quote of the Day section on July 18, 2001.

81. "Social and economic inequalities are to satisfy two conditions: first, they are to be attached to offices and positions open to all under conditions of fair equality of opportunity; and second, they are to be to the greatest benefit of the least-advantaged members of society (the difference principle)" (Rawls, *Justice as Fairness*, 42–43). If the difference principle is adopted, the maximin rule provides a procedure for determining how much inequality to tolerate in a particular case: "It tells us to identify the worst outcome of each available alternative and then to adopt the alternative whose worst outcome is better than the worst outcomes of all the other alternatives" (96). For an excellent introduction to Rawls and the various debates/refinements that his work has inspired, see Harry Brighouse, *Justice* (Malden, Mass.: Polity, 2004). Samuel Fleischacker's *A Short History of Distributive Justice* (Cambridge: Harvard University Press, 2005) tracks notions of justice in relation to distribution from the Greeks onward.

82. James, *Writings, 1878–1899*, 598.

83. Brian Barry, *Why Social Justice Matters* (Malden, Mass.: Polity, 2005), contrasts

the "neo-liberal" or (in the American context) conservative view "that whatever distribution of opportunities and resources arises within a framework of liberal rights is necessarily just" with a "social justice" view (which I see as generally characteristic of "modern liberalism" in the United States) that "we should also be concerned about equal opportunities" (25) and the capacity to exercise those rights. Barry illustrates his point by talking about "medical care. The absence of a prohibition on its being supplied to anybody does nothing to guarantee that everybody has the opportunity to receive it. If the opportunity depends on the ability to pay for it, some will get good medical care, some will get basic medical care, and some will get none. That people with the same medical condition will have such unequal opportunities to obtain treatment . . . raise[s] issues of justice" (25–26).

84. Quoted from a survey conducted by the Pew Forum on Religion and Public Life in the spring of 2004. "The American Religious Landscape and Politics, 2004," 6, <http://pewforum.org/publications/surveys/gree.pdf>.

85. In *The Subjection of Women*, Mill rests "the great modern spiritual and social transition" on the liberal planks of liberty and equality: "The burthen of proof is supposed to be with those who are against liberty; who contend for any restriction or prohibition; either any limitation of the general freedom of human action, or any disqualification or disparity of privilege affecting one person or kind of persons, as compared with others. The *a priori* presumption is in favor of freedom and impartiality. It is held that there should be no restraint not required by the general good, and that the law should be no respecter of persons, but should treat all alike, save where dissimilarity of treatment is required by positive reasons, either of justice or of policy" (Mill, *Three Essays*, 428–29).

86. Robert Heilbroner, "The Socialization of the Individual in Adam Smith," *History of Political Economy* 14, no. 3 (1982): 427–39, discusses how the social embeddedness of individuals in Smith's *Theory of Moral Sentiments* appears in *The Wealth of Nations*, thus complicating any simple notion of Smith as an extreme individualist.

87. Margaret Thatcher said (to an interviewer from *Women's Own* magazine on October 31, 1987): "And, you know, there is no such thing as society. There are individual men and women, and there are families." Quoted from <http://www.briandeer.com/social/thatcher-society.htm>. Gary Becker, *The Economic Approach to Human Behavior* (Chicago: University of Chicago Press, 1976), provides an excellent and influential instance of rational choice theory taken to extremes that Adam Smith never imagined.

88. Amartya Sen's essay, "Rational Fools: A Critique of the Behavioral Foundations of Economic Theory," *Philosophy and Public Affairs* 6:4 (1977): 317–44, remains the essential refutation of the work of Becker and his ilk. Sen shows quite convincingly that the "economic man" who pursues only his self-interest would not only be considered a monster by all with whom he interacts, but also would fail to last a week in a world where, for better and worse, every human is deeply dependent on other humans.

89. John Dewey's rejection of classic liberal individualism is everywhere in his work. "The idea of a natural individual in his isolation possessed of full-fledged wants, of energies to be expended according to his own volition, and of a ready-made faculty of foresight and prudent calculation is as much a fiction in psychology as the doctrine of the individual in possession of antecedent political rights is one in politics," he writes in *The Public and Its Problems* (1927; repr., Athens, Ohio: Swallow Press, 1980), 102. George Herbert Mead, *Selected Writings* (Indianapolis: Bobbs-Merrill, 1964), esp. chap.

12, "The Social Self" (142–49), presents the interactional theory of the self that stands at the center of his thought. Jürgen Habermas, *The Philosophical Discourse of Modernity*, trans. Frederick Lawrence (Cambridge: MIT Press, 1987), esp. chaps. 1–4, offers a critique of the "subject and consciousness centered" self of modern philosophy, which Habermas then contrasts to the more social self figured in his communicative model of social relations. For a succinct summary of Taylor's view, see Charles Taylor, "The Dialogic Self," in *The Interpretive Turn*, ed. David Hiley, James Bohman, and Richard Shusterman (Ithaca: Cornell University Press, 1992). For a full rendering of his position, see Taylor, *Sources of the Self: The Making of Modern Identity* (Cambridge: Harvard University Press, 1989). I agree wholeheartedly with Alan Ryan when he claims that these critics of a certain version of liberal individualism are, no matter what they may say of themselves, liberal critics of liberalism, firmly within the world of goods and fundamental principles identified by liberalism (as contrasted to De Maistre, Marx, and Nietzsche who are nonliberal critics of liberalism). Extreme individualism is a straw man by now (except for some rational choice theorists and libertarian thinkers, and both groups hardly qualify as liberal any longer, if they ever did, since they reject almost all liberal social policies). Mainstream liberalism fully accepts, in Ryan's words, that "individuals need communities, and liberal communities consist of associated individuals. Modern individuals need flexible, forward-looking, tolerant communities to live in, and such communities can be sustained only by modern individuals who are looking for a meaningful existence in association" with others. Ryan, *John Dewey and the High Tide of American Liberalism* (New York: Norton, 1997), 359. Ryan adds for good measure that Taylor "is for the most part a Deweyan without knowing it" (363).

90. Hume is the key modern philosopher who insists that the individual is always embedded in social relations that both form her desires and are a crucial good to be desired (i.e., we desire to be loved and we desire the welfare of those we love). Not surprisingly, it has been feminist thinkers, often pursuing what has come to be called an "ethics of care," who have been at the forefront of recent efforts to contest theories that posit an autonomous individual. Annette Baier, *Moral Prejudices: Essays on Ethics* (Cambridge: Harvard University Press, 1994), explicitly returns to Hume in order to further this feminist line of thought. See esp. chaps. 4 and 5, titled respectively "Hume, the Women's Moral Theorist" and "Hume, the Reflective Women's Epistemologist?" Virginia Held's *Feminist Morality* (Chicago: University of Chicago Press, 1993), chaps. 8–10, offers a superb overview of feminist critiques and reworkings of classical liberal themes of liberty, equality, contract, and individualism.

91. Ryan, *John Dewey*, 40.

92. Hume is quoted from Wills, *Explaining America*, 191–92. Wills, following the work of Douglas Adair, demonstrates at length the influence of Hume's thought on Madison and Hamilton.

93. Madison, *Writings*, 422.

94. John Dewey, *Freedom and Culture* (New York: G. P. Putnam, 1939), 22–23.

95. Bruce Ackerman and Todd Gitlin, "We Answer to the Name of Liberals," *American Prospect Online*, October 18, 2006, <http://www.prospect.org/web>.

96. Cass R. Sunstein, *The Second Bill of Rights: FDR's Unfinished Revolution and Why We Need It More Than Ever* (New York: Basic Books, 2004).

97. Madison, *Writings*, 420.

98. Richard Labunski, *James Madison and the Struggle for the Bill of Rights* (New York:

Oxford University Press, 2006), tells this story of Madison's changing views—and of his concrete actions to get the Bill of Rights written and passed by the first Congress. See also Gordon S. Wood's "Without Him, No Bill of Rights," *New York Review of Books*, November 30, 2006, 54–57.

99. Andrew J. Bacevich's *The New American Militarism: How Americans Are Seduced by War* (New York: Oxford University Press, 2005) is a sobering account of how, even against our self-image, American society is currently best understood as oriented toward war, not peace.

100. Strikingly, Russell Kirk, *The Portable Conservative Reader*, concedes that selfishness is the distinctly conservative vice. "Conservatism has its vice, and that vice is selfishness. Self-centered conservatives mutter, with Fafnir, 'Let me rest: I lie in possession'" (xxiii). The liberal drive to equality, which must always address existing inequalities and threaten those who benefit from them, should rule out this particular form of selfishness. But there remains the worry that the liberal (and bourgeois) division of private from public will underwrite a disengagement from public matters that effectively leaves current inequities undisturbed.

101. Gary Wills, *Explaining America: The Federalist* (Garden City, N.Y.: Doubleday, 1981), makes a strong case for Madison and Hamilton's reliance on "public virtue" in combination with "checks and balances" to ensure the well-being of the new government of the United States. See esp. pp. 186–87, 224–26. Wills reads the founders' notion of virtue (derived from Montesquieu and Hume) as "devotion to the happiness of the people" (186) and quotes Hamilton in Federalist No. 22 on the contrast between the public official of "superior virtue" whose "interest . . . in the common stock" overcomes any lure of personal benefits that could follow from "betraying [the people's or voters'] trust" (187). For Wills, it is the need to promote and preserve "public virtue" that motivates the founder's creation of a republic, not a democracy. My position is that the "civic virtue" tradition is important and that the existence of civic virtue is absolutely necessary. But I don't think, especially in our contemporary world, that much does—or can—ride on a distinction between a republic and a liberal democracy. Rather, the virtues needed—a concern for the general welfare, a commitment to reciprocity that rules out making an exception of oneself, and a capacious interpretation of what the value of equality requires of a polity—must be inculcated and practiced within the context of the governmental and legal forms that have evolved—and thus become our political reality—since 1787. I am agnostic about whether our current forms make public virtue more difficult now than it was for George Washington, but I would insist that our current forms hardly make such virtue impossible. That such virtue is currently so scarce is our sorrow as a nation—and a call for reform. Wills himself ends his book (265–70) admitting (lamenting?) that Madison and Hamilton's republicanism was obsolete within ten years after its articulation in the Federalist Papers.

102. Barry, *Why Social Justice Matters*, 269.

103. Immanuel Kant, *Grounding for the Metaphysics of Morals* [1785], trans. James W. Ellington (Indianapolis: Hackett, 1993). Page numbers for quotations from this text are supplied parenthetically in the body of my text.

104. Kant, "Perpetual Peace," 126.

105. Mill, *On Liberty*, in *Three Essays*, 14–15.

106. For a very useful overview of the debate between a Kantian and a consequential-

ist ethics, see Marcia W. Baron, Philip Petit, and Michael Slote, *Three Methods of Ethics* (Oxford: Blackwell, 1997). Baron's contribution to this volume (esp. 7–10) does a good job of explaining why Kant and Mill, despite working from different premises, will often arrive at the same conclusion about which action is "right." The "third method of ethics" offered in the volume is an Aristotelian "virtue" ethics. I am suggesting that there is a fourth tradition, one coming out of Hume, developed by the American pragmatists, and now most often championed by feminist thinkers. In the foreword to his *Human Nature and Human Conduct* (1922; repr., New York: Modern Library, 1957), Dewey writes that "this volume might be said to be an essay in continuing the tradition of David Hume" (v), and Jennifer Welchman concludes her book, *Dewey's Ethical Thought* (Ithaca: Cornell University Press, 1995), with a strong five pages (213–18) arguing that "Dewey's moral philosophy does continue the tradition of Hume" (217). On the ways in which Mill's version of utilitarianism depends on a fundamental assertion about the "evil" of any experience of suffering (no matter who suffers) and the "good" of any experience of happiness, see Geoffrey Sayre-McCord's "Mill's 'Proof' of the Principle of Utility: A More Than Half-Hearted Defense," *Social Philosophy and Policy* 18, no. 2 (2001): 330–60. My understanding of all these matters has greatly benefited from conversations with and classes taken from Professor Sayre-McCord.

107. Dewey's wonderful summary statement, "Morality Is Social," is the final section (pt. 4, sec. IV) of *Human Nature and Human Conduct*. James's view of morality, with the phrases I quote in my text, is found in "The Moral Philosopher and the Moral Life," *Writings, 1878–1899*, 595–617.

108. My thoughts here are influenced by a presentation I heard Richard Rorty make in Berkeley in 2002 in which he insisted that "bleeding heart liberalism" was all that liberalism consists in. Making due allowance for Rorty's love of overstatement, his comment does point us, once again, to a fundamental divide between liberal and conservative sensibilities, between those who are proud to have "bleeding hearts" and those for whom the epithet is a sneer. Stanley Cavell's reading of the famous passages on pain in Wittgenstein's *Philosophical Investigations* offers another way to dramatize this gap in sensibility. Cavell reads "pain behavior" (which we might equate with James's "cries of the wounded") as a call for help, a request for a response, from another human being. What kind of person, Cavell then wonders, finds that his first response is: "How do I know that person is really in pain? How do I know he is not trying to trick me?" I have paraphrased Cavell rather liberally here, but in ways that I do not think violate the spirit of his work, especially *The Claim of Reason: Wittgenstein, Skepticism, Morality, and Tragedy* (New York: Oxford University Press, 1979).

BOOK TWO

1. John Henry Newman, *Liberalism*, quoted from *Norton Anthology of English Literature*, 5th ed. (New York: Norton, 1986), 2:1032.

2. Thomas Babington Macaulay, "All Sail and No Anchor," in *The Portable Conservative Reader*, ed. Russell Kirk (New York: Viking Press, 1982), 215–16.

3. John Adams, "On Natural Aristocracy," in *Portable Conservative Reader*, 66–67.

4. James Fenimore Cooper, "On Equality," in *Portable Conservative Reader*, 183–202.

5. Donald Davidson, "Some Day, in Old Charleston," in *Portable Conservative Reader*,

532. Falwell is quoted from Naomi Schaefer Riley, "In Search of the Religious Vote, but Which One?," *Wall Street Journal*, May 12, 2006.

6. "We can say of the right in America that it exemplifies the tradition of big prop-ertied liberalism in Europe . . . a tradition which hates the *ancien régime* up to a cer-tain point, loves capitalism, and fears democracy." Louis Hartz, *The Liberal Tradition in America* (New York: Harcourt, Brace and World, 1955), 15.

7. Quoted from *Los Angeles Times*, November 15, 2005. For a more fulsome state-ment of contemporary American conservatism's leading values and obsessions, see the platform of the Texas Republican Party, <http://www.texasgop.org/site/PageServer?pagename=library_platform>.

8. My particular sources for characterizing each of the variants will emerge as I proceed, but I need to list here several general works on which I have relied in offering my account of conservatism: Michael Oakeshott, *Rationalism in Politics and Other Es-says* (Indianapolis: Liberty Fund, 1991); Robert Nisbet, *Conservatism: Dream and Real-ity* (Minneapolis: University of Minnesota Press, 1986); Ted Honderich, *Conservatism: Burke, Nozick, Bush, Blair?* (London: Pluto Press, 2005); Jerry Z. Muller, *Conservatism* (Princeton: Princeton University Press, 1997); and Noel O'Sullivan, "Conservatism," in *The Cambridge History of Twentieth Century Political Thought*, ed. Terrence Ball and Richard Bellamy (Cambridge; Cambridge University Press, 2003), 165–80.

9. Bloom sets himself against the "three-hundred-year-long identity crisis" that is modern individualism, understood as "the turn in philosophy away from trying to tame or perfect desire by virtue, and toward finding out what one's desire is and liv-ing according to it." The ultimate source of a true standard of virtue is, according to Bloom, "nature," and it is the task of philosophy to identify that nature and lead selves to govern their impulses according to its dictates. Bloom quite explicitly presents his position as derived from Plato's notion of the philosopher-king. See Bloom, *The Clos-ing of the American Mind: How Higher Education Has Failed Democracy and Impoverished the Souls of Today's Students* (New York: Simon and Schuster, 1987), esp. 173–79. Bork is more directly moralistic than Bloom. He decries "radical individualism (the dras-tic reduction of limits to personal gratification)" and looks to "traditional morality" to combat the "cultural and moral chaos" that are "both prominent and destructive features of our time." See *Slouching toward Gomarrah: Modern Liberalism and American Decline* (New York: Regan Books, 1996), esp. 1–13.

10. A good example is American attitudes toward freedom of conscience in reli-gious affairs. All the evidence indicates that Americans, even the most fervent evan-gelicals, accept that individuals have the final say in matters of religious belief. The liberal principle of religious freedom, in that sense, is not threatened in contemporary America. The liberal understanding of the separation of church and state is, of course, another matter altogether. I base these assertions on the extended discussion of these issues in Christian Smith, *Christian America?: What Evangelicals Really Want* (Berkeley: University of California Press, 2000), chap. 2.

11. Russell Kirk, Introduction to *Portable Conservative Reader*, argues that Burkean conservatives are pluralists because their "preference for the established order of so-ciety" comes with the recognition that the established order "must differ considerably from nation to nation, since any land's politics must be the product of that country's dominant religion, ancient customs, and historic experiences" (xiv). It is certainly

true that Burke is not a universalist and thus recognizes the existence of different cultures and nations. But the key issue here is pluralism within the polity, not the plurality of nations. And, despite Kirk's best efforts (see xvii), the emphasis on order makes deviance from "the paths that his father followed" suspect. "We human beings have learned certain ways and principles of order. Were we lacking these, we would lie at the mercy of will and appetite—in private life, in public concerns. It is this order, this old safeguard against private and public anarchy, which the conservative refuses to surrender to the evangels of Progress" (xxxv–xxxvi). In explaining why he is not a conservative, Friedrich A. von Hayek points directly to this conservative parochialism, the refusal of new knowledge or of foreign examples because they might suggest changing the ways my father followed. Hayek shrewdly indicates how conservative parochialism, which can look like pluralism, so often leads to imperialism: "Only at first does it seem paradoxical that the anti-internationalism of the conservative is so frequently associated with imperialism. But the more a person dislikes the strange and thinks his own ways superior, the more he tends to regard it as his mission to 'civilize' others." Hayek, *The Constitution of Liberty* (Chicago: University of Chicago Press, 1960), 406.

12. Kirk, Introduction to *Portable Conservative Reader*, xvi. Michael Oakeshott, especially in his essay "Rationalism in Politics" (*Rationalism in Politics and Other Essays*), has offered the most influential twentieth-century version of this Burkean position.

13. See Albert O. Hirschman, *The Rhetoric of Reaction: Perversity, Futility, Jeopardy* (Princeton: Princeton University Press, 1991).

14. Riley, "In Search of the Religious Vote" (on Falwell); Kirk, Introduction to *Portable Conservative Reader*, xxvi.

15. Jerry Muller, *Conservatism*, 423, is particularly incisive on what he calls the "perennial dilemma" in conservative thought about "when to declare the battle for a particular institution definitely lost." If conservatives eventually accept each change in the polity's institutions, they just seem persistently behind the curve, engaged "in a fighting retreat from one institutional outpost to another," but always eventually defending any institution that successfully establishes itself as part of the social fabric. Today's conservative defends what yesterday's branded a dangerous innovation. But the alternative path, "the defense of institutions that are irrevocably lost," leads to "the eccentric reactionary" or mere "crankiness."

16. "On 9 June 1998 the Southern Baptist Convention, in a national meeting of 8,500 delegates, amended its essential statement of beliefs . . . to include a declaration that a woman should 'submit herself graciously' to her husband's leadership, and that a husband should 'provide for, protect, and lead his family.' This was only the second amendment to the Southern Baptists' *Statement* in its entire history, and its first-ever declaration dealing with a social—and not strictly theological or church—issue. With it, the nation's largest Protestant denomination disavowed the idea of egalitarian marriage, in favor of functionally hierarchical marriage relationships in which husbands stand as authorities over and leaders before their wives." Smith, *Christian America?*, 160.

17. A prime example is Roger Scruton, *The Meaning of Conservatism*, 3rd ed. (South Bend, Ind.: St. Augustine's Press, 2002). My presentation here is derived from Scruton's book, where he takes up the issues of allegiance to authority, the sources of au-

thority's legitimacy, the rule of law, the family as the basic model of social relations, and the inevitability/desirability of a "stratified society."

18. Kirk, Introduction to *Portable Conservative Reader*, xxxv; Scruton, *Meaning of Conservatism*, 22.

19. Kirk, Introduction to *Portable Conservative Reader*, xxx.

20. Ibid., xv.

21. See John Gray, *Liberalism* (Minneapolis: University of Minnesota Press, 1986), chap. 4, for a succinct account of how Mill's and Green's "revisionist liberalism" signaled the end of English liberalism's association with laissez-faire economics at just about the time when such economic theories (mixed with the social Darwinism of Herbert Spencer) were introduced into America by, among others, William Graham Sumner.

22. Hayek, *The Constitution of Liberty*, 409, 531:n18. Subsequent references to this work will give page numbers parenthetically in the text.

23. John Micklethwait and Adrian Woolridge, *The Right Nation: Conservative Power in America* (New York: Penguin Press, 2004), 253–54, believe that there is a "logical contradiction between trying to be the party of both the free market and the heartland," and that the contrast "between libertarians and traditionalists," between "business conservatives and social conservatives," marks a strong tension in contemporary conservatism.

24. Tom Frank, *What's the Matter with Kansas?: How Conservatives Won the Heart of America* (New York: Henry Holt, 2004), offers the latest version of the by-now-familiar left-wing analysis that says that citizens who vote against their economic interests have been led to focus their discontent (or resentment) against either those more unfortunate than themselves (e.g., blacks or immigrants) or on the wrong elites (liberal eggheads instead of corporate nabobs). This line of thinking is both too pat and blames the people for our current political climate rather than liberals who have failed to make the case for liberal values and our liberal heritage.

25. Friedrich A. von Hayek, *The Mirage of Social Justice*, vol. 2 of *Law, Legislation, and Liberty* (Chicago: University of Chicago Press, 1976), 85. Compare with Roger Scruton's brisk dismissal of "the absurdity of the aim of 'equality of opportunity.' Such a thing is neither possible nor desirable" (*Meaning of Conservatism*, 143–44). We can take it as a sign of how "liberal" American political culture remains that no politician, no matter how conservative, would dare utter such sentiments publicly in the United States. That, of course, does not stop conservatives from caring little and doing less to address inequities resulting from the fact, as Hayek admits, that "is not to be denied": "the initial chances of different individuals are often very different" (*Mirage of Social Justice*, 84).

26. "The Rich, the Poor, and the Growing Gap between Them," *Economist*, June 17–23, 2006, 29. The studies referred to can be found at <http://www.economist.com/inequality>. Neal Acherson (in a review of a book by Tony Judt that he quotes) writes: "What binds Europeans together . . . is what has become conventional to call—in disjunctive but revealing contrast to 'the American way of life'—the 'European model of society'. . . . Its core is the Europeans' 'deliberate choice to work less, earn less—and live better lives.' In return for high taxes, they receive 'free or nearly free medical services, early retirement, and a prodigious range of social and public services.' They pay

to be better educated than Americans, to live longer and healthier lives and to encounter far less poverty." "The Atlantic Gap," *London Review of Books*, November 17, 2005, 8. Such statements infuriate American conservatives (especially of the laissez-faire variety), who always insist that Americans are better off than Europeans and that "old Europe" (especially France) is a half step away from total collapse because of its refusal to attend to the realities of global capitalism. For good examples of these views, see the unsigned editorial, "French Lessons," *Wall Street Journal*, November 11, 2005, which tells the French they can solve all their problems by "deregulating labor markets, reducing taxes, reforming the pension system and breaking the stranglehold of unions on economic life." As for which economic policies are more sustainable—and more in tune with economic realities—it might be worth taking these observations from the *Economist* into account: "In fact, Europe's performance has been better than the conventional wisdom says. Although America has outpaced Europe this year, over the past five years GDP per head, the best single measure of economic performance, grew at an average rate of 1.4% in the euro area, just behind America's 1.5%. Ah, but America is better at creating jobs, isn't it? Actually, no. Employment has grown a tad faster in the euro area than in America whether one looks at the past five years or the past ten. . . . Since 1996 the proportion of the population of working age with jobs has fallen from 73% to 71% in America; in the euro area it has risen from 59% to 65%. The fact that the euro area has achieved its growth without enormous increases in its current account and budget deficits might also indicate that its record is more sustainable than America's." *Economist*, November 19–25, 2005, 76. In addition to all of this, European countries also have far less economic inequality than the United States. (See Appendix, item 7.)

27. Irving Kristol's undocumented assertion about the failure of Sweden's social policies is indicative of the quality of conservative opinion on this subject: "The more egalitarian Sweden becomes—and it is already about as egalitarian as it is ever likely to become—the more *enragé* are its intellectuals, the more guilt-ridden and uncertain are its upper-middle classes, the more 'alienated' are its college-educated youth." That's because, Kristol tells us, people don't really want such equality; it's the spiritual emptiness of modern life, not its material inequalities, that people are really protesting against; the people—and their leaders—have simply misdiagnosed the problem. Does that mean they'd be better off if the society were more unequal? Kristol doesn't quite say that; he just tries to change the subject away from the fact that some societies are more materially equal than others because of deliberate state actions that, in fact, don't seem to have appreciably lessened freedom or introduced massive "coercion." Kristol, "About Equality," *NeoConservatism: The Autobiography of an Idea* (Chicago: Ivan R. Dee, 1995), 172. In *The Constitution of Liberty*, Hayek writes that "the rapidity with which rich societies . . . have become static, if not stagnant, societies through egalitarian policies, while impoverished but highly competitive countries have become very dynamic and progressive, has been one of the most conspicuous features of the postwar period. The contrast in this respect between the advanced welfare states of Great Britain and the Scandinavian countries, on the one hand, and countries like Western Germany, Belgium, or Italy, is beginning to be recognized even by the former" (49). Though perhaps true in 1960, this statement has not stood the test of time. Living standards in Scandinavia (and Canada) have consistently remained among the highest in the world, comparing favorably with those of the United States and Japan (this

last hardly a bastion of laissez-faire policies). Conservatives are so threatened by these facts that they continue to offer every argument they can devise to combat what they deem the "myth" of Scandinavian prosperity. Richard Posner, hardly a liberal, captures this conservative bias perfectly when he writes of Milton Friedman: "I think his belief in the superior efficiency of free markets to government as a means of resource allocation, though fruitful and largely correct, was embraced by him as an article of faith and not merely as a hypothesis. I think he considered it almost a personal affront that the Scandinavian nations, particularly Sweden, could achieve and maintain very high levels of economic output despite very high rates of taxation, an enormous public sector, and extensive wealth redistribution resulting in much greater economic equality than in the United States. I don't think his analytic apparatus could explain such an anomaly" (<http://www.becker-posner-blog.com/archives/2006/11/milton_friedman.html>).

28. Hayek, *Mirage of Social Justice*, 67.

29. Ibid., 69–70.

30. Hayek, *The Constitution of Liberty*, writes: Conservatives "did show an understanding of the meaning of spontaneously grown institutions such as language, law, morals, and conventions that anticipated modern scientific [i.e., his political economy] approaches" (400).

31. See Sebastian Mallaby, "The Return of Voodoo Economics: Republicans Ignore Their Experts on the Cost of Tax Cuts," *Washington Post*, May 15, 2006, for a discussion of Republican politicians' continued use of the claim that cutting taxes can increase tax revenues despite the fact that even conservative economists say that is not true. For a detailed refutation of the claim, see Aviva Aron-Dine and Joel Friedman, "The Capital Gains and Dividend Tax Cuts and the Economy," *Center on Budget and Policy Priorities*, March 27, 2006, <http://www.cbpp.org/3-27-06tax.htm>. For discussion of a recent study by the Cato Institute that indicates cutting taxes (the so-called starving of the beast) actually increases government spending, see Jonathan Chait, "Blind Trust: Conservatives and Tax Cuts," *New Republic On-Line*, May 15, 2006, <http://www.tnr.com/docprint.mhtml?i=w060515&s=chait050815>. It was Dick Cheney, of course, who said that deficits don't matter; for a defense of that point of view, see Robert L. Bartley, "The Dread Deficit," in *The NeoCon Reader*, ed. Irwin Stelzer (New York: Grove Press, 2004), 181–92, which is followed by Stelzer's "Neoconservative Economic Policy: Virtues and Vices," 193–98. Stelzer, himself a self-described conservative, writes: "President George W. Bush may be right when he shows his disregard for deficits with the flippant, 'It is clearly a budget. It's got lots of numbers in it.' But I rather doubt it"—and offers some good reasons to worry about massive government debt.

32. Larry M. Bartels, "Is the Water Rising?: Reflections on Inequality and American Democracy," *P.S.: Political Science and Politics* 39, no. 1 (January 2006): 39–42, uses Census Bureau data from 1948 to 2001 to show that "under Democratic presidents income growth has been fairly egalitarian (at least in percentage terms), with average real growth rates ranging from 2.6% for families at the 20th percentile to 2.1% for families at the 95th percentile. Under Republican presidents the pattern has been dramatically different. Affluent families have fared equally well during Republican and Democratic administrations; but middle-class and poor families have fared markedly worse, on average, under Republican presidents. For working poor people (at the 20th percentile of the income distribution), Republicans have presided over average income

growth of 0.6%—less than one fourth of the corresponding average under Democratic presidents" (41). Bartels concludes: "Over a period of more than half a century the policies of Democratic administrations have been significantly more effective than the policies of Republican administrations in generating economic growth, and in distributing the benefits of economic growth broadly to people across the political spectrum" (41).

33. Steven Lukes, "Epilogue: The Grand Dichotomy of the Twentieth Century," in *Cambridge History of Twentieth-Century Political Thought*, 612.

34. Muller, *Conservatism*, 316.

35. Kristol, "Capitalism, Socialism, and Nihilism," in *Portable Conservative Reader*, 640–42.

36. Robert B. Reich, *Reason: Why Liberals Will Win the Battle for America* (New York: Vintage Books, 2005), 43–69, has wonderful things to say about the conservatives' obsession with private morality and their almost complete blindness to "the real *public* moral breakdown" resulting from the "abuse" of authority at the top rungs of our society (77). Reich details a number of cases, ranging from CEOs to corrupt politicians and corporate malfeasance. And that doesn't cover the appalling lack of loyalty to employees shown every day by companies that outsource jobs, reduce benefits, and renege on pension commitments. For the gory details on pensions, see Ellen E. Schultz and Theo Francis, "As Workers' Pensions Wither, Those for Executives Flourish," *Wall Street Journal*, June 23, 2006. The title of this article nearly says it all, but here's one sample of the facts it reports: "45% of AT&T's pension expense" in 2005 covered 1,000 executives. "The other 55% of pension expenses? It covered 189,000 regular employees."

37. Kristol is the great example of this disconnect in contemporary conservative thought, and anyone who wants a nutshell picture of such thinking should read his short essay "About Equality" in his *NeoConservatism*, 165–78. In Kristol's view, everything and anything is wrong in our society today except capitalism itself. He never recognizes how capitalism tells us that we owe nothing to any other human being and that the only determinant of value is whether there is a "demand" for something in the marketplace.

38. Honderich, *Conservatism*, esp. 94–100. I can't reproduce Honderich's intricate argument here; I can only point my readers toward it, while quoting its conclusion that "here we have a real and fundamental distinction of conservatism . . . it assigns an overwhelming place to extrinsic as against any intrinsic incentives" (99).

39. Richard Sennett and Jonathan Cobb, *The Hidden Injuries of Class* (New York: Knopf, 1972), remains the classic statement of how the less well-off in America internalize this relentless message that they are to blame for their own economic position.

40. Frederick A. von Hayek, "Whither Democracy," *New Studies in Philosophy, Economics and the History of Ideas* (Chicago: University of Chicago Press, 1985), 157–58.

41. Not surprisingly, in the wake of contemporary conservatism's fixation on "responsibility," moral philosophers have examined the ways in which actual relations between the wronged and the wrongdoer are negotiated in human communities. Three essays that I have found particularly compelling on these issues are David Wiggins, "Claims of Need" (which addresses why society should address needs instead of fixat-

ing on deserts), *Needs, Values, Truth*, 3rd ed. (Cambridge: Cambridge University Press, 1998), 1–58; Margaret Urban Walker, "Moral Repair and Its Limits" (on the claims of forgiveness and punishment and their consequences), in Todd F. Davis and Kenneth Womack, eds., *Mapping the Ethical Turn* (Charlottesville: University of Virginia Press, 2001), 110–27; and Susan Wolf, "The Moral of Moral Luck" (on responsibility and the limits of "strict justice"), in Chesire Calhoun, ed. *Setting the Moral Compass* (New York: Oxford University Press, 2003), 113–27.

42. For the *Economist*'s cover story on growing economic inequality in America, see n. 26 above. David Wessel has been writing fairly frequently on the topic in the *Wall Street Journal*; see his "Inequality: An 80s Legacy or Worsening Now?," January 19, 2006, and "College Grad Wages Are Sluggish, Too," May 18, 2006. The *New York Times* ran a whole series on the subject in the summer of 2005, subsequently published in book form as *Class Matters* (New York: New York Times, 2005).

43. Stelzer, "Neoconservatives and Their Critics: An Introduction," in *Neocon Reader*, 16–17.

44. For the text of Bush's West Point speech, see <http://www.whitehouse.gov/releases/2002/06/20020601-3.html>. For an excellent discussion of the "preemptive strike" doctrine, including specifics on how it violates the United Nations Charter to which the United States is a signatory, see Richard Falk, "The New Bush Doctrine," <http://www.thenation.com/20020715/falk>.

45. Hannah Arendt's description of imperialism in Part Two of *The Origins of Totalitarianism* (San Diego: Harcourt Brace, 1966) carries new—and unsettling—resonance in our contemporary world. Arendt believes that the imperial experience in the nineteenth century of imposed power was then brought back home to Europe in the twentieth century, when totalitarian states adopted similar policies domestically. "The state-employed administrators of violence [in the colonies] soon formed a new class within the nations and, although their field of activity was far away from the mother country, wielded an important influence on the body politic at home. Since they were actually nothing but functionaries of violence, they could only think in terms of power politics. They were the first who, as a class and supported by their everyday experience, would claim that power is the essence of every political structure" (137).

46. Stelzer, "Neoconservatives and Their Critics," 17–18, explains that neoconservatives believe "containment might have been appropriate in its time, but . . . the policy outlived the era in which it might have been sensible."

47. Robert Sidelsky, "Hot, Cold, and Imperial," *New York Review of Books*, July 13, 2006, 55.

48. Michael Gove, quoted from Stelzer, "Neoconservatives and Their Critics," 16.

49. Robert D. Kagan, *Of Paradise and Power: America and Europe in the New World Order* (New York: Vintage Books, 2004), 136.

50. Kagan (ibid.) is particularly interesting on this score. He fully understands that the legitimacy of interventions is dependent on their not being unilateral, on their being sanctioned by either institutions that transcend the nation or by an alliance of many nations. But he thinks that, at least currently, Americans and Europeans view "the threat posed by terrorism and weapons of mass destruction" so differently that we are left with a "tragedy" of America's "need [for] the legitimacy that Europe can provide" and the Europeans' failure "to provide it [i]n their effort to constrain the

superpower" (158). Kagan thinks that the Europeans are wrong: they have lost "sight of the mounting dangers in the world, dangers far greater than those posed by the United States" (158).

51. Robert D. Kaplan, *Warrior Politics: Why Leadership Demands a Pagan Ethos* (New York: Random House, 2002), 113. Compare with Kagan: "It is time to stop pretending that Europeans and Americans share a common view of the world, or even that they occupy the same world. On the all-important question of power—the efficacy of power, the morality of power, the desirability of power—American and European perspectives are diverging. Europe is turning away from power, or to put it a little differently, it is moving beyond power into a self-contained world of laws and rules and transnational negotiation and cooperation. It is entering a post-historical paradise of peace and relative prosperity, the realization of Immanuel Kant's 'perpetual peace.' Meanwhile, the United States remains mired in history, exercising power in an anarchic Hobbesian world where international laws and rules are unreliable, and where true security and defense and promotions of a liberal order still depend on the possession and use of military might" (3).

52. William Kristol, "Neoconservatism Remains the Bedrock of U.S. Foreign Policy," in *NeoCon Reader*, 76–77. Kristol does realize that his use of the word "successful" is a bit problematic given the U.S. experience in Iraq. But he brushes off that gnat: "Of course, the Bush administration made the big mistake of trying to will the ends without the means. There was no big increase in the size of the military, no overhaul of our political, diplomatic, and intelligence institutions, no suitable commitment of resources, no radical adjustments of government bureaucracy and mindset needed to adjust to the post-9/11 world." But, granted the fantasy world in which all those "adjustments" were made (and their consequences within our society figured at naught), "the neoconservative analysis is, I think, broadly vindicated" (76). For a succinct and powerful description of neoconservatism's failure from a "former neoconservative," see Francis Fukuyama, "After Neoconservatism," *New York Times Magazine*, February 19, 2006, 62–67.

53. William Kristol and Robert Kagan, "National Interest and Global Responsibility," in *NeoCon Reader*, 72.

54. Kaplan, *Warrior Politics*, 4–6.

55. The relevant lines from Kipling's poem are: "Take up the White Man's Burden / And reap his old reward: / The blame of those ye better, / The hate of those ye guard."

56. Joseph Conrad, "Heart of Darkness," *Norton Anthology of English Literature* (New York: Norton, 1993), 2:1818.

57. Kristol and Kagan, "National Interest and Global Responsibility," 72–73.

58. James Gerstenzang and Alissa J. Rubin, "Bush Responds Angrily to Criticisms by Europeans," *Los Angeles Times*, June 22, 2006, <http://www.latimes.com/news/nationworld/world/la-fg-bush22jun22,1,7321965.stroy?coll=la-headlines-world>.

59. Irving Kristol, "The Neoconservative Persuasion: What It Was, and What It Is," in *NeoCon Reader*, 36.

60. Kenneth R. Weinstein, "Philosophic Roots, the Role of Leo Strauss, and the War in Iraq," in *Neocon Reader*, 201–12, offers a carefully nuanced account of Strauss's influence on the neocons. Weinstein is undoubtedly right that Strauss should hardly be blamed for the Bush administration's addiction to secrecy, but the fact remains

that Strauss did believe the masses cannot be expected to understand or appreciate the reasoning of the elites and thus should be kept in the dark. On how "classification activity has increased by 75 percent" under the Bush administration, see Steven Aftergood, "The Age of Missing Information," <http://slate.com/id/2114963>; on how the administration has used "the state secrets privilege" to block legal questioning of its actions, see Henry Lanman, "Secret Guarding," <http://slate.com/id/2142155>. Daniel Patrick Moynihan, *Secrecy: The American Experience* (New Haven: Yale University Press, 1998), offers a sober account of how government secrecy is counterproductive (because it eschews the benefits of the deliberation and debate that come with openness) as well as antidemocratic (and hence a violation of our political principles).

61. Niall Ferguson, *Empire: The Rise and Demise of the British World Order and the Lessons for Global Power* (New York: Basic Books, 2004), 314–17; Kaplan, *Warrior Politics*, 147–49.

62. Stelzer, Introduction to *Neocon Reader*, 18. "Many neocons—the so-called 'democratic imperialist' wing—regret America's unwillingness to adopt an explicitly imperialist role" (18).

63. The quoted passage comes from an internal White House memo written by John Yoo, a lawyer working in the White House Office of Legal Counsel. Quoted from Jane Kramer, "The Hidden Power," *New Yorker*, July 3, 2006, 51.

64. Ibid.

65. On the Bush administration's decision to bypass the special courts set up by the FISA to conduct warrantless intelligence gathering, see "Bush Authorized Domestic Spying," *Washington Post*, December 16, 2005, and "President Acknowledges Approving Secretive Eavesdropping," *Washington Post*, December 17, 2005.

66. Jess Bravin, "Justices Bar Guantánamo Tribunals," *Wall Street Journal*, June 30, 2006. Bravin's article is an excellent summary of the issues in the *Hamdan v. Rumsfeld* case. As Bravin explains: "Administration lawyers contended that the constitutional clause designating the president 'commander in chief of the Army and Navy' should be read broadly, so that the Executive Branch could take virtually any steps it deemed necessary for national security. At various times, administration lawyers have argued that the commander-in-chief power permitted the president to disregard laws prohibiting torture—and, in this case, provisions of the Geneva Conventions and other treaties protecting enemy prisoners."

67. For the *National Review*, see The Editors, "An Outrage," posted June 30, 2006, at <http://nationalreview.com>. The unsigned *Wall Street Journal* editorial of July 3, 2006, is entitled "After *Hamdan*."

68. See Elizabeth Drew, "Bush's Power Grab," *New York Review of Books*, June 22, 2006, 10–15, for a compelling summary of why many observers, on both the left and the right, have concluded that the Bush administration's actions constitute a constitutional crisis. See also Charlie Savage, "Bush Challenges Hundreds of Laws," *Boston Globe*, April 30, 2006, for a discussion of the same topic, focusing on the "signing statements" in which "President Bush has quietly claimed the authority to disobey more than 750 laws enacted since he took office" (<http://www.boston.com/news/nation/washington/articles/2006/04/3>).

69. To his credit, Niall Ferguson was appalled by Congress' action. Here's his description of the new bill: "Last week, both houses of Congress approved a bill—the Military Commissions Act—that would permit the indefinite, extrajudicial incarcera-

tion of terrorist suspects and their interrogation using torture in all but name. Does that sound shocking? What's really shocking is that this was a *compromise* measure. When President Bush signs this bill into law, a category of detainees will come into existence: 'unlawful enemy combatants,' who, regardless of their nationality, will be liable to summary arrest. Those detained will not have the right to challenge their interrogation by filing an application for a writ of habeas corpus. When—or rather if—they are tried, it will be by military tribunals. Classified evidence may be withheld from the accused if the tribunal judges see fit. My old friend Andrew Sullivan—who used to think he was a conservative until President Bush came along—calls it a bill to 'legalize tyranny.'" "Why Churchill Opposed Torture," *Los Angeles Times*, October 2, 2006, <http://www.latimes/news/opinion/la-oe-ferguson2oct02,0,4615277.column?coll=la-opinion-rightrail>. The Bush administration almost immediately filed papers in the Fourth U.S. Circuit Court of Appeals to make the new law applicable, not just to the detainees held in Guantánamo Bay, but to any foreigner arrested by the United States and labeled as an "enemy combatant." See Matt Appuzzo, "US: Immigrants May Be Held Indefinitely," AP wire story of November 13, 2006, <http://beit-bart.com/news/2006/11/13/D8LCIVL80.html>.

70. Kristol, "The Neoconservative Persuasion," 35.

71. Arendt, *Origins of Totalitarianism*, 153.

72. Irving Kristol, "A Conservative Welfare State," in *Neocon Reader*, 145–48.

73. "Condi's European Torture," *Wall Street Journal*, December 7, 2005.

74. Kirk, Introduction to *Portable Conservative Reader*, xv.

75. Erstwhile (and, perhaps not coincidentally, British) conservative Andrew Sullivan offers this eloquent lament for American conservatism's loss of all notion of the "rule of law" or the need to limit power. Responding to conservative outrage over the *Hamdan* decision, Sullivan writes: "Support of an unlimited executive power in a permanent war, and contempt for the critical role of the judiciary in a constitutional republic reveals the depth of the rot in the American conservative mind and soul. From conservatism being a political tradition rooted in freedom from government control, and in the checks and balances of a constitutional order, conservatism has now morphed in America into a defense of unfettered executive power, in which all judicial checks are regarded as a form of tyranny. Yes: an executive empowered to be judge, jury, torturer and executioner is no problem. A Court attempting to uphold the constitution, in contrast, is a sign of outrageous tyranny. We truly have passed through the Looking Glass" (blog entry, July 2, 2006, <http://time.blogs.com/daily_dish>). My only comment is that Sullivan overestimates the traditional conservative commitment to freedom; even in Burke, the fear of anarchy and the fetishization of order trumps freedom time and again. I am not so convinced that today's American conservatism is drastically out of line with the tradition.

76. James Weaver, the Populist Party candidate, received 8 percent of the popular vote in the 1892 presidential election. The Socialist Party candidate, Eugene Debs, captured 6 percent of the popular vote in the 1912 presidential election; the Socialist Party got between 3 and 4 percent of the vote in the 1904, 1916, 1920, and 1932 elections. Running on the Progressive ticket, Robert LaFollette received 17 percent of the vote in 1924 and Henry Wallace 2.5 percent in 1948. Since then, the left has never even topped 1 percent of the vote. Figures taken from the Encyclopedia Britannica online, <http://www.britannica.com/presidents/browse?browseId=242348>.

77. For a detailed account of how American politics has moved rightward in the past thirty years, see Jacob S. Hacker and Paul Pierson, *Off-Center: The Republican Revolution and the Erosion of American Democracy* (New Haven: Yale University Press, 2005).

78. See my *Postmodernism and Its Critics* (Ithaca: Cornell University Press, 1991) and *Democracy's Children: Intellectuals and the Rise of Cultural Politics* (Ithaca: Cornell University Press, 2002).

79. Jean-François Lyotard, *The Differend: Phrases in Dispute* (Minneapolis: University of Minnesota Press, 1988), presents an influential version of this argument. For a version that draws more on the work of Emmanuel Levinas than on the work of Lyotard, see Zygmunt Bauman, *Postmodern Ethics* (Oxford: Blackwell, 1993). That the anti-Kantian romantics who made such arguments—from Burke to Nietzsche—were almost all deeply conservative seems not to have bothered contemporary leftists who have appropriated their views.

80. "Communicability" plays a prominent role in Kant's *Critique of Judgment* and is, arguably, a central premise of his liberalism. The key contemporary liberal (and recognizably Kantian) theorist who relies heavily on communicability is Jürgen Habermas, especially in his two-volume *Theory of Communicative Action* (Boston: Beacon Press, 1984, 1987).

81. Those who have read Richard Rorty's *Achieving Our Country* (Cambridge: Harvard University Press, 1998) will recognize that my account of the cultural left jives with his in many ways. But I think Rorty's use of the conservatives' favorite accusation of a lack of patriotism greatly mars his book. Even more vituperative are Martha Nussbaum's attack on Judith Butler and Russell Jacoby's attack on Eric Lott. Nussbaum, "The Professor of Parody," originally published in *New Republic* (February 1999), <http://www.qwik.ch/the_professor_of_parody>; Jacoby, "Brother from Another Planet," *Nation*, April 10, 2006, <http://www.thenation.com/doc/20060410/jacoby>. I have discussed (and deplored) Nussbaum's attack at length on my blog, Public Intelligence, <http://www.mcgowans3.com>, posts of August 10, 23, 2005.

BOOK THREE

1. I take the term "state-action liberalism" from the English writer Matthew Arnold (1822–88).

2. Interestingly, John Gray's *Liberalism* (Minneapolis: University of Minnesota Press, 1986) traces the rise of modern liberalism to democratic pressure as well as the influence of Mill. Gray writes: "It is important to note that the decline of classical liberalism cannot be explained simply by a response to the abandonment of important classical liberal ideas by John Stuart Mill and others. Such developments in intellectual life reflected, and were in part caused by, the changes in the political environment brought about by the expansion of democratic institutions" (33). For the experiences and reasoning that led Mill to abandon the laissez-faire views of his father, see Robert L. Heilbroner's *The Worldly Philosophers*, 5th ed. (New York: Simon and Schuster, 1980), chap. 5.

3. James Madison, "Political Observations, April 20, 1795," quoted from <http://www.reclaimdemocracy.org/quotes/madison_perpetual_war.html>.

4. Marouf Hasian Jr., *In the Name of Necessity: Military Tribunals and the Loss of American Civil Liberties* (Tuscaloosa: University of Alabama Press, 2005), and Geoffrey

R. Stone, *Perilous Times: Free Speech in Wartime* (New York: Norton, 2004), offer accounts of the limitations of civil liberties that war has wrought throughout American history.

5. Reporting on the Bush administration's record in the handling of detainees in the war on terror, Mark Danner writes: What has occurred "rests ultimately on President Bush's controversial decision, on February 7, 2002, to withhold protection of the Geneva Convention both from al-Qaeda and from Taliban fighters in Afghanistan. The decision rested on the argument, in the words of White House Counsel Alberto Gonzales [who became attorney general in 2005], that 'the war against terrorism is a new kind of war,' in fact, a 'new paradigm [that] renders obsolete Geneva's strict limitations on questioning of enemy prisoners and renders quaint some of its provisions.'" Danner, *Torture and Truth: America, Abu Ghraib, and the War on Terror* (New York: New York Review of Books, 2004), 42. The Bush administration position, articulated by Gonzales in his confirmation hearings as attorney general, is that "because the Constitution makes the president the 'Commander-in-Chief,' no law can restrict the actions he may take in pursuit of war." Quoted from David Cole, "What Bush Wants to Hear," *New York Review of Books*, November 17, 2005, 8. See also David Cole, "Who They Are: The Double Standard that Underlies Our Torture Policy," <http://www.slate.com/id/2130028/?nav=tap3>, and Dahlia Lithwick, "Uncivil Liberties: Why Won't the Bush Administration Obey the Law?," <http://www.slate.com/id/2132983>. A transcript of the confirmation hearings for Gonzales is available at <http://www.washingtonpost.com/wp-dyn/articles/A53883-2005Jan6_5.html>. Gonzales, of course, talks at length of his concern for the rule of law and for civil liberties, but the key moment comes when he says that, despite the fact that the Geneva Conventions do not apply to the detainees in the war on terror, "that's not to say that we don't operate without legal limitations and that we don't treat people consistent with our values as Americans. The president was very clear in providing directions that even though Geneva would not apply as a matter of law, that we would treat detainees humanely and subject to military necessity and as appropriate consistent with the principles of Geneva." Gonzales does not seem to recognize that saying the law does not apply here but that we can be expected (or trusted) to follow the law is to violate the first principle of the rule of law: no one gets to be the judge of his own behavior. Karen J. Greenberg and Joshua L. Dratel, eds., *The Torture Papers: The Road to Abu Ghraib* (New York: Cambridge University Press, 2005), collect the significant Bush administration documents that have argued for the policies adopted for treatment of the detainees.

6. Ron Chernow, *Alexander Hamilton* (New York: Penguin Books, 2004), 628.

7. John Duffy, *The Sanitarians: A History of American Public Health* (Urbana: University of Illinois Press, 1990), provides a full history of the growing government involvement—first on the city and state levels—in public health matters. Significantly, "the first U.S. study on health [1837] . . . was Dr. Benjamin W. McCready's work on the influence of trades and occupations on the health of workers. . . . His essay on the general living conditions of the poor was . . . intended to awaken the public conscience" (95).

8. One good example is the drug company Pfizer's unauthorized sales of its drug Neurontin for various ailments it did nothing to alleviate or cure. Pfizer admitted in court in 2004 to a whole panoply of techniques that effectively added up to the bribing of doctors to prescribe the drug. The drug's consumers, of course, had no way of knowing that their doctors were giving them faulty information. Pfizer agreed

to pay a $430 million fine to the government for the Medicaid fraud, but that still left the company holding the profits—estimated at more than $1 billion in a single year—for sales to consumers not on Medicaid. Obviously, there is no economic incentive against fraud in this case. For full details, see "Pfizer Admits Guilt in Promotion of Neurontin," <http://www.ahrp.org/informal/04/15/16.php>.

9. David Montgomery, *The Fall of the House of Labor: The Workplace, the State, and American Labor Activism, 1865–1925* (Cambridge: Cambridge University Press, 1987), and Melvyn Dubofsky and Foster Rhea Dulles, *Labor in America: A History*, 7th ed. (Wheeling, Ill.: Harlan Davidson, 2004), are two excellent sources for tracing the struggles by labor to gain governmental support for setting minimum wages, outlawing child labor, establishing and enforcing workplace safety regulations, and protecting the right to unionize. As Montgomery emphasizes, "The history of American workers has not been a story of progressive ascent from oppression to securely established rights," but, instead, the story of a "movement" that "has grown only sporadically and through fierce struggles, been interrupted time and again just when it seemed to reach flood tide, overwhelmed its foes only to see them revive in new and more formidable shapes, and been forced to reassess what it thought it had already accomplished and begin again" (7–8). The government has, to say the least, been a most uncertain ally, but the constant effort of both employers and employees to get the government on its side belies any notion that the government can—or will be—a nonplayer in economic matters.

10. See John Rawls, *Justice as Fairness: A Restatement* (Cambridge: Harvard University Press, 2001), 59–60.

11. Joseph E. Stiglitz, *Globalization and Its Discontents* (New York: Norton, 2002), is a good place to start in considering the ill effects of globalization in non-Western parts of the globe. I also recommend the film *Stolen Childhoods* for a powerful account of the exploitation of children as laborers and slaves around the world. For more on the film, see <http://www.stolenchildhoods.org/>.

12. David Harvey, *A Brief History of Neoliberalism* (New York: Oxford University Press, 2005), argues forcefully that globalization provides a means for consolidating the economic and political power of elites in the West.

13. For useful overviews of this history, see Michael Freeden, "The Coming of the Welfare State," 7–44, and Robert E. Goodin, "The End of the Welfare State?," 202–16, in Terrence Ball and Richard Bellamy, eds., *The Cambridge History of Twentieth Century Political Thought* (Cambridge: Cambridge University Press, 2003).

14. Rick Fantasia and Kim Voss, *Hard Work: Remaking the American Labor Movement* (Berkeley: University of California Press, 2004), esp. chap. 2, and David Sirota, *Hostile Takeover* (New York: Crown Publishers, 2006), chap. 9, detail the various ways unions and union organizing are currently undermined by federal and local authorities who support the anti-union policies and activities of big business.

15. Truman's racial integration of the military kept him off the ballot in Alabama and Mississippi in 1948 because the Democrats there refused to endorse him. That split in the Democratic Party—and Strom Thurmond's presidential run on the States' Rights ticket—foreshadowed the switch of the South from a Democratic to a Republican stronghold. Thurmond, of course, was a Democrat at the time; he would only switch parties many years later. George Packer's *Blood of the Liberals* (New York: Farrar, Straus, and Giroux, 2000) tells this story well.

16. Here's a pessimistic reading of the rise of the American middle class from 1900 to 1970: It was a function of white solidarity achieved in the face of the ever-present racial strain in American society. Once the racial "compact" was broken and blacks began to enter the public square and the public workplace, all bets were off and the exploitation of workers—white and black—returned with a vengeance. In this interpretation, the end of the "post-war compromise" and the rise (and success) of the black civil rights movement are of a piece. I find this interpretation a bit too neat, but race continually bedevils any narrative we offer about American history. Liberalism is committed to effective freedom for all—and the achievement of that goal has been continually thwarted and diverted by the politics of race in the United States.

17. Charles R. Geisst, *Monopolies in America* (New York: Oxford University Press, 2000), chaps. 7–8, offers a succinct account of these developments in corporate America since 1970. Constant "deregulation" of one industry after another has had the predictable result of a return of oligopoly if not monopoly in American capitalism.

18. There are various ways to think and talk about what I have called here the "return of ruthless capitalism." My reference is to the aggressive driving down of labor costs domestically by an appeal to the exigencies of a global labor market, by the movement of jobs overseas, and by the undermining of unions, of benefits, and/or of job security by practices such as "outsourcing" and the hiring of temporary and part-time workers. The two most solid indicators of these current capitalist practices are the growing income/wealth disparities in American society and the decline in benefits (particularly health insurance and pensions) among American workers (see Appendix, items 6–7, 9). The most dramatic indicator of the contempt in which management currently holds its employees is the gap between what it pays itself and what it pays its workers. (See Appendix, item 8.) That the current upsurge in employer power over employees dates from the early 1970s is generally agreed, even if reasons for the shift are more contested. Unquestionably, the data indicate 1973 as the key turning point. "Between 1947 and 1973, American families in every income category enjoyed income growth—and the poorest families had the highest rate of all. Then, between 1973 and 1998, average income remained close to stagnant (adjusted for inflation) for the bottom 40 percent of families, growing robustly only for the top quarter. Indeed, in 1993, before the boom that followed, the bottom half of families were [*sic*] worse off than in 1973." Edward N. Wolff, *Top Heavy: The Increasing Inequality of Wealth in America and What Can Be Done about It* (New York: New Press, 2002), viii. After the gains made by the least well-off between 1994 and 2000, the U.S. economy has returned to increasing the income and wealth of the most well-off and to offering no gains in income and wealth to the remaining 80 percent of the population. (See Appendix, items 6–7.)

19. Of course, contemporary conservatives insist that they favor economic policies that will bring prosperity to all—and thus that they are not hostile to American workers. But we have had, since the Reagan presidency, plenty of time to judge the result of the economic policies that conservatives advocate. The consequences are unambiguous; none of the economic growth of the past twenty-five years has found its way to the lower 50 percent of American households, while the vast preponderance of the new wealth that has been created has gone to the top 5 percent. (See Appendix, items 6–7.)

20. Robert Higgs, *Crisis and Leviathan: Critical Episodes in the Growth of American Government* (New York: Oxford University Press, 1987), is a fascinating study that attends

to many of the causes for state growth (war, the Great Depression, the need to attend to labor conditions and to employer-employee relations) that I touch upon all too briefly here. Thomas Katsaros, *The Development of the Welfare State in the Western World* (Lanham, Md.: University Press of America, 1995), offers a highly useful outline of the major steps toward the creation of the welfare state. For a good brief summary of the "decline" of the welfare state and of the various forces and ideas that have worked against it since the 1970s, see Christopher Pierson, *The Modern State*, 2nd ed. (New York: Routledge, 1996), 98–105.

21. The classic essay on the failure of socialism to gain much traction in America is Werner Sombart's *Why Is There No Socialism in the United States?*, trans. Patricia M. Hocking and C. T. Husbands (White Plains, N.Y.: International Arts and Sciences Press, 1976).

22. Philip J. Funigiello, *Chronic Politics: Health Care Security from FDR to George W. Bush* (Lawrence: University Press of Kansas, 2005), 62–87, details the Truman administration's failed efforts to establish national health insurance.

23. "Civil Rights Focus Shift Roils Staff at Justice," *Washington Post*, November 13, 2005, reports that "prosecutions for the kinds of racial and gender crimes traditionally handled by the [Civil Rights] division [of the Department of Justice] have declined by 40 percent over the past five years, according to department statistics."

24. Two good books on the lost opportunity of Reconstruction after the Civil War are Eric Foner, *Reconstruction: America's Unfinished Revolution, 1863–1877* (New York: Harper, 2002), and W. E. B. DuBois, *Black Reconstruction in America, 1860–1880* (New York: Free Press, 2004). Nicholas Lemann, *Redemption: The Last Battle of the Civil War* (New York: Farrar, Straus, and Giroux, 2006), tells the story of what today we would call "an insurgency" by Confederate veterans during Reconstruction and of how their violence drove blacks from the political sphere and federal troops from the South. For a good short version of that story, see James M. McPherson, "The Great Betrayal," *New York Review of Books*, November 30, 2006, 47–49.

25. Robert Putnam, *Bowling Alone: The Collapse and Revival of American Community* (New York: Simon and Schuster, 2000), documents the decline of the American commons. Stephen Macedo et al., *Democracy at Risk: How Political Choices Undermine Citizen Participation, and What We Can Do about It* (Washington, D.C.: Brookings Institution Press, 2005), also addresses the withdrawal of Americans from the public sphere.

26. Because there are wide differences between the situation in cities, in suburbs, and in rural areas, aggregate school segregation (or desegregation) statistics for the nation are just about meaningless. Thus, there are no simple figures for me to offer in my Appendix about school segregation in the United States. The complex story is told fully and well in Charles T. Clotfelter, *After Brown: The Rise and Retreat of School Desegregation* (Princeton: Princeton University Press, 2004). Clotfelter shows that a large number of blacks in the United States today attend schools that are predominantly black, but also that contact (as self-reported) between black and white students in our nation's schools has grown since 1954 and continued to grow slightly through the 1990s. Indices of racial tolerance (again self-reported attitudes) among students have also shown modest increases (see chap. 7). In sum, school integration below the college level has been very uneven, with some modest successes to its credit, but also with some glaring deficiencies, especially in our cities.

27. Four good sources for beginning to think about how recent immigrants are simi-

lar to and different from the immigrants of the 1880 to 1915 period are "Immigration and American Values: A Dialogue on Policy, Law, and Values," *ABA Focus* 14, no. 2 (Spring 1999), <http://www.abanet.org/publiced/focus/immvalues.html>; Gregory Rodriguez, "Still E Pluribus Unum: Recent Immigrants Are Joining the American Mainstream," *San Diego Union Tribune*, July 18, 1999, <http://www.newamerica.net/index.cfm?pg=article&DocID=287>; Pia Orrenius, "Immigrant Assimilation: Is the US Still a Melting Pot?," Federal Reserve Bank of Dallas, January 2004, <http://www.dallasfed.org/research/indepth/2004/id0401.html>; and Mortimer B. Zuckerman, "Land of Opportunity," *U.S. News & World Report*, June 20, 2005, <http://www.us-news.com/usnews/opinion/articles/050620/20edit.htm>.

28. Jennifer Hochshild and Nathan Scovronick, "School Desegregation and the American Dream," in Stephen J. Caldas and Carl L. Bankston III, eds., *The End of Desegregation?* (New York: Nova Science Publishers, 2003), 25–50, document the positive educational and social results of school integration. Citing a number of long-range studies, Hochshild and Scovronick report: "Desegregated children are more likely than others to become integrated adults. Both black and white adults who attended desegregated schools have more close friends and casual acquaintances of the other race than do adults from racially isolated schools. They are also more likely to attend desegregated colleges, live in (or at least accept) integrated neighborhoods, hold jobs in integrated work settings, and be comfortable with racially-mixed work groups" (35). Hochshild and Scovronick's essay is the best thing I have read on America's mixed experience and mixed success in attempting to desegregate its schools. And I think they reach the right conclusion: "Winston Churchill once described democracy as the worst system of government—except for all of the others. School desegregation was like that. Few people outside the black community wanted it badly and districts sometimes did it poorly or were too constrained by political boundaries; but when coupled with educational reform, desegregation was always and still is the policy best suited to help all students pursue individual success and learn how to live in the multiracial and multiethnic future that will be theirs. Integration is not guaranteed to follow desegregation, but it is impossible without it" (42).

29. The biggest disappointment is that integration has made almost no dent in the economic gap between blacks and whites in this country. (See Appendix, item 2.) That fact is the main piece of evidence that integration has been a failure. At the fiftieth anniversary in 2004 of the *Brown v. Board of Education* decision, there was an outpouring of books assessing the fruits of integration. Most writers saw little or no betterment in the lives of black Americans. See esp. Derrick Bell's *Silent Covenants: Brown v. Board of Education and the Unfulfilled Hopes for Racial Reform* (New York: Oxford University Press, 2004), and Charles J. Ogletree Jr., *All Deliberate Speed: Reflections on the First Half Century of Brown v. Board of Education* (New York: Norton, 2004).

30. Alexis de Tocqueville, *Democracy in America*, trans. George Lawrence (New York: Harper and Row, 1966), vol. 2, pt. 2, chap. 1, 473.

31. Quoted from *The Moral Writings of John Dewey*, ed. James Gouinlock (Amherst, N.Y.: Prometheus Books, 1994), 191–92.

BOOK FOUR

1. James Madison, *The Federalist* (New York: Barnes and Noble, 2006), 210. Subsequent references to the Federalist Papers come from this edition, with page numbers given parenthetically in the text.

2. Quoted from Gordon S. Wood, *The Creation of the American Republic, 1776–1787* (Chapel Hill: University of North Carolina Press, 1998), 24. Wood supplies examples of similar sentiments expressed by Americans of the Revolutionary period—for example, Benjamin Church's (of Boston) statement that liberty was "the happiness of living under laws of our own making" (24). The Declaration of Independence declares that "it is the Right of the People . . . to institute new Government, laying its foundation on such principles and organizing its power in such form, as to them shall seem most likely to effect their Safety and Happiness."

3. My account of "pragmatic" democracy is deeply influenced by Ian Shapiro's *The State of Democratic Theory* (Princeton: Princeton University Press, 2003), although I inflect his notion of "competitive democracy" rather differently. In Shapiro's formulation, democracy stakes "its claim to our allegiance as the best available means for managing power relations among people who disagree about the nature of the common good, among many other things, but who nonetheless are bound to live together. To be sure, this view rests on a conception of the common good. But it is a comparatively thin one, best captured by the formulation that it embodies what those with an interest in avoiding domination share" (146). The key is that those who lose an election or a vote today may win one tomorrow. "It is institutionalized uncertainty about the future that gives people who lose in any given round the incentive to remain committed to the process rather than reach for their guns or otherwise become alienated from the political system" (14).

4. Max Weber introduced the notion of "legitimacy," which attempts to account for the fact that some authorities are voluntarily obeyed because their "right" to command is acknowledged. There are various ways to obtain legitimacy (Weber himself distinguishes three sources—tradition, rationally grounded institutional procedures, and charisma). My suggestion here is that democracy relies on procedures plus outcomes (stability and peace) and what Shapiro (*State of Democratic Theory*, 14) calls "the perpetual possibility of upsetting the status quo." This last feature is crucial because it enables people who disagree with legitimate authority to contest and, perhaps, even to supplant that authority within the recognized, and hence legitimated, procedures of the political system. For a good overview of theories of legitimacy, see Anthony H. Birch, *The Concepts and Theories of Modern Democracy* (New York: Routledge, 1993), 28–42.

5. In *State of Democratic Theory*, chap. 5 (esp. 124–39), Shapiro takes up the question of what leads people to lose faith in their political system and to rebel. The empirical evidence he surveys suggests that a sense of what is "just" or "unjust" in the distribution of power or resources is more crucial than actual inequalities. In short, people are moved to rebel when they perceive that a system is "unfair"; hence, that system loses legitimacy in their eyes, which, in turn, justifies rebellion against it.

6. Shapiro (*State of Democratic Theory*) writes: "The focus on incentives [to keeping people involved and invested] . . . underscores the importance of avoiding all-or-noth-

ing policies. Ensuring that the stakes in any given contest are comparatively low attenuates the incentive for losers to act on the impulse to defect. If issues can be raised periodically, if they can be pursued in different forums, if it is never the case that all issues are up for decision at the same time, and if candidates can run for a variety of offices, then they have more reason to remain committed to the system when they lose. To the extent that one wants to create incentives for those who do not prevail in a given contest to keep their opposition to the outcome 'loyal,' it is important that they perceive future or different avenues for pursuing their goals; otherwise there is no reason for them not to defect—whether this means alienated withdrawal, turning to crime, or becoming a politicized revolutionary" (90).

7. The pragmatist would add that consensus is most often achieved through experience (interaction with diverse others in public), not through intellectual persuasion prior to or apart from all experience. It is as we live out a particular social arrangement—and as we engage in various forms of democratic interaction—that we come to accept relationships and values that we formerly scorned or feared. Let me stress once again that such reconciliation doesn't always occur. The pluralist reminds us that we should expect that there will always be some conflicts in any society. But that is no reason to deny that some conflicts fade away over time; they become nonissues or even yield to agreement. The question of how that happens—and how its occurrence might be facilitated—is of relevance to any society that values peace and stability, just as the related questions of how to maintain peace in the face of conflict and disagreement are also relevant.

8. Because making sure that all parties have a stake in the system is of such practical importance, many democracies (especially those in societies with strong ethnic or other identity-based divisions) do not emphasize majority rule at all, focusing instead on guaranteed representation of all the different factions in the society. In fact, the United States is rather anomalous among contemporary democracies in not having some kind of proportional representation (although the "majority minority" congressional districts in the United States are a kind of proportional representation). For a good introduction to the "art" of creating a democratic system (along with a chart that shows what system is in place in 214 countries), see Andrew Reynolds, Ben Reilly, and Andrew Ellis, *Electoral System Design: The New International IDEA Handbook* (Stockholm: International IDEA, 2005). My thanks to my colleague Andy Reynolds for everything he has taught me about on-the-ground efforts to craft democracy in the new states of Africa, Asia, and the Middle East.

9. For an excellent overview of disputes over how polarized Americans actually are in their political attitudes (as contrasted to the obvious polarization among political elites), see John Leo, "Splitting Society, Not Hairs," *U.S. News & World Report*, December 15, 2003, <http://www.usnews.com/opinion/articles/031215/15john.htm> (accessed on January 3, 2006). Leo reports that some observers claim that only 7 percent of Americans now count as swing voters (which would be an ominous development), while other studies put the number as high as 20 percent.

10. Jacob S. Hacker and Paul Pierson, *Off-Center: The Republican Revolution and the Erosion of American Democracy* (New Haven: Yale University Press, 2005), offer an extended and sobering account of how the United States has reached its current frayed condition.

11. Gingrich's remarks—here and in the previous paragraph—are quoted from Rob-

ert B. Reich, *Reason: Why Liberals Will Win the Battle for America* (New York: Vintage, 2005), 35.

12. James Bohman and William Rehg, eds., *Deliberative Democracy: Essays on Reason and Politics* (Cambridge: MIT Press, 1997), Amy Gutmann and Dennis Thompson, *Why Deliberative Democracy?* (Princeton: Princeton University Press, 2004), and James S. Fishkin, *Democracy and Deliberation: New Directions for Democratic Reform* (New Haven: Yale University Press, 1991), provide important contemporary versions of the connection between democracy and processes of deliberation.

13. "On the view represented by such thinkers as John Stuart Mill and Hannah Arendt . . . this transformative power of politics makes democratic engagement an end in itself; deliberative democracy should be advocated precisely because of the beneficial educative effects it has on citizens." Bohman and Rehg, *Deliberative Democracy*, xiii.

14. In our own day, Jürgen Habermas has developed the most far-reaching version of this set of norms for fully democratic speech against which we can judge distorted communication that attempts to manipulate the deliberative process. For Habermas, a "regulative ideal" becomes the standard by which we can judge how far actual practices in *soi-disant* democracies fall short. For a succinct statement of Habermas's view, see his "Morality, Society, and Ethics: An Interview with Torben Hviid Nelsen," *Justification and Application: Remarks on Discourse Ethics*," trans. Ciaran P. Cronin (Cambridge: MIT Press, 1993), 147–76, esp. 163–65.

15. For an informative discussion of how deliberation and calling on the input of many different people improves results in a variety of settings, see James Surowiecki's *The Wisdom of Crowds: Why the Many Are Smarter Than the Few and How Collective Wisdom Shapes Business, Economies, Societies and Nation* (New York: Doubleday, 2004).

16. "Incumbents in the House [of Representatives] are fiendishly hard to dislodge— in a typical election year, more than 90% of those who stand, win. This is partly because both parties have shamelessly gerrymandered districts to protect sitting congressmen, and partly because incumbents outspend their challengers by a factor of 6.6. (Why give money to someone who's going to lose, and can't return the favor?)." "Will Lightning Strike the Republicans?" *Economist*, January 7–13, 2006, 27. For more on the lack of competition in contemporary elections and the role of money in our politics, see Appendix, item 10. See also Elizabeth Drew, "Fear and Loathing in Washington," *New York Review of Books*, February 12, 2004, 17–20, and "Washington for Sale," *New York Review of Books*, June 23, 2005, 24–27; and Jeffrey H. Birnbaum's *The Money Men: The Real Story of Fund-Raising's Influence on Political Power in America* (New York: Crown Publishers, 2000).

17. For a sobering overview of how the ability of the press to act as an independent source of information has been undermined, see Michael Massing, "The End of News?," *New York Review of Books*, December 1, 2005, 23–25, and "The Press: The Enemy Within," *New York Review of Books*, December 15, 2005, 36–44. Chris Mooney, *The Republican War on Science* (New York: Basic Books, 2005), documents the discounting of scientific information by today's partisans on the right.

18. The strong tendency in today's politics to circumvent the deliberative process— as particularly evident in various parliamentary maneuvers in Congress—reflects the equally strong desire to avoid compromise. For a detailed account of how Congress has avoided or curtailed deliberation over pending legislation, see Susan Milligan, "Back-Room Dealing a Capitol Trend," *Boston Globe*, October 3, 2004. Among other

practices, Milligan notes: "The House Rules Committee, which is meant to tweak the language in bills that come out of committee, sometimes rewrites key passages of legislation approved by other committees, then forbids members from changing the bills on the floor"; "bills are increasingly crafted behind closed doors, and on two major pieces of legislation—the Medicare and energy bills, few Democrats were allowed into critical conference committee meetings, sessions that have historically been bipartisan"; and "the amount of time spent openly debating bills has dropped dramatically, and lawmakers are further hamstrung by an abbreviated schedule that gives them little time to fully examine a bill before voting on it." In two follow-up articles—Milligan's "Energy Bill a Special-Interests Triumph," *Boston Globe*, October 4, 2004, and Christopher Rowland's "Medicare Bill a Study in DC Spoils System," *Boston Globe*, October 5, 2004—the decline in deliberation is also linked to the growing role lobbyists play in actually writing legislation.

19. Norberto Bobbio, *The Future of Democracy*, trans. Roger Griffin (Minneapolis: University of Minnesota Press, 1987), chap. 2, "Representative and Direct Democracy," offers a balanced look at the case against representative democracy and a persuasive argument that representation of some sort is unavoidable.

20. Robert A. Dahl's *How Democratic Is the American Constitution?* (New Haven: Yale University Press, 2001), 48–50, 87–88, 144–45, clearly lays out where and how the Constitution falls short of democracy, particularly in violating the one-person, one-vote principle in congressional representation and in the Electoral College votes awarded to each state in presidential elections. Jacob S. Hacker and Paul Pierson, *Off-Center*, describe how this undemocratic arrangement currently operates. "The mismatch between popular votes and electoral outcomes is even more striking in the Senate. Combining the last three Senate elections, Democrats have actually won two-and-a-half million *more* votes than Republicans. Yet they now hold only 44 seats in that 100-person chamber because Republicans dominate the less populous states that are so heavily over-represented in the Senate" (36).

21. Alan Wolfe, *One Nation, After All: What Middle-Class Americans Really Think* (New York: Penguin Books, 1998), has been the most vocal advocate of the view that political partisanship in Washington does not accurately reflect prevailing opinions or passions in the country at large. Hacker and Pierson, *Off-Center*, esp. chap. 1, from a very different perspective also challenge the notion that the partisan positions taken by today's politicians, especially those on the Republican right, actually reflect the mood or views of the country at large.

22. Douglas J. Amy's *Real Choices/New Voices: How Proportional Representation Elections Could Revitalize American Democracy*, 2nd ed. (New York: Columbia University Press, 2002), is a passionate and cogent call for wide-scale reform of how we organize representation in the United States.

23. As of January 2006, six states (Maine, Vermont, Arizona, New Jersey, North Carolina, and New Mexico) were experimenting with some version of publicly financed elections. For details, see <http:www.newrules.org/gov/clean.html> and <http://www.publicampaign.org>. Of course, we also have a mechanism for partial public financing of presidential campaigns, but its ability to limit the power of private dollars in politics is just about moot now that candidates have chosen to "opt" out of the system because it limits how much they can raise and spend on their campaigns. Bruce Ackerman and Ian Ayers's *Voting with Dollars: A New Paradigm for Campaign Finance*

(New Haven: Yale University Press, 2002) offers a variant of the public financing of campaigns that does not provide money to candidates directly but has voters choose which candidates will receive funding. This idea combines the effort to level the playing field with an effort to increase voter participation. Another ingenious proposal (and I have to admit I can't find my source for this one) is that all political donations go through a blind trust so that the candidates who receive the money have no idea who the donor is. Such a plan would at least let us see how many donors really do not expect a direct quid pro quo for their money.

24. "The United States is 'alone among 146 countries, according to one study, in refusing to provide free television time to political candidates.' Furthermore: 'a key provision [in proposals for campaign finance reform in 2002] that would have forced the networks to offer candidates their least expensive advertising rates [was] originally passed by the Senate by a 69 to 31 margin, [but] died in the House of Representatives following a furious campaign by the National Association of Broadcasters and the cable television industry.'" Quoted from Brian Barry, *Why Social Justice Matters* (Malden, Mass.: Polity, 2005), 239.

25. Bruce Ackerman and James S. Fishkin's *Deliberation Day* (New Haven: Yale University Press, 2005) combines the attempt to involve more citizens in deliberative processes while also addressing the issue of voter apathy. Stephen Macedo et al., *Democracy at Risk: How Political Choices Undermine Citizen Participation, and What We Can Do about It*, documents current voter alienation from political processes in the United States and suggests various remedies.

26. The recent Supreme Court decisions (*Vieth v. Jubelirer* in 2004 and *League of Latin American Citizens v. Perry* in 2006) that basically refused to intervene in gerrymandering practices were, I think, correctly decided because the Constitution explicitly leaves such matters to the states and to Congress. But the current situation reveals a deep flaw in the Constitution, a failure to provide a check to an abuse of power that the founders simply did not anticipate. The current setup is deeply corrupt—and we probably need a constitutional amendment specifying fair methods for legislative redistricting. The models for such an amendment already exist in Iowa and Arizona. I do not think campaign finance reform requires a constitutional amendment because the first amendment (free speech) arguments made against such reforms are specious. But it may prove necessary to go the constitutional amendment route for reining in the role of money in government if the first amendment objections to it continue to prevail in the courts. Of course, the prospects for passing redistricting and campaign finance amendments are pretty slim—and that fact is the one that I find most depressing when viewing the current American political scene. The marriage of corporate dollars and our politicians has concentrated power in the hands of the few, and they are using that power to accumulate more wealth and more power. The problem, of course, is that the very politicians who have benefited from the current system would have to approve any reform of that system, any constitutional amendments of the sort I am advocating.

27. Rousseau lists among the four conditions for successful democracy the stipulation that there be "a large measure of equality in social rank and fortune, without which equality in rights and authority will not last long." Rousseau, *The Social Contract*, trans. Maurice Cranston (New York: Penguin Books, 1968), bk. IV, chap. 4, "Democracy," 113.

28. As anyone who teaches at an American university knows, as do most middle- and upper-middle-class parents of children between the ages of 14 and 23, the anxiety about getting into the "right" or "most prestigious" college has grown tremendously over the past fifteen years, fed by ranking systems like the annual one produced by *U.S. News & World Report*. One sign of the anxiety has been the outpouring of books that tell you how to get your child into an Ivy League school; another sign is the growth of an ancillary industry that preps students for the SATs and offers a wide variety of other services for students who are applying to college. During the same period, college has become more expensive in the United States and thus, not surprisingly, as Gary Orfeld reported in 2000, "in contrast to the peak of access when the top quartile of families, in terms of income, were six times more likely than the bottom group to send their children to college, the ratio is now ten to one." Orfield, "Policy and Equity Lessons of a Third of a Century of Educational Reforms in the United States," in *Unequal Schools, Unequal Chances: The Challenges to Equal Opportunity in the Americas*, ed. Fernando Reamers (Cambridge: Harvard University Press, 2000), 412. Given that education is the surest avenue to social and economic movement upward in American society, it is not surprising that upward mobility is on the decline in the United States. (See New York Times, *Class Matters* [New York: New York Times, 2005], and Appendix, item 7.) For a good overview of current anxieties about college, see Andrew Hacker, "The Truth about Colleges," *New York Review of Books*, November 3, 2005, 51–54.

29. *Global Corruption Report, 2004* (London: Pluto Press, 2004), prepared by Transparency International, in its "global comparison of political corruption" ranks the United States as evidencing "low corruption" in regard to "irregular payments in government policy-making," as evidencing "medium corruption" in terms of "prevalence of illegal political donations" (with 18 percent of countries better than the United States and 41 percent worse), and as evidencing "high corruption" in "political consequences of legal political contributions" (worse than 80 percent of the 102 countries in the study). Not only do these results square with my own, admittedly unscientific, sense of American political culture, but they also suggest that campaign finance reform, if done right, could have real benefits since the tendency to follow the law is still fairly strong in this country. It is legal, not illegal, political donations that are the problem in the United States, and that's why the law needs to be changed. On the power of American business in the framing of legislation and in garnering "corporate welfare" (various tax breaks and subsidies from the state), see David Sirota, *Hostile Takeover* (New York: Crown Publishers, 2006); Noreena Hertz, *The Silent Takeover: Global Capitalism and the Death of Democracy* (New York: Free Press, 2001); and Mark A. Smith, *American Business and Political Power: Public Opinion, Elections, and Democracy* (Chicago: University of Chicago Press, 2000).

CONCLUSION

1. Fareed Zakaria, *The Future of Freedom: Illiberal Democracy at Home and Abroad* (New York: Norton, 2003), describes the possible tension between liberalism and democracy this way: "The tension between constitutional liberalism and democracy centers on the scope of governmental authority. Constitutional liberalism is about the limitation of power; democracy is about its accumulation and use. For this reason, many

eighteenth- and nineteenth-century liberals saw democracy as a force that could undermine liberty. The tendency for a democratic government to believe it has absolute sovereignty (that is, power) can result in the centralization of authority, often by extraconstitutional means and with grim results. What you end up with is little different from a dictatorship, albeit one with greater legitimacy" (101–2). Zakaria's book has helped me think about this issue of liberal versus illiberal democracy, and he attends to many of the same signs of deep trouble in current American democracy, especially the role of money and lobbyists in present-day Washington. (See his chap. 5.) But I couldn't disagree more with his conclusion that "what we need in politics today is not more democracy but less" (248). The difference between the ways we read our current situation hinges, I think, on his posing the choice as between "limiting" power and "accumulating" it. What Zakaria misses is the key liberal insight (ultimately derived from Montesquieu) that it is neither desirable nor possible to limit power. Power is desirable because it is capacity. So the way to safeguard against the abuses that power undoubtedly sometimes enables is to check any power with other counterbalancing (thus, necessarily roughly equal) powers. The solution to the dangers posed by power is not (primarily) limitation, but proliferation and distribution. Democracy can be a means for the proliferation and distribution of power, especially when democracy works hand in hand with a liberal commitment to effective freedom for all.

2. Thus Tocqueville, *Democracy in America*, bk. 2, pt. 2, chap. 1, writes: "Freedom is found at different times and in different forms; it is not exclusively dependent on one social state, and one finds it elsewhere than in democracies. It cannot therefore be taken as the distinctive characteristic of democratic ages. The particular and predominating fact peculiar to those ages is equality of conditions, and the chief passion which stirs men at such times is the love of this same equality" (474).

3. Stuart Hall, *The Hard Road to Renewal: Thatcherism and the Crisis of the Left* (London: Verso, 1988), 150–60, develops the concept of "authoritarian populism" to characterize the "new" conservatism introduced by Margaret Thatcher. Granting the differences between English and American politics, Hall's "authoritarian populism" is close to what I am calling "illiberal democracy." Especially relevant is Hall's characterization of the "'anti-statist' strategy of the 'new right'" that, he comments, is "not one which refuses to operate through the state; it is one which conceives a more limited state role, and which advances through the attempt, ideologically, to *represent itself* as antistatist, for the purposes of populist mobilization" (152). Also relevant is Hall's description of the new right as "a movement towards a dominative and 'authoritarian' form of democratic class politics—paradoxically, apparently rooted in the 'transformism' (Gramsci's term) of populist discontents" (153). The most celebrated American examination of similar dynamics has been Tom Frank's *What's the Matter with Kansas?: How Conservatives Won the Heart of America* (New York: Henry Holt, 2004).

4. For a full-scale analysis of how many Americans are a step away from financial disaster, see Teresa A. Sullivan, Elizabeth Warren, and Jay Lawrence Westbrook, *The Fragile Middle Class: Americans in Debt* (New Haven: Yale University Press, 2000).

5. Jacob S. Hacker and Paul Pierson's *Off-Center: The Republican Revolution and the Erosion of American Democracy* (New Haven: Yale University Press, 2005) insists that increasing economic inequality is directly linked to the decline of democracy: "The past three decades have witnessed an increase in economic inequality that has no precedent in modern US History or the recent experience of other affluent nations.

Over the same period, and not by coincidence, political inequality has also increased dramatically. Today money plays a much larger role in politics than it once did, and other forms of political participation appear to have become increasingly skewed in economic terms, too. In no other rich democracy has the playing field become so sharply tilted against citizens of modest means" (194).

6. Jeffrey K. Tulis's *The Rhetorical Presidency* (Princeton: Princeton University Press, 1987) and Craig A. Rimmerman's *Presidency by Plebiscite: The Reagan-Bush Era in Institutional Perspective* (Boulder, Colo.: Westview Press, 1993) are two books that track the fairly recent history of the president's by-passing the deliberative and legislative process by "going to the people."

7. Hacker and Pierson, *Off-Center*, 17.

8. For the Bush administration's account of the Clear Skies Act, go to www.epa. gov/clearskies/; for a more skeptical view, go to <http://sierraclub.org/cleanair/clear_ skies.asp>. On the Healthy Forests Initiative, see <http://www.healthyforests.gov> and <http://sierraclub.org/fires/healthyforests_initiative.asp>.

ACKNOWLEDGMENTS

I cannot think alone. I am spurred into expression by what others do and say—and I only discover what I think and believe in the process of struggling to articulate my inchoate ideas to friends, students, and projected readers. I dedicate this book to Allen Dunn, James Thompson, and Tyler Curtain as synecdoches, as representatives, of all my interlocutors. Allen has been my closest intellectual collaborator for some twelve years now, and I have learned more from him than anyone on the planet. His intelligence is matched only by his endless good humor; my friendship with him is one of the great good things in my life. My co-conspirator James has been the making of my academic life in Chapel Hill; from team-teaching graduate seminars to chewing the fat in the early hours before any of our colleagues are in the building, James and I have grown old together. Tyler made me write this book by asking me directly to codify my thoughts on liberalism. My conversations with him have changed my thinking time and again even though—maybe precisely because—we have such similar reactions to events, writers, and ideas.

The list of the many others who have contributed to this work is absurdly long, but I am going to indulge myself nonetheless. No one has to read these acknowledgments, although, of course, they will be the first—and perhaps the last—thing many readers will peruse. Michael Bérubé got me started by having me take over his blog for a month. His encouragement and his readers' responses gave me the impetus to morph those posts into this book. Pete Simon, Jeff Spinner-Halev, and (especially) John Holbo read big chunks of the manuscript, and I recast it dramatically in response to their reactions. I wrote the first draft during a semester's leave at the University of North Carolina's (UNC) Institute for the Arts and Humanities. My fellow fellows that term—Christopher Browning, Cori Dauber, Flora Lu Holt, Charlene Regester, Andrew Reynolds, Joyce Rudinsky, and our wonderful leader, Julia Wood—also read part of the book and suggested many improvements. I owe even more to Ruel Tyson, erstwhile director of the institute, whose job I have since inherited. This book reflects my internalization of Ruel's spirit over the past twelve years. Special thanks to John Burress, the donor who funded my semester's leave and who also cofounded (along with Knox Massey, to whom I also send thanks) the chaired professorship in honor of Ruel that I now hold. My thanks also to the institute's staff members for all their hard work and good cheer: Jane Brown, Jean Chandler, Mary Flanagan, Cathi James, David Kiel, Martha Marks, Marty Mitchell, and Sandy Smalley.

Meili Steele has, once again, read a book of mine for a publisher and improved it with his judicious comments. An anonymous reader went far beyond the call of duty, producing a forty-page report that buoyed me with praise before pointing out a thousand small improvements and the need to rethink entirely one of the book's main arguments. His or her fingerprints are all over the book you hold in your hands. Sian Hunter, Paula Wald, and Stevie Champion at the University of North Carolina Press are editors to live (and write) for, especially if you use the word "very" very often and are addicted to parentheses.

Now the pace steps up, although each of the people listed here deserves his or her special word. To my supportive colleagues—Nicholas Allen, Bill Andrews, Bob Cantwell, Eric Downing, Gregg Flaxman, Larry Grossberg, Jennifer Ho, Joy Kasson, Lloyd Kramer, Megan Matchinske, Della Pollock, Alan Shapiro, Bev Taylor, and Jane Thrailkill—thanks for making Chapel Hill hop. To the political theorists at UNC and Duke—Susan Bickford, Rom Coles, Kim Curtis, Peter Euben, Steve Leonard, Mike Lienesch, and Jeff Spinner-Halev—thanks for taking me seriously (at least some of the time) as a political theorist. To the philosophers at UNC—Dorit Bar-On, Doug MacLean, Gerry Postema, Geoff Sayre-McCord, and Susan Wolf—thanks for letting me sit— and stick my oar—in. To my students—Patrick Cooper, Jill Craven, Devon Fisher, Eric Iversen, Nancy Jesser, Gary Johnson, Brent Kinser, Andrew Lallier, Carrie Matthews, Will Nolan, Supritha Rajan, Barb Ryan, and Elizabeth Stockton—thanks for taking my obsessions so seriously. And then there's the antediluvians, the ones who have been there all these years whenever and wherever I needed them: Charles Altieri, Kath Anderson, David Brehmer, Tony Cascardi, Zach Cowan, Randi Davenport, Doug Dempster, Judith Farquhar, Daniel Hayes, Jim Hevia, Devon Hodges, John Kucich, Carol Lashof, Dan Latimer, Jeff Nealon, Bill Newton, Mary Papke, Lee Quinby, Bob Rice, Dianne Sadoff, Sarah Stadler, Jeff Williams, and Lynn York. A special word for my mother, Madeline, and for all my siblings is in order, for reasons they will understand. Barbara, Pat, Kevin, Mary, Jane, and Kathy, you are the best. I love you.

A number of causes, not the least of which was a broken wrist, made the writing of this book far more disruptive of family peace and sanity than any of my prior ones. Kiernan lost his room for a whole Christmas vacation to books strewn on the floor and father muttering at the computer. Siobhan missed dinners and her parent's undivided attention, not to mention some needed driving lessons. The brunt fell on Jane—and she bore it with a grace that her wayward husband hardly deserved. Luckily, she is filled with the liberal spirit that attends to need over desert. Such love is only had as a gift— and can only be appropriately acknowledged by a return in kind. The next one's on me guys.

INDEX

Canovan, Margaret, 218 (n. 33)

Cantor, Joseph E., 211

"Capabilities approach," 65–67, 73–74, 165, 224 (n. 66)

Capitalism, 11–12, 72, 103–4, 111, 115, 119, 127, 135, 141–42, 144, 146, 147–50, 154, 205–8, 236 (n. 37), 244 (nn. 17, 18)

Carlyle, Thomas, 103, 104

Carter, Jimmy, 153

Cavell, Stanley, 230 (n. 108)

Chait, Jon, 235 (n. 31)

Checks and balances, 3, 15, 17, 19–22, 35, 63, 108, 118, 129, 130–31, 141–42, 154, 164, 184, 189, 193, 215 (n. 14), 229 (n. 101), 240 (n. 75)

Cheney, Dick, 124, 133, 235 (n. 31)

Chernow, Ron, 67, 145, 225 (n. 71), 242 (n. 6)

Church, Benjamin, 247 (n. 2)

Churchill, Winston, 101, 246 (n. 28)

Citizenship, 38, 40, 68, 219 (n. 36); and political participation, 161–62, 167–68, 181–82, 245 (n. 25)

Civic republicanism, 12–14, 72, 168, 214–15 (n. 6), 229 (n. 101)

Civil liberties, 7, 13, 14–15, 19, 53, 99, 105, 130–31, 133, 139, 144–45, 168, 191, 239–40 (n. 69), 240 (n. 75), 241 (n. 4), 242 (n. 5)

Civil rights movement, 39, 149, 155, 161, 244 (n. 16)

Civil society/public sphere, 17, 26, 53–63, 158–64, 177–79, 187–88, 216 (n. 16), 223 (nn. 53, 54), 225 (n. 74), 245 (n. 25)

Civil war, 55–56, 63–64, 105, 174–75

Clinton, Bill, 170, 212

Clotfelter, Charles T., 245 (n. 26)

Cohen, Jean L., 216 (n. 16)

Cole, David, 242 (n. 5)

Columbus, Christopher, 11

Competition, 103, 164, 181; and democratic politics, 172, 174–76, 178, 247 (n. 3)

Conflicting interests, 26–27, 45–46, 72, 150–51, 179

Connolly, William, 221 (n. 50)

Conrad, Joseph, 128, 238 (n. 56)

Conservatism: and American South, 101, 243 (n. 215); in America today, 1, 6–7, 101–2, 142, 191–92; and antirationalism,

58–59, 103–6, 108–12, 116; and arguments for inequality, 100–101, 107–11, 118, 120–23, 131; and authority, 30–31, 48, 100, 103–5, 218 (nn. 28, 29), 232 (n. 17); and big government, 143–45, 153–54, 253 (n. 3); and change, 104–7, 110, 116–17, 232 (n. 15); and Christianity, 108–9; and civil liberties, 144–45, 240 (n. 75); and consolidation of power, 191–92; and Constitution, 14–15, 24; and divisive politics, 174–75, 192–93; and economic inequality, 117, 134, 149–51, 243 (n. 14); and European social democracies, 115, 233 (n. 26), 234 (n. 27); and fatalism, 107, 115–16, 121; and globalization, 148–49; and health care, 153; historical meaning of, 8, 99–101; and hostility to equality, 68–70, 73–74, 76, 84–85, 87–88, 100–101, 155, 191–92, 195, 225 (n. 73), 226 (n. 78), 234 (n. 27), 244 (n. 19); and hostility to pluralism, 47, 51–53, 62, 105, 113, 133, 161, 231–32 (n. 11); and individualism, 80–81, 88; and justice, 76, 113, 115–16, 119–22, 188, 226–27 (n. 83); and laissez-faire theories, 13, 214 (n. 5); and morality, 119–22, 217 (n. 23); and national identity, 35–40; and politics of fear, 161, 192; and responsibility, 119–21; and war, 144–45. *See also* Laissez-faire conservatism; Neoconservatism; Traditional conservatism

Constitutional crisis, 130–31, 239 (nn. 63–66, 68)

Constitution of the United States, 3, 14, 15, 16, 21–22, 23, 26, 35–38, 47, 53, 54, 62, 64, 67, 68, 71–72, 76, 100, 106, 130, 145, 157, 158, 183, 189, 215 (n. 7), 216 (nn. 19, 21), 216–17 (n. 22), 242 (n. 5), 251 (n. 26)

Constitutions, 193; interpretations and revisions of, 23–24, 216–17 (n. 22); as legal expedient, 21, 189, 252–53 (n. 1); and national identity, 38–40

Conti, Joseph, 222 (n. 51)

Cooper, James Fenimore, 100–101, 230 (n. 4)

Corrado, Anthony, 211

Corruption, 186–87, 251 (n. 26), 252 (n. 29)

Coulter, Ann, 139

Cultural politics, 137–39, 162–64

Dahl, Robert A., 215 (n. 7), 221 (n. 50), 250 (n. 20)

Danner, Mark, 242 (n. 5)

Darwin, Charles, 44

Davidson, Donald, 101, 230 (n. 5)

Debs, Eugene, 240 (n. 76)

Declaration of Independence, 3, 7, 14, 67, 68–69, 73, 225 (n. 73), 247 (n. 2)

Deficits in governmental budgets, 132, 143–44, 158, 184, 194–95, 235 (n. 31)

Deliberation, 4, 46, 60, 170; and democracy, 76–84, 193, 249 (nn. 12–15, 18), 251 (n. 25)

DeLillo, Don, 196

De Maistre, Joseph, 99, 228 (n. 89)

Democracy, 167–88; and accountability, 173, 182, 185; and citizen participation, 161–62, 167–68, 181–82, 185–86, 245 (n. 12), 251 (n. 25); and decision-making procedures, 170–71, 175, 176–77, 179, 193; and deliberation, 176–84; and economic inequality, 186–87, 253–54 (n. 5); and economic issues, 151–52, 181; and equality, 8, 70–71, 184–88, 191, 251 (n. 27), 253 (n. 2); and founders, 12, 16–17; and handing over power, 56, 167–68, 170–71, 176; historical emergence of, 11–13, 99–100, 213–14 (n. 1); as ideal, 178, 181; and "identity" political parties, 172–73; and inclusiveness, 180; and issues of representation, 182–84, 248 (n. 8), 250 (nn. 19–22); and legitimacy, 168–70; in neoconservative thought, 124, 127, 128; pragmatic view of, 169–70, 175, 247 (n. 3), 248 (n. 7); relationship to liberalism, 1, 5, 11–13, 19–20, 189–90, 252–53 (n. 1); and stability, 171–72, 176

Democratic Party, 112, 120, 153, 235 (n. 32), 243 (n. 15)

Dewey, John, 4, 8, 9, 43, 64–65, 81–84, 88, 96–97, 110, 113, 160, 164–65, 169, 177–80, 181, 213 (nn. 3, 6), 220 (n. 44), 224 (n. 64), 227 (n. 89), 228 (n. 94), 230 (nn. 106, 107), 246 (n. 31)

Disagreement, 23, 55–56, 59–60, 61, 63, 172

Discrimination, 76–77, 149–50, 155–64, 190, 245 (n. 23)

Disraeli, Benjamin, 103

Doctorow, E. L., 196

Dratel, Joshua L., 242 (n. 5)

Drew, Elizabeth, 239 (n. 68), 249 (n. 16)

Dubofsky, Melvyn, 243 (n. 9)

Du Bois, W. E. B., 245 (n. 24)

Duffy, John, 242 (n. 7)

Economic exploitation, 147–48

Economic inequality, 2, 14, 27, 66, 71, 72, 74–75, 93, 115, 117, 123, 127, 136, 147–49, 150, 160, 163–64, 186–87, 191–92, 194, 199–200, 203–8, 224 (n. 69), 225 (n. 78), 233 (n. 26), 234–35 (n. 27), 235 (n. 32), 236 (n. 36), 237 (n. 42), 244 (n. 18), 246 (n. 29), 252 (n. 28), 253–54 (n. 5). See also Equality

Edsall, Thomas, 221 (n. 47)

Egalitarian liberalism, 8, 9, 14, 18–19, 64–66, 73–76, 77, 104, 112, 115, 187–88. See also Equality; Liberalism

Eisenbrey, Ross, 205

Eisenhower, Dwight D., 143, 157

Elections, 46, 126, 167–68, 170–72, 177, 179, 180–82, 183–85, 249 (n. 16)

Elkins, Stanley, and Eric McKitrick, 12, 214 (n. 2), 216 (n. 22), 223 (n. 54), 226 (n. 78)

Ellis, Andrew, 248 (n. 8)

Ellison, Ralph, 61

Elster, Jon, 219 (n. 34)

Empires and imperialism, 125, 128–32, 231–32 (n. 11), 237 (n. 45), 239 (nn. 61, 62)

Employee-employer relations, 147–52, 181, 208, 209, 242 (n. 9), 243 (n. 14)

Equality, 227 (n. 85); and African Americans, 69–70, 77, 155–57, 199–200, 244 (n. 16), 246 (n. 29); and American liberalism, 8, 190–91; and "capabilities approach," 65–66; and civic life, 187–88; and conservative thought, 68–69, 84–85, 107, 110–11, 113–14, 120–23; and democracy, 185–88; and distribution of economic resources, 70–75, 147, 226 (n. 81); and distribution of power, 3, 18, 148–49, 154, 189–90; as dynamic principle, 68–69, 70, 87–88; and effective freedom, 66–67, 73, 139, 165, 224 (n. 64); as ideal often ignored, 87–88; as ideal that can be achieved, 123, 191, 195–97; and justice,

74–78; as liberalism's inspiring ideal, 7, 64–78, 84–85, 94, 118; mischaracterizations of, 73–74; and race, 154–55; and recognition, 96–97; and slavery, 67–68; various forms of, 68–71. *See also* Economic inequality

Equal opportunity, 85, 113, 207, 233 (n. 25)

Evangelical Christians, 104, 192, 231 (n. 10), 232 (n. 16)

Evil, 63–64, 126, 127, 230 (n. 106)

Executive branch, 130–31, 143–44, 242 (n. 5)

Falk, Richard, 237 (n. 44)

Fallibilism, 41, 45, 180, 220 (n. 39)

Falwell, Jerry, 101, 107, 231 (n. 5), 232 (n. 14)

Fantasia, Rick, 217 (n. 25), 243 (n. 14)

Federalism, 152, 155–58

Ferguson, Niall, 129, 239 (nn. 61, 69)

Fish, Stanley, 222 (n. 51)

Fishkin, James S., 249 (n. 12), 251 (n. 25)

Flathman, Richard E., 222 (n. 50)

Fleishacker, Samuel, 226 (n. 81)

Foner, Eric, 245 (n. 24)

Foreign Intelligence Surveillance Act, 130, 239 (n. 65)

Foreign policy, 124–26, 127, 129–32, 237 (nn. 44, 50), 238 (nn. 51, 52)

Frank, Thomas, 112, 233 (n. 24), 253 (n. 3)

Franklin, Benjamin, 67

Fraser, Nancy, 224 (n. 59)

Free, Marvin D., 199

Freeden, Michael, 243 (n. 13)

Freedom: as basic liberal principle, 7, 13, 54, 79–80, 86–87, 157; and capitalism, 142, 147; collective, 21, 93–94, 168–69; and diversity, 52; and economic resources, 27, 66–67, 73; as "effective freedom" (capacity), 18–19, 27, 64–67, 73–74, 82, 113, 135, 164–65, 168–69, 190–91; and equality, 165, 189–90; for founders, 64; in Hayek, 112–13; and individual self-determination, 20–21, 57–58, 65, 74–76, 78–80, 82–83, 84, 88–89, 160; as inspiring ideal, 70, 195; and international relations, 125, 127; and power, 18–19, 79–80, 148–49, 224 (n. 64); as social good, 93–94; and social order, 82, 86–87; threats to, 136–37. *See also* Liberty

Friedman, Joel, 235 (n. 31)

Friedman, Milton, 80, 119, 234–35 (n. 27)

Fukuyama, Francis, 238 (n. 52)

Funigiello, Philip J., 245 (n. 22)

Galeotti, Anna Elisabetta, 222 (n. 51)

Gallie, W. B., 213 (n. 4)

Galston, William, 221 (n. 49), 222 (n. 50)

Geisst, Charles R., 244 (n. 17)

Geneva Conventions, 130, 145, 239 (n. 66), 242 (n. 5)

Gerrymandering, 183–84, 185, 193–94, 211–12, 249 (n. 16), 251 (n. 26)

Gilbert, Dennis, 204

Gilded Age, 13, 118, 160

Gingrich, Newt, 174–75, 248 (n. 11)

Gitlin, Todd, 85, 222 (n. 50), 228 (n. 95)

Globalization, 1, 102, 127, 135, 137, 148–49, 151, 243 (nn. 11, 12)

Gonzales, Alberto, 242 (n. 5)

Goodin, Robert E., 243 (n. 13)

Gove, Michael, 237 (n. 48)

Grant, Ulysses S., 157, 174

Gray, John, 220 (n. 39), 233 (n. 21), 241 (n. 2)

Green, Thomas Hill, 112, 233 (n. 21)

Greenberg, Karen J., 242 (n. 5)

Grinstein, Yaniv, 209

Gutmann, Amy, 249 (n. 12)

Habermas, Jürgen, 81, 216 (n. 16), 219 (n. 37), 228 (n. 89), 241 (n. 80), 249 (n. 14)

Hacker, Andrew, 252 (n. 28)

Hacker, Jacob, 2, 193–94, 201, 208, 213 (n. 1), 241 (n. 77), 248 (n. 10), 250 (nn. 20, 21), 253 (n. 5), 254 (n. 7)

Hall, Stuart, 253 (n. 3)

Hamden v. Rumsfeld, 130–31, 239 (nn. 66, 67), 240 (n. 75)

Hamilton, Alexander, 3, 12–15 passim, 67, 72, 112, 145, 215 (nn. 9, 14), 216 (n. 19), 216–17 (n. 22), 220 (n. 41), 226 (n. 78), 229 (n. 101)

Hartz, Louis, 13, 101, 214 (n. 4), 231 (n. 6)

Harvey, David, 243 (n. 12)

Hasian, Marouf, 241 (n. 4)

Hauser, Nathan, 220 (n. 39)

Hayek, Friedrich von, 112–21, 138, 231–32 (n. 11), 233 (nn. 22, 25), 234 (n. 27), 235 (nn. 28–30), 236 (n. 40)

Health care, 152–53, 209–10, 245 (n. 22)

Hegel, G. W. F., 18, 216 (n. 16)

Heilbroner, Robert, 227 (n. 86), 241 (n. 2)

Held, Virginia, 228 (n. 90)

Hennessey-Fiske, Molly, 200

Hertz, Noreena, 252 (n. 29)

Higgs, Robert, 244 (n. 20)

Hirschman, Albert O., 106, 232 (n. 13)

Hobbes, Thomas, 11, 12, 82, 87, 126

Hochshild, Jennifer, 246 (n. 28)

Hofstadter, Richard, 226 (n. 76)

Hollinger, David, 40, 219 (nn. 37, 38)

Hollis, Martin, 218 (n. 30)

Honderich, Ted, 120, 231 (n. 8), 236 (n. 38)

Honneth, Alex, 224 (n. 59)

Hoover, J. Edgar, 134

Human nature, 41–42, 81, 220 (n. 41)

Hume, David, 9, 30–31, 34, 81–82, 88–89, 96, 110, 111, 133, 217 (n. 26), 218 (nn. 28–30), 228 (nn. 90, 92), 229 (n. 101), 230 (n. 106)

Identity: and access to civil society, 57, 159; and change, 110; as ethnic or national, 36–40; and immigration, 160–61, 245–46 (n. 27); in leftist thought, 137, 160; and pluralism, 221–22 (n. 50); and political parties, 172–73; and political unity, 47, 51, 107–9

Ignatieff, Michael, 40

Illiberal democracy, 1, 6, 9, 78, 133, 188, 192–95, 252–53 (n. 1), 253 (n. 3)

Immigration, 1, 39–40, 101, 151, 160–61, 163–64, 192, 245–46 (n. 27)

Individualism, 14, 20, 47–48, 52, 54, 58, 60–61, 94–96, 122; in American thought, 122, 152, 160; and conservative thought, 103–4, 109–11, 119, 154, 231 (n. 9); in democratic polity, 177–78; leftist critique of, 91–92; as modern (post-1600), 86–87, 88–89; in modern liberal thought, 79–84, 122–23, 227 (n. 89); and self-development, 88

Integration, 57, 160, 162–63, 245 (n. 26), 246 (nn. 28, 29)

International law and institutions, 124, 126, 128–29, 130, 238 (n. 51)

Ip, Greg, 205

Iraq war, 124, 126, 130, 156, 238 (n. 52)

Jacksonian era, 12

Jacoby, Russell, 241 (n. 81)

James, William, 43, 75–76, 96, 169, 220 (n. 43), 226 (n. 82), 230 (nn. 107, 108)

Jefferson, Thomas, 3, 7, 11, 14, 16, 67, 68, 72, 82, 85, 100, 112, 115, 164, 214 (n. 4), 215 (n. 12), 223 (n. 52), 225 (nn. 72, 73), 226 (n. 78)

Jones, Edward, 196

Judicial branch, 23–24, 34–35, 71, 216 (n. 19)

Judt, Tony, 233 (n. 26)

Justice, 25–26, 165, 196, 226 (n. 81), 226–27 (n. 83), 247 (n. 5); and conservative thought, 113, 115–16, 119–21, 127; and economic equality, 73; and effective freedom, 65; and law, 33; and modern liberalism, 73–75, 76, 77, 84; and public openness, 95; and social cooperation, 93–94, 187–88

Kagan, Robert, 127, 237 (nn. 49, 50), 238 (nn. 51, 53, 57)

Kahn, Si, 223 (n. 53)

Kamin, David, 206

Kant, Immanuel, 11, 21, 41, 94–96, 111, 126, 136, 137, 168, 214 (n. 1), 220 (n. 40), 229 (nn. 103, 104), 230 (n. 106), 238 (n. 51), 241 (n. 80)

Kaplan, Robert, 126, 127, 129, 238 (nn. 51, 54), 239 (n. 61)

Katsaros, Thomas, 244–45 (n. 20)

Keane, John, 216 (n. 16)

Kipling, Rudyard, 128, 238 (n. 55)

Kirk, Russell, 14, 104, 106, 107, 109, 110, 111, 132, 215 (n. 8), 229 (n. 100), 231 (n. 11), 232 (nn. 12, 14), 233 (nn. 18–20), 240 (n. 74)

Kramer, Jane, 239 (n. 63)

Kristol, Irving, 119, 127, 129, 131, 132, 234 (n. 27), 236 (nn. 35, 37), 238 (n. 59), 240 (nn. 70, 72)

Kristol, William, 238 (nn. 52, 53, 57)

Kymlicka, Will, 219 (n. 36)

110, 112, 115, 119, 143–44, 164, 168, 176, 214 (n. 3), 215 (nn. 9, 10, 12, 14, 15), 216 (n. 21), 216–17 (n. 22), 218 (n. 31), 220 (n. 41), 221 (n. 48), 221–22 (n. 50), 226 (nn. 76, 77), 228 (nn. 97, 98), 229 (n. 101), 241 (n. 3), 247 (n. 1)

Magleby, David B., 211

Mallaby, Sebastian, 235 (n. 31)

Mallock, W. H., 99

Markell, Patchen, 224 (n. 59)

Marx, Karl, 103, 119, 135, 138, 228 (n. 89)

Massing, Michael, 249 (n. 17)

Matthews, Robert Guy, 205

McCarthy, Joseph, 133, 134, 192

McLennan, Gregor, 221 (n. 50)

McPherson, James M., 245 (n. 24)

McReady, Benjamin W., 242 (n. 7)

Micklewait, John, 233 (n. 23)

Mill, John Stuart, 3, 13, 38, 80, 94–96, 112, 142, 177–80, 219 (n. 35), 227 (n. 85), 229 (n. 105), 230 (n. 106), 233 (n. 21), 241 (n. 2), 249 (n. 13)

Milligan, Susan, 249–50 (n. 18)

Minnich, Elizabeth, 223 (n. 53)

Mishel, Lawrence, 205

Modernity: characteristics of, 11, 21–22, 38, 219 (n. 35); traditional conservatism's suspicion of, 103–4, 107, 119

Modern liberalism, 66–67, 69–71, 74–75, 76, 80–84, 94, 118, 141–43, 151, 154, 164–65, 168–69, 187–88, 190, 226–27 (n. 83), 241 (n. 2)

Money in politics, 2, 159–62, 183–84, 185–87, 193–94, 211–12, 249 (n. 16), 249–50 (n. 18), 250 (n. 23), 251 (n. 26), 253–54 (n. 5)

Montesquieu, 11, 17, 119, 124, 229 (n. 101), 253 (n. 1)

Montgomery, David, 243 (n. 9)

Mooney, Chris, 249 (n. 17)

Morality: in conservative thought, 119–20, 218 (n. 29), 236 (n. 36); and foreign policy, 128; and justice, 25–26, 76; and liberalism's values, 94–96; relation to law, 24–25, 31–32, 76–77, 96–97, 133, 217 (n. 23); and responsibility, 120–23, 236 (n. 36), 236–37 (n. 41)

Morgensen, Gretchen, 209

Morrison, Toni, 196

Moynihan, Daniel Patrick, 238–39 (n. 60)

Muller, Jerry Z., 68–69, 214 (n. 5), 218 (n. 28), 225 (n. 73), 231 (n. 8), 232 (n. 15), 236 (n. 34)

Nagel, Thomas, 8, 213 (n. 5)

Napoleon, 124

Napoleon III, 193

National security, 105, 130, 132, 133, 143–45, 156, 193, 203

Nations and nationalism, 35–40, 47, 52, 56, 132–33, 141, 168–69, 218–19 (nn. 33, 34, 36, 37)

Nativism, 51, 101

Necessity: in conservative thought, 107, 113, 115–16, 119, 122, 132–33; in leftist thought, 135, 137–38; in liberal thought, 41, 46; and war, 144–45

Neoconservatism, 102, 124–33, 235 (n. 31), 237 (n. 50), 238 (n. 52)

Neoliberalism, 102, 126, 148, 243 (n. 12)

New Deal, 1, 8, 67, 102, 149, 152, 173

Newman, John Henry, 99, 230 (n. 1)

Nietzsche, Friedrich, 29, 89, 111, 228 (n. 89), 241 (n. 79)

Nisbet, Robert, 231 (n. 8)

Nixon, Richard, 133

Nozick, Robert, 80

Nussbaum, Martha, 4, 65–66, 73, 75, 213 (n. 3), 222 (n. 50), 224 (n. 66), 225 (nn. 68, 69), 241 (n. 81)

Oakeshott, Michael, 31, 133, 220 (n. 42), 231 (n. 8), 232 (n. 12)

Ogletree, Charles J., 246 (n. 29)

Opposition party, 72, 171–72, 226 (n. 76), 247–48 (n. 6)

Orfield, Gary, 202, 252 (n. 28)

Orrenius, Pia, 245–46 (n. 27)

O'Sullivan, Noel, 231 (n. 8)

Packer, George, 243 (n. 15)

Partisanship in contemporary American politics, 174–75, 179–81, 183, 211, 248 (n. 9), 250 (n. 21)

Paternalism, 80, 103, 108–9, 131, 177–78, 232 (n. 16)

Patriotism, 40, 52, 88, 107–8, 134, 144, 163, 241 (n. 81)

Patterson, Kelly D., 211

Peace: as basic liberal value, 25, 41, 51, 54, 62–63, 89–91, 97, 195, 197; and empires, 125; and foreign policy, 124–27; means of securing, 28–29, 90–92, 125, 161, 171–72, 174, 181, 223 (n. 56); and modern democracies, 169–71; and power, 127

Peirce, Charles Sanders, 220 (n. 39)

Performatives, 36, 218 (n. 32)

Persuasion: as form of political conflict and negotiation, 26, 56, 76–77, 178–79; limits of, 162–63, 248 (n. 7); in plural liberal societies, 48, 53–54, 62–63; and public reason, 58–60; as transformative, 58, 162–63, 177–78, 182, 249 (n. 13)

Petit, Philip, 230 (n. 106)

Pfizer Drug Company, 242 (n. 7)

Phillips, Wendell, 213 (n. 2)

Pierson, Christopher, 245 (n. 20)

Pierson, Paul, 193–94, 201, 241 (n. 77), 248 (n. 10), 250 (nn. 20, 21), 253 (n. 5), 254 (n. 7)

Pildes, Richard, 211

Plebiscite, 19, 193, 254 (n. 6)

Plessy v. Ferguson, 156

Pluralism: and conservatism, 231 (n. 11); and democracy, 169–71, 173–76, 177–78; developing taste for, 51; and equality, 73–74, 158–59; as ineluctable fact, 44–47, 50; and issues of representation, 182–84; and liberalism, 40–63, 133; and liberty, 78–79; in Madison's thought, 15–16, 45–48; and market, 119; and modern societies, 7, 11–12, 35, 44–45, 52, 58, 88–89, 161, 189; in moral views, 25–26, 133; and multiple goods, 44–45; in political theory, 221 (n. 50); and social stability, 55–56, 125

Politics: and citizen participation, 161–62, 181–82; and compromises, 180; as continual negotiation, 27–28, 149, 164, 193; defined, 4, 62, 189–90; in democratic polity, 172; as distinct from morality, 25; and fight against injustice, 136–37; and public persuasion, 77, 162–63; and state-market relations, 154

Popper, Karl, 41, 220 (n. 39)

Pork barrel spending, 183–84

Posner, Richard, 234–35 (n. 27)

Price, Richard, 168

Privatization, 160–61, 223 (n. 53)

Progress, 42, 73, 78, 196

Progressive Era, 8, 134

Promises, 30–31, 94

Property, 11, 26–27, 29, 102, 115, 135, 144

Proust, Marcel, 136

Public health, 145–47, 242 (n. 7)

Public/private distinction, 27–28, 53, 91–92, 154, 229 (n. 100)

Public reason, 58–62, 177–80, 223 (n. 57)

Punishment, 32–33, 105, 120–22, 168

Purposive action, 20, 42–44, 220 (n. 42); conservative distrust of, 105–7, 110–11, 116–18

Putnam, Robert, 245 (n. 25)

Quadagno, Jill, 209

Racial relations in America, 57–63, 244 (n. 16), 245 (n. 26), 246 (n. 29)

Racism, 69, 71, 87, 101, 149, 156, 157, 158–59, 162–63, 244 (n. 16)

Rand, Ayn, 113

Rawls, John, 4, 41, 75, 123, 147, 213 (nn. 3, 6), 220 (n. 40), 223 (n. 57), 226 (n. 81), 243 (n. 10)

Read, James, 15

Reagan, Ronald, 149, 202, 244 (n. 19)

Reagan Democrats, 112

Reardon, Sean E., 202

Recognition, 60–62, 81, 96–97, 224 (n. 59)

Reconstruction, 156–58, 245 (n. 24)

Regulatory laws, 114–15, 146–47, 150–51, 153–54, 162–63, 178–79

Rehg, William, 223 (n. 57), 249 (nn. 12, 13)

Reich, Robert, 236 (n. 36), 248 (n. 11)

Reilly, Ben, 248 (n. 8)

Religion, 38, 88, 103, 141, 150; plurality of in modern societies, 11–12, 231 (n. 10)

Representative democracy, 182–84, 185, 250 (nn. 19, 20)

Republican Party, 112, 120, 131–32, 133, 153, 163–64, 170, 231 (n. 7), 235 (nn. 31, 32)

Rescher, Nicholas, 222 (n. 50)

Resistance to law, 26, 56, 92, 247 (n. 5)

Reynolds, Andrew, 248 (n. 8)

Richards, David, 222 (n. 51)

Rights, 85–86, 137, 163; and Bush administration, 239 (nn. 65, 66), 239–40 (n. 69),
240 (n. 75); in neoconservative thought,
126–27

Riley, Naomi Schaefer, 231 (n. 5), 232 (n. 14)

Rimmerman, Craig, 254 (n. 6)

Rodriguez, Gregory, 245–46 (n. 27)

Roosevelt, Franklin D., 4, 64, 66–67, 85, 101,
149, 213 (n. 3), 224 (n. 63), 225 (n. 70)

Rorty, Richard, 230 (n. 108), 241 (n. 81)

Rousseau, Jean-Jacques, 12, 87, 182, 186, 251
(n. 27)

Rove, Karl, 47

Rowland, Christopher, 249–50 (n. 18)

Rule of law, 7, 17, 19–40, 48, 52, 62, 63,
103, 107–8, 133, 139, 189, 193, 196, 216
(n. 19); in democratic polities, 170–71;
as humanly contrived, 30–31, 109, 111;
and limits of compulsion, 92–93, 96–97,
114–15, 162–63; and rights, 86; subverted
by Bush administration, 130–33, 144–45,
239 (nn. 63–69), 240 (n. 75), 242 (n. 5)

Ruskin, John, 103, 111

Ryan, Alan, 81–82, 228 (nn. 89, 91)

Santayana, George, 38, 106

Savage, Charlie, 239 (n. 68)

Sayre-McCord, Geoffrey, 230 (n. 106)

Scalia, Antonin, 217 (n. 23), 218 (n. 29)

Schwarzenegger, Arnold, 193

Scovronick, Nathan, 246 (n. 28)

Scruton, Roger, 109, 232–33 (n. 17), 233
(n. 25)

Secrecy, 95, 129–31, 133, 145, 194, 238 (n. 60)

Security, 89, 91

Segregation, 56–57, 61, 63, 67, 156–57, 160,
202

Self-interested behavior, 34, 80, 82, 97, 117,
187, 196, 227 (n. 88)

Selfishness, 92–94, 96–97, 165, 187, 192–93,
229 (n. 100)

Sellers, Charles, 225 (n. 75)

Sen, Amartya, 65, 73, 75, 224 (n. 66), 225
(n. 67), 227 (n. 88)

Sennett, Richard, 236 (n. 39)

Shah, Anup, 203, 225 (n. 69)

Shapiro, Ian, 247 (nn. 3–6)

Shapiro, Isaac, 206

Shklar, Judith, 65, 224 (nn. 62, 65)

Sidelsky, Robert, 125, 237 (n. 47)

Siemers, David J., 21, 215 (n. 9), 216 (n. 20),
216–17 (n. 22)

Sirota, David, 243 (n. 14), 252 (n. 29)

Slavery, 26, 37, 66–67, 156, 157, 196

Slote, Michael, 230 (n. 106)

Smith, Adam, 11, 14, 80, 82, 178, 227
(nn. 86, 87)

Smith, Anthony D., 218 (n. 33)

Smith, Christian, 231 (n. 10), 232 (n. 16)

Smith, Mark A., 252 (n. 29)

Smith, Neil, 223 (n. 53)

Socialism, 115, 151–52, 240 (n. 76), 245
(n. 21)

Social order, 11, 36–37, 71, 79, 89, 103, 125;
in conservative thought, 104–5, 108–10,
116–18, 121–22, 132, 231–32 (n. 11)

Social relations: and civil peace, 248
(n. 7); in conservative thought, 107–8;
in contemporary America, 173–75;
and democratic deliberation, 180; individuals embedded within, 80–83, 87, 88,
163, 228 (n. 90); in liberal polities, 55–56,
61–62, 75, 86, 92–93, 149–50, 163, 187–88,
228 (n. 90); and questions of choice,
108–9; as source of value, 93–94, 96–97,
110–11

Sombart, Werner, 245 (n. 21)

Spencer, Herbert, 233 (n. 21)

Spinner-Halev, Jeff, 219–20 (n. 37)

Spinoza, Baruch, 18

State: and American federalism, 155–56; in
American liberalism, 14, 54, 78, 79, 82; in
conservative thought, 102, 105, 118–19,
131–32; in democratic polities, 189–90;
as distinct from nation, 132–33; and
economic inequality, 27, 123, 149–50, 243
(nn. 9, 14), 244 (n. 17); in Federalist era,
13; historical growth of, 143–44, 244–50
(n. 20); hostility toward, 85–87, 122; in
liberal polities, 133, 141–43, 164, 189, 195;
and market, 145–54; and national security, 105; and nondiscrimination, 155–56;
and rights, 85, 137; and war, 143–45

Stelzer, Irwin, 130, 235 (n. 31), 237 (nn. 43, 46), 239 (n. 62)

Stetson, Brad, 222 (n. 51)

Stiglitz, Joseph E., 243 (n. 11)

Stone, Geoffrey R., 241 (n. 4)

Strauss, Leo, 129, 238 (n. 60)

Suffering, 79–80, 94, 96, 97, 105–6, 148, 152, 230 (nn. 106, 108)

Sullivan, Andrew, 217 (n. 23), 239 (n. 69), 240 (n. 75)

Sullivan, Teresa A., 253 (n. 4)

Sumner, William Graham, 233 (n. 21)

Sunstein, Cass R., 85, 213 (n. 3), 228 (n. 96)

Sun-Tzu, 126

Surowiecki, James, 208, 249 (n. 15)

Taylor, Charles, 81, 88, 96, 224 (n. 59), 228 (n. 89)

Terrorism, 125, 132, 144, 156, 237 (n. 50), 242 (n. 5)

Thatcher, Margaret, 80, 120–21, 227 (n. 87), 253 (n. 3)

Thompson, Dennis, 249 (n. 12)

Thompson, E. P., 217 (n. 24)

Thucydides, 126

Thurmond, Strom, 243 (n. 15)

Tocqueville, Alexis de, 8, 15, 71, 74, 84–85, 164–65, 191, 214 (n. 2), 223 (nn. 54, 56), 225 (n. 74), 246 (n. 30), 253 (n. 2)

Tolerance, 12, 48, 49–51, 63, 97, 174, 221 (n. 49), 222 (n. 51)

Toobin, Jeffrey, 212

Torture, 130–31, 132, 239 (nn. 63, 66, 69), 242 (n. 5)

Traditional conservatism, 102, 103–11; and family, 103–4, 108–9; and morality, 119–20

Truman, Harry, 149, 152, 243 (n. 15), 245 (n. 22)

Tulis, Jeffrey, 254 (n. 6)

Tyranny, 141, 158, 164, 165, 239 (n. 69), 240 (n. 75); as effort to suppress pluralism, 45, 50, 55–56, 221 (n. 46); and founders, 16–17, 82; and inequality, 71, 108, 147; liberalism directed against, 63–64, 79, 94, 111; Madison's definition of, 15, 105; and rule of law, 35

United Nations, 124, 126

Varshey, Ashutosh, 223 (n. 56)

Violence, 97, 127–28, 164, 170, 237 (n. 45); generated by absolute victories, 28–29; and hostility to pluralism, 50, 54; international, 125–26; and law enforcement, 28–29; mitigated by civic interaction, 223 (n. 56); sectarian, 31

Voluntary associations, 61–63, 83, 158–59, 223 (n. 56)

Voss, Kim, 217 (n. 25), 243 (n. 14)

Walker, Margaret Urban, 236–37 (n. 41)

Wallace, Henry, 240 (n. 76)

Walzer, Michael, 222 (n. 51)

War, 89–91, 124, 125–27, 143–45, 156, 193, 229 (n. 99)

Warren, Elizabeth, 253 (n. 4)

Washington, George, 67, 72, 223 (n. 52), 229 (n. 101)

Weaver, James, 240 (n. 76)

Weber, Max, 124, 247 (n. 4)

Weinstein, Kenneth R., 238 (n. 60)

Welchman, Jennifer, 230 (n. 106)

Welfare state, 132, 148–49, 151–53, 243 (n. 13), 244 (n. 16), 245 (n. 20)

Wellmer, Albrecht, 216 (n. 18)

Wessel, David, 237 (n. 42)

Westbrook, Jay Lawrence, 253 (n. 4)

Westbrook, Robert, 224 (n. 64)

Wiggins, David, 213 (n. 4), 236–37 (n. 41)

Wilde, Oscar, 182

Wilentz, Sean, 13, 72–73, 214 (nn. 2, 4), 223 (n. 54), 226 (n. 79)

Williams, Robert B., 224 (n. 59)

Wills, Gary, 214 (n. 3), 215 (n. 15), 216 (n. 22), 218 (n. 31), 226 (n. 78), 228 (n. 92), 229 (n. 101)

Wilson, Woodrow, 101

Wittgenstein, Ludwig, 230 (n. 108)

Wolf, Susan, 236–37 (n. 41)

Wolfe, Alan, 250 (n. 21)

Wolff, Edward N., 203, 244 (n. 18)

Wolfowitz, Paul, 124

Wood, Gordon S., 68, 214–15 (n. 6), 225 (n. 75), 228–29 (n. 98), 247 (n. 2)

H. EUGENE AND LILLIAN YOUNGS LEHMAN SERIES

Lamar Cecil, *Wilhelm II: Prince and Emperor, 1859–1900* (1989).

Carolyn Merchant, *Ecological Revolutions: Nature, Gender, and Science in New England* (1989).

Gladys Engel Lang and Kurt Lang, *Etched in Memory: The Building and Survival of Artistic Reputation* (1990).

Howard Jones, *Union in Peril: The Crisis over British Intervention in the Civil War* (1992).

Robert L. Dorman, *Revolt of the Provinces: The Regionalist Movement in America* (1993).

Peter N. Stearns, *Meaning Over Memory: Recasting the Teaching of Culture and History* (1993).

Thomas Wolfe, *The Good Child's River*, edited with an introduction by Suzanne Stutman (1994).

Warren A. Nord, *Religion and American Education: Rethinking a National Dilemma* (1995).

David E. Whisnant, *Rascally Signs in Sacred Places: The Politics of Culture in Nicaragua* (1995).

Lamar Cecil, *Wilhelm II: Emperor and Exile, 1900–1941* (1996).

Jonathan Hartlyn, *The Struggle for Democratic Politics in the Dominican Republic* (1998).

Louis A. Pérez Jr., *On Becoming Cuban: Identity, Nationality, and Culture* (1999).

Yaakov Ariel, *Evangelizing the Chosen People: Missions to the Jews in America, 1880–2000* (2000).

Philip F. Gura, *C. F. Martin and His Guitars, 1796–1873* (2003).

Louis A. Pérez Jr., *To Die in Cuba: Suicide and Society* (2005).

Peter Filene, *The Joy of Teaching: A Practical Guide for New College Instructors* (2005).

John Charles Boger and Gary Orfield, eds., *School Resegregation: Must the South Turn Back?* (2005).

Jock Lauterer, *Community Journalism: Relentlessly Local* (2006).

Michael H. Hunt, *The American Ascendancy: How the United States Gained and Wielded Global Dominance* (2007).

Michael Lienesch, *In the Beginning: Fundamentalism, the Scopes Trial, and the Making of the Antievolution Movement* (2007).

Eric L. Muller, *American Inquisition: The Hunt for Japanese American Disloyalty in World War II* (2007).

John McGowan, *American Liberalism: An Interpretation for Our Time* (2007).